Banner in the West

A Spiritual History of Lewis and Harris

John MacLeod was born in Lochaber in 1966. After graduating from Edinburgh University, he began his career at BBC Highland in Inverness and quickly established himself as a freelance writer. He won Scottish Journalist of the Year in 1991 and contributed regularly to *The Scotsman* and *The Herald*. He is presently a columnist with the *Scottish Daily Mail* and is the author of several books, including *When I Heard the Bell*, which was shortlisted for the Saltire Book of the Year award in 2009. He has lived on the Long Island since 1992.

In memory of Doris Cumming

Banner in the West

A Spiritual History of Lewis and Harris

John MacLeod

BIRLINN

This edition first published in 2010 by
Birlinn Limited
West Newington House
10 Newington Road
Edinburgh
EH9 1QS

www.birlinn.co.uk

ISBN 978 1 84158 852 0

British Library Cataloguing-in-Publication Data
A catalogue record for this book is available from the British Library

Design and typeset by Iolaire Typesetting, Newtonmore
Printed and bound by MPG Books Limited, Bodmin

For

Duncan Angus MacLean

Do cheartas mar na sleibhtibh àrd',
do bhreth mar dhoimhneachd mhòir;
Air duine 's ainmhidh ni thu, Dhè
deagh-choimhead agus fòir.

O Dhia! is prìseil urramach
do chaoimhneas gràdhach caoin;
Fo sgàil do sgèith ni uime sin,
làn dòchas clann nan daoin . . .

Salm 36:6, 7

Contents

III. 'The Shore of Trouble is Hidden'

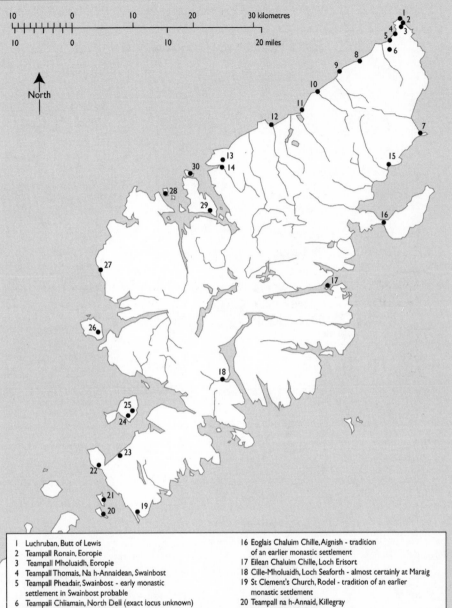

Early Christian sites on Lewis and Harris

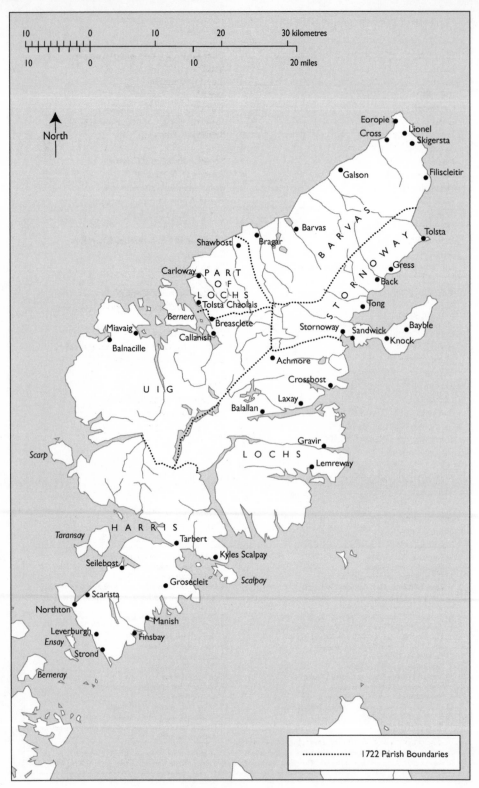

Present-day congregations on Harris and Lewis

Free Church of Scotland Congregations
Back
Barvas*
Callanish*
Carloway*
Cross*
Harris (Leverburgh)*
Kinloch (Laxay)*
Knock (Garrabost)*
Lochs (Crossbost)*
Park (Gravir)*
Point (Bayble)*
Scalpay
Shawbost*
Stornoway*
Tolsta*
Uig (Bernera) - services discontinued, 2002

Church of Scotland Congregations
Barvas*
Carloway*
Cross*
Harris (Manish, Scarista)*
Harris (Tarbert)*
Kinloch and Park (Lemreway)*
Knock*
Lochs*
Stornoway - High Church*
Stornoway - Martin's Memorial*
Stornoway - St Columba's Parish*
Uig and Bernera*

Free Presbyterian Congregations
Achmore
Breasclete - services discontinued, 2010
Harris (Leverburgh)*
Harris (Tarbert)*
Ness (Lionel)*
Stornoway*
Tolsta*
Uig (Miavaig)

'Free Church Continuing' Congregations
Cross*
Harris (Leverburgh)
Knock*
Scalpay*
Shawbost (service at Bragar, midweek only)
Stornoway (Sandwick)*

Scottish Episcopal Church
Stornoway (St Peter's)*
Eoropie (St Moluag's) with Tong
Harris (Christ Church, Grosecleit;
annual Eucharist on Ensay)*

Associated Presbyterian Churches
Stornoway*
Harris (Seilebost)

Roman Catholic Church
Stornoway (Church of the Holy Redeemer)*

Other Christian
Brethren, Salvation Army, Pentecostal and
Baptist groups in Stornoway

Cults
Mormon and Jehovah's Witness
groups in Stornoway.

*Congregations with a settled ministry in April 2010 marked **

Preface

The need for a comprehensive history of Long Island religion, from primal Mesolithic fears to the realities of twenty-first-century Evangelicalism, has been on my mind for a number of years. In the difficult summer of 2007, a project began to take clear shape in my head. The initial plan was a brief, most accessible history for a new generation of teenage believers on Lewis and Harris, but hardened into thoughts of one both detailed, researched and robust for a wider audience, written from within the culture and yet accessible to any educated layman.

I am most grateful to Hugh Andrew, Andrew Simmons, Jim Hutcheson and all at Birlinn Ltd for giving me the opportunity to write it and for much encouragement, wisdom and support. I have also deeply appreciated the editorial services of Lawrence Osborn, who went carefully through the script and whose observations and corrections have been invaluable. Peter MacAulay, son of Carloway and distinguished journalist, sacrificed a day to improve my execrable Gaelic; I can only thank him and blush. I owe much to my father, Rev. Dr Donald MacLeod, Principal of the Free Church College, Edinburgh, for his sustained support and passionate care for both accuracy and prudence, and to Dr Robert Dickie and Mr Norman Campbell: these three men heroically read an entire, early draft and made many excellent suggestions. My father also ran to earth some important source material and Mr Campbell provided other scarce matter – most importantly photocopies of rare nineteenth-century newspaper material, from a collection prepared by his late uncle, Donald M. Campbell. And I have much valued the informed interest of Rev. David Campbell, Tolsta, Isle of Lewis – amidst gruelling responsibilities and the joy of a new son; Rev. Iain D. Campbell, Back, Isle of Lewis; and Carl R. Trueman, Professor of Historical Theology and Church History, and Dean of Faculty besides, at Westminster Theological Seminary, Philadelphia, Pennsylvania.

Responsibility for the accuracy of any material in this book and for any opinion expressed in it must, however, be laid exclusively at my door.

Man is incurably religious and our finest Highland minds have always pondered the deepest questions of our existence and the indefinable mystery of being human, as well as engaging – often uneasily – in the perceived tension between orthodox Christianity and the problem of evil; and the occasional tension, at times, between the tenets of the faith and the conduct of some who profess it. I feel it important both to reflect this wider spirituality and to exemplify the achievement of our greatest twentieth-century Gaelic poets; and have chosen three outstanding examples to introduce the sections of this book. My kinsman Professor Derick S. Thomson, *Ruaraidh MacThòmais*, is, happily, still with us and I thank him for graciously granting permission to carry *Srath Nabhair*. I acknowledge, besides, the kind permission of Carcanet Ltd, Manchester, to include the powerful *Aig clachan Chalanais* by the late Iain Crichton Smith, *Iain Mac a' Ghobhainn*; and, in all its compressed purity, *Reothairt*, by the late Sorley MacLean, *Somhairle Mac Gill-Eain*, whose own kindness and hospitality – with his excellent wife, Renee, in their Skye home – it was my privilege on several occasions to enjoy. I appreciate such opportunity to enrich this book.

I am indebted, too, to Dr Donald M. Boyd; Rev. Andrew Coghill; the late Rev. Professor G.N.M. Collins (who was preached against by Neil Cameron); the late Mrs Peggy Gillies; Mr Bill Lawson; Mrs Chris Lawson; Rev. Iain MacAskill, South Uist, for encouragement on an early chapter; Miss Anna MacAulay; Rev. Donald MacDonald, lately minister of Carloway, for kindly provision of more nineteenth-century material; Mr Fraser MacDonald, University of Melbourne; the late Rev. John Angus MacDonald; the late Mrs Margaret MacDonald; the Rev. James MacIver, Knock, for the account of local Union difficulties in 1900; Mr Angus MacKay; Mrs Marsaili MacKinnon; the Rev. Donald MacLean, lately minister of Glasgow; Mr Duncan MacLean; the Rev. Malcolm MacLean, Scalpay, for comments on an early chapter; Mrs Margaret Anna MacLean; Mr Grant MacLennan of the Church of Scotland Media Office; the late Dr Jean MacLennan (who remembered Donald Mac-Farlane taking a service in her school); my late grandmother, Mrs Alice Thomson MacLeod; the late Mr Duncan John MacLeod; Rev. John MacLeod, London, for the loan of a rare book and rarer photographs; Mrs Marion MacLeod; my uncle, Mr Murdo I. MacLeod; Rev. William MacLeod; Mrs Annie MacSween; Mr Innes MacSween; Mr Kenneth MacSween; the late Mrs Catherine MacVicar (who died in 1994 at the age of 103, still incandescent about the 'UF' tactics in Carloway); Mr Angus J. Mitchell; my aunt, Mrs Christina Montgomery; Mrs Margaret MacKenzie Morrison; Mr Neil Murray; Mr Paul Murray; Dr Susan Parman; Mr Tearlach Quinnell; the late Rev. Robert R. Sinclair (whose

cradle had been rocked by MacDonald of Shieldaig and had himself
draped a rug over Donald MacFarlane); Mr Norman Smith; a number of
island Free Church ministers who, on terms of strict anonymity, answered
some demanding questions on the present religious interest of many local
schoolchildren; and many, many others, some for over two decades, for
detail, information, anecdote, correspondence, counsel and cheer.

The temptation to halt this work at the early 1950s was considerable
and – especially in relation to some subsequent, painful events – I have
said as little as possible, confining myself from that period to such
statements as are necessary to explain how certain new congregations
on Lewis and Harris came into existence. I have written elsewhere and at
length on the rather civilised 1989 division in the Free Presbyterian
Church and was too close a spectator in the Free Church difficulties a
decade later to choose, this early, to revive that infinitely more depressing
episode. I also – perhaps surprisingly – chose not directly to consult
formal Presbyterial records. In fact they have very little of value to
contribute. Pre-war kirk session minutes, especially, are largely a record
of church discipline – cases invariably humiliating and usually sexual –
and, though I was generously offered access to those of one island
congregation, I with all courtesy declined. Presbytery or Synod papers
– being courts of appeal and review as they are – would besides too readily
give the impression of a church in ceaseless, loveless strife. (This is
spectacularly exemplified in a little 1982 biography of Hector Cameron,
which drew overwhelmingly from such deathly Free Church chronicles
and, as a result, gives a most unattractive impression of its subject.)

In such a field as this, especially from the advent of Evangelicalism,
there is far more material than one could possibly use; and, had I explored
everything I might have wished to explore, the book would be three times as
long, few would seriously want to read it and it would be cheaper, frankly, to
hand out a £50 note to each potential customer. I have had to be ruthless.
Despite the dozens and dozens of ministers Lewis and Harris have exported
to the mainland and elsewhere, few of their careers can be touched on and
none followed. The Long Island has, besides, sent dozens of men and
women on evangelism and mission to just about every corner of the globe;
but that, too, has had to be overlooked. I could not indulge in a chapter on,
say, Highland Evangelicalism in Glasgow – though even in the 1980s there
were still six Presbyterian churches in the city, of three denominations,
where Gaelic services were weekly held – two of these almost exclusively for
people from Lewis; and a third by the sons of Skye. My biggest regret is how
little I have been able to say about women, of whom thousands had a vital,
prayerful and resourceful part in this story, but little voice in any written
history, and most long dead and their witness unrecorded.

Writing this book has been a highly educative project for myself and has disabused me of certain cherished notions, such as romantic proto-Calvinist regard for the Celtic, Columban order. The most striking lessons have been the incalculable debt the Highlands and Islands owe to others for the Gospel, especially the sacrificial endeavours of many from lowland Scotland; how sturdily men persevered to witness, evangelise and educate against hardship, oppression, and repeated reverse and discouragement, and the signal part played in awakening the glens and isles of the north by our national Church.

I have cited as much source material as possible without being either exhaustive or intimidating. Much more could be attested and any student or scholar is welcome to email me at the address below. I owe an incalculable amount to the late Rev. Murdo MacAulay, the first assiduously and in detail to write from the heart of the Lewis faith-community while bravely shunning the traditional rail-tracks of the genre: hagiography and cop-out. Almost as important – and a constant stimulus, especially as they wrote from the best of the Lowland, Moderate tradition – has been the majestic three-volume history of the Scottish Church by the late Rev. Andrew L. Drummond and the late Rev. James Bulloch. Mr Bulloch's death, in April 1981, deprived us of what would have been a definitive, fourth volume on the twentieth century.

I can only ask the reader's forbearance for occasional, sometimes blunt expression of my own opinion, joining Mr Bulloch's cheerful plea, in 1978, that 'to expect a historian to write without prejudice is like asking a man to go courting without a girl'.

John MacLeod
Shawbost, Isle of Lewis
July 2008
jm.macleod@btinternet.com

I

'Like Heaven Cracking . . .'

Aig clachan Chalanais

Aig clachan Chalanais an dé
chuala mi té ag ràdh ri t'èile:
'So far na loisg iad clann o shean'.
Chan fhaca mi druidhean anns na reultan
no grian no gùn: ach chunna mi
ball breagha gorm mar nèamh a' sgàineadh
is clann le craiceann slaodadh riutha
mar a' bhratach sna dh'ìobradh Nagasaki.

At the stones of Callanish yesterday
I heard one woman saying to another:
'This is where they burnt the children in early times.'
I did not see druids among the planets
nor sun nor robe; but I saw
a beautiful blue ball like heaven cracking,
and children with skin hanging to them
like the flag in which Nagasaki was sacrificed.

Iain Mac a' Ghobhainn
Iain Crichton Smith (1928–1998)
from *Biobuill is Sanasan-Reice*, Glasgow, 1965.

1

Last Stronghold

Religion, Landscape and Pre-History

It was a summer Sabbath evening, about 1975, damp and still and mild, golden sun misting over the outskirts of Stornoway in the sort of soft, summer weather we describe, in Gaelic, as *mosach*. We trundled towards evening sermon in the mustard-coloured, denim-seated Volkswagen Beetle which was our improbable motorised transport.

And we were, tonight, stuck in a snaking line of cars, as the world and his wife headed at once to sermon. By the side of the road, sturdy ladies and serge-suited men walked valiantly, clutching Bibles, to assorted places of worship. In Stornoway Free Church, these Sabbaths of the 1970s, the building filled early, swiftly; on occasion, so full that perspiring deacons had to bring in chairs, racking still more worshippers into the aisles, as all awaited the Reverend Murdo MacRitchie. His congregation was so huge it met in two separate buildings; the other was 'the Seminary', on Francis Street – accommodating parallel demand for Gaelic and English services, and each Sabbath attracting 1,600 to 2,000 worshippers. Thousands more in Stornoway, who seldom came to sermon, counted themselves Free Church people and MacRitchie as their minister.

Thirty years ago, those who shunned public worship were nowhere to be seen. They huddled from sight in their homes, through a Sabbath kept with a solemnity one can, in the twenty-first century, scarcely credit. Not a child played on the streets. No one toiled in his garden. Every shop, every filling station, every business was shut. The Ullapool ferry lay inertly at her berth in a calm, lifeless harbour.

I leaned forward and piped, 'Daddy, why does everyone go to church here, when they don't in Glasgow?'

His response was immediate, concise and true. 'Because, John, the Gospel was so late in coming to Lewis, and therefore it is late in leaving.'

In 1800, the great island of Lewis and Harris was, to all intents and purposes, a pagan community. A handful of ministers held desultory services in churches beyond ready reach of most of their parishioners.

They were left in impoverished ignorance, sustained only by illicit whisky, and by a vague, superstitious sacramentalism. *Why did this change?*

By 1850, this same community had been seized – transformed – by Evangelical revival. Huge numbers flocked to public worship and entire villages crammed into homes to hear the Bible being read. Thousands at a time would trek across pathless moor to gather for a Communion season. An entire new way of life had, with astonishing speed, come into being, and it substantially survives. *How did this happen?*

For, even in 2008, in all its wonders and terrors, far beyond an old subsistence economy and amidst accelerating innovation, religion remains a formidable force in Lewis and Harris. Here yet is the most Evangelical region in the British Isles, where all native Hebrideans have still a conscious, if often very nominal, attachment to the Presbyterian order; where Sunday is a day of shuttered shops and motionless ferries and closed amenities; where, out of all proportion to its size, the island continues to furnish many men for Scotland's pulpits. *What explains its survival?*

The spiritual history of Lewis and Harris is a roller-coaster ride of drama, upheaval, courage, endeavour, tragedy and joy, and a wonderful succession of larger-than-life personalities, each generation throwing up new and striking figures against a background of social revolution, global conflict, war and emigration, occasional oppression, denominational strife and – especially in recent years – the uncomprehending mockery of outsiders.

We meet illiterate peasants, some with undoubted learning difficulties, whose eerie wit could silence the educated and scornful. There is the wanderer from Tain, who could not even read the Gaelic Bible, and yet who proved a pivotal figure in spiritual awakening; the austere minister who eloped with a farmer's daughter; the parson's wife who fed the local serial killer in the manse byre; the Italian immigrants who opened the door for the unexpected return of an old faith; and the man who built a Brethren chapel in the middle of nowhere.

We explode the myths of denomination – for, far from being a fractious, quarrelling breed, island believers have proved remarkably resistant to schism; bust the legend of the post-war 'Lewis Awakening' that wasn't; and look at a whole new generation of teenage believers, in some respects disconcerting to their conservative seniors, but as ardently committed to the Gospel as any the islands ever bred.

And we examine real elements of paradox. Most supposedly distinctive features of religious life in the Outer Isles, for instance, are borrowed. The lengthy Thursday to Monday biannual Communion seasons were invented in the Lowlands. The distinctive 'giving out the line' style of

Gaelic precenting came to Scotland from England; of all the melodies launched by Gaelic precentors today, only one is of indisputably Highland origin. And these forms, indeed, had long reached Lewis and Harris before the fires of Evangelicalism took hold, with such energy and transforming power, in their myriad communities.

Still more startling, to outsiders, is the high view of the Lord's Supper. There is a deep Highland dread of superficiality in religion and hundreds of island believers have died without ever partaking of Communion – humble, holy Christian people. But the ranks of such 'adherents' – those connected to the church but who never become communicant members – include besides many with no meaningful, personal religion at all. Thus a thuggish streak has on occasion surfaced in local ecclesiastical history. There is, besides, an enduring, hedonistic paganism in these townships – and a persistent, paradoxical anticlericalism.

Remarkably, this is a story which has never really been written. The one authoritative account of Lewis ecclesiastical life after the 1843 Disruption is in immaculate Gaelic. Only a few hundred copies of a 1985 history of the Long Island's earlier religious development, by Murdo MacAulay, were ever printed.[1] The last century is a minefield hitherto shunned by authors. We have otherwise thin, formal records and a mass of obituaries, memoirs, pamphlets and articles, often hagiographical and usually partisan.

It is only in recent decades that Long Island religion has become increasingly unique. That reflects the secularising tide that swept through Skye and the Highland mainland since the 1960s. Until then churchgoing and Sabbath reverence were not particularly remarkable in terms of the wider region. In the new century church attendance has markedly fallen, a handful of Stornoway businesses now open on Sundays with seeming impunity, and the social authority of Christianity has significantly eroded.

These have always been religious islands, as ancient burial sites make apparent and mysterious standing stones; and the little ruined Columban churches; and the chapels of medieval Roman Catholicism. The personalities of a new Evangelicalism are still remembered, long discussed through protracted island winters when people had little occasion – and no practical need – to leave their snug thatched homes. Thus ministers and 'the Men' were woven into the tales and maxims and awful warnings of a rich old culture: a people who thought of themselves instinctively in terms of genealogy and community, people who never walked alone, worshipped alone or even slept alone.

Evangelical religion, in its late and mighty advent, brought literacy and aspiration to island people. It brought a dignity and cohesion which, within decades, shaped a new social consciousness; it begot disciplined, political action against oppression. Through an intensely communal people it had immediate, spectacular – and abiding – communal impact.

But Evangelical religion is not, of its essence, communal. Even eschewing such loaded terms as 'true religion' or 'vital religion' it is, indubitably, personal religion. It demands not 'confirmation' but conversion; not induction to the Church, but immediate encounter with the living God – as the Gospel is heard and the grace of Christ received, against the awfulness of 'death itself, and the pains of Hell forever'. Conversion is a crisis event; it is, of its nature, an acutely solitary one.

It is much easier to illustrate such solipsism than to explain it, and a recent obituary of one eminent Lewis Christian – Finlay Thomson, a greatly loved elder in Ness – is as neat a 'conversion narrative' as any, demonstrating not only the central loneliness in religious experience of this nature, but how one described his coming to faith to others, and how it was finally validated by his church and in his community.

Finlay Thomson was born in Ness, at the family home in Skigersta, on the seventeenth day of October 1938. Although neither his father nor his mother made a public profession of faith, their life and walk was exemplary to the extent that one would be inclined to cherish the hope that it was well with them at last. Theirs was a Christian home and under its roof the family of five boys and one girl born to them were taught to respect the Sabbath and to attend the means of grace. In those days almost every household in Skigersta was Free Presbyterian and in that village as, indeed, generally throughout the Ness community, there were not a few God-fearing men and women who sought to influence others for good. The presence of such had its own influence on the rising generation. In this connection, we are told that one Sabbath morning, while Finlay was still a little boy, he was allotted the duty of taking the cow along the road, presumably to pasture. On the way, he happened very briefly to play football with a stone which he came across on the road. This was observed and reported to his father. On Monday, Finlay, after having no doubt received paternal admonition, was summoned to appear before Christina MacDonald ('Banntrach Rudair'), a widow who lived nearby, and who is still remembered in Ness as a much-beloved, godly matriarch whose smiting did not break the head of any whose misconduct she felt obliged to reprove; on the contrary, it was a kindness remembered, as in Finlay's case, over a lifetime. It might be said of her what was said by one who appreciated the interest taken in him by the noted Separatist, John Grant: 'I'll get the rod from John, but then I'll get honey with it.'

At the age of seventeen, Finlay, like many of his contemporaries, joined the Merchant Navy and for some years he was employed as a deckhand by the New Zealand Shipping Company. It appears that he was at that time not found without thoughts as to his spiritual state, but these thoughts were transient, like the morning cloud. Out of regard to the minister concerned and also no doubt as a result of his upbringing, he several times, while his ship was berthed in Auckland, attended services conducted in that city by the Reverend William MacLean. Mr MacLean had visited Australia and New Zealand as a deputy in 1962 and the following year he accepted a call to Gisborne. In 1963, Finlay elected to give up deep sea sailing and having, with the help of his family, built a house in Skigersta, he married Catherine MacRitchie, whose home was very near the one in which he was born. For some time, he earned his living working as a weaver, but that was only until the opportunity of returning to sea presented itself, this time as a fisherman. In the port of Stornoway and further afield, he, in due course, became well known as a first-class seaman and expert fisherman. Strong in physique, manly and courageous, he was much respected by those who sailed with him and especially after he came to own and skipper his own boat. For seven years, until he suffered an injury to his right hand, he was a member of the group of intrepid Nessmen who annually visit Sula Sgeir to harvest the young of the solan goose (*an guga*), spending around fourteen days on that rocky islet 40 miles north of the Butt of Lewis. He used to dwell on the unity and friendship which prevailed among them and how he relished the 'family' worship in which they engaged morning and evening. In his time, this worship was conducted by Donald Murray, a much-respected elder in the Free Church, but Finlay took part and often led the singing. It was at the stage of his becoming a fisherman, that the Spirit of God began to strive with him and the salvation of his soul accordingly became the one thing needful. The Bible began to accompany him to the wheel-house. In seeking to enter into the kingdom, he was to discover that he had to contend not only with foes present within – there as a result of his fall in Adam and the corruption of his whole nature – but, also, the opposition of Satan without.

We are informed that he was much affected by a sermon he heard preached in the Lionel church in October 1972 and that from that time forth he turned his back on the world, although not yet having the assurance he sought. At this time, apparently, Chapter 23 in the book of Job became precious to him and he often quoted the words of verse 10: 'But he knoweth the way that I take: when he hath tried me, I shall come forth as gold.' He was wont to say that he did not understand the last part of the verse but towards the end of his life he confided that he was now beginning to do so and was to some extent able to enter into their depth of meaning. The following Spring, the Communion seasons in Lewis followed one another in due order and Finlay, if at all possible, was in attendance. We are told that he could never understand how anyone in health and having the opportunity to attend could be absent on such occasions. He was present at the Stornoway Communion in February 1973 and was a guest, with others, in Mary Ann Matheson's house between the services. Some verses from Psalm 107 were sung, with Dr Hugh Gillies leading the praise, and he was so much affected and overcome by the words of verse 29. 'The storm is changed into a calm at His command and will;/ So that the waves which raged before,/ now quiet are and still,' that he had to leave the room. It is thought that it was then that he obtained the assurance that he was indeed within the circle of the divine favour and thus on the way to the desired haven. Throughout his life he felt spiritually bound to the Lord's people present on that occasion. In March 1973, the Session gladly received him as a communicant member and, over the years which followed, his walk, life and conversation proved that its confidence in him was not misplaced . . .[2]

Finlay Thomson, a winsome man, died in August 2006. The story of religion on Lewis and Harris goes on; but such personal narratives – and there are many, many more – exemplify how an ancient culture quickly learned to socialise – and even to codify – a whole new and very personal kind of spirituality, most grounded in the land of their birth.

Introducing a volume of Gaelic spiritual verse, some years after the Second World War, the Free Church Publications Committee imprudently described Harris as 'the southern and most mountainous part of the Island of Lewis'. In strict geography, of course, Lewis and Harris are one land mass. But they are wholly distinct communities: divided by mountains, divided by clan, of different Gaelic vocabulary, of very different accent and of different social character and, indeed – until 1975 – even in different counties. Joannis Blaeu, who first mapped the Hebrides for his 1654 *Atlas Novus*, took good care to note 'Lewis and Herray of the numbre of the Western Yles, which two although they ioyne be a necke of land ar accounted dyvers Ylands . . .'[3]

In fact, he had mistaken the boundary: the narrow isthmus of Tarbert is well within Harris and the border is miles to the north, from Bowglass on Loch Seaforth to Kinlochresort on an indescribably lonely stretch of Atlantic coast. But the real barrier is the great rampart of the Harris hills, crowned by the Clisham and clamped by deep arms of the sea. While the intrepid could, with difficulty, cross this majestic terrain on foot, it was not lightly enterprised. There was historically very little interaction between Lewis and Harris. Thus the religious life of the two communities took, at times, very different turns, most recently in the 1890s. And Lewismen still talk of going 'up to Harris' and 'down to Ness' – counter-intuitive in terms of the compass, yes; but the natural language in terms of the land.

And all this is but one instance of how, even in spiritual affairs, the doings of men are shaped by soil, climate and topography.

The Long Island, the largest of all Britain's offshore satellites – bigger than Skye, or Mull, or Islay, or Man – sits at the north-west edge of the realm. Though so far north – further north than Mongolia, and as far north as Newfoundland and other ice-girt desolations – Lewis and Harris enjoy remarkably mild weather, thanks to the beneficence of the North Atlantic Drift, washing their coastal rocks in relatively warm sea.[4] Strictly, it is an oceanic climate, marked by winters relatively free of frost and snow and summers, as tourists quickly ascertain, apt to be cool and damp. The rainfall is an average sixty inches a year – Ness is the driest district, and mountainous North Harris, as one would expect, the wettest. Much more shocking – not least to the sort of well-intended incomer whose first act, on acquiring a crofter's cottage in the likes of Shawbost or Borve, is to lay out a garden and plant a few fruit trees – is the wind.

Gales gusting at sixty or seventy miles an hour are a regular feature of the island winter and speeds in excess of 100 mph have been recorded at the Butt of Lewis. A severe storm can hit the Outer Hebrides in any month of the calendar, but the Long Island's legendary blasts are largely a winter affair, with the first 'equinoctial gales' roaring in October and, not infrequently, blasting in the spring. The most terrible storms of all, though, are associated with the month of January. By contrast, deep frost and heavy, long-lying snow are rare, and there have been but two protracted episodes of extreme winter conditions since the war – in 1955, and the turn of 1995–6.

It is easy to hate the wind on Lewis and hard to credit, unless one has lived through it, how weeks of sustained storm and bluster can fray the nerves, frustrate outdoor endeavour, sap one's energies even in a few minutes of walking, tending to livestock or performing some essential outside chores; how incessant winds off the ocean cake windows with salt, burn shrubs and crops, rapidly corrode any exposed iron, can cast shreds of seaweed and wrack miles inland. But it is only one element of a profoundly stripping environment.

Though overlaid – especially at Ness and around Stornoway – by more complex geology affording better land, Lewis and Harris are fashioned of an ancient metamorphic stone: a mess of gneisses, schists and granites called 'Lewisian'. It makes pitiable soil, save in such districts as eastern Harris where you might wonder if there is any soil at all – 'much of the landscape', muses Stewart Angus in his definitive guide to this geology, 'is gnarled and knobbed, crushed and creviced, seeming to reflect the great age of the island rocks'.[5] That people have survived on such land testifies to their ingenuity and their resilience.

This rock has besides been scoured by glaciation, left bare in Harris and some western corners of Lewis and otherwise draped in boulder-clay. It is no more fertile than concrete and is, of course, impermeable to water, which is why there are so many freshwater lochs. Indeed, of the total acreage of Lewis – 437,200 acres – inland water comprises 24,863; and most agree that the name 'Lewis' itself is from a Norse word, *Leodjus*, 'a place abounding in pools'. ('Harris' – which is actually a plural name in Gaelic, *'Na Hearadh'* – stems from 'the harries', or grounds for deer-hunting by the clan chief and other notables.) Lack of drainage, heavy rain and limited evaporation – with the added factor of an acidifying bedrock – have averted decomposition and, instead, embalmed millennia of moss and grasses as peat.

Peat immediately impacted the human ecology. For one, though it provides ample, if rather poor, grazing ground, blanket-bog will not yield crops. For another, peat dries readily, if with considerable loss of mass, and makes very good fuel; the best, 'black' peat has a calorific value almost as high as brown coal.[6] In a community with no significant woodland, this was a signal bonus. But people could not live on the peatlands and feed their families.

Nothing, accordingly, defines Lewis and Harris more than the sea: it is their highway and their larder, and all but two island villages are coastal. (These two, Achmore and Lochganvich, were laid out only in the nineteenth century, as a by-product of eviction and – most unusually – have Gaelic names rather than ones of Norse origin; that is invariably a clue, on the Long Island, to a very modern settlement.)

The sea provided shellfish for the earliest settlers and, especially after a winter storm, throws up great masses of seaweed. Gathered, well-rotted kelp, mixed with dung and mixed further into peat, makes remarkably fertile soil – if at considerable labour – but still more important, especially on the Atlantic edge of Lewis and Harris, is the shell-sand of the great beaches. Exceedingly rich in lime, windblown sand has long sweetened the land within a mile or two of the coast. Still more hospitable, in those areas where great tracts of sand have been colonised by marram and other grasses, is the terrain we call *machair* – excellent grazing, readily ploughed for crops, and through summer ablaze with a wonderful variety of flowers.

The traditional economy was pastoral, not arable, and centred on cattle, for in a mild, damp place so far north and with protracted summer daylight nothing grows like grass. All centred on the cow. She provided milk, butter and cheese; her winter dung manured your crops. By May, with the corn growing and without the security of fencing, the cattle were led out to grazings deep in the moor, to be tended by the women and children as the men rethatched the homes (conserving the lower, older layer of peatsmoke-saturated thatch for the cow's winter bed). The women walked home nightly with the day's dairy produce to feed their men, leaving small offspring in the doubtful but exuberant charge of older siblings. The thatching done, all then engaged in the communal chore of the peats – cut, dried, stacked and finally borne home, for aromatic winter fires.

These days of *na airighean*, 'the shielings' – a form of transhumance practically as old as humanity – endured until the catastrophe of the First World War and, in some form at least, to the final and weary protraction of the Second. And, though the house-cow has all but vanished from island villages since the 1970s, Sabbath services are still held at noon and 6 p.m., surviving from days when the family cow had to be milked, every twelve hours, without fail, and many had to walk a good distance to sermon.

But the sweet grass and clover that sustained the cow, and the seaware that melded with her dung to grow the bare crops of subsistence – barley and oats (the climate is far too windy for wheat) and, in much more recent times, potatoes – were, at the last, but fruits of the sea. So, indeed, was the precious timber swept ashore, without which islanders could not have roofed their houses.

Roads are a most recent development and – beyond Stornoway, which has been a substantial settlement for centuries – there were no roads anywhere on Lewis or Harris capable of bearing a wheeled vehicle until well into the nineteenth century. The wealthiest might have a pony. Everyone else walked. And how they walked! When Oighrig MacLean of Leurbost died in 1928, her obituary in the *Free Presbyterian Magazine* records that she once walked 'from Leurbost to Breasclete, in a storm of wind and rain to the Communion there'.[7] Mrs MacLean was then eighty-two. Dan Morrison, in 1955, took a splendid photograph of the sprightly Jessie Morrison, Knockaird, herding home her cows from the distant Ness shielings.[8] She was ninety-four. Alexander Carmichael, compiling a compendium of Highland lore that became his *Carmina Gadelica*, found a valuable source in Mary MacRae – *Mairi Bhanchaig* – in South Harris; a native of Lochalsh, she had come with her niece to Northton Farm. Years later, Carmichael recorded her passing in 1877, when she was 100 – even the previous year, she had still regularly walked over the sands to the distant church at Scarista.[9]

The relative ease of waterways affected even the invigorated Presbyterianism. The new Free Church buildings at Crossbost and Tarbert were both erected hard by the shore, where they stand to this day – most of the congregation, after all, arrived by boat. And when, inheriting that Tarbert building, Rev. Donald A. MacRae became the local Church of Scotland minister in 1961, he found himself responsible not only for the vast district of the North Harris mainland, but for three then-inhabited offshore islands.[10] He had preaching-stations at Kyles Scalpay, Rhenigidale (to which there was then no road), Maraig, Ardvourlie, Bunavoneader, North Meavag and Amhuinnsuidhe. That was just the north. In the Bays of Harris, he had meetings besides to keep in South Meavag, Drinishader, Scadabay and Grosebay, with the occasional jaunt to Luskentyre. And on top of that he had the island of Scalpay, the island of Scarp (till its evacuation late in 1971) and Taransay (until the last family quit in 1974.)

He had, admittedly, at least five salaried lay preachers or 'missionaries' to help him; local elders besides kept many routine services and by then, at least, there were metalled roads and the use of a car. But he still bore a crushing pastoral responsibility for a vast district – and several times a year, besides, he had to attend Presbytery in Uist. It would be 1996 before a car ferry shuttled back and forth over the Sound of Harris, and so treacherous and tidal are these waters that passage by motor-launch could be fraught. Travelling to a 1975 ordination, Mr MacRae's boat ran aground on a sandbank, and he and the Harris party were stranded for hours.

In serene retirement, MacRae made light of these toils, always recalling fondly his 'fee' for the annual Sabbath jaunt to Taransay – 'two chickens, a lobster, a bag of carrots and a bag of potatoes!' But just how punishing the life of an island minister could be, especially in a generation still further past, is evident.

In the Hebrides all such practicalities – rocky, infertile land; an oppressive climate; the uncertainties of wind and ocean – spectacularly underline the frailty of man. It is small wonder if, from earliest times, their inhabitants have sought for meaning, have looked for God, have pondered what lies beyond death.

There have been people on the Long Island for five millennia. One Mesolithic settlement at Northton, excavated in 1964, has been reliably dated to about 3000 BC.[11] The remains of an oval-shaped dry-stone house were uncovered, with fragments of bone and neat little tools – flint and antler – scattered on the sandy floor. The central hearth was encircled in stone: no trace of the roof survived, but it was probably of animal skins over a light frame. Other, earliest human sites have almost certainly been lost to the encroaching sea.

That ancient life may at first have been most fragile. The earliest settlers – who seem to have drifted to the Hebrides from Ireland – chose a location much as one today would choose a camping-site. The Western Isles had, too, one signal advantage over the contemporary Highland mainland – they had neither wolves nor the still more dangerous brown bear.

Yet even these people had tools – scrapers, choppers and hammers of chipped flint have been found on Oronsay in the Inner Hebrides – and jewellery, for pierced cowrie-shells have been found at assorted Hebridean sites. And they had transport – the coracle, which in South Uist at least endured as a means of getting about into the nineteenth century. It is no exaggeration, though, to say that the advent of Neolithic – or New Stone Age – people was perhaps the most important single event in the history of the British Isles – 'they were farmers,' writes W.H. Murray, 'with arts and crafts ready for development . . . expert seamen and boat-builders . . . the first earthenware pottery made by man . . .'

Certainly that pottery is poignant still, unearthed from a new grave or gathered from storm-ripped shore here and there on the west side of Lewis, indented often with the pads of careful, crafting fingers from some nameless soul long dead.

What has endured are their works in stone and, especially, their great chambered cairns which, though heavily despoiled by later generations for stone, are still found all over the Hebrides: Islay, for instance, has fourteen, and there is a notable example at Gress, on the Broad Bay coast a few miles north of Stornoway. These seem to have been the sepulchres of notable families; the dead being both cremated and inhumed, the remains interred with pottery, ornaments and even animals. Such 'megalithic' architecture bears witness to a maturing culture – one with religion, engineering, organised leadership and a strong social order. And by 1800 BC these doughty stone-movers had graduated to still more spectacular development – mighty standing stones, in avenues and alignments, in henges and in circles. The speed with which such endeavour spread strongly supports the theory that some sort of missionary community – moving northwards and sharing at least some language with these islanders – was directing the work, in a society now so organised that its ablest did not have to catch or grow their own food. And their greatest monument is at Callanish.

Callanish is best visited on a kind day in the island winter, when the coaches have ceased for the season, when visitors are few and intrepid and there is good prospect of having the standing stones to yourself. In fact, the famous site – where the megaliths walk up a ridge from the old township, with commanding views over Loch Roag and Loch Ceann Hulabhig to the hills of Pairc, Harris and Uig – is but the principal in a great complex of ancient works in this district.[12]

There are other, smaller stone circles within sight of 'Callanish I'; two of the most evocative are linked to it by footpath. There are still more at Garynahine, Achmore, Great Bernera and – though largely dismantled – even by Loch Raoinebhat, near South Shawbost. And there are half-circles, and solitary stones, such as the one rather sweetly incorporated into a modern council-housing scheme at Breasclete, and no doubt many others long since overwhelmed by peat. But it is Callanish I, with its radiating wings, southern avenue and central circle and huge central monolith and its central, ravaged chambered cairn, which attracts the tourists by the bus-load.

There is much confusion about dates. It was generally and for many years assumed that the Stones were erected around the second millennium before Christ – between, roughly, 2200 and 1800 BC – but of late it has become fashionable to assert the complex began 5,000 years ago, a view unfortunately stated with authority in the interpretative plaques. In fact this claim apparently rests on carbon-14 evidence outlined in a study by Edinburgh University in papers that have never been made public. Suffice to say that the standing stones of Callanish have stood for thousands of years and are very, very old; they pre-date Christianity by many centuries and were long obsolete when the Gaels came to Scotland.

A number of stones have vanished; one – found and 'reinstated' by the Victorians – is certainly in the wrong place; and another, at the end of the east row and on the other side of the perimeter path, was found by Gerald and Margaret Ponting and duly reinstated – correctly, in its original stone socket – only in 1982. Even after a quarter of a century, it is still visibly bleached from its long horizontal burial; the Pontings also retrieved the tip of a stone at the very end of the avenue, which they found in a nearby dyke, and this was sensitively mortared back onto its due megalith in 1978. The tip of another stone in the avenue was broken after 1860 and has quite vanished. These casualties aside, Callanish I is a remarkably intact site, and is best studied with a detailed, numbered plan and in relation to the closest natural feature, the rocky knoll beyond the southern end called Cnoc a Tursa.

In local tradition, all these standing stones were known as *na tursachan*, translating as either 'place of pilgrimage' or 'place of mourning'. The megaliths at the main site were called, besides, *Na Fir Bhreige*, the 'false men'. With one ancient and tantalising exception, their earliest reference in written history is to be found in the 1680 manuscript of John Morrison of Bragar, who retails the widespread belief that these ancient Lewis pillars of gneiss were 'men turned to rock by ane enchanter' – though he nowhere mentions Callanish by name. Martin Martin, visiting in 1703, 'enquired of the inhabitants what Tradition they had from their Ancestors concerning these Stones; and they told me it was a Place appointed for Worship in the time of Heathenism, and that the Chief Druid or Priest stood near the big Stone in the center, from whence he address'd himself to the People that surrounded him.'

Martin's dark conclusion – 'ye Heathen Temple' – has fed into our knowledge of the Druids and the persistent belief that the standing stones were a centre for human sacrifice. Certainly there are vague – very vague – stories retailed in the Callanish district of the stones' use in historic times, though it is by no means easy now to distinguish genuine Lewis tradition from traditions of other megalithic districts in the British Isles cheerfully imposed upon Callanish.

'About a hundred years ago, certain families in Callanish were known to be "of the Stones",[13] records Otta Swire, in her colourful little book of Outer Hebridean lore, 'and though the ministers had expressly forbidden reverent visits to the Stones on the days of the old festivals, they still made these visits in secret, "for it would not do to neglect the Stones." At midsummer sunrise, "the Shining One" was thought to walk up the avenue, heralded by a cuckoo's call . . .' While we are on cuckoos, Swire notes besides that 'the cuckoo, it is said, also gave its call in time to convene the Druidical May festival. Nowadays each cuckoo, on first reaching Lewis in the spring, is supposed to fly to Callanish and give its first call from the Standing Stones.' This is scarcely more credible than another barnacled tale, that *Na Tursachan* are ancient giants turned to stone by St Kieran, who cast the fateful incantation after they refused to convert to Christianity.

In fact, Morrison and Martin Martin – to say nothing of other lofty scholars of the period, who happily postulated Callanish theories while never quite finding the time to visit the site – saw far less of the stones than we can view today, so engulfed were the megaliths by inexorably growing peat.

In October 1857, prevailed upon by the Society of Antiquaries in Scotland – and alerted further as local peat-digging cut into the complex and exposed much buried stone – the laird of Lewis, Sir James Matheson, had the peat cleared completely from Callanish I in what one suspects was a rough, exuberant operation that destroyed much archaeological evidence. A full five feet of the stuff was removed, an accumulation sufficient to prove *Na Tursachan* had stood for millennia. Only then was the chambered cairn at its heart uncovered, to say nothing of quite a number of smaller megaliths that had been quite buried – and photographs of the exposed stones taken then, and for many years afterwards, still show clearly the newly uncovered and peat-bleached gneiss of their base, contrasting with their weathered, lichened uppers.

And rigorous archaeological investigation in 1980 and 1981 confirmed that the Callanish complex evolved over a long period.[14] A curved ditch had been dug long before their erection, and crops grown on rigs about six feet apart. A piece of pottery found suggested a date of around 3000 BC. Decades after this, the site was fenced, for holes and trenches suggest some sort of wooden palisade. This may well have been a ritual enclosure, for soon afterwards the first megaliths were hauled up the brae and erected, forming a circle of thirteen stones with one tall, central megalith – precisely as we see them now. Any of the local rock-faces could have furnished the gneiss, but tradition has long asserted that the slabs were prised from a cliff at Na Dromannan, about a mile away and certainly convenient. They were probably dragged by sledge, and eased up the more awkward slopes on timber rollers. Only a fifth of each weighty megalith is actually underground – secured in 'sockets' of boulder-clay and packing-stones, raised a little proud of the surface – and yet each has withstood the formidable gales of Lewis for thousands of years. (This also knocks on the head a notion still widely butted around; that the Stones have moved or 'drifted' over the centuries. While some, especially in the southern avenue, have tilted a little, they stand precisely where they have always stood. Astonishingly, the very stars – from Earth's perspective – have moved more.)

Because the foundations of the central cairn lie over ground disturbed when the standing stones were raised, we can be sure it was built much later – probably centuries later – and was at first a rather basic crypt. It was later expanded and then – perhaps a little before 1000 BC – deliberately opened and despoiled, before being subsequently embellished again. Soon afterwards, the peat began rapidly to enclose the area and by 500 BC the Callanish complex seems to have faded from use or great communal significance.

As the Druids had by then barely got going – their rites and activities are later detailed by the Romans, whose invasion of Britain was driven largely by their desire to smash the power-base of Druid-led resistance in Gaul – we can discount them from any Callanish activity and certainly dismiss visions of the Stones dripping with human blood, to the screams of sacrificial infants and the wailing of wretched mothers.

We can equally ignore the report of one Rev. A.C. MacLean, whom an old man of seventy-five assured – in the 1920s – that 'at Beltane time a great procession, led by white-robed priests chanting songs, approached the Callanish Stones. In the procession the most beautiful woman in the land carried her first-born child for sacrifice. After the child was handed over, the mother (who was not permitted in the temple) was led to the "place of wailing".' The kindly pensioner even pointed out this 'wailing place', by the end of the west row, and a 'conduit which led the blood away', going eastwards from the burial chamber. Actually, this ditch has been proved to be a Victorian addition, and it is hard to disagree with the Pontings when they suggest the old man had his tongue firmly in his cheek. They add that the Druid cult only arose around a thousand years after the last stone circle was built; that Druid rites centred on oak groves; and that there is not the least evidence that the cult ever reached the Hebrides.

Nevertheless, the Druid notion was rather less fatuous than many others touted over the ages – that the stones were a megalithic court of law (1814); that they made up a Norse temple to Thor (1824); that they were, rather, a fertility temple with the tallest megalith as a central phallus (1857); that it is a Christian site built as penance (1863); that Martian surveyors in search of minerals built Callanish and other sites as landing-marks for flying saucers, additionally guided by 'bio-electric potential' generated by exuberant dancing (1973); and that they served as theatre for assorted rites to awaken the White Goddess, combining with other megalithic sites to make one 'Chakra system' of earth energies, 'a network of communication, involving the vital forces of life, for universal enlight-enment' (1981). One inevitably wonders what that lady was smoking.

We need secondly to remember that Lewis has changed a very great deal since the turn of the second millennium before Christ. 'Our ancestors of 500 years ago knew a Callanish landscape very different from that of today,' writes Margaret Curtis:

> The sea level was lower and there was more machair – the coastal fringe of land where alkaline shell sand and heavy acidic peat mix to create a well-drained fertile soil attractive for farming. The climate was milder, warmer and drier, probably similar to that of central France today. The terrain was less harsh, with less peaty moorland, more grassland, and scatters of trees; mostly birch, hazel, willow, rowan and alder, and a few elm, pine and oak trees among the numerous rocky outcrops and lochs. It was quite unlike the dense forest on the mainland, where bears, wolves . . . still roamed. A climactic deterioration from about 1500 bc with cooler, wetter weather caused peat to grow more rapidly and to spread across grassland and scrub woodland, destroying them: a process which has carried on more or less continuously to the present day.

Confirmed by pollen grains in peat-core samples, this explains much: a rich, developed agriculture, and clear, generally cloudless skies, for if there is one thing on which most now agree these stones were built by men keen on astronomy.

And two other constants survive at Callanish. The standing stones are in the far north, where sun and moon can be observed over a very wide arc of the horizon; and the outstanding view of the Lewis and Harris landscape is more than merely an aesthetic consideration: the assorted peaks, hills and vales of all these hills allow the movement of all the celestial bodies to be plotted precisely, using this bearing and that sight-line and other distant landmarks, over months and years, to compile an accurate almanac.

The hypothesis that Callanish, at least in its practical aspects, thus functioned is not new. As long ago as 1726, Joseph Toland thought the 'temple' dedicated to 'the Sun', and in 1808 James Headrick mused that it was a 'rude astronomical observatory . . . the priests could mark out the rising of the Sun, Moon, and stars; the seasons of the year; even of the hours or divisions of the day.' But it was Alexander Thom, who first saw the stones in 1933, who truly advanced the idea.

Professor Thom was an engineer: as Duncan MacMillan notes, a 'trained visual thinker' who immediately saw astronomical significance. Indeed, he was so entranced that he devoted the rest of his life to studying Callanish and other prehistoric sites, founding a new discipline – archaeo-astronomy. He convincingly argued that Megalithic Man was entirely capable of complex mathematical and astronomical thought; and – less credibly – that he used a common unit of measurement, a length of 2.72 feet or 0.829 metres, which Thom dubbed the 'megalithic yard'.

More recent scholarship has cast doubt on many of Thom's conclusions. The 'megalithic yard' is not universally apparent in such sites, and is suspiciously close to the average adult-male pace – which is almost certainly what these people used. More seriously, Clive Ruggles – for one – has shown that many claims of precise alignment at Callanish are not accurate; and those which are so demonstrable are so few they could have occurred even by chance.

But Margaret Curtis' essay[15] in *Calanais*, published in 1995 to accompany a major art exhibition in Stornoway, provides the most useful navigation through a complex and occasionally fraught subject; she has built on, and largely overtaken, Thom's work but is careful to respect him.

Alexander Thom – who first saw the Stones on a moonlit summer evening – was immediately struck by one obvious feature; when viewed in exact line from a spot on Cnoc a Tursa, the pillars of the south row –

aligned on the high central monolith – run true from south to north. That is particularly impressive because, in the second millennium before Christ, the star we now call Polaris – the Pole Star – was not, four millennia ago, near the North Celestial Pole; our planet's axis of rotation has shifted in relation to the night sky, a phenomenon called the 'precession of the equinoxes'. How had the builders of the Callanish stones come to fix so accurate a bearing?

They may have done it by patient, regular observation of the night sky, using peaks and notches in the circling hills much as one would use the near-sight of a gun, and recording a position of – say – moonrise from a given viewpoint by something as simple as two wooden stakes. In due course, stones could be erected to mark the alignment. In short, Thom argues, Callanish is a megalithic calendar, of evident use in a society that depended on climate and tides, whose priests had grasped a connection with the Moon.

One Callanish hypothesis, outlined in depth by Margaret Curtis, is that they were ideally placed, and expressly designed, to follow all the movements of the Moon through the so-called 'lunar year'; a period of 18.61 years from 'major standstill' to 'minor standstill' and back again, as the Moon works through every possible variation of swings in moonrise and moonset over all those months, these variations arising from a slight irregularity in its orbit. And, as Margaret Curtis has now twice demonstrated on the Callanish site, the standing stones of Callanish I – aligned on Cnoc a Tursa – are perfectly placed for a spectacular display of the Moon, combined with a little human showmanship, on the night of the major lunar standstill – or south extreme of the Moon's movement – which last occurred in 2006. On such a night the Moon sails low, low, low over the hills south and west of Callanish.

Mrs Curtis makes a great deal of the Pairc Hills – the ridge of which apparently resembles a pillowed, recumbent woman and is said to be known locally as *Cailleach na Mointich*, 'the old woman of the moors' or the 'Sleeping Beauty'. But no documentary evidence of this pre-dates the 1970s, and it is hard not to feel that only then were imported New Age notions of the Earth Mother hung hopefully on the Callanish Stones.

Curtis is surely on much firmer ground in arguing that each of the six stone circles in the district 'appears to have been determined by the people's need to watch the Moon rise out of the stones of the circle from outside the ring; then, about two and a half hours later, from a different stance outside the same ring, to watch the Moon's brief re-gleam in the valley through the circle with the silhouette of a living person inside the Moon's orb.' And she dramatically describes the spectacle in June 1987, the first occasion on which she could test the 'major lunar standstill' hypothesis at Callanish I, with a willing actor to stand on Cnoc a Tursa and provide the eerie silhouette – and then parading down the stones, looming ever larger and larger against the lunar light.

By all accounts, it was a hammy affair. Yet may this have been how tales of a Shining One, walking up the avenue, took root? And then, there is that extraordinary note from Diodorus of Sicily, writing in 55 BC and quoting Herodotus, a long-dead Greek historian:

> Beyond the land of the Celts there lies in the ocean an island . . . situated in the North . . . inhabited by the Hyperboreans . . . and there is . . . both a magnificent sacred precinct . . . and a notable temple . . . spherical in shape . . . the moon as viewed from this island appears to be but a little distance from the Earth . . . and the god visits the island every nineteen years and . . . he plays on the cithera and dances continuously the night long until the rising of the Pleiades.

We need certainly once and for all to get out of our heads one notion: that our ancient forebears were pitiable, shambling things in skins, both fearful and stupid. These people could feed themselves, cure and sew leather, light and maintain fire, weave fabric, breed animals, hunt game, recognise ores and smelt the metals, mould tools and ornaments and jewellery, frame laws and order a society. We cannot blithely dismiss their astronomy. Plutarch, in the first century AD, may well have sneered at the Druids of his day for celebrating the feast of Saturn every thirty years 'because they contend that Saturn takes thirty years to complete his orbit round the Sun.' Plutarch in his wisdom 'knew', of course – as the Papacy would still absurdly contend 1500 years later, to the point of judicial murder – that Saturn and everything else revolved around the Earth. But the Druids were right. W.H. Murray, too, cites Herodotus, mentioning the visit of one Abaros to Greece, a philosopher 'from the Winged Temple of the Northern Isles' – and, more, that Abaros took the trouble to visit Pythagoras. It is hard to disagree with Murray's firm conclusion – 'the only winged temple in northern latitudes was Callanish'.

But Callanish bears useful lessons. Even in prehistoric Lewis, religion was not something entirely ring-fenced from the rest of the daily round of life. The standing stones of Callanish fitted neatly into the entire order of the society that built them – a place of observation, of gathering, of consecration, of honour, of adjudication and of funerals, of social and agricultural and sacerdotal significance. One must concur with Duncan MacMillan, 'the function of these stones seems to have been eminently practical in a world where the practical was not divorced by definition from the spiritual. There was no such thing as religion as a separate mode of consciousness, special for Sunday.' And, on this island, there never has been.

Yet, secondly – to resort to the language of Christian theology – Callanish was a religion founded on natural revelation: on close, detailed, painstaking study of the physical environment. We do not know whether the men who erected the stones were permanent, settled members of the local community or a travelling elite. But it is difficult to believe they could have resisted the temptation to priestcraft, presenting science as magic in predicting an eclipse, for instance. There can be little doubt they used their secrets to manipulate all about them to their advantage and it is improbable they would have had the least interest in, for instance, any programme of general education that would have forfeited their mystical status.

And the final lesson is, of course, that this man-made religion of Callanish failed, so entirely that the society about it collapsed; so completely that its traditions are lost.[16] One suspects the mounting corruption of its elite had much to do with the final disintegration, especially as advancing climate change – the marching peat, the remorseless waterlogging, the clouding of once-clear astronomical skies – imperilled the economy and their own claim to authority. Perhaps indeed, in the last centuries, they resorted to bloodier rituals. Invasion and conquest may have overwhelmed that society. But the real vulnerability lay in a metaphysic with no answers to the deepest human question of all: the immortality – or otherwise – of the individual human spirit.

And in all this we largely speculate. 'Archaeology tells us something about how people lived,' warns Patrick Ashmore, who deserves the last word, 'but it does not tell us what they felt, nor what they thought. We seek to understand their ideas through analogies with better known societies, assuming that tools and buildings reflect the beliefs of those who fashioned them; but present perceptions of past peoples are not the same as past people's perceptions of their present.'

Even today, rather more survives – if at the edges, in the twenty-first century, of the Hebridean consciousness – from this pre-Christian era than interesting stone structures. Paganism still echoes – and much more superstition and even downright witchcraft survived well into living memory than is readily admitted.

An enduring emphasis is sun worship, in human terms eminently understandable at so northern a latitude. Forms of it survived far into the Christian era, most notably in the custom of *deiseal* – that, most propitiously, any enterprise should be done, or at least begun, sunwise. A boat heading to sea was always at first rowed sunwise; people walked

sunwise around places of veneration, such as the old monuments and
cairns, and so on. More strikingly, the prehistoric calendar survived.
There was Samhain in early November, a feast of the dead; Imbole, or
Imbolc, on 1 February, celebrated fertility; Beltane, on 1 May, became
May Day; and Lughnasad (1 August) endures as Lammas Day, for virility
and harvest.

There was a degree of perhaps calculated conflation. The Celtic
goddess of stock and fertility, Brigit − or Bride − became St Bride,
most venerated of the Celtic saints, and the tradition took strong hold
that she had served as midwife to Mary, mother of Jesus − 'over whom,'
Anne Ross notes wryly, 'she would, in fact, appear to have taken
precedence in popularity, possibly because Candlemas (2 February)
which so closely coincides with her feast day, was the date of the
purification of Our Lord's mother.'[17] There are still localities all over
Scotland and Ireland centred on ancient dedication to Bride − from the
bonny East Kilbride, at the southern tip of South Uist, to the eponymous
New Town in Lanarkshire.

Notionally, of course, such little Celtic churches were dedicated to the
memory of a real woman, such as Brigit of Kildare, who lived from about
452 to 525. There is at least one other credible candidate − but Bill
Lawson asserts that 'the Bride who was most revered in the islands was
neither of these,' and relays a tradition recorded by Alexander Carmichael, presumably from Argyll or the Catholic Hebrides, that she was a
serving-maid in the Inn at Bethlehem, *'bean-chuideachadh Mhoire'*, aid-
woman to Mary; and that this Bride not only delivered the baby Jesus but
'put three drops of water from the spring on His forehead, in the name of
God, in the name of Jesus, in the name of the Spirit.' And even that
tradition is only to overlay improbable Christian myth on the worship of a
pagan goddess. Significantly, Lawson relates these matters in his engaging history of the old parish church at Scarista, on the west coast of
Harris − 'a religious site even in pre-Christian days, as is shown by the
standing stone of Clach Steinigrie, which with its companion stones −
now fallen − may originally have formed a stone circle . . . the dedication
there is to St Bride, or Bridget.'

But what survived most powerfully, and on Lewis at least till after the
Second World War, were ancient customs associated with Hallowe'en −
naturally overlaid on Samhain − and especially the rites associated in
living memory with the 'old New Year' on 12 January, a hangover from
the 1752 transition in Britain to the Gregorian calendar. A neighbour in
South Shawbost,[18] for instance, born in 1920, vividly recalls the bannock
still baked for children at New Year celebrations, known as *Oidhche na
Challain* (Night of the Kalends) or *Oidhche na Bhannaig* (Night of the

Cake) – 'a special scone, with sugar and butter, and currants and raisins. It was tasty!'

But such a bannock was a staple of ancient Celtic rituals. A bannock – deliberately scorched in one portion – was a staple of Beltane ceremonies in Scotland, such as one enacted until well into the twentieth century at Glenlyon, Perthshire. 'The one whose lot it was to receive the blackened piece of the bannock,' records Anne Ross, 'was ritually beaten out of the *temenos* – sacred area – as the scapegoat of the community. In earlier times his or her fate would no doubt have been more sinister. The festival likewise to mark the summer solstice (21 June) was likewise celebrated by the lighting of great bonfires, the baking of a special cake, dancing and rejoicing.' Hector MacIver and Calum Ferguson – writing respectively of pre-war customs in Shawbost and Point – detail *Oidche na Challain* chants and a leading, 'scapegoat' figure draped in a calf-skin, ritually (if lightly) beaten and leading his pack of happy youngsters away to another house with more goodies in their sack.[19] 'Celebration of the *Callain* finally petered out at the time of the Second World War,' Ferguson wistfully concludes. But its roots in Celtic paganism are unmistakeable.

There endures besides the veneration of springs and wells. There are still healing wells on Lewis, and many still quietly resort to them – one, in the sea-cliffs at South Shawbost, for instance, is said to be particularly rich in iron; another, by Galson some fifteen miles to the north, was supposed to be most efficacious for epilepsy.[20]

Not all traditional medicine on the Long Island can be dismissed as superstitious nonsense. Shawbost, for instance, had an eminent tradition of herbal medicine. Lewis folk still head into the moor to collect *lus nan laogh*[21] – the bogbean; *Menyanthes trifoliata* – which, duly boiled to a fare-thee-well, is strained and the liquor bottled with a healthy glug of spirits. A little glass of this mixture – which, of course, tastes vile – is said to work wonders for gippy tummies and illnesses of lassitude. I have met too many strong, clever women who attest to this remedy lightly to dismiss it.

Only desperation, though, amidst the terrible tuberculosis which proved such an island scourge, could explain the stubborn belief in a certain cure for *tinneas a Righ* – the King's Evil, or scrofula, a tubercular affliction of glands in the neck. It was maintained – at least in the absence of local royalty – that the touch of the seventh child of a seventh child (or, being realistic, just the touch of a seventh child) was a sovereign remedy.[22] Such were besought for that mystical touch, or asked to rub a silver sixpence, or even to wash their hands in water then later deployed as an affusion. The belief, even among professing Christians, in this cure was so inveterate that a district nurse appointed to the care of Barvas and Brue – around 1940 – remembers ruefully what the local doctor said when she

asked how best to win the confidence of her charges. 'Och,' said he, 'just
tell them you believe in *tinneas a Righ*, and you'll be fine . . .'[23]

And there is still a tacit cult of the rowan tree on Harris. When I
moved to Maraig in 1993, one grew near my door; repairing two years
later to Tarbert, another grew by that door too. In wider Celtic lore, that
tree is believed to ward off the 'evil eye'. And some have even boldly
argued that the Celtic Cross itself combines with the tree of Calvary the
circle of the Druids,[24] which leads us neatly to the coming of Christianity.

2

Pro Christo Peregrinari Volens

Myths and Reality of the Celtic Church, the First Millennium

Near the Butt of Lewis, on the Atlantic coast of Ness, is the ancient graveyard of Swainbost, a few hundred yards to the south of the modern cemetery (opened in 1922) and in the quiet, lovely glen of a little river, its dark water cutting through the shore into the great rollers of the Atlantic Ocean. Few have been buried here since the Second World War: the last, in February 1971, was my own great-grandfather, who insisted on lying with his first, beloved wife, whom he had survived by fifty-six years.[1]

It is a quiet, timeless spot, with remarkably few engraved headstones; most of the numberless dead, buried here through at least a thousand years, are marked only by small boulders, one to the head and feet of each interment, and quite a hazard in the long undergrowth of a Lewis summer. And Swainbost cemetery is dominated by *Teampall Pheadair*, now open to the winds and with only the eastern gable still standing – an old, old church, once the second-biggest on Lewis, and where services only ceased in the 1820s.[2]

'St Peter's' is a very obvious Roman Catholic dedication, which would suggest – at first – that this site, secluded and sheltered and fertile, with its ready landing from the ocean, was a stranger to Christianity until well into the Middle Ages. And archaeologists – who have of late taken a keen interest in the tumbled kirk – confirm its medieval construction.

Yet the Ness district bristles with ancient, tiny churches – the immaculately restored *Teampall Mholuaidh*, and the founds nearby of *Teampall Ronain*; the folk-memory of *Teampall Chliamainn* at North Dell; the forlorn, tiny cell of some ancient Christian hermit on Luchruban, or 'Pygmy Isle', near the Butt itself; or another still bleaker cell on lonely Sula Sgeir, many miles out to sea and where, to this day, the men of Ness sail each August to cull (by special licence) gannet chicks, that local delicacy of *guga*; or a remarkably well preserved church on North Rona, forty-four miles north of the Butt.[3]

And we know from clear local recollection that when Teampall

Pheadair was extended late in the eighteenth century, the roof was cannibalised from Teampall Mholuaidh and the stone pillaged from the ruins of still another church, Teampall Thomais, only two or three hundred yards away, on a striking knoll overlooking the shore. Apart from a distinct hollow, perhaps shaped by turf-entombed foundations, nothing of this place of worship can now be seen.

All this ecclesiastical construction, in so confined a parish, suggests some intense Christian activity long, long ago. And there are other clues that a Gospel witness was known here before the late Middle Ages. For one, oral tradition in Ness relates that a mound within the Swainbost cemetery, just east of the church, is the mass grave for the casualties of a battle – a skirmish with the Norsemen; or, indeed, between Norsemen. But, most telling of all, a hillock between this walled, faintly eerie cemetery and the shore is known locally as *Na h-Annaidean*, or *Cnoc an Annaid*. That name occurs more than once throughout the West Highlands – in Skye; near Shieldaig in Wester Ross (Annat); the Annat Narrows of Loch Eil, between Corpach and Ardgour, where a black tide flows strong at the flood. And it is used invariably of something much more complex than a church – a religious foundation, a monastery. We may be confident that here, well before the first millennium, was a mission of what we know today as the Celtic Church.

To ascertain how Christianity reached Lewis and Harris, we must first examine how the Gospel reached the British Isles and, specifically, the origins of the Christian order – flooding and overflowing from Ireland – that we call the Celtic Church. And we should bear in mind, besides, another most significant population movement – the migration of German tribes into England, Angles and Saxons who, by pillage and conquest, drove the indigenous British west into the fastnesses of Wales and Cornwall and, no less significantly, for some centuries made contact between the Christians of Gaeldom and the church on the mainland of Europe extremely difficult.

There are extraordinary difficulties in exploring the early Christian history of Britain.[4] For one, documentary evidence is scant and extremely unreliable. And what survives is heavily coloured by the literary conventions of the time, and often most partisan. It was difficult enough for Adomnan to write his great *Life of Columba*, around 640, when that redoubtable figure had already been dead for half a century; but Adomnan had no intention of writing what we would regard as a biography, or even notion of the concept: he was determined to prove the sanctity and abiding, supernatural powers of his subject. And nothing at all, contrary to widespread belief, survives of Columba's own writings.

Some writers, like the Venerable Bede, who wrote his history of the English church around 731, had axes to grind: he hated the Welsh Christians (whom, like his contemporaries, he called the British) and naturally emphasised Anglo-Saxon Christianity over its Celtic brethren; others, like the self-righteous and creepy Gildas, a sixth-century Celtic moralist, are more interested in vituperation than the faith once delivered to the saints.

But the real problem is our own perception, looking back over centuries through layer upon layer of denominationalism, propaganda and mythology; as generation upon generation reinvented a past British Christianity and especially the Celtic saints for their own purposes. What we generally understand today as the 'Celtic Church' is little more than a confused myth.[5] Roman Catholic scholars have naturally projected their own recent tradition – with all its egregious errors – back upon the early Irish church of Gaeldom. Modern Protestant propaganda has taken still greater liberties, suggesting that Iona operated in a kind of proto-Presbyterianism, with Columba – naturally – an eminent proto-Calvinist.[6]

And – since the Ossianic romance of Victorian times, and especially since the 1960s, an extremely fashionable 'Celtic Christianity' has emerged from a variety of peacenik, feminist, New Age strands. The Iona Community, founded in 1938 by a posh Church of Scotland minister, Rev. George MacLeod, was at least robustly practical. Today, the Community resembles nothing so much as the Liberal Democrats at prayer.[7] Beyond that is a wider Celtic spirituality, and even some modern sects: a quick Google search, for instance, introduces us to the Holy Celtic Church, the Celtic Catholic Church, the Celtic Episcopal Church and (not to be outdone) the Independent Celtic Episcopal Church.

All cherish the same fond beliefs: in the inherent virtue of the Gael and the old Celtic culture – primitive wisdom and the 'Noble Highlander'; in a sort of aboriginal, apostolic Christianity that took root of itself in the British Isles without any 'patriarchal' or 'imperialist' intervention from a wider Europe; in a Celtic Christianity that cherished the environment, loved all God's creatures and practically worshipped nature; in a Christianity that not only lived tolerantly alongside an older pagan faith but actively borrowed from it in a peaceful syncretism, especially in its veneration for wood, water and female sexuality – in all, a holistic, sustainable way of life, utterly uncontaminated by anything Roman or Teutonic or Angle or Saxon, supervised in benign tolerance by wholly non-confrontational monks.

Alas, such a picture bears not the least relation to reality. For one, Christianity was no more 'indigenous' to these islands than – beyond Jerusalem and Galilee – it is anywhere else. The Gospel was brought to

Britain, and it was brought, of course, by the Roman occupation. 'The importance of the Roman presence in creating a structure conducive to the introduction of Christianity to these islands cannot be overemphasised,' writes Donald Meek. 'Any attempt to dismiss it and to afford a primary place to our "aboriginal apostles" cannot be supported by the evidence.' Of course, it was the fourth century before Rome officially sanctioned (and indeed adopted) the Christian faith and, practically since the Resurrection, there were outbursts of sporadic but intense persecution. There was certainly no uniform spread of the new faith – which drifted in unofficially, with Roman administrators, slaves, tradesmen and camp followers – and, despite attempts to argue otherwise, there was no Christian organisation to speak of, such as a diocesan structure, when the Romans left shortly before the fall of the Western empire.

Yet there can be no doubt that Christians were in Britain at a very early point, probably before the end of the first century. The evidence is largely archaeological – Communion silver; imagery; assorted inscriptions. Gravestones in the far north of England, for instance, attest to Christian activity within the Roman era, and this area generally, into Scotland and around the Solway, affords our strongest evidence of a continuous, surviving faith after the legions sailed out. At Whithorn, what is almost certainly a fifth-century gravestone is inscribed, in Latin, 'To The Praise Of The Lord' and records one Latinus and his daughter, as well as the man who raised the stone. At Kirkmadrine in the Rhinns of Galloway, two more tombstones – replete with *chi-rho* symbols, and the Alpha and Omega – record several 'holy and distinguished priests'; the names still legible are Viventius, Mavorius and Florentius. They are confidently ascribed to the fifth century and, by this point, we have some historical knowledge of Christian personalities in contemporary Britain – Pelagius, Ninian and Patrick.

Pelagius was born in Britain around AD 352 and is immortalised by his round denial of 'original sin'. He argued, in optimistic contrast, that everyone is born with a free and unpolluted moral nature, capable of pursuing God and good – or disobedience and evil – by the untrammelled exercise of free will. Pelagianism has been rightly called the 'English heresy' and, as Andrew Bulloch noted in 1961, 'to learn a modern version of it no more is needed than attendance at a few of our most popular city churches.'

As for Ninian, all we know is what is claimed by the Venerable Bede,[8] who maintains that

the southern Picts who live on this side of the mountains had, it is said, long ago given up the error of idolatry and received the true faith through the preaching of the Word by that revered and saintly man Bishop Nynia, a Briton by birth, who had received orthodox instruction at Rome in the faith and mystery of the truth. His episcopal see is distinguished by the name and church of St Martin the bishop, and there his body now lies along with those of many saints; this see now belongs to the English race. This place, belonging to the province of the Bernicians, is commonly called 'at the white house' inasmuch as he built there a church of stone in a manner unusual among the Britons.

Tradition and archaeological evidence do suggest Ninian established a Christian base at Whithorn and, from this, Christianity may well have spread through the Lowlands and – by dint of easy terrain – up into the East Highlands and even as far as Shetland, where a church was certainly dedicated to him. But we can emphatically assert that the West Highlands and the Hebrides – the whole western seaboard north of the Firth of Clyde – were evangelised not from England, nor the Roman Empire, but from Ireland; and the very first Christian witness was probably one as much of simple population movement as of conscious mission.

From the first century AD the Gaels of Ulster began to settle in increasing number in the south-west corner of the West Highlands; this is why, to this day, we call that county Argyll; *Earra-Ghaidheal*, the territory of the Gaels.[9] Their homeland in northern Ireland they called *Dail Riata* and, confusingly, applied the same name to their burgeoning base in Argyll; New Dalriada became, by the sixth century, Alban or *Alba*, and Gaelic-speakers to this day use that name for all Scotland. For this new language is the enduring legacy of the migration; that Gaelic which survives – in much vulnerability – even in the twenty-first century. Certainly these Gaels, or – as the Romans called them – *Scottii*, became in time not only established, but dominant, to the point that their polity finally commanded the whole country and gave it the name that endures today.

But these Gaels brought more than language: from the middle of the fifth century they brought besides a new religion. And how the Christian faith first took root in the Emerald Isle is lost in the Celtic mists. Though one of the most famous of British saints, virtually everything about Patrick is mired in dispute. Some even contest the authenticity of his own writings. He was certainly not the first to evangelise Ireland, and never pretended to be. The chronicle of Prosper of Aquitaine records unambiguously, in 431, that 'Consecrated by Pope Celestine, Palladius is sent as the first bishop to the Irish who believe in Christ.' Again, the primacy of Rome is evident; the first missionary-bishop is a Palladius, not a

Patrick; and there were Christians there already, among the Gaels or *Scottii* of Ireland, before even Palladius was commissioned. We can sure of little else about Palladius; the only biography appeared 600 years later and is not remotely reliable.

Cutting through the confusion, we can be fairly certain that Patrick was born in what is now Scotland (contemporaries refer to him, accurately, as a Briton, from Welsh-speaking Strathclyde); that he reached Ireland as a consecrated bishop; and that he is emphatically the founding father of the historical Celtic Church. And, even to the Christians of the present day and especially those of that Reformed, evangelical stamp on Lewis and Harris, and taking his surviving writings – some letters and a *Confession* – as authentic, there is something immensely appealing about him. Nor was he any stranger to Ireland.

Assuming that Patrick really did write the memoirs that survive and if we adjust for the difficulty he faced in adapting Celtic terms to his Latin text and trust to stubborn, enduring tradition, he was apparently born towards the end of the fourth century in what is now Old Kilpatrick in Dunbartonshire; his father, a farmer, was an important local official; and the family had been Christian for some time: Patrick tells us his grandfather, Potitus, was a priest.

But contented childhood was cruelly ruptured. As a lad in his teens, Patrick was captured by Irish pirates and borne away to that country to be sold as a slave. In that wretched situation, Patrick's Christianity became personal and vital:

> Day by day I used to pasture the flock, and I used constantly to pray in the daytime. More and more the love of God came to me, and the fear of Him. My faith was increased and the Spirit wrought within me, insomuch that in a single day I would offer as many as a hundred prayers and nearly as many by night, while I abode in the fields or on the mountains. Before sunrise I used to wake to pray, in spite of snow or frost or rain, and I felt no ill, nor was there slothfulness in me, as I now see, because the Spirit was then fervent within me.

After six years he managed to escape, and talked his way aboard a ship bound for the Continent. Patrick wandered around Gaul and the Mediterranean, revelling less in the comforts and dignity of a new freedom than in all the Christian fellowship he found, and duly settled for some years in a monastery on the island of Lerins, off the Riviera coast. He gained an excellent grasp of theology and, of still more importance, an astonishing knowledge of the Bible. He was ordained deacon by Amator and, when Germanus came puffing back from Britain in 431, he duly consecrated Patrick as a bishop. The following year, he sailed for Ireland.

The mission of Patrick quickly prospered, despite inevitable hardship and some disappointments. An early convert was an influential local chief, allowing him to establish his first church in Down and 'a Christian community, a permanent base for his work and an assured income,' observes Bulloch. He also found – and himself records – signs of earlier Christian activity: a stone cross in the far west of the country, a tiny sanctuary with altar and chalices. His travels – around Ulster, Meath and Connaught – were unceasing, his labours constant. But Patrick was used in the conversion of many, many groups, and would ordain and leave behind one of his retinue to serve as pastor, complete with a textbook of basic Christian truth; a light in a land still dominated by animistic worship of woods and wells, crude idols, phallic symbolism and human sacrifice to gods associated with sex and the harvest. 'Milk and corn,' notes a chilling Irish verse, 'they used to ask of him urgently, for a third of their children: great was the horror and wailing . . .'

Patrick's significance was not that he was a missionary, blasting through utterly pagan territory, but a bishop, bequeathing a viable, enduring church structure, advancing Christianity from beleaguered irrelevance to a confident faith. 'Whatever had been before he came, Patrick had virtually created the Church in Ireland,' concludes Bulloch, leaving 'the imperishable record of a devoted and fearless man of God, tempestuous, and ever in conflict with heathendom . . . of an evangelical faith and reliance upon God . . . Patrick will live in the memory of men so long as there are Christians who know what it is to venture all for the Gospel.'

The Irish Church, Meek points out, was 'firmly contextualised within early Irish society. It took much of its outward, physical shape from that society, and its clergy were accommodated within the prevailing social hierarchy and value-system.' It had besides robust discipline, not least because on occasion there were robust problems. One abbot, in Caldey, had a drink problem so bad that one night he fell down a well to his death. A 'penitential' – a manual for church discipline, produced by Gildas in the sixth century – prescribed a penance of three years, excommunicate, for 'a presbyter or deacon committing natural fornication or sodomy,' which suggests the Celtic order was no more stranger to such spectacular lapses than any church is today.

It was at once sturdy and intimate, a typical Celtic Church community being run – quite deliberately – as a sort of large extended family, or rather small clan, with the abbot as father-figure, and new foundations, if they

were planted out, duly looking back to the founding monastery for
succour, authority and guidance. It is impossible to overemphasise the
centrality of monastic life to the Celtic Church. On the Continent,
monasticism operated within the wider Catholic order. In the Celtic
order, monasticism defined it.

Monasticism itself – men and, in later centuries, women forsaking
family relationships and secular calling for full-time, communal religious
service – began as a reaction to what Bulloch describes as the 'unexpected
and embarrassing popularity' of the Church after Constantine made
Christianity the official faith of the Roman Empire. A new way of
Christian living took root in Egypt – enclosed brotherhoods with a
common refectory, church and library and under the unquestioned
authority of a superior. These early, Eastern monasteries, advocated by
Anthony, Jerome and others, were not centres for engagement with a
wider community, but retreat from it.

In Gaul, though, Martin of Tours – whose early Christian life was
shadowed by his past as a soldier, a calling the Church then and for
centuries afterwards viewed with utter disdain – founded a different sort
of monastic life, less cloistered, less bound by a detailed rule. To be sure,
Martin and his followers – about eighty of them – lived behind a
boundary fence, held to a loose but clearly understood discipline, wore
the poorest clothing, denied themselves wine and ate but one meal a day.
But they sallied forth regularly; Martin himself, an ordained bishop, went
on great preaching jaunts around the adjoining countryside.

And it was this sort of outgoing monastic mission which took such
enthusiastic root in Ireland – just before Anglo-Saxon hegemony so
established itself in England that for very many years the Church was
effectively cut off from the Continent.

A Celtic monastery, such as Columba would in 563 establish on Iona,[10]
was nothing like the establishment we might envisage today – mighty
walls, great Gothic arches, long echoing cloisters and magnificent architecture. The buildings presently hallowed on Iona are of the much later
Benedictine foundation, in the Middle Ages, and the oldest surviving
building – St Oran's Chapel, or Reidhlig Oran – dates only from the late
twelfth century. Columba's monastery, like any other Celtic Church
monastic community, had much more in common with the sort of
mission compound the Free Presbyterian Church, for instance, would
plant with such success in Southern Rhodesia.

A Celtic monastery was not a single, large, grandiloquent building
accommodating a great many monks, but a collection of several small
buildings constructed, depending on what was readily to hand, of turf,
stone or wattle, all enclosed behind a *vallum*, which could be a dyke or

palisade but, in some instances, simply a ditch, and served not as a barrier
but as a line of demarcation, beyond which – for instance – a sword was
not to be carried. Indeed, sections of the original *vallum*, now a low
rampart of grassy sod, are all that today can be seen of Columba's original
Iona foundation, rightly described by John MacKay as an

> unpretentious little village . . . The small church, or oratory, with its
> side-aisle or *exedra*, is built of oak. So is also the abbot's house, which
> stands on rising ground near by. At a little distance from these buildings
> we see the requisite number of circular creelwork huts, thatched with
> rush or heather, and placed at regular intervals round an open lawn, or
> *faithche*. Our attention is also attracted by their common dining room
> (*pronntigh*) and kitchen (*coitcheann*). In process of time a library, reading
> and writing rooms, schoolrooms and workshops would be added, and
> the whole surrounded by a wall of stone and turf.[11]

The church building, of course, was most prominent; but anything other
than the smallest monastery in time usually built several; the architecture
of the day did not lend itself to great buildings and mighty roof-spans,
and the churches 'of the Celtic West, taken on the whole, are the poorest
in Christendom', notes Bulloch, noting of the oratory at Gallarus in
Kerry, for instance – an extended beehive cell consisting entirely of
corbelled, interlocking stone, that 'it looks not unlike a well-built peat-
stack'.

The ruins of these first, primitive cells can still be found in the
Hebrides and, even in later centuries, buildings in the Irish tradition
were tiny. A ninth-century church still surviving on Iona, and known as
St Colm's House, measures – internally – but nineteen feet by fifteen feet
six inches. And, of course, these buildings were almost unlit, with the
tiniest of windows – if there were windows at all. Whatever their later
connotations, candles at the altar served an evident practical purpose. But
how could a congregation have been assembled in such a space? In truth,
congregational worship as we understand it was unknown. Churches
accommodated only the celebrant and a server, and a handful of onlookers,
and the building itself was but a strongroom for the Communion vessels –
there is often an obvious niche where they were kept – and where the
Eucharist could be enacted in some dignity and comfort. Preaching, and
administration of the sacrament, was done outside.

The church apart, a Celtic monastery boasted a common house or
domum, combining a refectory and kitchen and, no doubt, space for
fellowship and relaxation. There was a hospice, for receiving guests, and a
school, and a *scriptorium* – where manuscripts were copied meticulously

and beautifully decorated; and workshops for smiths, engravers, stone-masons and so on. Celtic monks slept not in dormitories, but in individual cells, the better for meditation and private devotion, and seem to have been free to venture into the communities of a wider world beyond. The main structures were erected of wood and wattle – Columba bought timber from a chief on Mull, in exchange for barley – but monks built their own dwelling-huts, from wood and reed and sods, and the cell occupied by Columba himself for his daily routine was neither bigger nor any less austere.

Neither Ireland nor Scotland had known any literacy until the coming of Christianity; within a few generations, there was a huge clerical caste lettered not only in Latin, but able to write in a newly scripted Gaelic. Their surviving verse, notes and journals show a surprising breadth: love of landscape, a tender eye for nature, a keen sense of place and a quiet pleasure in the wonders of the creation around them. By the sixth century, a typical Celtic monastery comprised 150 monks, though these included lay brothers who did not wear an ordinand's undyed, woollen cloak over a white tunic. The Celtic – or any – tonsure – sounds eccentric to us; but it had the same function as a modern clerical collar, being both the badge of a servant and readily identifying one as an unarmed man of God in, possibly, fraught situations beyond that community.

But the bounds of this western Christendom were already advancing beyond Ireland. And the Gospel preceded Columba to the Hebrides, taken by other hardy Irishmen who, their piety apart, were skilled and resourceful seamen, capable of daring and, on occasion, prodigiously long voyages in their hide-hulled coracles and curraghs. For one, Lugad reached the new Dal Riata before the Ulster prince, founding his community on Lismore in the Firth of Lorne. This man of God is still remembered in the Hebrides as Moluag – the possessive *mo* being a term of half-endearment, half-beatification – and it is to him that Teampall Mholuaidh at Eoropie is dedicated, but he is still more notably memor-ialised in assorted Kilmaluags on Lismore itself, on Tiree and Skye and Raasay, and almost certainly the great parish of Kilmallie, in Lochaber. And what may well have been the very first Christian structure on Harris is recorded in the 1851 *Origines Parochiales*, a chapel on the shores of Loch Seaforth, dedicated to 'St Luke'. The founds of such a cell are evident in the ancient burial ground of Maraig, the name of Moluag being mangled to Luke by the nineteenth century. Lochaber and the Inner Hebrides were an immediate and successful field for Moluag in his lifetime, but he also founded a sub-monastery at Rosemarkie, on the east coast, and his reach extended to Banffshire, Buchan and Deeside.

He may have been beaten to the Firth of Lorne by Brendan of

Clonfery, who founded a monastery around 542 on an island – 'Hinba' – not now readily identified; it may have been Eilean an Naoimh, but the surviving ruins are just as likely to be Columban, and the tidal island of Oronsay, adjoining Colonsay, is more probable. Some, though, doubt Brendan's historical existence. An ancient life of St Bridget mentions a visit, in 523, from 'a priest named Ninidh of Mull', who administered her last Communion. One Kieran had established a monastery on Tiree before Columba's arrival, though this did not prevent Columba from establishing his own mission on the island.

It is unlikely that such early agents of Christ viewed word of Columba's imminent arrival with unalloyed joy; and it is still more probable that in Dal Riata generally many shuddered at its political implications. Columba is, of course, the most famous of all the Celtic saints in Scotland; a man whose zest, energy and flair for leadership still crackle through even the treacly pages of Adomnan; a man whose name has been appropriated, time and again, for assorted causes through succeeding history – the new, united Scottish kingdom of Kenneth mac Alpan; for Bruce's victory at Bannockburn; for the energies of the Scottish Reformation. New churches in Scotland's industrial cities would be dedicated to this Columba – in one Edinburgh street, a St Columba's Free Church and a St Columba's Episcopal Church are but yards apart – and, in 1997, the saint's name would even adorn *Iomairt Chaluim Cille*, the 'Columba Initiative', designed to foster close new ties between the Gaels of Scotland and Erin, and blessed by the President of Ireland herself.

Columba's real importance in Scottish history is political, not spiritual. He had an intense interest in affairs of state, as became one of his background – born in 521, in Donegal, and son of Fedilmith mac Fergus, of *Cenel Conaill*, the 'lineage of Connell', whose great-grandfather had been Niall of the Nine Hostages, founder early in the fifth century of the Tara dynasty in Ulster. It is also believed that Columba's mother, Eithne, was a direct descendant of Cathair Mor, a king of Leinster; and his given name was Crimthann: he adopted Colm, or Columba, on baptism. It means 'dove'; but scarcely reflects his temperament. Devout, principled and kindly as the churchman would prove, this was a man of passion: one who spoke his mind, one of force and purpose – 'kin to princes, soldiers and warriors', says James Hunter, 'and it showed'.

And we know that in 563 Columba 'sailed away from Ireland to Britain *pro Christo peregrinari volens;* "choosing to be a pilgrim for Christ"', and moreover – something on which Adomnan places curious emphasis, for he states it twice, that this was about two years after 'the battle of Cul Drebene', when Columba's Ui Neill kinsmen of Ulster's north won a bloody confrontation with the forces of Diarmait mac Cerbaill, the southern Ui Neill king and notional overlord of them all. The *Annals of Ulster* assert besides that this victory was 'through the prayers of St Columba'.

And, reading between the lines of Adomnan's cagey text, it seems that Columba quit Ulster for Scotland under a cloud – perhaps even, at least for a season, excommunicate – having alienated a good many brethren by explicit, partisan, political engagement in a way they naturally deemed inappropriate in a priest ordained. Nevertheless his venture to Dal Riata seems to have been carefully planned, perhaps by direct negotiation with King Connall himself. And Iona – a small, fertile island at the tip of the Ross of Mull – was a deftly chosen location for a new foundation. Today, from a southern and urban perspective, the little place is in the back of beyond. In Columba's time, when the sea afforded the most swift and ready transport, it was at the heart of his world and by his own formidable leadership could readily win a place at the centre of affairs – convenient for Ireland, for all the Hebrides, and by direct passage up the Firth of Lorne and Loch Linnhe and then by easy portage through the Great Glen and its linked lochs, to the Pictish capital itself by modern Inverness.

Columba, as we have noted, did not bring Christianity to the Hebrides. And – though he twice visited Skye – he never set foot on any of the Outer Isles. By example, by vision, and by force of personality he did bring a whole new confident vigour into the lately established West Highland mission. He also, famously, made that long and daunting journey to Inverness, where he was graciously received by King Brude of the Picts and seems to have been able to communicate without an interpreter. He even engaged – and won – a competition against the 'magicians' of Brude's court. What is generally overlooked in the compounded mythology of the Celtic Church is that he did not 'convert' the Picts. There is not even any evidence that he converted King Brude. His aim, which he secured, was an accord that allowed the Christian mission from Dal Riata and Ireland to found further monasteries and to expand in the Highlands without Pictish molestation – no mean achievement: the Picts, and the Scots of Dal Riata, had just concluded a war.

The learning and literacy of the Irish churchmen no doubt did much to secure this understanding: the Picts revered knowledge, as they hallowed their own Druids – jurists, scholars, accomplished bards. According to Caesar, it took a full twenty years of oral instruction to become a Druid and become thereby priest, judge and a walking database. Of their religious rites, we know they favoured oak groves and were especially fascinated by mistletoe, because it never touched the ground; they followed the old megalithic festivals – Lughnasad, etc. – and certainly practised animal and, on occasion, even human sacrifice. Many of their superstitions, and especially their bardic talent and a vigorous 'oral tradition' of memorised history and song and story, survived far into modern Gaeldom.

Columba's other great personal achievement was no less political: he not only secured Christianity in Dal Riata, but quickly established it, in the sense of making it a State religion, in binding it up with all the legitimacy of secular power. This was spectacularly underpinned when the new King Aedan travelled to Iona, and Columba, in 574 'to be consecrated as king of Dalriada – the first occasion in the history of Europe when elements of the rituals of priestly ordination were used as part of the process of royal inauguration,' records Richard Sharpe. There may well have been a special relationship between Columba and Aedan's dynasty, the Cenel nGabrain, and no doubt Columba borrowed consciously from Old Testament narratives of kingly anointing by the Prophets. But his new religion – in its coherence, in its liturgy, in its confident narrative – had, even in human terms, a potent power to legitimise a sovereign and reinforce kingly government, and this has much to do with the rapid spread of Christianity through Europe and its remarkable, near-entire triumph over idolatry and animism.

Columba made more visits to Inverness. One source suggests he travelled and preached as far to its east as Buchan, and he certainly established two missions, at Snizort and on an island in the bay of what is now Portree, on the Isle of Skye. Otherwise his personal missionary endeavours centred on Mull and the adjacent headlands of Moidart and Morvern. But the enterprise, which, if he had not actually begun, he certainly fashioned into a confident and going concern, survived him for centuries. It is no exaggeration to say that the unity of Scotland – substantially accomplished by King Kenneth mac Alpan in the ninth century, and completed by the reign of Malcolm Canmore from 1058 – is a Columban achievement. And, of the sixty-three kings who reigned from Fergus of Dalriada to James VI a thousand years later, forty-eight lie buried on Iona. Even then, the little place was still known as *I-Chaluim-Cille*, the Island of St Colm. 'He, rather than Andrew,' W.H. Murray rightly concludes, 'should have been Scotland's patron saint,' and when a Scots army marched against Edward II at Bannockburn in 1314, they bore a reliquary of St Columba with them.

It seems probable that Lewis and Harris were first claimed for Christ by missionaries, many years after his death in 571, from a new monastic community in Wester Ross. This Applecross mission was founded around 670 by Maol Rubha, and is recorded in the Irish annals of 673. Maol

Rubha was born in Bangor, Ireland, in 642 – where there was a massive
Celtic monastery – and his West Highland foundation was so important,
and so influential, that to this day the Gaelic name for Applecross is
A' Chomraich, 'The Sanctuary'. And sorties to the Outer Isles were all the
braver as, by then, the Western Isles were increasingly a summer-squat for
landless, ruthless Vikings. Maol Rubha spent forty-nine years at Applecross and it is said his monastery – which prospered – had a right of
sanctuary within a six-mile radius. Another tradition suggests that the
Kingdom of Dalriada – which now extended as far as Loch Broom –
granted Maol Rubha's mission all the land between Loch Broom and
Loch Carron. And, Skye and the Long Island apart, Maol Rubha sent
missionaries throughout Ross-shire, Caithness and Sutherland.

The chaos that broke out on Lewis and Harris in the ninth century,
the absence of any significant written records and – much later – the
overlaying of Celtic chapels, in many instances, with Roman ones re-
dedicated to Roman saints makes it difficult to assess the earliest
Christian development on the Long Island.

But the ruins of chapels survive, especially in the north-west of Lewis,
which endured in their dedication to Celtic saints – Teampall Mholuaidh
and Teampall Ronain in Ness, for instance, or Teampall Bhrighid in
Melbost Borve; or the dedication of the remarkable church at Aignish, by
the isthmus to the Eye Peninsula, to St Columba himself; and records
of another Cille Chaluim-Cille at 'Garien' – almost certainly Garry, by
North Tolsta; and so on. There is even a church dedicated to a Norse
saint, Teampall Aulaidh, at Gress, and that the ruins of many others
dedicated to Peter, Thomas, Michael and so on in the Roman Catholic
adherence were built on Celtic sites seems probable.

Very often general physical evidence suggests the base-camp presence
of a Celtic mission – several churches very close together in a locality, as
at Ness or in Carloway; this is counter to the parochial model of Roman
Catholicism. The Ness mainland alone, from South Dell to the Butt, held
six sites of worship. In a very small area of Carloway there are two:[12]
Teampall Chiarain and Teampall Mhicheil. Wells can be a big clue; of
practical use for a religious community, and held in mystical honour since
ancient times. And an adjacent or surrounding burial ground is again
indicative of first-millennial development. Carloway has it all: two tiny
ruined churches, one in honour of a Celtic evangelist, an abandoned
cemetery (around Teampall Mhicheil, with only a handful of recent
legible headstones and very difficult to reach) and a special well near by,
Fuaran Chiarain; Martin Martin was told that water from this spring
could not wash linen.

Names on the map, too, tell us much. As the Norse occupation preceded the imposition of Roman Catholic religion, religious sites labelled by them certainly indicate Celtic Christianity – and they identified eight of the Outer Hebrides as 'priest's islands', named Pabbay to this day.[13] One might cautiously note that the Norsemen had heathen priests of their own, and that they too liked island retreats; but too many of these islands have clear traces of Christian activity. We have, besides, the odd priest's village – Paible in Uist; Bayble on Point; or a locality named after a church, such as Kilbride – *Cille-Brighid* in South Uist; *Teampall Brighid* at Scarista. And one or two islands may have been named for Celtic churchmen: a Pictish saint, Taran or Ternan, is generally thought to be honoured in Taransay,[14] off Harris. Certainly it boasts the ruins of two churches, Eaglais Tarain and Teampall Che, each with its own burial ground and in which, respectively, men and women were buried – a tradition noted by Martin Martin, and enduring even to 1700, when the islanders maintained any corpse put in the wrong cemetery for its gender would be cast to the surface by the following day. And it may well have been this Taran who carved a cross into the ancient megalith that still stands on the Uidh of Taransay.

Still another clue for early Christian endeavour in these islands is that word *annaid*, anglicised in some Highland localities to Annat – 'the name means "mother church",' notes Ian Armit, 'and was commonly used in Ireland and Scotland to denote the earliest monastic establishment within a given district.' On Waternish in Skye, for instance, Annait is one of the earliest known ecclesiastical sites in the Hebrides, making use of a ruined prehistoric fort; a chapel and domestic buildings can still be traced. We have noted Cnoc an Annaid – or Na h-Annaidean – at Swainbost. The name survives too on Eilean Garbh in the Shiants – Airighean na h-Annaid – and on a little island off Staffin in Skye. The other Teampall Pheadair on western Lewis, at Shader, now very difficult to identify amidst much half-buried stone, is by a headland called Rubha na h-Annaid. There were, besides, two wells at this Shader site – Tobar Anndrais and Fuaran an Deidih; one now deliberately blocked, and the other long buried by a minor landslip. And, at Melbost, only a couple of miles up the coast, Tobar Bhrighid (by the founds of that church to St Bride, and its little burial ground) is still neatly maintained and still in use; its waters are said to be most efficacious for jaundice.

There were churches besides on Uig and Point and Lochs, and on assorted offshore islets. There seem to be far fewer sites on Harris. *Cille-Mholuaidh*, which we can reasonably place at Maraig,[15] was evidently one; Scarista another, though until after the Reformation it was long neglected in favour of the church at Ui, on the Northton machair. Though roofless, that is still otherwise relatively intact, and is known locally as An

Teampall – and nearby is a priest's well, Tobair an t-Sagairt. But there is besides An Teampall on Scarp; Eaglais Tarain and Teampall Che on Taransay; Teampall na h-Annaid on Killegray; Teampall Easaigh on Ensay; Teampall Mhuire and Teampall Mholuidh (Moluag again) on Pabbay; another Teampall Mholuidh, and a Cill Aiseam, on Berneray; Scalpay – remarkably – boasts no ancient church, but there may have been no ancient community. The basalt-columned Shiants, though, had two – perhaps even three – and, in the distant Atlantic, we have already noted chapels on Sula Sgeir, the Flannans and St Kilda – where Martin Martin notes three dedicated respectively to Columba, Brendan, and Christ himself, all on Hiorta. There is reference in oral tradition to a fourth, on Boreray. Details and directions to all these old, old sites for worship in the Western Isles are given in Finlay MacLeod's little book and another, by Michael Robson, considers in special detail those of Ness.

One of these, most evocative and unspoiled of all the known Celtic sites, is Cill Ronain, on North Rona,[16] which MacLeod rightly describes as 'one of the most important of its kind on Europe'; it has survived, intact in much detail, precisely because the island is so inaccessible. (Indeed, I can claim direct descent from the last family who lived on it, MacLeods from Gress who took up temporary shepherding residence in 1834, but moved to the Ness mainland the following year after losing a child over the cliffs.)

Ronan is a historical figure, mentioned in passing by the Venerable Bede, but only oral tradition attests to his Rona labours, and that with considerable embroidery. Making landfall round the turn of the seventh and eighth centuries, he soon built the little, corbelled chapel that can be seen today. It has two parts, an eastern oratory or 'St Ronan's Cell', about ten feet by seven externally, and to the west a larger western cell, some fourteen feet by ten. Both were roofed by, presumably, driftwood, turf and straw or marram, and the external wall of the lesser eastern chapel is concave (traditionally, after the Devil himself tried to blow it down). The base of a stone altar still stands against the east wall – a telling detail; the celebrant evidently consecrated the sacrament, in priestly fashion, with his back to the tiny congregation – and in the south wall beside it is a niche; this can be seen in many of the ruined little churches, and was probably where the Communion vessels were stored. Presumably the larger cell was added as the community expanded; but it may have been simply Ronan's living-quarters. Outside, the little churchyard has the remains of a stone *cist*, for either a grave or a shrine, and assorted cross-marked grave-slabs of two distinct periods, seventh to ninth century (Celtic) and twelfth to thirteenth (Roman). That strongly suggests Rona's people, or at least its clergy, quit the island for a long period, probably during the Viking threat. Some significant artefacts – a font, and the most striking grave-stone with three unusual holes – have been removed to Ness for safe-keeping; but this building, on this rather pretty but most marginal little island, 'is one of the most complete groups of buildings of the early Celtic Church to survive anywhere in Scotland', notes an Historic Scotland guide. Michael Robson has published much detailed history of Rona, with description of its chapel.

But such a tiny church is really a hermitage, and the proliferation of so many scattered, minuscule Celtic Church structures in the Western Isles reflects both how long it took the Irish missionaries to reach them and in circumstances that seem to have precluded any substantial mission-bases on the Iona or Applecross models. And a good number were manifestly built for occupation by a single individual, often in ludicrous and most uncomfortable isolation – clear signs that the work of Calum-Cille reached the Outer Hebrides late, in turbulent times and when the mother church was in serious trouble.

The mounting, violent depredations of the Norsemen were certainly a factor. But the Irish, Celtic Christian order was by the eighth century increasingly fractious and demoralised. In Iona's greatest achievement, in 635 a Celtic missionary – Aidan – travelled to Northumbria, at the invitation of King Oswald, to set up as local bishop and head a whole new mission. His foundation at Lindisfarne – a daughter-house of Iona – grew and prospered, and became a Christian light to all the north of England. But there was a tiny, parlous Christian witness already, in York, in the person of James the Deacon – a representative of another English church launched from 597 by another Augustine, an Italian who began his labours in Kent at the commission of Pope Gregory the Great. Augustine, chill and self-important, was not one of nature's diplomats and is not a particularly likeable figure. Yet he is the apostle of the Anglo-Saxons; his base, at Canterbury, is to this day the heart of the Church of England; and his mission met with undoubted and enduring success through that England south of the Thames. After a long separation, the Celtic Christian order had inevitably to re-engage with the wider, Catholic Church – and not just in Northumbria, for Celtic missionaries now probed the Continent, with Columbanus, for instance, founding monastic houses in Gaul and Lombardy; others reaching the wildest parts of Germany, into Thuringia, Franconia and Bavaria with the Gospel; and some even sailing into the territories of the Norsemen. Roman clergy inevitably followed them.

By this point, there was little love lost. 'Distinctiveness and suspicion remained,' muses Andrew Bulloch, 'but isolation had ended. Nothing made this so evident as the historic decision at Whitby.' Continuing in terms eerily reminiscent of a much later Edwardian unease, between the Free Presbyterians and a reconstituted Free Church, 'No doctrinal basis existed for a continued breach but suspicion on one side and arrogance on the other fostered an atmosphere of ill will in which small but obvious differences became the pretexts for strife. Men who have little to fight about, but no inclination to friendship, quarrel over trifles.'

The Whitby confrontation, in 664, centred on two trifles – the tonsure and the calculation of Easter. The Roman churchmen, who shaved the crown of the head, viewed the Celtic tonsure with almost comical horror. But the feeling was mutual. Rome, too, had adopted the 19-year Dionysian cycle for calculating the date of Easter, that movable feast; the Celts, long out of the loop, had adhered to an ancient 84-year mechanism – though not all of them; a substantial party in the south of Ireland had adopted the Roman Easter, another reminder that there was never such an ecclesiastical monolith as the 'Celtic Church'. King Oswiu of Northumbria had been raised in the Celtic tradition, but his queen and her Kentish chaplain followed Rome, and – with the elaborate self-denials of Lent – the domestic inconveniences of two different Easters honoured in the same palace are obvious. Whitby was the showdown, and the new Bishop of Northumbria – Colam – was readily outflanked by Wilfred of York, speaking for the Roman order. The Gaels lost the argument and, swayed by Papal claims to hold the very keys of Heaven, Oswiu accepted the Roman Easter and the primacy of the Roman Church.

Whitby is not the Armageddon popularly portrayed in Protestant folklore. It was certainly not the end of a Celtic Christian system, which endured in its distinct, recognisable forms until at least AD 1100. Yet it was pivotal, precipitating division and decline. Iona increasingly floundered. A new and self-consciously virtuous order of monks, the *Celi De*, or 'Companions of God', took root in Ireland, at Tallaght, near Dublin, marked by personal austerity, legal discipline and not the least interest in evangelism: by the time of Norman settlement in Scotland, these 'Culdees' were the main representatives of religious life. As for Whitby, Wilfred moved swiftly to install a new breed of monk. 'Did I not arrange the life of the monks in accordance with the rule of the holy father Benedict which none had previously introduced there?' gloated Wilfred. 'Did I not instruct them in the rite of the primitive church to make use of a double choir singing in modes and with assonance, with reciprocal responsions and antiphons?' So the Church of the British Isles turned in on herself, and the world outwith her walls went to the Devil.

There has been sustained Roman Catholic endeavour through the centuries to minimise the distinctives of the Christian tradition which flowered from Ireland, and many attempts to adduce evidence of later Roman Catholic peculiarities in ancient Celtic practice. Great scholars, for instance, have tried to prove that the Celtic saints believed in Purgatory, but there is not the slightest evidence for such a doctrine in Ireland before at least the tenth century.

But there has been a still more determined Protestant bid to portray the Celtic, Columban order as a native, unadulterated and proto-Protestant Christianity that had spread Gospel blessings throughout the isles and glens when, by some perfidy at Whitby, it was overthrown and the Highlands abandoned to the iniquities of Papists and Norsemen. Such a view was explicitly articulated by Scots divines in the seventeenth century, in a bid to find some sort of indigenous, historical validation against a persecuting Episcopacy. And it is still advanced today.

'The Columban students were licensed and ordained in the Presbyterian fashion,' insisted Murdo MacAulay in 1985. 'The sacrament was given to the laity in both kinds, and not as in the Roman Catholic Church which gives only the bread to the laity, on the pretext of the doctrine of Transubstantiation . . . the offices of Bishop and Presbyter were synonymous. It did not practise celibacy, nor auricular confession, nor did they pray for the dead. The Church of the Reformation in Scotland can thus trace her evangelical succession "back through Columba and Patrick to the apostolic age."' Douglas MacMillan, in a 1989 foreword to his father-in-law's memoir of Highland Evangelicalism, is still more apocalyptic: that the teaching of Columba 'was warmly evangelical and under his labours the north and west of Scotland became the cradle of a robust, literate Church which in its best days sent many Christian scholars and preachers out across Europe . . . under the invasion of Norse paganism and medieval Roman Catholicism, the darkness of a long spiritual night settled over the Scottish Highlands . . .'[17] Free Church ministers both, MacAulay and MacMillan only padded in the footsteps of Nigel Mac-Neill, who in 1892 explicitly asserted that the 'Celtic Church' was the 'early Free Church . . . comparatively early and aggressive'.

It is untenable. Nothing in the Irish or Celtic order of ordination is reminiscent of Presbyterian practice, save that the necessity of three bishops to consecrate a new one has an echo in the quorum (two ministers and an elder) required to constitute a Presbytery. The Celtic clergy certainly administered Communion in two kinds; but so did their Roman contemporaries on the Continent, and the Roman Catholic order has recently revived it. The Celtic Church had many bishops but – largely because the social geography dictated a monastic structure, rather than a parochial structure organised by diocese – they had no civil authority nor any powers of church discipline, existed only for ordination and consecration, and were entirely marginalised by the abbots, to whom they were answerable. (Columba, significantly, was never consecrated a bishop.)

Celibacy was widely practised and certainly imposed in Celtic monasticism. Auricular confession actually began in the Irish Church and, by the eleventh century at least, was known in the wider Church as the 'Irish penance'. Prayer for the dear departed had certainly emerged by AD 1100; the veneration and invocation of saints is self-evident in Adomnan's *Life of Columba* and, indeed, the book is explicitly written to bolster his cult. Veneration of Mary, Mother of Our Lord, is apparent in the surviving *Book of Kells* – one of the greatest cultural achievements of the Celtic order, apart from its magnificent high crosses; it is rather sweeping to insist that any meaningful Christianity was obliterated by the Norse invasion, and silly to equate Scandinavian paganism with contemporary Roman Catholicism, whatever that order had become by the Reformation.

Whatever their isolation and occasional tensions, Celtic believers were essentially as Roman as they were Catholic. For one, the African chromosomes of their monastic system left a heavily ascetic bent; a fondness for *peregrinatio*: monks taking themselves off alone into utterly isolated, rugged situations, self-indulgent and at times self-righteous; this eremitic tendency became so destabilising a practice that there was a sustained effort to limit and regulate such excursions, which did neither the Church nor the heathen community about it any practical good.

Much more obviously, Celtic Christianity was spectacularly sacramental and, though the Council of Trent lay centuries away, had an inchoate but evident doctrine of transubstantiation, that in some real sense the bread and wine became the true body and blood of Christ. The surviving church on North Rona, and its altar hard by the wall, is plain evidence of a liturgy much more like the Roman Mass than the Presbyterian Lord's Supper, where the elements are but symbolic. Adomnan writes incessantly of the 'sacred mystery of the Eucharist', 'the sacred mystery of the oblation', 'the solemnities of the Mass', 'the Body of Christ' and even 'the sacrifice'. Any Free Church minister who spoke in such terms would be out on his ear.

A 'mixed chalice' was used, in the enduring Roman practice of blending wine with holy water; the sacrament was reserved for private administration to the sick; salt and other rituals of exorcism were used in baptism and the Christian calendar – which, later, Protestants would overthrow entirely in Scotland – was assiduously followed. And so on.

The real legacy of such ardent Reformed propaganda is the myth of an indigenous and somehow singularly blessed Christian religion in the Celtic regions of the British Isles, and this in turn – from the late nineteenth century – has increasingly encouraged mystical revival of what is purported to be a reborn Celtic faith: fey, syncretistic, non-judgemental and environmentally friendly, founded not on any intelligent knowledge of the early Church in Ireland and certainly not on study of the original sources. Few acolytes of purported Celtic religion care to master any of the surviving Celtic languages, and Donald Meek has systematically demolished the historical argument for 'Celtic Christianity'.

For all their faults and sacramentalism, the manifest holiness of the notable Celtic churchmen is the most devastating rebuttal of all. They were tough: as capable, when circumstances called for it, of malediction as well as kindly blessing. (Columba slew a wild boar with a word, according to Adomnan; cursed a tidal rock which had proved inadequate mooring for his coracle. On another occasion, to help some hungry folk, he magically ordained sharp wooden stakes to sprout from the ground, whereon – equally magically – assorted tasty beasts promptly impaled themselves. This is scarcely Greenpeace.)

They were unhesitatingly confrontational: they sought no concord with paganism, but to overthrow it. Columba did not sit down in King Brude's court and make friends with the magicians. He challenged them to a competition in power, which – whatever it was – he won; enough to debunk the New Age compromise, surely, of present Celtic mysticism. Their orthodox hard-line theology was so pounded into Gaeldom that, many centuries later, emphatic Trinitarian doctrine runs through the invocations and prayers and runes Alexander Carmichael collected, late in the nineteenth century, for *Carmina Gadelica*.

Men like Patrick, Columba and Aidan gave themselves wholly over to Christ and Patrick's personal experience, at least, would resonate with any Christian today in Lewis, in his awareness of God's grace and an explicit experiential religion. These were men of conscious, disciplined holy living, marked by poverty, chastity, self-denial and an ability to live without common comforts. They were men much given to private prayer. They loved the Scriptures and certainly knew them thoroughly; they had particular regard for the Psalms, and Columba was inscribing the Thirty-Fourth Psalm when he died. 'The young lions do lack and suffer hunger,' he scratched, 'but they that seek the Lord shall not want any good thing.' Then he laid his work aside, and wrote no more.

These are not men who can be readily claimed for some sort of vaguely baptised, Scottish Green Party white witchcraft; or vaunted in modern Roman Catholicism; or sanitised for historic Presbyterianism. They were men of their time, their age and their landscape and for whom, within the lights of their knowledge and the emphases of their tradition, Christ was all, and in all.

In his name, they were prepared to put their lives on the line. Hundreds of Irish and Scottish missionaries must have been lost at sea. We know, for instance, that Maol Rubha's successor at Applecross, Failbhe mac Guarie, drowned in 737 with twenty-one of his brethren as they tried to cross the Minch – almost certainly for Lewis.

Many more besides perished in remote, isolated situations of cold, illness and starvation. At Chester, in 613, annals record that 1,200 Irish believers were slaughtered by the forces of King Aethelfrith, in his battle to retain power in Northumbria: only fifty of these 'prayer warriors' escaped. Four years later, at Eigg in the Small Isles, Donnan and his entire community were massacred to a man, probably by Norsemen. And, in 795, the Vikings sacked Iona.

3

'Bitter is the Wind Tonight'

Norsemen, Rome and the Medieval Church, 795–1560

For three centuries the Norsemen battered the British and Irish coasts and all but ruled the seas swirling around them. What at first seemed only a passing storm of Viking terror proved to be much more. It was a war of conquest, waged for the most part against defenceless communities on Scotland's edge with neither the means nor – at length – even the mind greatly to resist, sensibly choosing serfdom as preferable to death. For a time the survival of the Gaelic language – and certainly the Christian faith – in the Western Isles seemed in serious doubt.[1]

Ironically, the Celtic Church had served in part to tempt these first Viking forays. Its monasteries were wealthy places – stockpiles of cattle and grain and dairy produce and tools. Then there was the Communion ware in their church buildings; the famous manuscripts, gorgeously decorated, with a blaze here and there of fine leaf-gold.

In that 795 raid from the north, Iona Abbey was destroyed. It was sacrificially rebuilt – and again burned, in 802. Only four years later, in 806, it was levelled once more – the Vikings butchering sixty-eight monks. Next year, planning a retreat to the east of Ireland, the surviving community at Iona started to erect a new monastery at Kells; from this base they tried repeatedly to re-man the Iona foundation, 'and the persistent courage with which they did so commands admiration,' says Murray, 'for Kells itself was seven times ravaged.' The famous Book of Kells – with the Lindisfarne Gospel, the only surviving illuminated texts of the Celtic Church – survives today in Trinity College, Dublin; it was almost certainly begun on Iona.

On still another Viking expedition in 825, they killed the abbot. In 849 Kenneth mac Alpan prudently removed some of the relics of Columba to Dunkeld, and Iona seems from this date to have ceased to be a 'mother-church', though Dunkeld itself was assailed and the mac Alpan dynasty thereafter based their principal church at St Andrews, which would remain pre-eminent in Scotland until the Reformation. Not that Iona was abandoned entirely – nor had it been forgotten by the Vikings. In

986, on what proved their last descent, they murdered another abbot and, on this occasion, only fifteen monks.

It was the same everywhere, whenever the winds blew from the east and north-east and afforded swift, ready passage from the coasts of Scandinavia. What lingers in Hebridean consciousness is not so much the bloodshed as the bloodlust. Certainly, Viking verse of the period – be it by Egil Skalla Grimmson, Bjorn Cripplehand or other resonant names – exults in gore: the latest king is a 'destroyer of Scots', by whose grace the wild beasts can feed on corpses, and after whose endeavours the eagles may tear and the wolves may feast, even by the glow of 'house-destroying fire' – as the Hebrides run with blood, and as they sail yet southwards to Man, or Ireland, and enjoy the pall of smoke they have left over what were once homes on Islay. One can readily appreciate the momentary relief of an unknown ninth-century Celtic scholar, whose note in the margin of a Latin grammar survives – in its archaic Gaelic – to this day.

Is acher ingaith innocht fufuasna fairge findfolt
ni agor reimm mora min dondlaechriad lainn ua lothlind . . .

Bitter is the wind tonight, loosening the white tresses of the ocean
I fear not the fierce warriors of Norway, coursing on the Irish Sea . . .

Yet, in due time, slaughter became settlement. And one has only to glance at a map of Lewis, or any of the Outer Hebrides, to see how the human geography – the names of townships and communities – unmistakably attests to permanent, widely spread and enduring Norse occupation – a *stadir* or farm (Grimersta, Tolsta and Mealista); a *bolstaedr*, homestead (Garrabost, Crossbost, Shawbost and Leurbost), a *setr* or summer pasture (Guershader, Grimshader, Kershader and Sheshader). And even the physical topography, with simple and self-explanatory suffixes, was comprehensively labelled by the Vikings: all the little coves (Marivig, Meavag, Islivig and Brevig) and the bigger coves (Floddabay, Grosebay, Finsbay and Lingerbay), most of the mountains (Roneval, Chaepaval, Uisneaval and Suineval) and very many freshwater lochs (Langavat, Bacavat, Raoineabhat and Grinnavat). For the most part – and it explains most of the Gaelic exceptions in this otherwise Nordic tapestry – features the Vikings thought merited a name were either plainly visible from sea or of relevance to a portage, such as a well-placed loch – like Langavat in South Harris – which, granted a sturdy crew and a light boat, was a convenient shortcut.

Tradition tells that Swainbost, for example, was named for – and no doubt held by – Swein Asleifson, a noted Orkney freebooter who sought refuge in the Ness district and was subsequently killed on a raid in Dublin.[2] His sister was Ragnhildis; one of many personal names the Norse left behind – Gaelicised to Raghnailt and, far later and unconvincingly, anglicised to Rachel.[3] Others include Tormod (Norman), Torcuil (Torquil), Raghnall (Ronald) and Gormul (Gormelia). And eminent clans on Lewis and Harris – the MacLeods, the Morrisons of Ness, the MacAulays, even the Nicolsons – are of Norse descent.

Of the 126 village names in Lewis, 99 are of purely Scandinavian origin.[4] And there is an interesting north-south division. The further south one goes in the chain of Outer Hebrides, the lower the proportion of Norse to Gaelic settlement names. Was the later Gaelicisation of place-names more comprehensive in Barra and the Uists, for instance, than in Harris and Lewis? Or – as seems more probable, for in the far north of Lewis even features far inland bear a high proportion of Norse names – was Viking settlement at its most intense near the Butt? It used to be said that the people of Ness and Tolsta were remarkable for their blond and blue-eyed colouring and indeed their height, reflecting a very strong dose of Norwegian blood; and, even in the 1990s, watching a summer evening's football fixture in Tarbert, I used to be struck how fair the lads of Lewis seemed in contrast to the generally darker, stockier appearance of the *Hearraich*.

Indeed, one still hears a Gaelic word, *Spàinneach*, for a very dark island type – folk of olive skin and brown eyes and steely blue-black hair, especially on Scalpay – which has fed into the widely believed tale that many islanders are descended from shipwrecked survivors of the Spanish Armada. Certainly, many were cast on island shores, and it is quite possible a few at least survived and settled down; but it is really a legacy of the earliest pre-Celtic arrivals on island shores, of very Iberian appearance and probably a Mediterranean origin.

But the Viking onslaught opened a chaotic period in Long Island history. These are the centuries that saw – effectively – a resident Norse elite; its repeated battles with the Norwegian crown, and its reassertion of control; a successful 1156 rebellion which saw all the Sudreyar south of Ardnamurchan Point wrested away into an autonomous polity led by successive Lords of the Isles; that Lordship's own faltering – and ultimately unsuccessful – tussles with the Scottish Crown; and Norwegian defeat at the Battle of Largs, in 1263, when their last bid to recover the southern Hebrides and the Clyde islands faltered and collapsed. Three years later, in the 1266 Treaty of Perth, the entire kingdom of Man and the Isles was ceded to Scotland's king, Alexander III, by a new King Magnus of Norway – finally ending Norse domination of Lewis and the Hebrides.

Farquhar MacTaggart, Earl of Ross, who had played some part in the struggle against Norway, shortly had Lewis, Harris and Skye bestowed upon him by a grateful king. Not that the Earl's authority counted for much across the Minch. Leod, son of Olav the Black, King of Man and the Isles, of the blood of Godred Crovan, was given extensive lands in the Western Isles by his father – Harris, and the islands of the Sound of Harris, including Berneray and the most fertile Pabbay. His son Tormod – Norman – later acquired extensive lands in Skye, by a deft marriage to a Norse heiress; *Siol Tormoid* hold the Dunvegan estates to this day, and finally forsook Harris only in the nineteenth century. Tormod's son Murdo, however, enlarged his estates by rather less reputable alliance, seizing the only daughter of Clan Mac Neacaill, or Nicolson, whom he 'did violentlie espouse', John Morrison chronicled late in the seventeenth century, 'and cutt off immediatlie the whole race of Macknaicle and possesed himself of the whole Lews.' Bill Lawson adds another nasty detail to this virtual rape. 'The tradition that the takeover of Lewis by the MacLeods was not wholly peaceable is repeated in another story in which MacLeod's galley comes across that of the Nicolsons in a fog off the Shiant Isles, and MacLeod takes the chance to run the other galley down, drowning all the Nicolsons, and so disposing of any possible contenders for the succession to Lewis.'[5]

But the MacLeods were long denied official recognition by the Crown, long enough to allow real Hebridean power to be garnered by Clan Donald. *Siol Torcuil*, a more hapless and latterly murderous line, did belatedly acquire from King David II a charter confirming title to the lands and castle of Assynt, in Sutherland, gained by another fortuitous marriage; in the sixteenth century, a cadet branch was established on Raasay. The fortunes of MacLeod of Lewis did not long prosper thereafter; what had been seized by violence would be destroyed by violence, and their history generally is one of vicious little scraps, routs, feuds and sickening brutality, with the Morrisons of Ness and the MacAulays of Uig and, ruinously, with each other.

But there were still more momentous consequences of the Viking invasion. It accelerated the union of the Gaelic kingdom – Alba – with that of the Picts, under Kenneth mac Alpan, and in turn hastened the triumph of the Gaelic language itself in the Highlands and the extinction of the Celtic tongue of the Picts. The political and religious centre of gravity shifted rapidly from Argyll to the east of Scotland, especially the Tay valley. And the continued turmoil broke, decisively, the bonds between the Scots and northern Ireland – to say nothing of the protracted and near-entire isolation of the northern Hebrides.

We cannot accurately assess just how vicious the Norse assault on

Lewis and Harris was. Some believe it was, at least first, a policy of genocide; it is probable that most of the menfolk at least were slaughtered, and the survivors all but enslaved. Such written records as survive in Norse saga relate, naturally, to their own fraught internal politics and the archaeological evidence is extremely limited, for two reasons – the Vikings preferred to build in timber, and the communities they founded have endured, sites being built over again and again.

We can, however, explain why so many Norsemen began late in the first millennium to go berserking around Scotland's islands and, indeed, around Europe. The first reason was demographic. The country was bursting at the seams with restless, land-hungry young men. The second was political. In 872 Harald Haarfager, by force and guile and luck, became king of all Norway and promptly resolved to impose a feudal order on the newly united land. Presented with imminent vassalage, very many minor lairds sailed into exile. And, duly established in turn on the Scottish islands, the latest Viking arrivals began raiding not the coasts of Scotland and Ireland and England, but their own country villages on the shores of their native land. Harald, of course, did not put up with this; in 891 he raised a fleet and, with yet more violence, soon brought the islands of Scotland under the firm authority of his Crown. It is, no doubt, from a dimly remembered rout in this period, near a well-harboured inlet in the Bays of Harris, that local topography has still a bleak echo – a pretty shingled cove is Moll Bheagh, the 'shore of calamity'; a boggy plain near by, where battle was wrought, the 'Field of Blood'; both hard by what is now the village of Scadabhagh, or Scadabay, 'the bay of destruction'.[6] These are, of course, Norse names.

But there fell a still more famous little local difficulty between Norway and its Hebridean colonies, recorded with distinct relish by a contemporary scribe. Assorted *jarls* – effectively, viceroys – governed Shetland, Orkney and the Hebrides in the name of the Norwegian crown, of whom Godred Crovan, who died in 1095, is the most eminent. His *birlinn*, or galley, is still commemorated in a Gaelic song popular to this day. Godred's successor, though, had all his chutzpah and far less judgement. He declared himself King of Man and the Isles, and Magnus III of Norway had already – in 1093 – visited Scotland to assert his suzerainty. In 1098, rattled and furious, he amassed an enormous fleet and fell upon his Hebridean kindred.

Magnus, still only twenty-five, ravaged all the islands of Argyll as well as Skye, Uist and Lewis. He forced the King of Scots, Edgar, to cede his claim to the islands, though made no attempt to recover the extensive Norse possessions on the mainland. Yet he was not immune, amidst all the butchery, to the charms of this country and, when he turned his back on Scotland, he went home wearing the national dress. For a century, at least, Norwegians wore a kilt-like garment and remember this genial terror as *Barfod* – Magnus Bareleg.

Somerled, descended from Dalriadan nobility and a Celto-Norse ruler of Lorne, whose father Gillebride was true King of Argyll, finally drove the Vikings out of their last mainland holdings in 1156, by deft redesign of the traditional Scots galley and some guile in statecraft. He was less successful, though, on his other front – a protracted battle against an increasingly Anglo-Norman monarchy and its determination to impose feudalism on the Hebrides. Somerled was encamped at Renfrew, at the head of a large force preparing to confront King Malcolm IV in 1164, when he was found murdered in his tent, and with him any hope to rebuilding a united Celtic kingdom. A Highland/Lowland divide was already well advanced, and now irrevocable.

Nearly a century later King Alexander III, as we noted, duly completed the Viking overthrow and negotiated terms for Scottish sovereignty over the northern Hebrides.[7] On his mysterious death at Kinghorn, Fife, in 1286, only an infant grand-daughter survived to succeed him. The 'Maid of Norway' died on her way home, in Orkney, in 1290, and the confusion afforded the perfect opening to England's Edward I. It was 1314, at the end of a protracted War of Independence and detested English occupation, that the forces of Robert the Bruce routed the army of Edward II at Bannockburn, with substantial support from Highland clans.

But the male line of Bruce died with his son, David II, and the old warrior's grandson, Robert II, succeeded as the first of a long and distinctly hapless line of Stewarts. Meanwhile the Lordship of the Isles – in Somerled's heirs, Clan Donald – was virtually an independent state, constantly intriguing against the King of Scots and treating privily with, for instance, the English court. In 1411, these forces of Gaeldom marched into Aberdeenshire, as Donald of Islay fought to secure his wife's claim to the Earldom of Ross, including Skye, and waged a messy battle at Harlaw – it was not a rout, but it was a defeat, and they retreated in order through the western glens.

This was a fateful turning point; Clan Donald had initiated a protracted, bitter feud with the Scots crown, and overextended their power. Donald's grandson, John, lost all, plotting ineptly with England's Edward IV for the dismemberment of Scotland and then falling out with his own son, who waged successful revolt. He met his final match in James IV, the ablest and one of the most ruthless of Stewart monarchs, the last who could speak Gaelic, and who outmanoeuvred him brilliantly. The Lordship of the Isles was forfeited to the Crown in 1493 and the title, ever since, has been enjoyed by the heir to the Scottish throne. Twenty years later, in 1513, James IV fell at Flodden with the flower of Scotland's nobility, leaving a baby son – James V – who, at the conclusion of his own much more inept reign in 1542, left a baby daughter. It was this infant Mary, Queen of Scots, who would return from France, a simpering widow, in 1560 and amidst the Reformation, which broke late but most decisively in Scotland.[8] And there we have quickly outlined a wider, national history.

Harlaw marks more than the high tide of Gaelic polity; it marks that generation when frightened, resentful Lowlanders had begun increasingly to mock and slander the Gael, when the Highlanders and their language became more and more marginalised from national life. The ignorance and hatreds begotten endure, most quietly, to this day. But what of faith in this period, and in particular that Christianity of Lewis and Harris?

The Vikings were keen, competent farmers; outstanding seamen; they loved music, poetry and stories, and their craftsmanship shows both a keen aesthetic sense and the highest attention to detail – most famously, the delightful Lewis Chessmen, unearthed in the sands of Ardroil, Uig in the late 1820s, brilliantly executed from walrus ivory and combining intricate skill with droll effect.[9] And it would be the twentieth century before the robustly defined rights of Viking women – to hold property, to share property acquired after marriage, and to be protected or at least guaranteed redress against wilful desertion – would be enjoyed by their female, British descendants.

Later Icelandic sagas give a detailed description of Norse religion. Like all the Teutonic peoples, they believed in a pantheon of gods, headed by Odin (as the Vikings called him) – he was Woden to the Saxons – and with particular veneration for his son, Thor. There was a priestly caste in Norway, but not in the Hebrides; a chieftain usually oversaw sacrifices, in their little wooden temples. There were great sacrificial feasts, in seasons pretty close to those of local pagan tradition – spring, autumn, midwinter. In crises, the Norsemen made human sacrifice to Odin, but seldom to Thor. They believed in life after death – in the mildly pleasant realm of Hel; but the great thing was to die in battle, for then you went to Valhalla and made most merry with Odin himself. Yet even that, intriguingly, was not an abiding eternity. Vikings believed in a final 'end of days', when even Odin and Thor would fall and Valhalla be consumed with fire. Then a new, younger generation of gods would order and command a better world.

So what possessed these capable people – whose strict honour code forbade the plunder of unarmed *kaupships*, merchantmen, at sea – so savagely to attack Christian foundations? The culprit is Charlemagne, prince of the Dark Ages in northern Europe. He had deliberately persecuted the old Teutonic religion, forcing the Saxons – for instance – to choose Christianity or death and, in 782, even butchering 4,500 Saxon prisoners after his victory of Verden. 'Until then, Norsemen had taken no action against the Christian Church. Thereafter, as fellow-followers of Odin, they hit back and spared no one,' records Murray. 'Once again, events far from the Hebrides, of which the islesmen were unaware, brought disaster.'

Yet these Vikings seem, within a few generations, to have adopted Christianity and by the Millennium, indeed, the new faith was imposed by decree: in 995 Olaf Tryggvasson, King of Norway, forced Sigurd, his Jarl of Orkney, to abandon paganism for the Christian faith, and it was legally established in Iceland by the century's end. It had to be reintroduced, then, to Orkney and Shetland, where it had evidently been utterly extirpated. But it is more convenient than convincing to assert that Christianity was established everywhere through Norse territories by top-down, political pressure. Grave evidence in the Western Isles suggests it had already and for some time been accepted by most of the Norse communities.

The faith somehow survived, one suspects, for much the same reason that Gaelic survived; the marauders arriving in such waves, lusty and acquisitive young men, had settled down with local women and, probably within three generations, the Norse communities of the Western Isles espoused at least a nominal Christianity – though it is alleged by a contemporary that, even if they prayed to Christ in their homes, early converts were apt to invoke Thor *in extremis*.

Viking topography certainly reflects the Christian landscape they first encountered and, indeed, their word for a place of worship not only survives in some island place names – Kirkibost on Bernera; Claddach Kirkibost in North Uist – but entered the Scots language itself. They noted, besides, dozens of islands occupied by a priest, or more likely a Celtic anchorite, a *papar*; and so we have a Pabbay, for instance, in Loch Roag, and Pabbay in the sound of Harris, and Pappa Westray in the Orkneys, and so on. The names of other islands, too, such as Taransay, indicate Viking knowledge of past saints associated with them.

Now a maturing Norse culture in the Western Isles was ready to found churches of its own. They often built on sites already established by Celtic missionaries, and in turn some genuine Norse foundations may have been lost below the structure of medieval Catholicism. But the ruins of St Barr, by Eoligarry in Barra and today in the care of the Roman Catholic Church, are certainly of late Norse construction. And in 1865, an inscribed rune-stone – incredibly rare in Scotland – was uncovered in the ancient cemetery. The irregular slab is a little over four feet high and engraved on one side with a cross of Celtic type, richly interlaced. On the other is the runic inscription:

[. . .]TIR THUR KIRTHU S[. . .] in [. . .] R
[. . .]R IS KURS SIA RISTA
[. . .]A

After Thorgerth, Steiner's daughter,
this cross was raised.

But Lewis, too, has Norse chapels. The most obvious is within the large burial ground of Gress, by Broad Bay, on the road to Tolsta; its walls and gables are still intact (though a shelter has been built against one end for gravedigging implements) and it is dedicated to St Aula – Olaf, whom the Royal Commission inaccurately declared in 1928, listing these ancient buildings on Lewis, to be 'the only Norse saint' among the dedications. Of comparable vintage to those at Cille Bharra, Teampall Aulaidh measures barely nineteen feet internally, but the lintel above the main door is inscribed '1681 1B MK', suggesting repairs that year, when it was still in use.

Much less obvious, at least to the Royal Commission, was the pretty little church in the old burial ground at Bragar, on the opposite side of the island; the present ruin is tentatively judged to be of fifteenth-century construction and is known generally as Teampall Eoin; St John's Chapel. But it is also known, in Bragar and Shawbost, as Cille Sgàire, as the late Murdo Murray of 1 New Shawbost, a winsome tradition-bearer, told me in 1992: 'Cill' is of course Celtic, but 'Sgàire' is a Norse name still found on Lewis and usually anglicised to Zachary. Finlay MacLeod notes that it is 'an attractive building and it is better preserved than many other chapels . . . approximately twenty-nine feet long and has two rooms; the nave and chancel.' A central arch over the division has long collapsed, and nineteenth-century gravestones attest to bold, recent burials within its precincts. MacLeod records wistfully that there used to be a special well nearby, Fuaran Buaile Dhomhnaill – 'the spring of Donald's enclosure', some 200 yards from the chapel; a film of fine oil could be seen on its rippling surface, and locals remember bottles of this water being taken to the sick and even to patients in a Stornoway hospital; one Bragar worthy related that it could cure toothache. Around 1980, it was irresponsibly destroyed.

As the Norse turned native, and Europe to the Middle Ages, the ecclesiastical landscape was rapidly altering and, from the first attack

on Iona to at least the late eighteenth century, it is difficult not to see the
spiritual history of the West Highlands, and especially of Lewis and
Harris, as one of sustained moral and spiritual decline, unchecked even by
a most notional Reformation and compounded by mounting oppression
and exploitation from the south.

After all, when the Norsemen themselves were converted to Christianity, it was to their own Scandinavian take on Roman Catholicism, and
– likely – a most nominal one at that. Certainly, monastic communities on
Lewis and Harris, such as there had been, were not restored, nor any sort
of intelligent Christian mission, or any quiet endeavours for social good.

It was also under the Norsemen that an ill-fitting episcopacy was
imposed on the Hebrides. A diocesan structure was laid over the Norse
realms and territorial bishops installed, for instance, in Orkney, Water-
ford, Limerick, Dublin and Man – well before any such hierarchy on the
Scottish mainland.

A diocese of Sodor – the Hebrides – seems to have been decreed by
Rome as early as 838, at the height of Norse adventures on the Long
Island. It counted for nothing, of course, until Norway embraced
Christianity; a diocese of the Hebrides is, however, evident by 1094,
and then Magnus Bareleg himself united Sodor to Man in 1098, as one
bishopric. He was also able – from a position of spectacularly reasserted
strength in the Hebrides – to force King Edgar to cede ecclesiastical
authority in the islands to Trondheim; or, more accurately, the arch-
bishopric of Nidaros-Trondheim. And, though the Scots crown recovered
the islands in 1266, to Trondheim the Hebridean church would answer
until around 1350.

The Norse influence, Meek argues, 'broadened cultural and ecclesiastical horizons in the Gaelic west, while helping to change the formal
organisation of the church in these parts'. Indeed, the Lewis Chessmen
were almost certainly carved at Trondheim, late in the twelfth century –
the town was a centre for the walrus-ivory trade, and workshops for ivory
goods have been identified there – and a widely accepted theory for their
final fate was that they were somehow lost off the Uig coast (by shipwreck
or piracy or pilferage) while on their way as a gift to the Bishop of Sodor
and Man: as a game of skill, rather than chance, by 1050 chess was a most
respectable diversion for clergymen.

But it is difficult not to agree with W.H. Murray's assertion that, by the
time of the Lordship of the Isles, men 'of every rank were not so much
religious as deeply reverential . . . easily led by the clergy, for their faith
had the simplicity of a child's'. Things had taken a sharp step backwards.
Few beyond the ranks of priesthood were literate; worship itself, from
what we can adduce, was still more sacramental, still more Latinate,

increasingly formal. No sense of mission seems long to have survived the breach with Ireland and the protracted Viking brutalities, nor any proper culture of priestly vocation and supervised training.

By 1350, after all, when the Hebridean church came under a Scottish episcopal control – Lewis, at least, under the Bishop of Ross; the isles in the south under Argyll – the Church nationally was of very different character from the old Irish order. In an echo of Whitby, centuries before, a royal marriage proved consequential. In 1070, King Malcolm III of Scotland – Malcolm Canmore, or 'Calum of the Big Head' – met a Saxon princess, Margaret, among a clutch of unhappy royal refugees from England. Sister of Edward the Atheling, descendant of Alfred and kin to the unhappy Harold of Hastings, she had expressly been excluded from the English throne even before his accession, and had grown up in Hungary. She was still more *persona non grata* in the new, Norman England. And she was a formidable character, who 'possessed an in-domitable will, a restless conscience, and clear-cut and definite ideas of what was right and wrong', sighs R.L. MacKie. 'She had no sense of humour and no sense of proportion.'

Queen Margaret brought costly tastes, French wine, fancy foods and elegant manners to the Scottish court. And she loathed Gaelic, still the language of the royal household, court and statecraft. She made no effort whatever to master it. Of their eight children, none bears a Gaelic name. She seems to have had a remarkable hold over her husband, for she dragged him into ill-fated adventures in England. And her effect was still more baleful in religion, especially as Malcolm III – a crude warrior who had, after all, overthrown MacBeth and would even take on the Con-queror – had no meaningful faith of his own and was quite overawed by the Church Militant embodied in his wife.

Insofar as there had ever been a 'Celtic Church', and insofar as it still survived, its order perished in this reign. Margaret loathed everything strange and unfamiliar she beheld in Scotland's religion – the plain if practical buildings, the married priests, the open and comfortable and – by this point – very slack monasteries, and the liturgy. She had no difficulty persuading her credulous husband to summon an assembly of the clergy, and King Malcolm translated doggedly into Gaelic as the queen ranted on and on, focusing especially on the Scottish manner 'of celebrating Mass with a barbarous rite, contrary to the custom of the whole Church.' (It was of course enacted in the vernacular – in Gaelic, which everyone understood – rather than Latin, and this simply infuriated her.)

Her main achievement was the renewal of Scottish monasticism, in the enclosed and ascetic model of the Continent. She is said to have begun the restoration of the monastery at Iona and she brought the Benedictines to Dunfermline. In short, Queen Margaret secured the kingdom for medieval Roman Catholicism, and a grateful Mother Church duly canonised her, in 1250. Her policies, too, were sustained by her sons, three of whom (David I, Edgar and Alexander II) served in turn as king. David had been brought up in the English court – a sister, Matilda, had married King Henry I – and when he came into his royal inheritance, he brought with him many fortune-seeking Norman nobles, including Walter Fitz Alan – whom David elevated as High Steward of Scotland, and granted rich lands in Renfrewshire – and the first Robert de Brus. Apart from the great houses these men founded, David thus introduced that feudalism which Somerled and the Gaels so angrily resisted.

New monastic orders followed: Augustinians at Scone, with tiny Highland outposts at Inchmohome, Strathfillan and Oronsay; Cistercians at Melrose and Saddell; the most severe Valliscaulians and their three Highland foundations at Beauly, Pluscarden and Ardchattan; Premonstratensians by Fearn, in Easter Ross. In 1188, a decree or Bull of Pope Clement III again asserted the sovereignty of Rome and divided Scotland into nine dioceses, which survive to this day. As for what remained of the past Irish order, the murder of Somerled ended his attempts to maintain a distinctive, traditional Christian foundation at Iona. In 1200, it was converted into a Benedictine monastery, though never a very strong or successful one; the adjoining Augustinian nunnery did no better. The light of Columba had failed.

But even this faltering, thoroughly Romanised church in Scotland had some sort of order and respect. Things took a very different turn when, in the fifteenth century, the Stewart monarchy assumed the power to appoint Scotland's bishops. The consequence was eminently predictable: by the final cataclysm in 1560, the 'Scottish church had long been remarkable for the depth of its corruption,' notes T.C. Smout, a respected academic who can by no measure be dubbed a Protestant propagandist. Even by the end of the fourteenth century, the laxity of Scots monasteries was scandalous, and 'the incumbent of a chaplaincy at Linlithgow in 1456 was obliged to find security that he would neither pawn the books, plate and vestments of the town kirk nor maintain for his enjoyment a "continual concubine." It does not sound somehow as if his sponsors would have had much objection to his enjoyment of an occasional concubine.'

By the sixteenth century, Scottish monasteries had ceased to be the vehicles for spirituality. They had become nothing more than property-owning corporations, often controlled entirely by laymen. Royal bastards, even when young children, were appointed to rich livings. Beyond the monasteries, friars roamed the streets of little Scottish towns as, effectively, professional beggars. Most Scottish nuns were so illiterate they could not even sign their own names.

David, Cardinal Beaton, Archbishop of St Andrews, who was murdered by Protestant zealots in 1546 – it would be 1969 before there was another resident Scottish cardinal – held three rich benefices at the same time and had a litter of illegitimate children. The Scottish parish priesthood had, in the main, a character to match – accounts abound of priests swaying drunkenly to the altar, priests who could barely read; a 'profane lewdness of life' at all levels. Even a Jesuit, in 1562, damned Scotland's clergy as 'extremely licentious and scandalous'. 'That this was no overstatement,' asserts Smout, 'is shown by the fact that, in mid-century, when perhaps two Scotsmen in six hundred were priests, no less than two legitimised children in seven were the bastards of priests. In these circumstances society at large treated the church and its services with open irreverence.'

Murdo MacAulay rightly notes that 'we know little of the pre-Reformation churches' history in Lewis. Of these old churches, the few that are left are in ruins.' But some identifiable priests flicker in the scant pages of medieval island history. In MacAulay's native Carloway, there is a tradition of a chapel at Kirivick, and that Teampall Mhicheil mentioned by Martin Martin: all that today can be seen, though, is a long-neglected burial ground, extremely difficult to reach and with only a few legible gravestones. The ancient graveyard was on Little Bernera, a straightforward sail from Loch Carloway and where the remains of two chapels suggest, perhaps, a Columban foundation. But storm often impeded the crossing and bodies awaiting passage had to be stowed in a Kirivick bothy, *Taighe nan Corp*, the 'house of corpses', until winds and seas abated. If the delay was lengthy, things must have become unpleasant. According to village tradition, a young priest learned of the problem and sailed over from Little Bernera to investigate. Sticking his walking stick into the ground, he tipped a little earth into his hand and declared, 'Undoubtedly this is St Michael's dust, and this spot will henceforth be your burying ground.'

We know of another Carloway cleric, the Red Priest – Patrick O Beolan – who was among the casualties of Harlaw. In 1506, the Rector of Uidh – Eye, or the peninsula of Point – was a John MacLeod, and his cure was promised by James IV himself to Sir John Poylson, a 'precentor of Caithness', once Uidh became vacant through the 'irregularity or inability' of MacLeod. By 1536, though, the Rector of Uidh was Sir Magnus Vaus, Commissary of Inverness, and who probably came no nearer Lewis in his life than the Kessock ferry. Another record, in 1536, has James V presenting Mr Roderick Farquhar to 'several churches' vacant upon the death of Martin MacGilMartin, including Teampall Mhoire, or St Mary's at Barvas, and presumably the other chapels up the West Side.

In the late 1540s, Roderick MacLean – Archdeacon of the Isles – became Bishop, and was succeeded in the archdiaconate by Sir Donald Monro, a native of Kiltearn (the district of Evanton, in Easter Ross) who had in 1526 become vicar of Snizort, in Skye. Monro thus took immediate charge of the rural deaneries into which the scattered diocese was divided, and probably did most of the bishop's work. 'Dean Monro' decided graciously to acquaint himself with his great district, and the little record he wrote up afterwards of that 1549 jaunt is the first helpful description of Lewis and Harris. He himself was, by then, Rector of Uidh, which no doubt afforded some land and income. Monro tells us that there were four 'parish churches' in Lewis; Uidh apart, the others were in Ness, Uig and Barvas. He makes no mention of Stornoway – then no more than a collection of huts around a promontory dominated by the crude MacLeod castle – and there is no evidence of any place of worship there until after the Reformation.

But a Master Lauchlan MacLean – the title tells us he was a University graduate – was presented to Barvas in 1559; we know of two of his predecessors, the Master 'Mertin mcGilmertyne', or Martin Martin, who was succeeded by a Master 'Roderic Farquhar Hectorisonne' in 1536. This Teampall Mhoire, or St Mary's in the old Barvas cemetery, had long been an established place of worship, for a Papal letter from Rome – in 1403 – solemnly declared, 'To all the Christian faithful – Indult granting an indulgence to visitors to the church of St Mary in Barwas in the isle of Lewis, diocese of Sodor, on certain feast days and those who contribute to its reparation,' which suggests both that the church was not as popularly frequented as Mother Church wished and that it was rather decrepit besides. By the Reformation, sand-blow increasingly threatened the little kirk and, in 1803, James Hogg noted of this 'ancient place of Popish worship' that it 'had formerly been on the very summit of the eminence, but the sand is now heaped up to such a height as to be on a level with the gables. Yet the eddying winds have still kept it nearly clear, so that it appears as a building wholly sunk underground. The baptismal font is still standing in a place in the wall prepared for it.' It sounds much as Teampall Cro Naomh, the 'Chapel of the Sacred Heart' up the coast at Galson, now appears today, half-buried in the machair. By 1861, Teampall Mhoire at Barvas had entirely disappeared, with most of the old cemetery besides.

There may have been two priories on the Long Island at the time of the Reformation – one at Uidh, and one at Rodel on the south-east toe of Harris – but neither was by then manned, so to speak, and no trace of any monastic buildings can be seen at Rodel today. And there is a local legend of a convent or nunnery at Uig – *Taighe nan Cailleachan Dubha*, the 'House of the Old Black Women', is supposed to have flourished near a Mealista chapel dedicated to St Catyn (a sixth-century Celtic missionary who is said first to have founded the church at Uidh) – but it is documented nowhere and it is unlikely it ever existed. There must, besides, be real doubt as to the survival of any Rodel foundation into the late Middle Ages.

Dean Monro tells us besides that the inhabitants of remote St Kilda are simple creatures, 'scant learned in any religion', and that when MacLeod's Steward sailed each summer to the little archipelago (presumably to relieve the poor natives of a good proportion of their produce), a chaplain accompanied him. Otherwise, the St Kildans baptised their own infants – indeed, several rites for this sort of lay baptism, usually executed by the 'knee-woman' or midwife, were noted centuries later by Carmichael. As for the people of North Rona, Monro records them 'scant of any religion'. He sees Luchruban, with its ruined cell, and even clambered onto that stack, but reports the local tale of a 'Pygmies' Isle . . . with their own little kirk in it, of their own handiwork' and that past visitors had even apparently dug up 'certain bones and round heads of very little quantity', said to be those of the long-gone pygmies. He himself sounds less than convinced.

Of Lochs, Dean Monro does mention Eilean Chaluim Cille; St Columba's Isle, in Loch Erisort, which certainly bears a few low ruins to this day, and strong tradition of a chapel and, besides, a monastery. An early chapel is probable, but it seems later to have served primarily as a verdant kitchen garden for MacLeod of Lewis, and is said to have boasted a fine orchard. Swordale, on Loch Leurbost, seems to have boasted the first parish church in Lochs, and – though a new parish church was opened at Keose in 1831 – was revived for that purpose after the Disruption in 1843.

As for Harris, Monro remarks that there are no wolves there – a disturbing reminder they were then still found elsewhere in the Hebrides, probably on Skye – and he gives interesting details, too, of the 'Council of the Isles' that had once advised the Lord of the Isles himself – it met regularly on Eilean na Comhairle, the 'Isle of Council', at the north end of Loch Finlagan on Islay, near the Lord's headquarters on Eilean Mor, and had comprised fourteen chiefs, including MacLeod of Harris and MacLeod of Lewis.

We know something of a rough and ready rule of law on the Long Island at this period, for this was the era of the Brieves[10] – not a sacred office, but a civil, judicial, hereditary one, in the person of the Chief of

Clan Morrison in northern Lewis, which would endure into the seven-teenth century. These Morrisons – *Na Moireasdanaich*, known as Clann a' Bhreithimh in Lewis – should not, by the way, be confused with the Morrisons, *mac Ghille-Mhoire*, of Harris; they are completely different clans. 'The Brieve is a kind of judge among the islanders,' Sir Robert Gordon recorded 'who hath an absolute judicatory, unto whose authority and censure they willingly submit themselves, when he determineth any debateable question between party and party.' The Brieve, who lived at Habost in the Ness district, thus resolved civil disputes as well as dispensing criminal law.

Dr Donald MacDonald of Gisla rightly warns against romantic, exaggerated notions as to the hallowed origins of this office and the geographical scope of its authority. It was really a legacy of the Norsemen, probably an echo of the *log-maor*, or speaker of their local but mighty community council, the Thing – reduced, over many years, to something like the *Deemster* on the Isle of Man, who presided not over the framing of law, but the execution of its 'doom', or judgement. Certainly, this Brieve 'was judge in cases of life and death, as well as in the most trifling contentions. His presence, whether in house or field, on horseback or on foot, constituted a court; his decisions were guided either by what he could remember of like cases, or by his sense of justice, and this *lex non scripta* was called "breast law". On assuming office he swore he would administer justice between man and man as evenly as the backbone of the herring lies between the two sides of the fish . . .'

MacDonald rightly doubts if any Brieve ever spoke a word of English, or that any laws made by a distant king and Parliament had the least bearing on his pronouncements, though it is reasonable to suppose that he was at least literate in Gaelic. What is still remembered in Lewis is that all submitted unhesitatingly to his final pronouncements; and that his criminal justice was dispensed unsparingly: every significant district has a Beinn na Croiche, or Cnoc na Croiche (sometimes corrupted, as in Shawbost, to Cloiche) – a 'gallows hill', or place of execution. And that was just Clan Morrison at work; they were fearsome warriors – and needed to be, for they were cordially loathed by the MacLeod chiefs and had at least one memorable set-to with the MacAulays of Uig, on a slope by the Shawbost river still known as *Cnoc nan Cnamh*, the 'hillock of bones'. North of the modern Habost cemetery is Clach na Fola, the 'blood stone', where they executed their prisoners of war; a few hundred yards from the present lighthouse at the Butt, they threw others over what is still *Creag an Uigich*, the Uigman's Cliff.[11]

Thus some order was kept in wider island society. Yet alongside this rule by Brieve there still flourished gross superstition. Only yards from the ruins of what was the Brieve homestead is the Clach na Gruagaich – the Fairy Stone – where the prudent returning from a milking on the machair left a libation in its hollow for the 'little folk', in the hope of good crops and healthy animals or, at least, as a placating gesture to avert the malevolence of pixies, brownies and bogles.

As for its Christianity, it is only fair to point out that, whatever the squalor of the Scottish church generally, there is no evidence of sexual corruption, simony (the buying and selling of benefices), demanding money for priestly duties or other gross declension among the Hebridean clergy. What is striking is that there seem, at least by the sixteenth century, to have been very few of them. And there was probably a great deal of 'curacy', as well-connected priests acquired rich livings and waged some lesser brother to perform its limited duties.

No doubt some were occasionally caught up in the intrigues of their kindred; certainly, in such areas as Lochaber, it was by no means unknown for a priest imperiously to summon clansmen to a rare Mass in some nook or glen – and thereby straight into an ambush by their enemies. There is no evidence of a preaching ministry, no signs of any education (save for the wealthiest and most important, who could retain private tutors) and but the dimmest folk-memory of infrequent visits by itinerant clergy. They disappeared into the tiny, venerable churches, celebrated the Eucharist and then emerged with the Host. It is probable that public worship was for centuries reduced in the Hebrides to something faintly pathetic. The summons spread when the priest was in the locality: you gathered, whatever the weather, in the churchyard as he and his server dealt in sublime mysteries within; and, at length, he emerged to display the wafer – probably in some sort of monstrance – as all bowed humbly before.

Munro, an able and evidently humane man, supported the Reformation and was still Archdeacon of the Isles in 1563, but had not long retained Uidh. He secured a better living as minister of Kiltearn and two rectors (or, more probably, a rector and a curate) are noted for Uidh in 1559, Sir John Finlay and Mr Lachlan MacLean. Monro died at Kiltearn, unmarried, around 1576.

Though records are thin, medieval Christianity on the Long Island has left us some striking monuments in stone. Take Teampall Mholuaidh, in Eoropie, Ness, which may well occupy the site of the very earliest Christian witness in the district, and – though later in construction than any of the surviving ecclesiastical ruins in the parish, is the oldest building still used for public worship in Lewis. Erected, probably, in the fourteenth century, on top of a far older cell, and – like its predecessor – dedicated to

Moluag, this Teampall had by modern times become associated with all sorts of neo-pagan practice, which we will note later. When it was examined in May 1852, by Second Corporal Michael Hayes of the Ordnance Survey, it was derelict and roofless; sixty years later, shortly before the Great War, it was restored with reasonable sensitivity, by the architect J.S. Richardson, for occasional Scottish Episcopal worship and, with more and more English settlement in recent years, regular services are now held there.

Angus Gunn of North Dell – an eminent tradition-bearer who proved a fount of local lore for Malcolm MacPhail[12] – could, in the late 1860s, talk of the original church's construction and with vivid colour, a millennium on, of the Norse terror:

> The Scandinavians were wild people, without compassion, without mercy, without the love of God, without the fear of man. They were wild as wolves and merciless as bears, and murdered and killed and robbed and plundered wherever they went. They came down upon these coasts, slaying the people in their houses and the saints at their altars, burning churches, killing the living and desecrating the dead.
>
> A son of the King of Scandinavia became a good man and, wishing to perform good deeds for the evil deeds he had done, he built a church down at Ruadh Eoropaidh and called it Teampall Mholuag . . . the walls of which are still entire. When the walls of the temple were built, the King's son had no roof to put on and he was in great straits. He did not know in all the living world what to do for a roof for the weather was so stormy that his father's galleys could not go to Lochlann [Norway] for wood to make a roof. The prince prayed and prayed, and when he prayed his best a voice came to him in a dream of the night and he would find a roof then. The prince arose and went down to the Stoth [a pleasant sandy cove near the Butt, on the Minch coast] and there he found a roof floating in the pool prepared and of the size required for his temple. The roof was taken up and placed on the walls of the building, which it filled.

Gunn's story, so beautifully narrated, is by no means incredible; timber cargo was frequently washed up on the shores of the Western Isles, and I have heard too many stories, by island believers in our own day, of no less remarkable provision in answer to prayer.

Much more famous – the architectural treasure of the Outer Hebrides – is St Clement's Church at Rodel.[13] Its name is, in fact, a misnomer: the structure has not been used as a regular place of worship since the Reformation. Built early in the sixteenth century – probably between

1520 and 1540 – by Alexander MacLeod, Chief of Harris and Dunvegan, it was conceived primarily as a rather splendid family mausoleum, and it is the tomb of Alasdair Crotach, 'Hunch-backed Alasdair' – which occupies the most prestigious position, on the south side of the choir. Alasdair Crotach may well have spent his last years at Rodel, in quiet and rather religious seclusion, but he had expended his youth in warfare, and it was in combat with the MacDonalds of Clanranald that he was grievously wounded with a battle-axe, leaving the muscles of his back permanently severed. He was not, of course, the first old Highland rogue given a mind in his last years to amass some sort of credit with Heaven; and a 1498 note survives in the accounts of his Lord Treasurer for good black cloth of Resolis, bestowed upon the son of the MacLeod family chaplain at a value of £7. Nor was he the first to build at Rodel. Affording excellent vantage over the Sound of Harris, the Little Minch and down the Outer Hebridean coast, there was almost certainly an Iron Age dun on this site; it is also very possible – though cannot now be proved – that there was some sort of later, monastic foundation, as Harris folklore retails.

Alasdair Crotach, still of military mind and with, no doubt, an interesting collection of enemies, certainly took care to include a mighty tower in his plans, and seems to have ceded chiefly authority to his heir, William, before his death around 1547. (His sepulchre is confusingly dated 1528, probably when that area of the church was completed.) We know that one transept was completed by 1540, when a David John MacPherson is recorded as chaplain of 'St Columba's altar' – a detail only compounding confusion as to the original dedication. Clement, the third Bishop of Rome after Peter in Roman Catholic mythology, was a popular choice for medieval churches. But it may also have been a twelfth-century Clement, Bishop of Dunblane; and some MacLeod historians insist (despite explicit, sculptured evidence to the contrary) that it was really founded in honour of Columba himself.

Public worship ceased at the Reformation, though assorted Hearraich would be buried around St Clements until after the Second World War. By the eighteenth century, the church was roofless; Alexander MacLeod of Berneray – 'Captain MacLeod' – selflessly restored it, in 1784, and the job was no sooner finished than it was consumed by a fire. Gamely, he restored it again, in 1787. By 1841, in a peculiarly low and wretched point in Harris history, St Clement's was once more derelict; works were carried out in 1873 by the patronage of the Countess of Dunmore and by the direction of Alexander Ross, an architect of many important Victorian churches, such as the new Free North in Inverness and that town's Episcopalian cathedral.

Constructed in rubble masonry, with finer dressing making use of freestone and a striking black schist – probably imported from Mull – St Clement's has a classic cruciform plan and the distinctive high, rectangular tower, reminiscent of that on the Benedictine Abbey of Iona. This tower is elaborately decorated, and bears some disconcerting features for any Christian foundation. Bull's heads (the MacLeod crest) project from the corners between the third and fourth storeys. Above the door, within a canopied niche, is the robed figure of a bishop, probably St Clement. The east elevation boasts a badly weathered representation of two fishermen in a boat – perhaps Peter and Andrew; the north has a bull's head; and the south a nude female nursing a child in a squatting posture that, naturally, displays her genitalia – this sort of *Sheela na gig*, a crude fertility symbol of pagan origin, is notable within the Irish sphere of ecclesiastical or cultural influence; the Augustinian nunnery at Iona is likewise secured against the evil eye by an explicit female sculpture. In another panel on the west face her brother flaunts himself beneath the feet of the innocent bishop, though his full priapic glory was much reduced, in gleefully retailed Harris recollection, when the Countess ordered one of her men to blast the offending member with his shotgun. There is still another figure, in a kilt.

St Clement's is an evocative building with fine windows, assorted effigies and grave-slabs, and a splendid view from atop its tower; but the tomb of Alexander MacLeod himself is rightly described as 'the finest ensemble of late mediaeval sculpture to survive anywhere in the Western Isles'. A stone effigy of Alasdair Crotach lies in repose, dressed in his best armour and guarded by recumbent lions, over the *kist* that holds his remains. Neatly taking advantage of the arch over this little sarcophagus, the sculptor has made of it the 'arc of the firmament', with God the Father holding the crucified Christ at its peak. Vandalism or a souvenir hunter may have removed a dove at the foot of the cross, representing the Holy Spirit. There are symbols of the four Evangelists surrounding this Trinity, and the twelve apostles – St Paul, of course, in place of Judas Iscariot – and two angels bearing censers.

In the panel or 'register' below this, the saints – by whom alone, in Roman Catholic thinking, mortals may approach the Most High – are represented by the Virgin Mary, who has two be-mitred, crozier-wielding bishops in her honour: one, holding a skull, is identified by inscription as St Clement, patron of the church. And, in humanising and still poignant detail, are carved emblems of the MacLeod world itself – Dunvegan Castle; and a galley under splendid sail and cut in striking detail. In the bottom register is sweet Highland life itself: at distinctly sedate pace, a knight in mail and helmet pursues two stags, with the support of ghillies and dogs. To the right of this, Michael the Archangel shares a pair of scales with Satan as they solemnly weigh the souls of the departed, for Heaven or Hell. And to the right of that, lamentable Latin records the completion of this tomb for Lord Alexander, son of William MacLeod, Lord of Dunvegan.

In stark contrast to this jewel of Harris is the desolate Eaglais na-h-Aoidhe at Aignish, Lewis – St Columba's Church of Uidh, once that living of Dean Monro. In local tradition, it occupies the site of the cell of St Catyn, a Celtic saint who bridged the sixth and seventh centuries. But the present church is no earlier than the fourteenth century; it fell into disuse nearly 200 years ago; and is not only roofless and dangerous but at real peril, some day, of finally tumbling into the sea that has already consumed most of its surrounding burial ground. Despite much talk, little has been done and there is no sign of anyone prepared to take practical responsibility for what is not only a historic church but, as Rodel, a tomb for the MacLeods of Lewis.

St Columba's is an elongated rectangle in plan, built originally in three compartments – mausoleum, nave and chancel – and the latter would originally have had a timber screen before it, with a loft above; a doorway survives for an adjoining vestry. It is built in rubble masonry, with later works in red sandstone, and seems to have been re-roofed in the sixteenth century as there is evidence the upper part of the north wall was rebuilt. From the fifteenth century, MacLeod of Lewis chiefs and their families were buried here, and other interments took place, well into Victorian times, of local people whose connection with that lost house must have been well known and demonstrable. And two grave-slabs have long since been raised from the floor and mounted on the wall, for their own protection.

One portrays a male figure, tall and lean and oddly vulnerable in his gait, wearing a long quilted coat, a pointed helmet and cape – 'camail' – of mail; he bears a spear (or pike?) in one hand, and clutches a sword with his left. Though identification cannot be certain, he is probably Roderick – Ruaraidh – MacLeod of Lewis, who died around 1498. His successor, Torquil, involved himself ineptly against the forces of James IV in the struggle to save the doomed Lordship of the Isles, and when he refused afterwards to knuckle under, the Earl of Huntly descended on Lewis at the head of a royal force, seizing and destroying Stornoway Castle before advancing across the island and smashing the scarcely less rumbustious MacAulays of Uig. Naturally, Torquil MacLeod's estates were forfeited to the Crown, and duly granted to his brother, Malcolm – whose own burial at Iona bears bleak evidence that Lewis did not agree.

The other slab is certainly that of their sister, and shows an interlaced cross with assorted beasts in the foliage. The Latin inscription identifies her as Margaret, daughter of Roderick MacLeod, widow of Lachlan Mackinnon, and that she died in 1503 – and its detailed carving, so like the Celtic monuments of Argyll and its vigorous tradition of sculpture even in the Middle Ages, is easily explained, as well as Malcolm's latter exile: this Margaret was, besides, mother of John, the last Abbot of Iona.

4

'No Religion for a Gentleman'

Reformation and Presbyterianism, 1560–1742

The Reformation came late to Scotland. When it did, though, it broke with all the power of a social and political revolution – which it was – and swept all before it with astonishing totality.[1]

In 1559, Scotland was a Roman Catholic country. That faith was the only game in town. The Church decided whose children were legitimate; whose marriages were lawful; whose wills were legally binding. It touched life at every turn in its entire corruption. By the end of 1560, the hierarchy had been smashed, the Roman order overthrown, celebration of the Mass banned by law, and the faith reduced to a few remote fastnesses – Galloway; the remoter dales of Banff and Aberdeenshire; the 'Rough Bounds' of western Inverness, in Lochaber, Moidart and Morar. Scotland was now a solidly Protestant country. When Roman Catholicism, three centuries later, began seriously to recover, it would be not by argument but by immigration.

On 11 May 1559, John Knox – who combined a sharp intellect and outstanding courage with the formidable new theology of Geneva – preached a sermon at the venerable Church of St John in Perth, denouncing Roman error. There followed direct action by a congregation who, depending on later perspectives, have been viewed as the righteous populace or a thuggish mob. They smashed assorted statues and ornaments in the kirk and then betook themselves away to sack religious houses nearby. From Edinburgh, a furious Regent – Mary of Guise, who had run Scotland in the name of her young daughter since the early death of her husband, James V, in 1542 – ordered her forces to muster at Stirling before marching on Perth to make an example of Knox and that city's burgesses.

Knox in turn called up an army of his own, from all corners of the Lowlands – 'the Faithful Congregation of Christ Jesus in Scotland', to all intents and purposes a radical Soviet – and took on the Crown. Their forces included all the important or influential individuals whom the Regent had alienated. But, behind them, lay vast popular support –

'articulate men of every class,' records T.C. Smout, 'discontented with the political and religious environment in which they lived.' They were genuinely outraged by the astonishing decay of the Scottish Church, which we have noted. And they were in tune with a much greater European movement – the revolutionary theology of Martin Luther, first expounded at Wittenberg in 1517, and given still more impetus by one of the greatest technological breakthroughs in human history, the invention of the printing press. Half the Continent had already thrown off Papal supremacy and others – Switzerland, the Low Countries, parts of France and Germany – were enchanted by the still clearer teaching of John Calvin, a French divine who now reigned in Geneva.

Fully aware of the scale of the crisis, Rome had moved – far too late – to clean up her affairs. The biggest problem of all was political: the Roman order in Scotland was now thoroughly identified with the detested Regent, her French court, her French troops and France herself, bound up thoroughly with a persecuting Papacy. For a decade, Scotland had been a pawn of Paris. The stage was now set for a new, startling alliance with England and, of course, the later and progressive integration of Britain.

The Scottish Reformation was no coup d'état by a fanatical elite. It enjoyed massive, entrenched support – in the burghs, for instance, where many merchants and mariners had already been exposed to Protestant teaching abroad. These literate, resourceful men particularly liked its democratic edge, the new doctrine repudiated clericalism, the Roman notion of a superior priestly caste, and asserted not only that laity were equal to the clergy but could ascertain divine truth, for themselves, in their own Bible. Towns, besides, had invariably an underclass – a mob who quickly 'could be whipped up into a rabble,' points out Smout, 'by demagogues dwelling on the hatefulness of idols and the abundance of salt beef in the friars' kitchens,' before pointing out that a strategy of carefully orchestrated spontaneous uprisings – as well as Perth, there were others in Dundee, Scone, Stirling, Linlithgow and Edinburgh – well served much later revolutionaries in the twentieth century.

But success hinged on the support of Scotland's nobility, if any armed resistance to a hostile and still more formidably armed Crown could succeed. Knox and his allies duly cultivated it and in 1557 the first 'Protestant Lords' signed a covenant, pledging their 'power, substance and our very lives' to securing the Reformed faith. The final, critical element – early in 1560 – was the arrival of an English fleet in the Forth, cutting off French supply lines and, at a critical juncture, relieving the Lords of the Congregation and their forces as all teetered on the balance. In short order, in February 1560, the Reformation was secured. The timely death of the Regent, and the inadequacies of her returning daughter, completed all.

The central question of the Reformation was that of spiritual authority. Roman Catholicism taught that true religion – as it teaches to this day – is informed by three sources of equal weight: the Holy Scriptures, the teaching of the early Fathers, and the ongoing authority of the living Church. The problem of Roman Catholicism has never been that she denies the central truths of the Christian Gospel. The trouble is that she has added a great deal of junk. It is only fair to point out that Christians have always been prone to complicate the Gospel – a plain message of saving faith in Jesus Christ – and that Protestantism has its own besetting sin, the virus of 'Pietism', centred on subjective experience and supposed attainments in personal holiness, too readily excuse for neglect of doctrine, the shirking of evident moral duty and a tedious brand of self-righteousness. Pietism is generally rooted, as a trend in European Christian thought, in German Lutheranism; but Highland Evangelicalism, at its weakest, has a fair dose of it.

The Reformation mantra is *sola scriptura* – Scripture alone – and the Scots took to it with singular enthusiasm, practically overnight ridding themselves of, for instance, an episcopal hierarchy; veneration of the Virgin Mary and the saints; the observances of the so-called Christian calendar; enforced clerical celibacy; monastic orders; and the five assorted, bogus Roman sacraments. Church buildings were remodelled and worship restored to the New Testament pattern – no choirs, man-made hymns, elaborate music, fancy vestments or funny Latin. Scots would thereafter praise their God in the unaccompanied singing of the Psalms, in metrical translation, to easy tunes.

From the very first, John Knox and his allies sought 'a school in every parish', grasping that strong, popular faith required popular literacy. His vision for national education, to say nothing of sensible sanitary laws and measures for poor-relief – outlined in the *First Book of Discipline* – seems astonishingly modern, but reflects the Reformed concept of 'Two Kingdoms' – a close partnership between the political order and the spiritual one, the Church's authority alive and alongside that of the 'civil magistrate', and in mutual interdependence.

The new Kirk would exercise real, judicial power within the rural parishes of Scotland, and have charge besides of schooling and welfare provision; she would retain these responsibilities until after the Disruption and even today, despite the best endeavours of Donald Dewar, there is still a national Church of Scotland with some real and abiding privileges. So the fathers of the Scottish Reformation advocated the 'Establishment' of religion – the duty of civil authority to support, and indeed to fund, the true faith; but they also advocated popular religion, and the right of heads of households, at least, in a congregation to choose their own minister.

It is worth here demolishing the myth of Scottish intolerance.[2] The Scotland of John Knox and the Reformation is often thought to be a realm of murderous bigotry, by contrast to civilised England. Nothing could be further from the truth. The Reformation – and even the decades that preceded it – are remarkable for their bloodlessness. In total, only twenty-one men were put to death by the pre-Reformation Church in Scotland, the burnings of Patrick Hamilton (1528) and George Wishart (1546) affording the most celebrated Protestant martyrs. And only one Roman Catholic, John Ogilvy was definitely put to death for his faith (1615, when he was hanged at Glasgow Cross); there may have been two others. Scotland has, besides, an enviable record on its treatment of the Jews, who have never been harassed or persecuted.

Compared with the slaughter of English Protestants, especially under Mary Tudor, or the torture and execution of Roman Catholics under her successor, or the pogrom against Jews under Elizabeth and her medieval predecessor, Edward I, this is an enviable record. Yet one must acknowledge the hysterical persecution of 'witches', most of whom were but innocent, terrified old women – though the scale of casualties is hard accurately to ascertain, the last was burned at Dornoch in 1727[3] – and, if infrequently, heretics: in January 1697, Thomas Aitkenhead was hanged in Edinburgh for asserting that Christianity was a 'rhapsody of feigned and ill-invented nonsense'. Denied legal counsel at his trial, Aitkenhead was only eighteen. That a witch was burned in France as late as 1780, and that Roman Catholic persecution could flame bloodily in the Balkans even during the Second World War, is no defence.

More characteristic of the true Scots temper are Knox's own words in the Preface to the Scots Confession, which would remain the subordinate standard of the new national Kirk for almost a century:

> Protesting that if any man will note in this our confession any article or sentence repugnant to God's Holy Word, that it would please him of his gentleness and for Christian charity's sake to admonish us of the same in writing; and we upon our honours and fidelity by God's grace do promise unto him satisfaction from the mouth of God, that is, from His holy scriptures, or else reformation of that which he shall prove to be amiss . . .

John Knox was not able, as he had hoped, to secure the monastic revenues for a network of popular education. Nobles collared most of them and their continued assent was vital if the Reformation were to survive. And the issue of church government itself was to prove fraught. Emerging from what had been one 'Christendom', under the Papacy, peoples across Europe had barely our concept of our modern nation state, far less such notions as freedom of conscience or limited government. The first instinct of kings and dynasties was that they themselves had an entire right – and, before God, a duty – to control the national Church and impose their own faith. Scotland was no exception.

Even before the century's end, James VI strove to impose episcopacy (with himself at its head) on the Scots Kirk. Once he had assumed the English throne, succeeding his childless kinswoman Elizabeth in the 1603 Union of the Crowns, he prosecuted the scheme with still more vigour and success. His successor, Charles I, sought in addition to impose a new, Anglican-style written liturgy, uniting its opponents in the National Covenant. He lost his kingdoms, and his head. Cromwell – who later duly humiliated Scottish forces and occupied the country – was a Congregationalist, with no time for Presbyterianism; but he now allowed divines from all sides of the border to meet and draw up (as promised in his deal with the Scots, the Solemn League and Covenant), a detailed creed for a British Presbyterian order. He had no intention of delivering one, and did not, but this Westminster Confession of Faith has since been the subordinate standard of the Church of Scotland and, indeed, of Presbyterians throughout the English-speaking world.

And a Stuart restoration, in 1660, saw a renewed bid by two royal brothers, Charles II and James VII, to force an Episcopal order back on Scotland; when hundreds of Scots were harried, tortured, shot down and judicially murdered, as they betook to the countryside in illicit Presbyterian 'conventicles' rather than sign up to a debauched church. The casualties included the 'Two Margarets' – the elderly Margaret MacLauchlan and the teenage Margaret Wilson, tied to a Solway stake and drowned by the tide, refusing to the last to abjure the Reformed order.

Yet out of all this, in the struggles of Covenant and Commonwealth, the writings of Samuel Rutherford and the heroism of the Cameronians, were hammered such abiding concepts as the right of private judgement, the spiritual independence of the Church, religious toleration, the first motions of representative democracy, limited government and the determined conviction – in 1689 and afterwards – that even the king was subject to the law. And it is generally believed that the use of Scotland's distinctive Communion tokens – small engraved things, usually of pewter, distributed to intending communicants and handed back at the Table – dates from this time, for spies were everywhere and such a thing was a useful security measure for the persecuted and desperate.

James VII, perhaps the most stupid of all the Stuart monarchs, and a
convert to Rome, lost England in 1688 to his son-in-law and nephew,
William of Orange, who acted swiftly when the king managed earlier that
year to beget a healthy baby son and thus displace William's wife, Mary,
from immediate succession. At first reluctant to rid themselves of King
James, a characteristically arrogant letter from their sovereign, now exiled
to France, made up the minds of the Scottish establishment for them.
Without great enthusiasm, in 1689 they accepted William's authority.

He had hoped to retain Episcopacy in Scotland, but thought again
when the Scottish bishops made plain their loyalties lay with James and
his house. So Presbyterianism was restored, and what we record as the
'Second Reformation' was at last accomplished – after decades of war,
invasion and upheaval, and on top of a deteriorating climate, dreadful
harvests and a ruined economy. William, who never saw fit to visit his
northern realm, died childless in 1702, and was succeeded by his sister-in-
law, Anne. Her seventeen heroic pregnancies had failed to spare any child
by that date surviving and – with an abiding threat from the exiled Stuarts
(supporters of King James, *Jacobus* in Latin, were quickly styled the
'Jacobites') – the Scots assented uneasily to the 1707 Treaty of Union.
They accepted, besides, the English Act of Settlement, which expressly
excluded a Roman Catholic or the spouse of a Roman Catholic from the
British throne and, on the demise of Anne, would bypass the 'Old
Pretender' (that surviving 1688 Stuart heir) and indeed a good many
others to bestow the succession on the House of Hanover, direct
descendants of James VI. George I duly inherited in 1714.

And that, briskly, is the history of the Scottish Reformation. But one
time-bomb still remained, and had in 1712 been unjustly reimposed on
the Scots in express defiance of one Article of Union – the system of
patronage, or the right of a local laird or 'heritor' to appoint a minister to
the parish church, whatever the wishes of the people. This 1712 measure
was got up in Parliament by English Jacobites, who remained powerful
and knew many Scottish landlords still supported James Francis Edward
and could be relied on to choose like-minded clergymen. That all
ministers had to swear loyalty to the Sovereign and the Protestant
succession upon induction to a charge was a minor inconvenience.

Practically all the Kirk's divisions were born of patronage and the
related issue of the Establishment principle. It provoked the birth of the
Secession Church in 1733, the constitution of a few Lowland Covenanting zealots into the Reformed Presbyterian Church of Scotland in 1745,
and still another breakaway, the Relief Church, in 1761. A tiny remnant
of the Reformed Presbyterians survives to this day in the Scottish
Lowlands; the Secession and Relief Churches broke over time into

factions, and at length their liberal wings united in a body utterly opposed to the Establishment principle, with real consequences for the Highlands. It would be 1874 before patronage was abolished, and by that point the Scottish church had much more insidious problems.

The Highlands are, at first glance, the disgrace of the Scottish Reformation. It is only fair to point out that the fragile Protestant order inherited a bad situation. 'Medieval parishes in the Highlands were impractically large,' Bruce Lenman points out, 'priests were few, religious houses were scarce and scattered, while bishops were often non-resident and non-consecrated, or both,' perhaps 'because of inescapable factors of geology and climate, this agricultural society was poorer than most.'[4] The ablest churchmen of the day went where the money was, and 'the Reformed Kirk tended to continue along the same ineffectual lines as its medieval predecessors.'

Though so forthright on education, on literacy, on the imperative of Scripture reading both in public and in private, the new Protestant Kirk failed for decades to provide anything like enough ministers. It would be the eighteenth century before there was any sustained effort to plant schools throughout the vast region; 1801 before there was even a complete Gaelic translation of the Bible; 1828 before it was readily affordable. Indeed, in terms of the provision of the most basic Christian ordinances, things actually became worse.

For over a hundred years the Reformed Church failed to furnish pastors for Kilmallie and Kilmonivaig – two vast Lochaber districts covering, between them, more than half a million acres and, then, thousands of people. Kilmonivaig, alone, was larger than eleven modern counties. Lewis was reduced, by the end of the sixteenth century, from four parishes to one, and even these would endure long vacancies. There was no resident minister of the Reformed Kirk on North Uist until 1626; South Uist had to wait until 1633.

'For long, the West Highlands were close to paganism,' Andrew L. Drummond and James Bulloch record, 'and when every allowance has been made for exaggeration by enthusiasts, it remains true that until the end of the eighteenth century the impression made by the Church was trivial. Change, when it came, was due to men of intensely evangelical faith, and the advance of the Church in Gaelic Scotland coincided, more or less, with its failure in industrial Scotland. For the first time the Highlands were not merely a problem for the Church, but a factor within it.'[5]

That, though, would be in the nineteenth century. In 1560, the Highlands and Islands of Scotland were to the fathers of the Reformation as remote and sinister as the Indies. Language was, of course, a formidable barrier in itself. We forget how recently Gaelic has retreated in Scotland.[6] The last native speaker in Aberdeenshire survived until 1985; the last of the Perthshire dialect, the Gaelic singer Petrina Stewart, until 1991. Gaelic was still to be heard on the Dunbartonshire shores of Loch Lomond into the reign of Edward VII, and on Arran until the late 1960s. Even today, it is not quite extinct – as a community language – on the Scottish mainland, and elderly native speakers can still with difficulty be found in one or two pockets of the eastern seaboard.

In fairness to the Reformers, there were not a few priests in this area whose Gaelic may have been lamentable. Roman worship, after all, was conducted in Latin. But the protracted delay even in translating Reformed material into Gaelic is still astounding. Initial labour fell to John Carswell, a native of Kilmartin in Argyll and one of the very few Gaelic speakers with a place in these early, Reformed circles. In 1544, he had graduated from the University of St Andrews. By 1551, he had taken holy orders and was treasurer at the Cathedral of Lismore – not nearly so grand a building as it sounds – and became rector of his native parish in 1553 before winning another living, on the Isle of Bute, in 1558; more importantly, he was chaplain to the Earl of Argyll. Argyll, head of Clan Campbell – who had prospered mightily, by dint of great care to cultivate the favour of the Crown, and their geographical importance as a counter to Clan Donald – was an eminent Lord of the Congregation, high in the leadership of the Reformed revolution.

So the well-connected Carswell became Prebendary and Chancellor of the Chapel Royal in Stirling and, in 1560, was chosen as one of the five Superintendents of the Scottish Kirk, taking oversight of the old dioceses of Argyll and the Isles; and in 1567 was installed as Bishop of the latter. That year, he completed a Gaelic translation of Knox's Liturgy – the Book of Common Order – and it has a footnote in history as the first Gaelic book ever printed. Few Highlanders, though, would have made much of the Irish-based and very grand classical Gaelic of Bishop Carswell, who was a trained Campbell bard.

Decades passed before anything more was issued. Calvin's Catechism appeared, in Gaelic translation, in 1631; the Shorter Catechism, drawn up by the Westminster divines, in 1659. The Synod of Argyll had the previous year completed a Gaelic rendition of the first fifty metrical Psalms – a work initiated in 1653; the scholars were Revs Dugald Campbell of Knapdale, John Stewart of Kingarth and Alexander Mac-Laine of Strachur and Strathlachan. Their task was difficult, notes R.L. Thomson, 'the common metre required by the tunes being unfamiliar to the Gaelic ear in demanding, like classical Gaelic, a fixed number of syllables to the line and, unlike it, a regular patterning of stresses. Synod published it together with the Shorter Catechism; but the restoration of the Stuarts in 1660, and the return of episcopacy, stopped the project for thirty years. In 1690 Kirk's Edition of Bedel's Irish Bible – in the Roman alphabet – was published, but few could have afforded a copy and, in any event, its language remained in the esoteric, increasingly alien tradition of Carswell. By 1694, at least a Gaelic Psalter was complete.

Centuries, then, would pass before the Reformation could even take root in the Highlands through the ready availability of the Scriptures 'in the vulgar tongue'. We should not forget, besides, a barrier no less formidable to the new, militant Protestantism – the plain realities of geography. The incredible isolation of the West Highlands, in particular, is manifest from the memoirs of contemporary travellers. It was the nineteenth century before, beyond Stornoway, there were any roads on Lewis capable of bearing a wheeled carriage, and after the Second World War before some Harris communities enjoyed any sort of road at all: West Scadabay was not granted a road until 1977 and Rhenigidale, notoriously, until 1990. Even today, the South Uist hamlet of Glendale can be accessed only by a rough track.

Drummond and Bulloch outline the scale of the difficulties in even penetrating – far less evangelising – the West Highland terrain.[6] In the 1740s, travelling from Dunkeld to his fastness near Blair Atholl, the Duke of Atholl had to be carried in a sedan-chair. At century's end, another duke could make the trip in a coach-and-six – but it still took twelve hours to cover the twenty miles. Poolewe, in Wester Ross, was long the port for anyone heading to Lewis; but when Lady Seaforth left from Contin, in 1799, to visit that part of the family estate, her coach was an entire wreck fifteen miles beyond departure. Communications long remained fraught. Even after the Great War, word of family bereavement was as likely to come from, say, Skye to Lewis by letter as by telegram. A Free Church minister who chose to drive from Glasgow to Gairloch,[7] say, in the late 1930s, would have not only to negotiate narrow, winding and at times precipitous roads but had to cross three crude little ferries, at Ballachulish, Dornie and Strome.

The Kirk, pathetically under-resourced, was slow to find ministers for many Highland parishes. It was still slower in providing new, better churches at more sensible locations; a Stornoway kirk apart, it was the last decade of the eighteenth century before a new church was erected anywhere on Lewis. At South Laggan, in the Great Glen, the medieval church was long ruinous when, as a consequence of Thomas Telford's Caledonian Canal, it was drowned in a rising Loch Lochy. Twenty years later, MacDonnell of Glengarry bestirred himself to build a little church

for Episcopalian worship. When that tedious parakeet died and his estates
were sold, it lay unused and derelict for years, until at last adopted by the
Free Church.

Even the most basic pastoral work seems to have been minimal and
infrequent. In the nineteenth century, for instance, we read of a boy at
Kinlochhourn, deep in the wilds of Knoydart, about five or six, and who
was belatedly to be baptised. 'He did not know what baptism was,'
Andrew Bulloch dryly observes, 'but did not like the sound, and as the
minister's boat drew in to the shore the boy took to the hills and could not
be caught until the minister had sailed. Thus he was not baptised till his
teens when the minister next returned . . .'

So most limited, infrequent ordinances were depressingly familiar to a
grieving man from Harris, cleared as so many of his neighbours from that
island in the nineteenth century and who, in a most isolated community
in the woods of Cape Breton, found himself standing by the open grave of
his young wife. By great good providence a minister happened to be in the
locality, and had appeared to conduct funeral worship. A woman plucked
at the widower's sleeve. 'With the children, you'll be looking to marry
again.' 'I suppose I will that, yes.' 'And had you anyone in mind?' 'I cannot
say that I have yet given it any thought.' 'Well,' she said diffidently, 'I'd
take you.' He looked up. He looked at her. 'Would you, now?' 'Gu dearbh;
indeed.' 'Go quickly,' he said, 'and fetch that minister back.' And so they
were married, that same afternoon that he buried his first wife; but, had
they delayed for the sake of some show of decency, it might have been
years before another minister hove in sight of that new, struggling
township.[8]

In 1598, fine-tuning a mission to the Isle of Lewis, King James VI
appointed Mr Robert Durie, minister of Anstruther, to accompany the
expedition of a carefully picked band of men to Stornoway. The king,
though, had not the least interest in the care of souls in the Long Island.
He had not even a mind for evangelism. The 'wisest fool in Christendom'
wanted genocide.

The Fife Adventurers, and their brutal fate, is one of the nastiest episodes
in island history,[9] driven by the murderous contempt of King James VI
for his Highland subjects, recorded so shamelessly by this King of Scots.
James VI embodied all the prejudices of his Lowland acquaintance against
the Gaels. Having subverted the Lordship of the Isles to their own
advantage, and thus exchanged the only effective West Highland authority for decades of chaos, feuding and massacre, they had naturally
concluded that Highlanders were nothing but trouble. And the king
genuinely believed the Long Island abounded in riches and was ripe for

colonisation, once cleared of a people who, as James Hunter suggests the king evidently thought, 'were no more part of civil society than were the Cheyenne or the Sioux.'

Lewis, burbled James, was 'inrychit with ane incredibill fertilitie of cornis and store of fischeings and utheris necessaris, surpassing far the plenty of any pairt of the inland.' It was, however, entirely wasted on its natives, who should accordingly be eliminated and new Lowland colonists installed in their stead, who could be relied on to 'advance and set forwardt the glorie of God, the honour of their native countrey and His Majesties service.'

But what of the MacLeods? The latest and longest-serving Chief, Ruaraidh, Tenth of Lewis – who had been unable even to sign his own name – had finally died at the ripe old age of ninety-five, after decades of domestic misfortune, a litter of children by different wives, and an increasingly bloody policy towards other upstarts of his house. What really undid him, though, was the ill-judged marriage around 1542 to Janet MacKenzie of Kintail, who duly bore a son not to him but to Uisdean Morrison, the latest Brieve, and then ran away before the hapless 'Old Rory' could beget her with a child of his own. The MacKenzies of Kintail had already designs on Lewis, and this bogus claimant, when he attained manhood, afforded the perfect opportunity and certainly caused untold trouble. The saga that follows is violent, bloody and involved, but came to a head when Old Rory breathed his last in 1595. That year, King James summoned his noble subjects for military duty, and two Torcuils turned up – the real MacLeod heir, son of Ruaraidh X by his third wife (a MacLean of Duart) and the bogus one, the Brieve's bastard by the first Mrs MacLeod. The services of these MacLeod rivals, in the event, were not required, and the true Torcuil hastened to prop up his claims by marrying a sister of MacLeod of Dunvegan, which Chief was high in the good graces of James VI.

The pretender resorted to one of the oldest tricks in Highland intrigue. He sailed to Stornoway and cheerfully invited the other Torcuil to a drink aboard his ship. The true MacLeod had the wit to turn up with seven companions, but not the wit to choose men who could actually fight. They were immediately seized, bound and borne over the Minch to Lochalsh, where MacKenzie, Laird of Kintail, murdered the lot of them. Shortly, too, he had kidnapped a still younger, legitimate son of Ruaraidh. He was never indicted, far less brought to justice; for King James was already making as deft use of the MacKenzies in the north – in the furtherance of his own purposes – as the Stewarts had long deployed the Campbells. He had, however, no intention of actually letting the MacKenzies take Lewis. And – without any MacLeods around to attend a

Privy Court summons and produce titles to their land (which, as the Council knew perfectly well, had been stolen by duress for the bogus heir during an earlier, Edinburgh jail adventure of Old Rory) King James took direct and personal possession of the island, and promptly bestowed it on twelve Lowland venture-capitalists we remember as the Fife Adventurers. To legitimise all, moreover, the king got up an Act of Parliament.

So the men who ran the country solemnly assembled to pronounce the people of Lewis beyond the bounds of civilisation – 'voyd of any knowledge of God or His religoun,' folk 'gavin thameselfis over to all kynd of barbaritie and inhumanitie.' Later, in 1600, the Privy Council would reiterate that these wild men of Lewis delighted in 'blude, murthour and all kynd of barbarous and beastlie crueltie'; and a new Bishop of the Isles, Andrew Knox, would happily describe all those Gaels in his pastoral care as a 'falss generation', a 'pestiferous' people, devoted all together to 'barbaritie and wickedness'.

Against such ruffians, the Adventurers were naturally granted all powers for 'ruiting out the barbarous inhabitantis' by Act of the Scots Parliament. There is nowhere the least suggestion of any bid to win them for the Reformation and the Gospel. It was tacitly understood that the people of Lewis would be put to the sword, as merely the first step in sustained settlement of the Hebrides where henceforth no lands were to be 'disponit in feu, tak or utterways bot to Lowland men'. The king put his own cousin, the Duke of Lennox, in charge of the adventure, backed up by Gordon of Huntly and with full and entire authority in Scots law for whatever 'slauchter, mutilation, fyre-raising or utheris inconvenieties' might prove necessary for the subjection of Lewis, and happily drafted plans for similar projects elsewhere in the Outer Hebrides, 'not be agreement with the country people bot by extirpation of thame'. The Adventurers first landed at Stornoway in October 1598 – and were beset, harassed, outmanoeuvred and finally overthrown. The islanders fought with sustained and determined courage. They captured ships in the Minch, took Stornoway Castle – twice – and at last slaughtered the entire garrison. King James and his sleazy little band of speculators had been comprehensively beaten and, as for that cocky little chaplain, Rev. Robert Durie, he was no doubt thankful to return home with his life.

So the king had finally, after all, to sign over Lewis to the MacKenzies, who would hold the island until the nineteenth century. His other Hebridean experiment, much more tentatively, at Islay, came to nothing, and from his accession to the English throne his ambitions for a policy of 'plantation', on a much larger scale, quickly focused on Ulster, begetting hatreds that redound to this day. He had to content himself with his Statutes of Iona, in 1605, imposed under duress on assorted Hebridean chiefs and which (though honoured more in the breach than the observance) were spitefully engineered both to neutralise any military threat and to extirpate the language and culture of Gaeldom. The gravest consequence of James VI's bigotry was that entire failure, by anyone throughout his long reign, to translate and publish either a Gaelic Bible or any Gaelic Gospel literature.

It took some years, of course, to confirm the MacKenzie grip on Lewis, and to hunt down and eliminate every possible claimant to the MacLeod chiefship; those who escaped detection naturally kept their kinship quiet, and – today – no one knows who, for truth, could lay claim to the title, though there must still be many descendants of the last chief about. There were some, though, brave enough to assert a late relation's right to burial at Aignish, in the Church of the Uidh, and it is said that a band of MacKenzie thugs tried to stop one such funeral: tempers flared, until John Morrison – tacksman of South Bragar – quipped

> *Leodhas gu leir aig MacCoinnich,*
> *ach leud a dhrom' aig MacLeoid . . .*

> Let MacKenzie have all of Lewis,
> but MacLeod the breadth of his back . . .

and the interment was permitted; indeed, scions of the last MacLeod chiefs, or folk who said they were, were interred inside the ruinous church into the 1890s. The very last burial of all, though – perhaps fittingly, recalling how that family had been robbed of its Lewis inheritance first by MacLeods and then by MacKenzies – was in 1897, and a Colin Nicolson.

The brave Neil, holed up at Dun Berisay in Loch Roag, was finally caught and executed in 1613, and that was the end of the MacLeods of Lewis, who may have been outmanoeuvred by an evil monarch but who had in truth consumed one another. 'The Clan Torkil in Lewis were the stoutest and prettiest men,' wrote the Rev. James Fraser in 1699, 'but a wicked bloody crew whom neither law nor reason could guide or modell, destroying one another, till in end they were expelled that country, and the McKenzies now possess it.'

> *'S e mo bharail air Clan Leoid*
> *gur cosmhuil iad ri poir an t-uisge:*
> *An te is sine, mas i is mo*
> *ithis ian te is oige dubhse . . .*

It is my opinion of Clan Leod
that they are like pikes in the water:
The oldest of them, if the biggest,
eats the youngest of them . . .

As for the MacKenzie chief, he became Lord MacKenzie of Kintail; and his son and successor the first Earl of Seaforth, after the long green-grey fjord dividing Lewis from Harris. And, in that odd but gratifying yin and yang of history, the Seaforth line would also go to perdition.

Slowly, patchily, amidst the turmoil of the seventeenth century and the occasional excitement of Jacobite uprising in the eighteenth, the Kirk moved to impose her own structure and order in the Hebrides.[10] Dean Monro tells us there were four parishes in Lewis. Within a few years of the Reformation, however, these were reduced to two monstrous charges, as if someone had drawn arbitrarily a line across the primitive maps of the time, from Fevig by Shawbost in the west to the mouth of the Laxdale river on the island's Minch coast. Everything north of that line – including Ness, Tolsta, Back and Tong – was the parish of Barvas. Everything south of it, including Point and Lochs, Uig and Carloway, was Stornoway. These ludicrous bounds endured until 1722.

Of the earliest Reformed ministers we know little more than their names. Sir Patrick MacMaster Martin is noted as minister of Barvas in 1566, having conformed to the Reformation, and took that confession off Uisdean, the Brieve – shortly before his 1556 execution – deponing to his own paternity of the MacLeod pretender. The other is Ronald Anguson – which sounds more like a patronymic than a surname – who had been minister of Uig and had at least some education, for he had 'subscribed an obligation' for Old Rory, Roderick MacLeod of Lewis, to John, Bishop of the Isles, on 16 April 1573, and took care to note in it that he penned it at the Chief's behest, 'because he could not write himself'.

The enormous disruption of the seventeenth century, with Stuart kings coming and Stuart kings going and Episcopacy at times in the ascendant, was another complication. Bishops had been restored to their temporal estates in 1606 – like the unpleasant James Knox – and a full Episcopal order in 1610. Presbyterianism came back in 1638, but was again dethroned in 1660. Today it is fashionable to bewail our Calvinist past and to talk darkly of the 'theocracy' of Covenanting times. There is no doubt the Stuarts cordially loathed the Kirk: Presbyterianism, sneered Charles I himself to the Earl of Lauderdale, 'was no religion for a gentleman'.[11]

But their antipathy had little to do with doctrine, Scripture or fine points of ecclesiastical polity. James VI hated the Kirk because its authority and popular support reminded him, at every turn, how limited by contrast was the power of the Scottish crown. In time, though Parliament moved effectively to oust Charles I in England, it was the Kirk who opposed him in Scotland, and in 'contemporary eyes Scottish Presbyterianism in the seventeenth century had been a political movement akin to social democracy, a revolutionary force opposed to strong central government. Its spokesmen, John Knox, George Buchanan, Andrew Melville and Samuel Rutherford, were reckoned dangerous men.' Through the Disruption, through 1893 and 1900, and even in present tension over Sabbath ferry services, the essentially popular character of the Scots Presbyterian order – now surviving, in our century, only on the Long Island – has never been lost.

Only in 1690 was the old order restored, and enshrined in the 1707 Articles of Union; as recently as February 1952, the Queen – like all her British predecessors – had to swear an oath to uphold that Presbyterian order in the Church of Scotland. As for the supposed benevolence of Episcopacy, there is hard evidence that even the most basic Christian ordinances vanished from many Highland districts at the height of its sway. In Lochbroom, Communion was administered only once in seven years; at Fodderty, once in twelve; at Glenurquhart, not once in twenty-four years. The requisite white linens, and the Communion vessels themselves, had not been got – or had mysteriously disappeared – and had to be borrowed.

Lewis and Harris were little troubled by the protracted stramash between Presbytery and Episcopacy; and, for that matter, between the Stuarts and Cromwell. Only the latter rudely intruded; in 1654, Cromwell's forces destroyed Stornoway Castle – its rubble can still be seen, at low water, beneath the town's main pier – and for some years occupied the town. But a popular bent to Episcopacy survived well into the eighteenth century. And the Risings themselves, or at least their aftermath, could intrude. After the collapse of the first Scottish Jacobite bid in 1689, when Claverhouse won the Battle of Killiecrankie but lost his life, not a few grand refugees sailed for Lewis after the final reverse on the Haughs of Cromdale, including an eminent MacLean of Coll, *Iain Dubh*, or Black John, and the Earl of Seaforth himself. It is said they held a muster on Stacashal, a hill in central Lewis, and tried to figure out what next to do. Iain Dubh settled permanently on Lewis and his descendants, in Shawbost and Ballantrushal and Tolsta Chaolais and even in Tarbert, are on the island to this day.

And the very first Reformed church built in Stornoway, around 1610 – St Lennan's – at the expense of Lord Kintail, was effectively an Episcopalian one. It stood on North Beach Street, on a site now occupied by the Royal Bank of Scotland, and served as the town's parish church until late in the eighteenth century, when the present building – St Columba's Parish Church – was erected. A door ended up in a shoe-maker's shop in the town, and the bell of St Lennan's – which seems to have been acquired, or even purloined, from a Cromwellian garrison at Stornoway – has had an exciting history, going first to the Manor Farm, and used, during the Aignish Riot of 1888, when local crofters laid moral claim to new holdings on the eponymous farm and drove off its cattle, to summon a resident detachment of the Royal Scots to parade. After a sojourn at Galson Farm it came into the possession of Canon Meaden, and hangs today in St Peter's Episcopal Church on Francis Street. This Lord Kintail, shortly elevated to the Seaforth earldom, seems to have been a decent and pious man, for he adhered sufficiently to Knox's Reforma-tion ideal to, besides, provide Stornoway with a small but rather good school.

What was more, he brought with him in 1610 a minister, Farquhar MacRae, who was already settled as minister of Gairloch, and later served from 1618 to 1662 as minister or priest (the title varies with the form of church government then in vogue, which oscillated wildly through the century) at Kintail itself. He was only thirty when he landed on Lewis and his main preoccupation seems to have been to regularise domestic life; it seems that cohabitation was rampant, and he quickly married a vast number of couples and thus legitimised their children: more, he stuck up for woman's rights, forbidding men to desert – or throw out – their partners on any ground short of adultery. He had, besides, to engage in wholesale and frantic baptism; scarcely a soul under forty had been christened. 'Mr MacRae did not stay for any length of time,' says Murdo MacAulay, 'but he left a lasting impression on the people. His presence helped to induce the people to submit to Lord Kintail. That aside, the state of affairs Mr MacRae found on Lewis only attests to the gross neglect of the island, and the general collapse of spiritual provision, since the Reformation half a century before.' And it would be the nineteenth century before the last, native Roman Catholicism died out on Lewis.

What is striking, once a regular Presbyterian ministry was established on the Long Island, is how it was utterly dominated by just two families.[12] The MacAulays have more than left their mark on history – one, Thomas Babington MacAulay, practically wrote it, and his 'Whig' interpretation of British affairs and a new, post-Stuart national character, when Scots had a Union and lived happily ever after, survived in our schoolrooms even in the 1970s. But he was not only a direct descendant of one Lewis hero, Donald *Cam* MacAulay, who successfully scaled the Carloway broch with the aid of two dirks to wreak most unpleasant revenge on some Morrison rustlers, but of a veritable dynasty of clergymen.

The Reverend Aulay MacAulay, ordained to Coll and Tiree in 1702, became minister of Harris and is most notorious for his determined bid, in 1746, to capture Charles Edward Stuart on Scalpay and collect the magnificent reward. His cousin, Donald MacAulay, was minister of Kilmuir in Skye, and Aulay's son John – grandfather of the historian – became minister of Cardross in Dunbartonshire. Another MacAulay descendant, Iain MacLeod, had a notable career in post-war Conservative politics and died in 1970 as Chancellor of the Exchequer.

But the MacAulays are quite eclipsed in the local ecclesiastical landscape by a particular line of Morrisons – the house of the Brieves, already skilled in leadership, and with (no doubt) a taste for it. 'After the office of the Judgeship had become extinct in the Morrison clan,' writes MacPhail, 'the immediate descendants . . . became the tacksmen, middlemen, farmers, and the learned class in Lewis, especially clergymen. Morrisons were not only the clergy of their native island, but supplied various parishes on the mainland with ministers, some of whom were men of note in their day.'

Take Donald Morrison, insofar as we can from incomplete and atrocious records. Born around 1614 and admitted to Barvas by February 1643, his manse seems to have been in Ness; but by 1649 he was minister of Stornoway, and for at least seventeen years he was the only minister on the island. A grandson of Allan, the last Brieve, he was still in Stornoway in 1676 and 'was bred an Episcopalian, but conformed to Presbyterianism'. One son, Allan, duly filled his own shoes at Barvas. And another, Kenneth, born at Barvas in 1647, duly succeeded him at Stornoway, for he was certainly minister of Stornoway by 1689 and seems to have died in 1720. And by his day, feelings between 'Papists and Protestants' evidently ran high, for he took to wearing a sword by his side as he walked from his manse to his church, and two more men – with swords drawn – guarded the door of St Lennan's Kirk as he conducted divine worship.

The Reverend Kenneth had to confront superstition on the one hand and a baleful Roman Catholicism on the other. He was once shaken at a baptism when, the sacrament barely concluded, a woman plunged her hand into the basin and flung water full in the face of her servant. The scullion, she explained, was prone to see visions, but this was the recommended cure.

But the Laird of Kildun was a real threat, holding lands at Aignish and Aird for his estate and a scion of Seaforth. Seaforth, however, was an

Episcopalian: Kildun was a Roman Catholic, and had already dealt robustly with a priest, Cornelius Con,[13] who, retained in the household as a family tutor, had slept with Kildun's daughter and got her pregnant. The furious laird promptly seized Father Con and banished him to the most desolate place he could think of – to Fladda in Loch Roag in 1694, under the custody of a shepherd, without adequate food or clothing. The glee of local Protestants can be imagined, and a note still survives from the delighted minister of Contin, Angus Morrison – 'Kildins daughter Jean is wt child and as the report goes she has declair'd to some friends, priest Conn is the man ha ha.'

The Privy Council got to hear of it, whereon Kildun hastily removed the unhappy Con to the still more remote North Rona; but the rumour grew that the priest had in fact converted to Protestantism, and the business became a cause célèbre, as the authorities strove with increasing vigour to find him. Father Con did, somehow, escape his Atlantic fastness and made it, incredibly, to Edinburgh – where he was promptly in-carcerated in the Castle. By this time – perhaps understandably – he really had become a Protestant, but had sufficient wit to write, 'this castle is a poor place for a weak purse, yet is a paradise to me in respect of the Papisticall Purgatory the last eight years. I question if the Pope will so soon get out of his purgatory if he goes there.' He was freed shortly afterwards, a wiser and – no doubt – rather thinner man, and sent a gracious letter of thanks to the Synod of Argyll.

The laird now bore such enmity to the local minister, and so resented a local Protestant ministry, that he sent a few bruisers out one night to seize Rev. Kenneth Morrison and bring him to Aignish. But Mr Morrison was a brave, self-possessed character. He neither panicked nor offered any resistance when the heavies appeared and told him robustly of their errand. 'Oh, very well,' he murmured, 'but let us first drink to the Laird's health.' No one thought to object, and a great drinking-horn was filled and passed about. The laird duly toasted, the minister invited them to drink to Mrs Morrison's health and, again, this was heartily agreed. Then he suggested they drink to his own health, and then they could all head along to Aignish. 'By this time,' MacPhail waggishly observes, 'they would have drunk anybody's health.' Meanwhile, of course, word had somehow been got out of the manse to the neighbours, and in short order the drowsy intruders were overwhelmed and bound hand and foot. They were then borne – this was still a roadless island – over the bay to Aignish by boat, and dumped quietly in the lobby of the laird's own house. Be it said to the lasting credit of the Laird of Kildun, a man of evidently uncertain temper, that when he literally stumbled over the aghast victims in the small hours – hastening to see what had become of the expedition –

he was stoical, rather than murderous. It was, he sighed, another of 'black Kenneth's' tricks, and at least they could be thankful the minister had not ordered they be left on the shore below the high-water line.

Black Kenneth's near kinsman, John Morrison – tacksman of Bragar – was evidently a clever man and one of those profane, golden-hearted rascals Lewis throws up from time to time. Born in 1630, he was also a grandson of Allan, the very last Brieve, and himself would be the progenitor of still more Morrison ministers.

We have already seen John Morrison averting trouble at a MacLeod funeral in Aignish. And he took time out in the 1680s to write a very short but illuminating little book, *Description of the Lewis*. He tells us of advancing literacy, at least among such minor gentry as himself – the children of tacksmen, ministers and so on, so that in their own families 'at least the master can read and write . . . I do remember in my tyme, when there was not three in all the country [of Lewis] that knew A b by a Bible.' He has quaint tales of the Flannan Isles, still so reverenced in his day that visitors kept together in pairs; and that a robber exiled to the place, whose fire calamitously went out, was delivered by a vision of St Flannan himself, who kindly left a flaming peat on the altar of his derelict chapel; and how the men of North Rona caught sea-fowl, and made a salve from the fat of gannets 'good for the healing of any sore, wound or cancer, either in man or beast'.

'Indweller', as John Morrison called himself – in those days, gentlemen were too modest to identify themselves on their own books – is an immensely appealing figure because we have the testimony of Martin Martin himself that he was a good man, 'of unquestionable sincerity and judgement'; but also enough anecdotes of the fellow to assure us he was tough, practical, shrewd and very funny. During the Cromwellian occupation of Stornoway, from 1653, he deftly befriended Major Crispe – the resident governor – and used to call by at the garrison for cards and drinks, mentally noting details of the defences and sentries and, later, suitably briefing Seaforth and assorted raiding-parties. He ran rings around a factor who dared to overcharge him for rent, and bore cheerfully with a red-haired wife – the sister of Donald MacKenzie, tacksman of Dalbeg, and who had a ferocious temper – by resorting to witty Gaelic rhyme.

One of John's sons, Roderick, himself became a celebrated Gaelic bard – *An Clarsach Dall*; the 'Blind Harper' of Dunvegan, minstrel to Iain Breac MacLeod, whose greatest work, foreseeing the doom of an old Highland order, is *Oran Mor Mhicleoid*, the Great Song of MacLeod. Another brother, Angus Morrison, settled as minister of Contin and who had thought Father Con's indiscretion so funny, proved an ardent

Episcopalian; he refused to conform to Presbyterianism, was duly ejected, ended up living at Doire na Muic by Loch Broom and is best remembered as the author of smutty verse. The Rev. Malcolm Morrison served as a chaplain at Poolewe and Murdo Morrison, who did not aspire to the cloth, became a respected blacksmith and, according to Dr MacDonald of Gisla, was like his father a 'very strong, inventive engineer'.

His brother, another John Morrison, was also a minister, but a much more respectable fellow than the raffish Angus of Contin, though he failed to win induction to his rightful charge of Gairloch in 1710 – he was resisted by a mob and locked up in a byre for several days, before being ordered out of the district by Sir John MacKenzie of Coul, Episcopalian and Jacobite, who told him pleasantly that 'no Presbyterian would be settled in any place where his influence extended, unless Her Majesty's forces did it by strong hand.'

John Morrison, a quaint but holy man, had to content himself at length as minister of Urray, in Easter Ross. One of his sons, yet another John Morrison, became minister of Petty, and the 'Petty Seer' is still remembered both for his pious ministry and unsettling prophetic gifts. But another, Norman, was in 1742 inducted to Uig in Lewis. There he served for thirty-five years, pastoring an enormous district that then included four inhabited islands, and for which cure he had to retain a large boat and six of a crew for exposed, Atlantic passages, dangerous whatever the season of the year; that expense alone consumed over a quarter of his stipend. In addition he had to negotiate three long sea-lochs and, besides, three broad rivers, readily forded only in summer – tending over 1,200 people. In a letter of May 1763, Rev. Norman confided to a Skye publisher that only he himself, in the entire parish, could read. Once, around harvest-time, he made the fraught trip to Great Bernera to preach. The attendance, that Lord's Day, was so thin he angrily called on the west wind during prayer – '*Duisg thusa O' ghaoth gholach an Iar, agus seid agus duisg as an cadal-sabaid na paganaich nach duisg gu eisdeachd ris an fhuaim aoibhneach!*' – 'Awake O hollow west wind, and blow and rouse up the pagans out of their Sabbath slumbers, who will not wake to hear the joyful sound.' It is said that the wind did indeed rise, and with such force that it was long remembered on Bernera for the damage it did to their standing corn – yet another outing in Columban malediction.

In fact, Norman Morrison and all his reverend kin laboured, at times bitterly, in what remained to all intents and purposes a heathen community. They were long denied any effective Presbyterial structure. The Synod of Argyll sought ineffectually to run all the West Highlands, and neither the Long Island nor the Outer Hebrides had even their own

Presbytery; the harried ministers were under Skye. Far into the eighteenth century, a fitfully reviving Roman Catholicism and, especially, an Episcopalianism supported still by most West Highland lairds, gave the Kirk and her servants a torrid time.

Patronage, dominant generally from 1606 to 1843, was a complication, especially as in much of the Highlands the local heritor might not be a Presbyterian at all.[14] Yet he was obliged to maintain church buildings and, where necessary, provide a manse and a place of worship. (Most very old parish churches in Scotland can still display the 'laird's loft', where the great man sat.) But many did not; some, indeed, and especially those of Jacobite and prelatical sympathy – which, in 1690, was most of them – would resort to violence; yet their 'approval and financial support were indispensable if vitally needed new parishes were to be established,' as Lenman points out. A distant Parliament had imposed an alien system of appointing ministers, only maximising the power of chiefs and lairds who dreamed daily of overthrowing the Protestant succession and the entire political order, while refusing to offer a desperate Presbyterianism any practical sustenance.

And the region was besides boiling with Jacobite support. 'All of this would have mattered less had the State thrown its full weight behind the Church of Scotland,' sighs Bruce Lenman:

> In the Western Highlands, for example, the religious situation was still so complex and fluid, and ordained clergy of any kind were still so thin on the ground, that had William of Orange meant what he said about being determined to effect a real Reformation in the Highlands and Islands there would probably have been at the least a significant swing in the confessional balance there. The new Presbyterian settlement was anxious to train and deploy Gaelic-speaking ministers in the Highlands, to distribute copies of the Irish Bible . . . and to conduct a vigorous campaign against "seminary priests, Jesuits and trafficking Papists." In practice very little happened, because intentions could not become realities without the active support of civil authority, which was not forthcoming.

It was 1724 before the General Assembly – so far away that few ministers beyond ready horseback ride of Edinburgh could ever take their seats – deigned to devise a new, north-western Synod of Glenelg, which, as Lenman observes, was 'designed to bring fresh vigour and effectiveness to the work of the Established Church in the western Highlands and Islands.' And the chief motive was not, of course, the winning of souls but the dishing of Jacobitism.

The new Synod's records begin on 7 July 1725. At first there was but

one Presbytery of the Long Island in its bounds, comprising all the Outer
Hebrides, though Lewis at least had, in 1722, been divided once more
into four realistic parishes: Barvas, Lochs, Stornoway and Uig, with
Stornoway gaining the Broad Bay townships from Barvas. Following his
open part in the 1715 and 1719 Jacobite Risings, the Earl of Seaforth –
though now actually skulking on the island – had come 'under attainder';
his estates were forfeit, and the ardent Episcopalian could not resist. From
8 May 1742 the 'Long Island' was divided further into a Presbytery of
Uist (including Harris) and a Presbytery of Lewis. The structure was at
last in place for effective Gospel ordinances; the scaffolding in readiness
for education and Evangelicalism.

5

'Moderation is What Religion Enjoins'

Ministers and Moderates, 1742–1820

In 1737, eight years before the great Rising of 1745, a man called James Thomson arrived on Lewis.[1] He was a teacher of an earnest, well-intended organisation which seems to have originated in an Edinburgh prayer group around 1690, when good men grasped that only systematic education of the young could properly address the social, political and religious crisis of the Highlands. They determined to plant charity schools in every parish. It had taken an abortive Jacobite effort in 1708, however – with the real if fleeting prospect of a French invasion – before anyone in authority took the least notice; the following year, though, they won 'letters of incorporation' as the Society in Scotland for Propagating Christian Knowledge.

The SSPCK[2] avowed itself (at least for the satisfaction of politicians) to be determined on an offensive against 'barbaritie, Jacobitism and Poperie . . . to erect and maintain schools to teach to read, especially the Holy Scriptures and other good and pious books: as also to teach writing, arithmetic and such like degrees of knowledge in the Highlands, Islands and remote corners of Scotland.' It was, then, primarily missionary and evangelistic; and no one sensible doubted the need for such an endeavour, for the existing parish school system in the region was risible.

Its stated aim was less than adequate – for instance, one school would not have counted for much in Kilmonivaig, stretching in all its vastness from Invermoriston to Spean Bridge and then east to the wilds of Rannoch; nor in the parish of Ardnamurchan, fully ninety miles long. It was inclined to chortle over its own achievements, such as the school planted in 1711 on St Kilda, where 'nothing had been taught for many a dark and dreary generation, but the art of catching fish and solan geese'. Until 1766, its official and stated policy was to teach absolutely nothing in the medium of Gaelic. And it was perennially strapped for cash, allowed only to spend the interest accumulated on its meagre capital, and cheated of funds promised to it (from forfeited Jacobite estates) after the Rising of 1715. Nevertheless, by the 1750s, there were over 180 of its schools in the

Highlands, and it was exceptionally well directed – 'an efficient central organisation,' writes John A. Smith, 'a shrewd combination of missionary zeal and business expertise.' And it has been much maligned, especially by modern Gaelic lobbyists remarkable for their hatred of Highland Presbyterianism, as some sort of bigoted, imperial crusade to smash Roman Catholicism and extirpate the Gaelic language and culture.

But the SSPCK was of its time and the genuine, widespread fear of Jacobite restoration and the renewal of 'Popery and arbitrary government'. From meagre resources it founded and directed not only a great many elementary schools but, emboldened by a new Royal Charter in 1738, a large number of spinning and sewing schools, particularly for young girls. There were sewing schools in England; but they did not offer girls a literate and numerate education besides; SSPCK foundations did, and this was not only most unusual in its day but had real impact in the community. By 1795 there were 229 ordinary schools and 96 'working' schools, and as late as 1872 there were still 272 SSPCK schools in Scotland. With the advent, that year, of a compulsory State system, its operations were of course obsolete and the Society was finally wound up in 1890.

From the beginning, Smith notes, SSPCK establishments were 'also remarkably accessible to all and helpful to other schools'. In any event, SSPCK statutes forbade the teaching of Latin as well as Gaelic (lest, no doubt, it be perverted to the service of Rome). The anti-Gaelic policy itself was, from the start, honoured more in the breach than the observance. As far as the language of Eden was concerned, indeed, the SSPCK 'early became one of its earliest benefactors,' points out Smith, 'encouraging and subsidising Gaelic publications on an extensive scale and, latterly, developing in Raining's School, Inverness, a training ground for a succession of notable Gaelic scholars like Alexander Mac-Bain, George Henderson, and for more Gaelic-speaking pupil-teachers than all the other schools put together . . .'

Over two centuries, 'the SSPCK developed and maintained a complete self-supporting system of education in certain areas, which constituted a credible alternative to the parish school system and which actually cost the nation nothing. The influence of these schools, in generation after generation, must have penetrated every aspect and corner of individual and communal life in the areas served . . . The beneficial influence of this voluntary system of education, whatever its minor shortcomings, has been incalculable.' And, beyond the social and material benefit, there was a marked spiritual one: later, vibrant Evangelicalism stood, humanly speaking, on the shoulders and because of the accomplishments of the SSPCK. Others, as we shall see, would follow, and there were later still more ambitious schemes. In 1817, for instance, a new Stornoway academy, subscribed by local gentry, would offer classes in Latin, Greek, French and Italian; mathematics, astronomy and navigation; natural philosophy and chemistry; drawing and stenography – all on top of the usual subjects and a sharp rebuke to persistent, Lowland taunts about the backwardness of Gaeldom.

But this was well in the future. We know sadly little of James Thomson, save that he first toiled in the Lochs district – at Keose – and, by 1749, when his signature survives as witness to a document drawn up by Rev. Murdo Morrison, minister of Barvas, he was in charge of a little school at Swainbost in Ness, teaching Scripture, arithmetic, English, geometry and so on. Scant details of it still survive on an SSPCK log at the Scottish Records Office. We cannot even be sure where he was from. He was for long enough believed to be a native of Banffshire – Speyside – but some have recently suggested he actually came from south Perthshire. My late great-grandfather always maintained 'our people were from Lochcarron'; perhaps, early in his career, James Thomson had taught there too.

Yet his was the first light of learning, of communal literacy and Reformed Gospel endeavour, in the townships of Ness by the Butt of Lewis. And there he raised a large family. James Thomson is the progenitor of all the Thomsons of rural Lewis, descendants founding lines of their own in Ness (at Swainbost, Habost and Skigersta); in Bayble; in Tong. They would include eminent elders and ministers of the Highland church, Donald Thomson (1907–1980), a noted Oban head-master for Gaelic education; another James Thomson (1888–1971), also an eminent Gaelic writer; and James' still more influential son, Derick, born at Stornoway in 1921 – Gaelic academic, the founder of the *Gairm* periodical, and the 'major voice of Gaelic poetry throughout the second half of the twentieth century'.

There was great need of such a programme as that of the SSPCK, and for such men as James Thomson. For one, the Highlands were more christened – and that most nominally – than evangelised. A generally unchurched, massively unlettered and fearful populace remained largely in the grip of ignorance and, indeed, heathen superstition.

In Ness alone, the locals, only thirty years before Thomson's arrival, practised rites more appropriate to the coconut-kickers of the South Sea.[3] Teampall Mholuaidh had become stage to fantastic practices. Even in 1630, an unpleasant southern officer, Captain Dymes, recorded that the people 'are very ignorant and have been given to the idolastrous worshipp of divers Saints . . . now most especially devoted to one of their Saints called St Mallonuy. This saint was for cure of all theire woundes and sores.' When unable to visit Teampall Mholuaidh in person, they 'were wont to cutt out the proportion of their lame armes or leggs in wood with the forme of theire sores and wounds thereof and send them to the Saint where I have seen them lying vpon the Altar in the Chapell.' In addition, there was another area of the building 'soe holy in their estimation that not anie of their weomen are suffered to enter therein. Anie woman with child dareth not to enter within the doores of the Chapell, but there are certain places without where they goe to theire devotions.'

It was no better at Galson, several miles to the south, where the natives 'had two generall meetings in the yeare at this Chappell, the one at Candlemas and the other at Alhollautide [Hallowe'en] where theire custome was to eat and drincke vntill they were druncke. And then after much dancinge and dalliance togeather they entered the chappell at night with lights in their hands where they continued till next morninge in theire devotions.' But lately a local minister – probably the formidable Rev. Farquhar MacRae, whom Seaforth had brought to Stornoway – had sought to cure them of 'theire Idolatrous worshipp,' travelling to Ness 'to reason with them, then to admonish them, and afterwards to threaten them both with God His Judgments and the Lawes of the Realme, insomuch as divers of the better sort of them promised to forsake that wonted Idolatry of theirs.'

Such reformation did not last long, for – in his 1703 *A Description of the Western Islands of Scotland* – Martin Martin has left notorious record of the goings-on in Ness, only a generation before the arrival of James Thomson:

> The Inhabitants of this Island had an antient Custom to sacrifice to a Sea-God, call'd *Shony* at Hallowtide, in the manner following: The Inhabitants round the Island came to the Church of St *Mulvay*, having each Man his Provision along with him; every Family furnish'd a Peck of Malt, and this was brew'd into Ale: one of their number was pick'd out to wade into the Sea up to the middle, and carrying a Cup of Ale in his hand, standing still in that posture, cry'd out with a loud Voice, saying, *Shony, I give you this Cup of Ale, hoping that you'll be so kind as to send us plenty of Sea-ware, for inriching our Ground the ensuing Year*: and so threw the Cup of Ale into the Sea. This was perform'd in the Night time. At his Return to Land, they all went to Church, where there was a candle burning upon the Altar; and then standing silent for a little time, one of them gave a Signal, at which the Candle was put out, and immediately all of them went to the Fields, where they fell a drinking their Ale, and spent the remainder of the Night in Dancing and

Singing, etc. The next Morning they all return'd home, being well satisfy'd that they had punctually observ'd this Solemn Anniversary, which they believ'd to be a powerful means to procure a plentiful Crop. Mr *Daniel* and Mr *Kenneth Morison*, Ministers in Lewis, told me they spent several Years, before they could persuade the vulgar Natives to abandon this ridiculous piece of Superstition; which is quite abolish'd for these 32 years past.

Was it? Nearly two centuries later, in the 1890s, Rev. Malcolm MacPhail of Kilmartin – a native of Shawbost and who himself taught briefly at a school in Ness – insisted he had personally known the grandson of a man who regularly took part in a very similar rite 'addressed to St Brianuilt . . . being scarce of manure for his land at the end of the sowing-season, he went on the 15th day of May – old style – being St Brianuilt's Day, to the point of a promontory, near which he lived, and shouted, "Brianuilt, Brianuilt, send seaware; send seaware!" The legend goes on to say that his prayer was speedily answered, but it was accompanied by such a tremendous snowstorm as caused the affair to be remembered for many a long day.'

And the inveterate belief that the very stones and sanctuary of Teampall Mholuaidh could cure the diseased, and especially the insane, evidently persisted. A 1792 writer had noted enduring 'superstitious veneration' of the church and that the 'country people send their friends that are long lingering in sickness, to sleep here of a night, where they believe the Saint grants them a cure, or relief by death . . .' Mr MacPhail insisted that, when he had worked in Ness, such things were still remembered:

One of my earliest recollections in connection with the temple was one day, hearing people remarking that a young man, whose mind happened to be unhinged at the time, had been seen passing through the district in which I lived, in the custody of friends, on his way to 'Teampull-Eoropie'. It was even then believed by some that if one afflicted with insanity could be coaxed to sleep within the precincts of the temple, he was sure to be, at least, partially restored after a sleep there . . . After arriving at the temple at dusk the patient was made to walk around the temple seven times 'sunwise' – 'deiseal' – and to drink water from the 'Holy Well of the Temple', and was then freely besprinkled with the same water; but unless the patient slept after this treatment, there could be no cure. I was slightly acquainted thirty-five years ago with the individual in question. He was then quite sane; and, as far as I know, was so ever afterwards . . .

Sir Arthur Mitchell had similar horror-stories, adding the detail that patients were bound hand and foot and left for the night on the site of the altar; and that water from the well was brought in an old stone cup of its own significance, left 'in the keeping of a family, regarded as the descendants of the clerk of the temple.'

Ness was not, in a wider Highland context, in the least eccentric. By the 1690s the Presbytery of Dingwall were appalled by reports of rituals associated with the vague folk-memory of St Maol Rubha, who had founded that Columban mission at Applecross and who, a thousand years later, was practically venerated as a pagan deity in Wester Ross. Votive cloths were tied, in his invocation, to shrubbery on an island on Loch Maree – as they are to this day, in vaguer superstition, at the 'Clootie Well' near Munlochy, on the Black Isle – and on at least one occasion a bull was sacrificed. Indeed, Martin Martin assures us that the custom of *tamnadh*, or *tamradh*, survived in Ness – when a sheep or a goat was ritually slaughtered at the start of the fishing season – and also describes the ritual use of fire, being borne about in circles to protect crops, livestock and buildings, or to bless unbaptised infants and newly delivered mothers against evil spirits.

So inveterate and endemic were such beliefs in the region that, despite the best endeavours of a much more capable and dynamic ministry, some elements of superstition would persist through decades of rampant Evangelicalism, especially when people remained materially poor, medical science generally inadequate and certain conditions could make families desperate. When my uncle, Rev. Angus Smith, was inducted to Cross Free Church in 1968, a Mrs MacKenzie of Habost – born in 1870 – was still well remembered. 'At the age of four years she saw a woman from the West Side being taken in a cart by her husband to the Temple, in an attempt to find a cure for her insanity. That would be in 1874. The small girl was terrified, but her mother, who was with her, explained the situation to her. The woman was shouting. She had to sleep all night in the Temple with her head on the stone.'

In 1962, Rev. William Matheson told a still more appalling story to Anne Ross, in connection with persistent elements in ancient Celtic paganism – the power of a severed head or skull, allied to the still more persistent belief in healing wells. The story is all the worse because it involves a professing Christian – indeed, an office-bearer.

An elder of the United Free Church in Ness had an epileptic daughter. He eventually decided to try to cure her of her epilepsy in a traditional manner. Between sunset and sunrise and without speaking to a living thing, he walked five miles to the family burial ground at Teampall Cro

Naoimh [the Church of the Sacred Heart] at . . . Galson. There he dug up the grave and removed the skull from it. He came back home with the skull, awakened the epileptic girl and made her drink from the skull. He then walked back to Teampall Cro Naoimh to re-bury the skull. My informant did not know the name of the well from which the water was taken, but it is likely to have been a healing well and its name should still be ascertainable.

It could have been a scene from *The Wicker Man*. And far into the twentieth century, as tuberculosis devastated Lewis communities and particularly the young, we have noted already the persistent belief that the touch of a seventh-born child could cure scrofula. Queen Anne was the last British sovereign actually herself to touch for this affliction, the 'King's Evil' – one child who could recall the experience grew up to be Dr Samuel Johnson, who himself deserves a footnote in Highland church history. But there was another and almost as disturbing issue for anxious Presbyterian evangelists in Gaeldom – the startling recovery, at least in the far west, of Roman Catholicism.[4]

By 1600, the Western Isles were all – officially – Protestant; even South Uist and Barra. But these southern districts of the Outer Hebrides were within the realm of Clan Ranald, a solidly Roman Catholic stronghold of the MacDonalds whose mainland territories – Moidart; Ardnamurchan; Arisaig, Morar and Knoydart would long be known as the 'Rough Bounds' and which, even today, include the most inaccessible and isolated communities in mainland Britain. And the family of the Clan Ranald chiefs themselves were a proud, staunch, highly conservative bunch. A proverb is still retailed in modern Lochaber – 'Blessed Morar, where no Protestant minister ever preached a sermon!'

A priest who had laboured for decades in Moidart, Fr Charles MacDonald, acknowledged the region's extraordinary isolation before his death in 1894. 'It is no doubt partly owing to this difficulty of access that the inhabitants of these districts are about the most conservative in the kingdom – conservative in religion, conservative in those old-fashioned notions of loyalty to the crown and of respect for their landlords . . . When the old faith went down under the Revolution which swept over Scotland in the sixteenth century, the changes which were brought about can scarcely be said to have acquired a footing north of the River Shiel.' And the Rough Bounds, as Joshua Dickson records, in a recent, most detailed and interesting study of this Hebridean Counter-Reformation, 'were seen as a place of relative safety by priests and travelling missionaries throughout the turbulent seventeenth century, from the Irish Franciscans in the 1620s to the visitations of Bishop

Gordon in 1707.' Indeed, there was constant sea traffic from the isles and capes and fjords of Clan Ranald to the distant, friendly shores of Ireland, and it was from Ireland that, in 1619, a determined Franciscan mission was launched to the West Highlands and the Outer Hebrides. It would last for twenty-seven years in its first, most intensive phase and, by 1633, claimed some 10,000 conversions.

After initial reconnaissance, four young priests were approved for the mission, Dickson relates, and were sent forth in 1623 to reclaim the Hebrides for Mother Church – Frs Cornelius Ward, Edmund McCann, Patrick Hegarty and Paul O'Neill. Ward – who targeted Moidart and the Small Isles, South Uist and Barra – sent back regular and fascinating reports, in immaculate Latin, and had more than a bouncy voyage to the West Highlands in common with St Columba: he, too, was a son of Donegal, and an accomplished bard from a noted bardic family.

Ward soon happily reported that most of the folk he encountered in this region 'retained strong elements of Catholic veneration' despite protracted Roman neglect. No priest had visited Eigg in seventy years;[5] Uist had not seen one in a hundred. But roofless churches were still standing and saints were still venerated. The folk of Canna, Ward found, regarded Columba as a 'second God' and maintained that no frog or poisonous creature could come there, as Columba had powerfully blessed it – though one bold toad had wandered over from Rum and had instantly turned to stone on the beach. Word got swiftly over the Sea of Hebrides, for Ward was invited to Barra by a MacNeil gentleman who wished his child baptised, and found the ruins of Cille Bharra still held in reverence. By October 1625 he was in South Uist and, later that month, as a large and curious crowd converged, 'sent a messenger to the leading men of the island to come and listen to him; they agreed to do so, and promised to accept the faith if they found Ward's arguments more convincing than those put forward by the ministers . . .' As there was no minister anywhere in the Uists, it was a safe enough bet, and the focus on gentlemen and those of local influence is more than an echo of Columba's general approach to Highland evangelism; it is a tactic since adopted by modern cults.

Ward would, of course, have readily found some sort of enduring Roman Catholic veneration even in early nineteenth-century Lewis; and it is probable that his subjects had done little more than gone through the motions of Protestant worship before his arrival. Certainly, once they were promised priests, South Uist and Barra happily re-embraced the old faith. And priests continued to visit, despite harassment and occasional arrests: in 1630, Fr Hegarty was captured on South Uist by John Leslie, Bishop of the Isles, though quickly rescued by a Ranald MacDonald of

Benbecula, at the head of thirty armed clansmen. Another priest, Donald MacDonald, was battering about the place in 1650, despite a recent stretch in an Edinburgh prison, and in 1697 two Irish Jesuits were seized at the behest of the Synod of Argyll.

Roman Catholic worship – sensual, theatrical – naturally appealed more to untutored Highlanders than long Presbyterian preaching by ministers they did not have from Bibles they had never seen and in a language they could not read. Priests cynically incorporated local super-stitions into their new religious order, rather than educating folk out of them. Martin Martin certainly describes yet another of those magical wells, on Eigg, to which folk had long resorted; but of late a Father Hugh had 'obliged all the inhabitants to come to this well, and then employed them to bring together a great heap of stones at the head of the spring, by way of penance. This being done, he said mass at the well, and then consecrated it; he gave each of the inhabitants a piece of wax candle, which they lighted, and all of them made the dessil, of going round the well sunways, the priest leading them.' And they had been ordered to do this every 15 April.

Camille Dressler suggests 'Father Hugh' sought to undermine island veneration of a Celtic saint – probably Donan – uncanonised by Rome. Alexander MacBain was probably nearer the truth in 1890 when he observed that 'what is religious passes imperceptibly into what is purely superstitious, especially if the culture of the people is not high. Super-stition is nearly all a survival of Paganism into Christian times; and in the incantations the names of Christ, his apostles, and the Virgin Mary took those of the old heathen gods.' And Fr Ward's own accounts show an entire willingness to sanction assorted rites, customs, incantations, and belief in second sight if it would further the extension of his Church. Like a later and still fondly remembered Eriskay priest, Fr Allan MacDonald, as Dickson concedes, Ward 'probably identified with it culturally and did not think of it at odds with Christian teaching. These and other instances lead one to conclude that, when compared with the Reformed ministers of the period, Catholic missionaries in and around South Uist were savvy in the art of conversion, more attuned culturally to the Hebridean way of life and quick to realise how powerful a Christianity made tangible with pagan ceremony could be among the West Highland Gaels. "For this reason unbelievers are daily attracted to Catholicism," writes Ward. It is impossible to say how great a number of people, for this reason alone, acquire a reverence for Catholic ceremonies.'

Much less tenable is Dickson's concluding thesis in what is, after all, but part of an absorbing history of piping in South Uist: that this and other aspects of a rich folk-culture survived in these Catholic Hebrides precisely because, unlike unluckier northern neighbours, they never fell under a repressive Calvinism. This is an old libel. The Uists have no monopoly on fine piping – Lewis has produced champions of its own, such as the late Pipe Major Donald MacLean of Ballantrushal[6] – and the tradition's abiding strength on South Uist stems from complex historical and social factors, the place of South Uist in a wider Clan Ranald territory being far more important than priest and prayer book.

It is certainly true that, once recovered for Roman Catholicism, the 'Rough Bounds' – together with Uist and Barra – proved generally impervious to Presbyterianism. These are still the Catholic Highlands. Only in Ardnamurchan was a strong and enduring Evangelicalism ever established. A vulnerable Free Church congregation in Arisaig had the building sold from under them by their minister in the late 1950s. The SSPCK could not break Roman Catholicism in South Uist. Later Free Church and, even – albeit briefly – Free Presbyterian activity in South Uist and Barra did not long survive the chaos of 1900 and a critical shortage of manpower.

There is no doubt that South Uist – and especially the 'South End' – is a special place; an enchanting environment still notable for the vigour of its Gaelic and musical culture and the warmth, merriment and kindliness of its people, despite generations of political and institutional neglect. It is probably the last spot on earth where one can still hear teenagers conversing in Gaelic, and where young people in the twenty-first century prefer the traditional dance and ceilidh to the lights and bam-boom of the discotheque. And when, in May 2005, an affable Roman Catholic schoolmaster from Barra, Angus MacNeil, won the Western Isles parliamentary seat for the Scottish National Party, ousting a Labour incumbent, a Lewis Presbyterian, by a substantial margin and with very many Protestant votes, no one locally thought it even worthy of comment, far less alarm.

But Highland Catholicism (without for a moment forgetting the cruelties inflicted even in present-day Presbyterianism) can have fangs too. In 1842 Neil MacLean,[7] a native of the Isle of Coll, was SSPCK teacher at Corribeg, by the shores of Loch Eil in Lochaber, and that year his endeavours were blessed to a sheep-farmer, *Domhnall Ruadh*, or Donald Cameron. 'Red Donald', a prosperous man who rode a handsome grey horse, had long and at times ferociously argued with MacLean. Now, converted, he joined the Kirk and left the Roman Catholic Church with his family, including his seven-year-old son, Hector. For this Donald Cameron, and all his, were cursed in the most ferocious terms, from the altar, by the local priest, and with such venom as to shake the Roman Catholic congregation. These were still days in Lochaber when, seeking a night's shelter in the hamlet of Dochanassie, a wanderer asked, 'Is there any Christian here that will give me a night's lodgings?' 'No,' he was sharply told, 'there are no Christians here. They are all Camerons.'

Fr Ward, his friends and their successors might have accomplished a great deal more, granted time and resources. 'Had they been more numerous and less dependent in trivial matters on the authority of Propaganda in far-off Rome,' observes Roderick MacDonald, 'where the needs of the Highland Church were quite unknown, the religious history of Gaeldom would have been different.' As things began truly to move, renewed revolt brought all Roman Catholic progress in the Highlands to an entire and permanent halt; otherwise Skye and even the Long Island might have been recovered for Mother Church.

The Rising[8] of 1745 was launched by Charles Edward Stuart, grandson of King James VII, with audaciously scant resources and with neither the forces nor the very real advantages enjoyed by the biggest previous attempt, in 1715. But he was of much more compelling personality than his father, enjoyed – in Lord George Murray – a gifted general and, at first, astonishing good luck. The Rising came much closer to success than it is generally fashionable to admit. But it failed, of course, amidst the grapeshot of Culloden, having drawn a great and fearful British army into the heart of the Highlands.

The brutal reprisals are still bitterly recalled. But the '45 is also a watershed in the religious history of the region. A rattled Whitehall at last grasped the importance of universal education, especially to advance the Reformed faith and, by imparting English, to achieve full social and religious integration with the rest of the kingdom. And hitherto feeble efforts to support Presbyterian church extension were accelerated. A Committee for the Reformation of the Highlands had already been formed by 1728 and – armed with all of £1,000 from King George I – could spend this annual Royal Bounty, as it was known, to support itinerant Gaelic preachers.

For too long, though, despite their 'public commitment to the cause of Reformation in the Highlands,' says Bruce Lenman, 'the London government was basically indifferent, except when frightened, and it regarded the Church of Scotland with a detachment bordering on contempt'. Now, if largely by the generosity of private individuals, rather more aid was forthcoming to the Established Church and the SSPCK. And, of course, all authority bore down hard on continued Roman Catholic schemes. Pro-Hanoverian clans entirely closed their lands to Roman missionaries; assorted troops and snoops watched like a hawk for renewed priestcraft in the Jacobite territories, and Bishop Hugh MacDonald was driven into exile, though by 1764 he had quietly returned to Glengarry. That year he could report only six priests in all the Highland District, to serve 13,166 Roman Catholic souls, including infants. By the restoration of the Roman hierarchy, in 1878, Scotland's indigenous Catholics were already out-numbered, enormously, by Irish immigrants, and neglected accordingly. There was little energy to translate and issue Gaelic Catholic literature. It was 1875 before there was even a Catholic, Gaelic New Testament, prepared by Fr Thomas MacEachan and based on the Latin Vulgate; and, outwith the Western Isles – and that now infrequently – the Gaelic language is scarcely used in Roman worship. The faithful have through centuries been ill served by the Vatican.

Of immediate relevance to Lewis and Harris, it was only the '45 which finally lent vital impetus to a deplorably delayed project: a complete, properly translated Bible in Scottish Gaelic, under the auspices of the SSPCK; there were generous donations by public figures, including Dr Samuel Johnson, whose 1775 *Journey to the Western Isles of Scotland* is still striking, amidst his fondness for the sententious, for insight and genuine compassion.

But it was, nevertheless, 1767 before a Gaelic New Testament became available, translated by Rev. James Stuart of Killin and, naturally, in the Perthshire dialect; he was helped by Rev. James Fraser, the long-suffering and gracious minister of Alness who is best remembered for an eminent work on sanctification and the ghastly, loveless wife who did much to advance his own, and Dugald Buchanan, schoolmaster at Kinloch Ran-noch and the outstanding Gaelic poet of advancing Evangelicalism. Even so, the new translation was heavily influenced by Kirk and had a strong *blas*, or taste, of an old, high and Classical Gaelic – 'a vocabulary and style that was significantly different from that of contemporary Gaelic,' says Donald Meek. Indeed, there was real consumer resistance, as Dr Johnson reports in 1773 after a visit to the minister of Coll in the Inner Hebrides. 'Mr MacLean said he did not use it, because he could make the text more intelligible to his auditors by an extemporary version. From this I inferred that the language of the translation was not the language of the island of Coll.' Ministers in many districts continued to make their own extempore renderings of Scripture, from the Authorised Version or the archaic and unfamiliar Kirk, as – indeed to the present day – do men who are native, fluent Gaelic speakers but can read only the English Scriptures.

Work on the Old Testament ground on, in four volumes. The first three were prepared by the minister of Luss on Loch Lomond, Rev. John Stuart, a son of the pastor of Killin. The fourth was translated by the Rev. John Smith of Campbeltown, who took a much bolder approach with great use of modern commentaries and recent textual scholarship. At first enthusiastic, the SSPCK grew critical of his approach and the work was finally adjusted by another noted Evangelical, Rev. Alexander Stewart of Dingwall. Thus, in 1807 a pocket edition of the Scriptures, in Scottish Gaelic, was at last available, and at a popular price by 1828; be it said besides that it was a scrupulously executed and outstanding translation, taking full advantage of the latest learning and superior in many important respects to the King James Version of 1611.

Other worthwhile works were translated too – Bunyan's *Pilgrim's Progress* and, later, the essays and studies of assorted great divines – Richard Baxter, John Owen, Robert Murray McCheyne and Charles Haddon Spurgeon. Rev. John MacDonald of Ferintosh, the most eminent Highland Evangelical of all, produced a superior Shorter Catechism in Gaelic, but the most influential works – in Gaelic translation – were William Guthrie's *The Christian's Great Interest* and Thomas Boston's *The Fourfold State*, which till most recently could have been found, in solid Gaelic, in practically every home on Lewis and Harris.

In the 1980s the National Bible Society of Scotland, who now hold copyright on the Gaelic Bible and Psalter, issued more informal translations of Mark's Gospel and four of the Pauline epistles, in the colloquial style of the Good News Bible. A new and convenient edition of the Gaelic Psalter was released in 1987 – it is now practically unobtainable – and, for the first time, without Roman numerals; this was reflected too in a slightly updated, and wholly reset, edition of the Bible in 1992. By that point, however, the Gaelic Catechism had long since ceased to be generally taught, in Lewis or anywhere else, and without that highly specialised theological vocabulary – and on top of its phonetic and dialectical peculiarities – the Bible itself has become increasingly incomprehensible to fluent native speakers, even those who can follow and enjoy a Gaelic sermon.

But, even as those good men ground on in their slow work of finalising an accurate Bible in the language of most Highland people, and the SSPCK doubled its efforts to ensure that, in time, almost all Highland people would be able to read it, formidable barriers remained to the furtherance of the Gospel. Churches were few and far-flung; Gaelic-speaking ministers in short supply. And there was the baleful impact of patronage. The natural bent of lairds to install biddable placemen scarcely fostered Christian advance.[9]

Such was the status of the ministry, and so comfortable and agreeable was the lifestyle – the easiest way for anyone, granted education and sufficient endeavour, to aspire to the ranks of the gentry and enjoy power, housing and comforts denied to most – that Scotland was by the late eighteenth century almost awash with 'probationers', divinity students who had completed their studies and been granted a 'licence to preach the Gospel'. But they were not true ministers, nor could they be until presented to a church and, by due process, set aside and ordained. And there were far more probationers than there were charges available – fretting men who taught in schools, or hired themselves out as tutors in the households of the wealthy, or took this and that job as a clerk, or an estate manager, or studied further for a position in law – so many that, to this day (though few Scots now know what it originally meant) the jibe of 'stickit minister' is still recalled.

For want of good social contacts, some very fine men were denied ordination. By contrast, others of very different stamp found themselves readily accepted, and appointed to most comfortable livings by comfortable men. The Highlands, too, found themselves in the age of the Moderates.

It is generally agreed that King James VII himself had coined the word 'Moderate', in an Indulgence issued in February 1687. But, as immediately conceived in the Kirk, its earliest use is in a letter from his indefinably creepy son-in-law, King William, to the General Assembly of October 1690. William of Orange would have been far happier to retain an Episcopal order – with he himself, of course, appointing the bishops – but political expediency had forced him to accept a revived Presbyterianism, and he can scarcely have relished something so unpredictable as a General Assembly, especially when it had threatened, at the height of the Covenant in the late 1640s, not merely to be the governing body of the Church but of Scotland itself. Apprehension is manifest in his 1690 letter. 'We expect that your management shall be such as we shall have no reason to repent of what we have done. A calm and peaceable procedure will be no less pleasing to us than it becometh you. We never could be of the mind that violence was suited to the advancing of true religion; nor do we intend that our authority shall ever be a tool to the irregular passions of any party. *Moderation is what religion enjoins*, neighbouring churches expect from you, and we recommend to you.'

In the early 1700s, to be called a 'Moderate' was almost a compliment. The Kirk had still obdurate Episcopalians, in certain fastnesses of the north and west; its manifest nutters; its Vicars of Bray. Archibald McLauchlan, minister of Arrochar, had been in 1658 inducted as a convinced Presbyterian; but he happily accepted the Episcopate of the Restoration and, at length, the Presbyterianism of 1691, and died – quite unmolested and in all his importance – as senior minister of Arrochar many years later, in 1731. A Presbyterian minister was sent scuttling to Glenorchy, in wildest Perthshire, with the edict for the deposition of Dugald Lindsay: Lindsay's parishioners met him in the parish, their swords drawn, and drove him from their bounds to the accompaniment of two pipers playing the Death March. And there was Daniel MacLachlan of Ardnamurchan, who – no doubt a little giddied amidst the Rough Bounds – had what Lenman dryly describes as 'a brief but colourful ministry . . . a ministry which did not long survive MacLachlan's pamphlet *An Essay upon Improving and Adding to the Strength of Great Britain and Ireland by Fornication*. He died in Jamaica. Then there was Robertson of Lochbroom who in the 1750s ran a shebeen from which he dispensed illicitly distilled whisky to his flock . . .'

It is easier to recognise Moderates than to define one. And the great Lachlan MacKenzie of Lochcarron had a whisky-still on his premises. Yet Moderates abide – affable, respectable, unthreatening clergy. By the Disruption, of course, 'Moderate' had become a term of abuse – short-hand for a lazy jobsworth – and, by the time partisan Free Church history was written, it was used lazily of any minister of the Kirk who had not 'come out' at the Disruption, and any minister of the Auld Kirk since. Certainly Dr John Kennedy, Free Church minister of Dingwall, went too far in his description of a typical Moderate minister – 'the great cattle-dealer at the market, the leading dancer at the wedding, the toast-master at the farmer's dinner and, if the last to slide off his chair at the drinking bout, it was because he was more seasoned than the rest.' A wiser, more measured summary came in 1753 from John Witherspoon, son of East Lothian and minister of Paisley, in his satire, *Ecclesiastical Characteristics*. The Moderate ministers were, he scorned, indeed 'moderate in ability, showing a moderate amount of zeal, and doing a very moderate amount of work.'

Witherspoon, an outstandingly able man and a fine Christian, is today all but forgotten in his native land. In 1768, though, at the age of forty-five, he accepted the invitation to become President of the Theological College of New Jersey, and sailed the Atlantic. He ended up as President of Princeton, a founding father of the United States – the only clergyman to sign the Declaration of Independence – and a member of the first Congress. He is an abiding American hero and the actress Reese Wither-spoon is a direct descendant.

In 1805 a gifted but arrogant young minister at Kilmany, Fife, Thomas Chalmers, happily described the joys of Moderate ministry. 'The author can assert, from what is to him the highest of all authority, the authority of his own experience, that after the satisfactory discharge of his parish duties, a minister may enjoy five days of the week of uninterrupted leisure for the prosecution of any science in which his taste may dispose him to engage.' Chalmers would bitterly regret these words. In 1809, amidst bereavement and serious illness, he read a recent bestseller by a noted politician – *A Practical View of Christianity*, by William Wilberforce. The book changed his life. Chalmers was, as we would say, 'born again'; the Moderate became the Evangelical.

Evangelicalism is not easy to describe in naturalistic terms. It has also become a grossly debauched word in modern usage – associated in England with inane, irreverent worship and, especially in America and in the popular media, with right-wing politics and ugly prejudice. But true Evangelicalism is Christianity as a vivid and vital personal knowledge of Jesus Christ, the 'liberty of the Gospel', usually – though not always – obtained by a process of crisis and a sense of entire, Hell-deserving guilt described as 'conviction of sin'. It is urgent, believing that this, our brief earthly life, is our only opportunity to embrace Jesus Christ as offered in the Gospel; that there is no other way to Heaven, of any kind – not good works, not sincerity, not ignorance, not any other religion or god – and that there is no renewed opportunity after death. Christians of this stamp are characterised, or ought to be, by most careful and scrupulous living, profound humility, great tenderness to others, delight in Scripture and in secret prayer and public worship – the 'means of grace' – and by very great earnestness. And this Evangelicalism – marked by clarity, commitment and conviction – was on entire collision course with the Moderates; by 1760, 'Evangelical' and 'Moderate' were, within the Kirk, the labels of organised party.

Most of the Highlands were still pagan. But the SSPCK was rapidly engineering a widespread literacy. A Gaelic New Testament had appeared in 1767. And Evangelicalism had, in fact, long been established in one corner of the Gàidhealtachd – the shores of the Moray Firth.[10] As early as 1564, the infant Kirk sent Donald Munro as its 'Commissioner' to Ross-shire. He toiled for nearly a decade and established an enduring Christian witness in Easter Ross and the Black Isle, and is the true father of Highland Evangelicalism. In 1605, James VI inadvertently reinforced it by banishing Robert Bruce, minister of St Giles in Edinburgh, to Inverness – a man 'of aristocratic lineage, an outstanding theologian', remarks Donald Macleod, 'and author of a very important book on the Lord's Supper, a great preacher and a great statesman'. King James could imagine no fate worse than to be dumped amidst the savages of the north. But Bruce made the most of his opportunity, despite widespread hostility and attempts on his life. Though he had no Gaelic, Scots was widely spoken on the Moray Firth coast. Soon multitudes came from all over the north to hear him preach and there were hundreds of conversions.

We can even credit a Swedish monarch, King Gustavus Adolphus. In the Thirty Years War he fought in defence of the Protestant cause and

Lord Reay, chief of Clan MacKay, raised a great Scottish regiment in his aid, packed with Highland soldiers. In Continental endeavour they found themselves in a greater army of conscious spiritual mission and full of soldiers who were committed Christians. These fighting men from Sutherland, Caithness, Ross-shire and the north were thus exposed to a new and powerful religion – and brought it home. It is possible, besides, they imported that militant streak that has often marked Highland religion.

But northern piety was strengthened further by persecution in Covenanting times, when several Easter Ross ministers – Thomas Hog of Kiltearn, John MacKillican of Alness and James Fraser, Laird of Brea – refused to affirm Episcopacy. Hog and Fraser both did time on the dreaded Bass Rock. Yet Hog, for instance, had a remarkable ministry at Kiltearn. 'His people,' says his successor, 'were awakened to hear, and he was encouraged to preach Christ Jesus to them, so that the dry bones began to revive, and pleasant blossoms and hopeful appearances displayed themselves everywhere through the parish.'

Thomas Hog died on 4 January 1692, broken by his sufferings; he is buried, at his express wish, in the very doorway of his church, and his tombstone ends with the inscription:

> THIS STONE SHALL BEAR WITNESS
> AGAINST THE PARISHIONERS OF KILTEARN
> IF THEY BRING ANE UNGODLY MINISTER
> IN HERE

. . . and such has since been general Evangelical sentiment in the Highlands of Scotland.

Lewis and Harris enjoyed, of course, godly and industrious ministers long before the presentation of Alexander MacLeod to Uig, in 1824; though that curious son of Assynt is often described as the island's first Evangelical minister, it is – of course – by then as much a political label, though he may well have been at ordination the only converted minister on the Presbytery.

But there is no reason to doubt the piety of the Rev. Donald Morrison,[11] son of that Rev. Kenneth who so deftly got out of trouble by plying the Laird of Kildun's henchmen with drink, and who succeeded his father in 1724 as minister of Stornoway. His first charge was Kilbrandon and Kilchattan, in Argyll, where he was ordained in 1705, and two gracious men from Ness are said to have gone to hear him there one Sabbath, and been so astonished by the depths of his Christian experience that they asked him how he had so acquired such teaching. 'Come to the manse with me to dinner, and I will show you how I got it,' said he. They were no doubt startled when, on arrival, he donned an apron himself and prepared a filling meal – then, repast concluded, he led them into a room and showed them his wife, stretched out in a drunken stupor. 'This, with the Bible, and the throne of grace,' says MacAulay, 'made him a very exercised man, and he made good use of these in his preaching.'

Called to Stornoway in 1724, a 1743 'visitation' by Presbytery noted that 'the heads of families showed an entire regard and love for their minister.' He also acquitted himself with grace and prudence when the Laird of Kildun – the son of the last one – tried to provoke him into a shouting match over the merits of Protestantism versus Rome, at a Stornoway function attended by the Earl of Seaforth; the civil debate delighted the Earl, who made them shake hands and part as friends. Yet this Donald Morrison was hounded by his fellow-churchmen for refusing to put away his alcoholic and increasingly embarrassing wife. Ministers increasingly railed on him to separate from 'such a notorious woman' or be himself suspended from the functions of his office. The Synod of Argyll was persuaded to raise the case and, in 1731, threatened him with discipline. He had to appeal to the General Assembly, and got himself an advocate who made a blistering speech against that sort of Christianity which would have Morrison 'abandoning his wife, and withdraw all his care and attention from her, and throw her out of doors to be a public burden.' The General Assembly not only found for Morrison, but ordered his pursuers to pay expenses.

One Sabbath afternoon a little later, Mrs Morrison was on a boozy rampage through the house, as her husband ignored her and sat placidly reading his Bible. Furious, she seized it from him and dashed it into the fire. He did not lose his composure but, instead, drew his chair in, and spread his hands as the book burned, and said quietly, 'Well, wife, this is the best fire I ever warmed myself at.' She stood, stared, then left the room and took to her bed – and never drank again. It is said that Mr Morrison afterwards maintained that her final years, and deportment, more than compensated for all past suffering.

There is something profoundly attractive about this man; and a later Stornoway minister, Rev. Colin MacKenzie, who served from 1789 to 1815, was also a good pastor.

But the most vivid glimpse we have of Moderate religion on Lewis is from Lord Teignmouth, who spares us no detail of a high-society 1827 funeral at the Church of the Uidh, in Aignish – the burial of Mary Carn MacKenzie, a descendant of those Lairds of Kildun.

During my stay in Stornoway, I received an invitation to attend the funeral of a wealthy old lady, who had made numerous and liberal bequests . . . Immediately after the decease of this lady, a cask of Madeira was opened in her house, a wake had been kept up, and the house nightly illuminated according to the custom of the country. The chief mourner, who arrived in an open boat from the mainland, was a minister, and the funeral was attended by all the principal inhabitants of Stornoway. Our party from the Lodge arrived too late at the house of the deceased to partake of the preliminary refreshments, but we over-took the procession on the road to the ancient cemetery of Stornoway, which is situated on the beach of Broad Bay, about four miles from the town. Another burial place used by the people of Stornoway, near the town, has been so encroached upon by the ravages of the sea, that the bodies will probably soon be consigned to a watery grave.

The graves of the principal families are enclosed by four walls forming a sort of mausoleum. That of the lady, whose obsequies we were celebrating, contains a marble monument to the memory of Colonel Colin MacKenzie, bearing a highly panegyric inscription . . . In Scotland, the funeral ceremony is celebrated without any religious rite. The minister of the parish attends only when invited, and not officially. He sometimes embraces the solemn opportunity of offering up a prayer among the assembled mourners at the house of the deceased, previous to the departure of the procession, though he may not accompany it. On the present occasion, as soon as we reached the cemetery, the coffin was deposited in the grave with all possible decency, and the whole body of mourners instantly adjourned to a tent pitched in the cemetery, within a few yards of the mausoleum, where we found the tables groaning beneath a plentiful repast. As soon as we were all arranged, a hundred and twenty in number, the minister, who presided as chief mourner, delivered a grace in the form of a prayer; and the minister of the parish offered up another, accompanied by thanksgiving, after dinner. The bottle was then circulated and many loyal, patriotic, and complimentary toasts followed; nor was the memory of the deceased forgotten, while the toasts were as usual accompanied with appropriate speeches. The presence of several ministers, and one acting as chairman, no doubt tended to preserve a certain degree of sobriety in the midst of revelry and merriment, inseparable from such a meeting, as the occasion would be necessarily speedily forgotten by the greater part present. But at length the chord was touched, to which the bosoms of the Islanders responded, amidst the flow of wine and whisky, with resistless accor-dance. 'The Chief of the MacIvers' was proposed amidst loud applause. The guests now became quite tumultuous, and the Rev. Chairman immediately rose up and left the tent, accompanied by all the party.

The expectations of the gleanings of so plenteous a repast had attracted to the spot a multitude of people of all ages, who thronged around and closed in upon the tent, eager for the signal for rushing in upon the remains of the feast. A man was constantly employed in walking round the tent, armed with a long whip, with which he inflicted perpetual, but almost fruitless, chastisement on intruders.

A few of the guests, who had not heeded the example of the chairman, continued long carousing, and one of them was brought to Stornoway on the bier which conveyed the body to the grave.

Successive ministers at Barvas were, as far as can be ascertained, a hard, dry, bunch of jobsworths, till we reach the remarkable William MacRae – as we will. And Aulay MacAulay of Harris – who transferred the parish church from Northton to Scarista – we have met already, chasing Charles Edward for much gold. He had angered his colleagues in Argyll by stealing the library at his previous charge, Coll and Tiree; and he pompously left a sum of money to his church officer (or beadle) to show future visitors the grave where the great Mr Aulay was buried. MacAulay can safely be labelled a Moderate.[12]

We know little save the dates of arrival, departure and death of four successive ministers of Lochs, but in 1789 Rev. John Simson, who came from Ferintosh, arrived as 'colleague and successor' to a sickly incumbent, and duly succeeded him after his premature death in 1793. Apart from a genuine interest in education – 'By the acquaintance of their native tongue, the Highlanders obtain possession of a key to other languages, and with the ability to read Gaelic is born the anxiety to learn English' – Simson is not at first glance a particularly admirable fellow. A big portly bear of a man, he was widely suspected to be a drunkard. Once, tramping to preach in some corner of his vast charge, his hat suddenly took off and bowled far away in the wind. He declared at once they should return home: later, he confessed the script of his sermon had been stowed inside it. And he was prone to bizarre intimations – 'Donald MacLeod, if you don't make a heather rope for me, I shall refuse to baptise your child.'

A true Stornoway Christian, Murdo MacDonald – who everyone called *Murchadh Rìgh*, or 'Murdo the King', was once hailed by Simson at the Bayhead burn: the minister had walked to town from Lochs, and demanded that MacDonald physically carry him through the stream, then high in spate. Though no easy task with Simson's bulk, MacDonald readily agreed, but could not resist teasing him. He asked innocently, a few paces across, who his passenger was. 'Oh, ho!' he carolled on the reply. 'Is that the big drunken minister of Lochs I am carrying on my back?' He had quickly to assure an alarmed cleric he had no intention of dropping him in the flood.

'Of this minister (and some of his elders were his match),' says Malcolm MacPhail, 'his people might say what the parishioners of another parson said, "Bad as we are, we are not as bad as the parson." So dense was the darkness of these people, and so gross their ignorance, that they were as well pleased with their minister as he was with them.' Yet it was probably at Simson's urging that a mission-house was built at Carloway, for use of an assistant in that district so far from his manse; and when his own son Kenneth duly laboured there, and became 'so disheartened and discouraged by the callous indifference and heathenism of the Carlowegians,' says MacAulay, 'that he threw up his work as a missionary, returned to his father and said that he would have nothing more to do with such pagans,' Simson was furious. 'How dare you speak thus of my people! – for they are an exceptional people, who are very precious to myself.'

The second, Reformed minister of Uig – Rev. John MacLeod, a native of Skye – was presented in 1726 and seems to have been a fine man of Evangelical disposition, who may have owed his charge to friendship with one of Seaforth's sons. 'He soon endeared himself to his parishioners,' writes MacAulay, 'but discovered to his sorrow that, with very few exceptions, they laboured under spiritual darkness. After labouring there for twelve years he began to see some fruit of his ministry. He used to exhort his parishioners regarding their state and, on one occasion, while speaking to some of them in the neighbourhood of the manse, he stated that Adam's sin brought both original and actual sin on the human race. One of the tenants replied, "Though Adam's sin had such disastrous consequences for us, yet it was good for the likes of you, Mr MacLeod . . . had Adam kept his first estate, there would be no need for ministers such as you to preach to us."' There was no ready answer to that.

We have met his successor in Uig – Rev. Norman Morrison – but the next minister, Rev. Hugh Munro, inducted in 1778 after a four-year stint as a missionary in Tarbert, Harris, was both a Moderate and a buffoon. 'Uig seems to have made little intellectual or spiritual progress during his ministry,' laments MacAulay. 'According to [Rev. Malcolm] MacPhail, Mr Munro was an easy-going gentleman, a mild ecclesiastic, who seemed to keep a respectable distance from the conscience and daily life of his parishioners.' He encouraged sports on Sabbath, after sermon, and retailed delicious gossip from the pulpit. Still more spectacularly, Hugh Munro once simply cancelled public worship when he heard a school of whales had just been spotted swimming into the bay. *'Mach a seo sibh; mach a seo sibh. Tha na mucan air a thighean a steach do'n bhaigh. 'S iomadh*

la gheibh sibh searmoin, ach chan ann tric a gheibh sibh na mucan,' he
bellowed happily. 'Out of here, everyone; out of here. The whales have
come into the bay. You can get a sermon any time, but you cannot often
get the whales.' A later good man from Uig, Angus MacIver, has left his
damning verdict on Munro. 'The minister was ignorant of the Gospel,
and of the nature of true godliness, and therefore could not impart to
others that gospel of which he was not a partaker himself, by the teaching
of the spirit of God in his own soul. The name of Christ was not to be
heard in his sermons.'

But a new sort of religion was at last to vault the Minch.

II

'The Peace of God'

Srath Nabhair

Anns an adhar dhubh-ghorm ud,
àirde na sìorraidheachd os ar cionn,
bha rionnag a' priobadh ruinn
's i freagairt mireadh an teine
ann an cabar taigh m'athar
a' bhlianna thugh sinn an taigh le bleideagan
    sneachda.
Agus siud a' bhlianna cuideachd
a shlaod iad a' chailleach don t-sitig,
a shealltainn cho eòlach 's a bha iad air an
    Fhìrinn
oir bha nid aig eunlaith an adhair
(agus cròthan aig na caoraich)
ged nach robh ait aice-se anns an cuireadh
    i a ceann fòidhpe.

A Shrath Nabhair 's a Shrath Chill Donnain,
is beag an t-iongnadh ged a chinneadh am
    fraoch àlainn oirbh,
a' falach nan lotan a dh'fhàg Pàdraig Sellar
    's a sheòrsa,
mar a chunnaic mi uair is uair boireannach
    cràbhaidh
a dh'fhiosraich dòrainn an t-saoghail-sa
is sìth Dhè 'na sùilean.

In that blue-black sky,
as high above us as eternity,
a star was winking at us,
answering the leaping flames of fire
in the rafters of my father's house,
that year we thatched the house with
    snowflakes.
And that too was the year
they hauled the old woman out to the dung-heap,
to demonstrate how knowledgeable they were in
    Scripture,
for the birds of the air had nests
(and the sheep had folds)
though she had no place to
    lay her head.

O Strathnaver and Strath of Kildonan,
it is little wonder the heather should bloom
    on your slopes,
hiding the wounds that Patrick Sellar, and
    such as he, made,
just as time and time again I have seen a
    pious woman
who has suffered the sorrow of this world,
with the peace of God shining from her eyes.

Ruaraidh Mac-Thòmais
Derick S. Thomson (b. 1921)
from *Creachadh na Clàrsaich*, Edinburgh, 1982.

6

'The Boy with the Bible'

Finlay Munro and the Rise of Evangelicalism, 1820–1824

The Gospel took powerful hold on the Long Island from 1820. But there were already a few redoubtable if isolated Christians, remarkable for their spirit and their austerity, and we have already met Murdo MacDonald, who so frighted the minister of Lochs at the Bayhead river.

Murdo MacDonald came from Guershader, a hamlet of the Laxdale district, outside Stornoway.[1] He was a weaver to trade, and a thinker, and of a plain bluntness of speech. He was not converted by an Evangelical sermon: like all his island contemporaries, he had never heard one. The 'saving change' came about when he heard a teacher reading aloud a famous work by Thomas Boston, *Human Nature In Its Fourfold State*, in Gaelic translation; even before 1820, he seems to have been a professing Christian and had become known as *Murchadh Mor nan Gràs* – 'Big Murdo of the Graces', or *Murchadh Righ*. MacAulay tells us that 'for piety and talent he developed into one of the most outstanding men in the Stornoway district at this time.' MacDonald remains the nearest Lewis has ever produced to the ferocious Separatists of the North Highland mainland, who had by this time established almost a parallel society to the Church of Scotland in Caithness and Sutherland and whose anticlericalism still casts a long shadow in the Highlands. MacDonald had little time for ministers. Going once to hear a sermon from a Moderate of the time, he afterwards confronted the preacher. 'In church today there was one small Christian – me – and one great hypocrite, you!'

MacDonald was not readily outwitted. A Stornoway scoffer once confronted him. 'Do you think, Murdo, that the *Siaraich*, the "West Siders" of this island, will go to the same Heaven as the enlightened people of Stornoway?' 'I don't think they will,' said Murdo, like a flash, 'but I think they will go to the same Hell.'

A godless Harris tailor jeered, 'You think you have great faith, but you cannot walk on the sea as Peter did.' Murdo said, 'You put Christ on the sea before me, as He was before Peter, and you will see if I do not walk on the sea before Him – but, poor man, you had better make sure that you yourself get faith, or else I shall wash my feet in your blood.' Shaken, the tailor gasped, 'Is that the way a man of your profession speaks?' 'Yes,' said Murdo MacDonald, quoting Matthew's Gospel 'for it is written, "He shall wash his feet in the blood of the wicked."' But he is best recalled for his distrust of ministers.

For even as Evangelicalism advanced through the Highlands, the worse the Moderates – and, indeed, the West Highland church itself – seemed to be. Alexander MacRae does not greatly exaggerate when, describing Skye, he records that

> Druidism, Romanism and Protestantism each contributed an element of the grotesque superstition that went under the name of religion. The island was peopled by witches, fairies and ghosts . . . At funerals great quantities of ardent spirits were consumed before lifting the body. The most outrageous orgies were indulged in: bagpipes were played, songs sung, filthy tales and jests recounted. The gatherings of the Lord's Day were fully utilised for business and pleasure. Sales and fairs in the parish were advertised at the church door. . . . At Communion seasons . . . pedlars, spirit-dealers and others erected their booths around the churchyards, and pushed a lively trade.

Presented to his first charge of Bracadale, in 1823, Rev. Roderick MacLeod would later grimly remember 'that the first presbyterial act after his ordination was to assist his co-presbyters to find their beds. They were so helplessly intoxicated. That is an indication of their morals.'[2] Things were little better on Lewis.

Murdo MacDonald was once asked, 'How can you tell the ministers who are sheep from those who are goats?' He replied, 'I look at their lips, and at their feet; I weigh their words and watch their conduct.' But he could be vindictive. Praying at a schoolhouse at Bayble in the Point district in 1823, he 'lifted up his voice in an earnest cry that God would remove, by death or otherwise, those feather-bed shepherds who fed not their flocks.' That was bad enough, but shortly afterwards Mr Munro finally declined and died in the manse of Uig; and, in November 1824, Rev. Simon Fraser – minister of Stornoway – was drowned in the Minch. There was some commotion and – behind his back – rattling tongues accused MacDonald of killing them. One Stornoway gentleman was bolder, telling him to his face that 'you never stopped praying until you drowned our minister.' 'Do you believe, man,' said MacDonald, in his quiet way, 'that God will listen to my prayers requesting that a man be drowned?' 'I do,' said his accuser. 'Well,' said *Murchadh Mor nan Gràs*, 'you be careful lest you be the next!'[3]

Before 1820, vital – as opposed to formal – Christianity was here all but unknown. From 1820, and through a variety of individuals and influences, Lewis and Harris flamed in full-blown Christian revival, culminating in 1822 with such fervour that it is still remembered as *Bliadhna an Fhaomaidh*, the 'year of swooning'.

'Revival' is an unfortunate word, almost as debauched in modern meaning as Evangelical. It conjures up visions of hysteria and fervour; weird people in West Virginia, burning their record collections and dancing with snakes. But there is not the least doubt of the new forces that burst on Lewis and Harris in the 1820s, leaving a distinctive and abiding Christian culture. The nineteenth century was in general, for Lewis, a time of benevolent landlords, population growth and real material progress. For Harris, it was a time of awful landlords, active and dreadful oppression, social turmoil and wholesale clearances overseas. And yet both flamed to the same faith, and glow with it to this day.

But there were necessary preconditions. The first essential element was a reliable Bible in Scottish Gaelic. That, as we have seen, was completed by 1807, though it was 1828 before it was widely available at a popular price. The second was general literacy.

We have noted the undoubted achievements of the SSPCK, but a glance at a 1755 map of SSPCK activity – furnished by Charles Withers in his *Gaelic Scotland* – shows there were still only two schools in all Lewis, and one at Harris. SSPCK activity was clustered along the Highland border and, significantly, in those districts where English was already advancing, in the east and the south and in Caithness. The SSPCK was also bedevilled by its abiding ambivalence to the Gaelic language. The breakthrough, especially for Lewis and Harris, came – as many good ideas still see daybreak today – in an Edinburgh coffee-house, in 1810, where concerned Christians got together and quickly established the Edinburgh Society for the Support of Gaelic Schools.[4]

This new body did not quite so assertively bear the self-conscious and militant Protestantism of the SSPCK, nor did the ESSGS envisage a complex, broader education geared to a wider political agenda. It was itself a product of the new Evangelicalism now advancing in the Lowlands, and its focus was admirably simple: it would have only one goal – to teach Highlanders to read the Bible in their mother tongue, and would draw heavily on the success of a similar scheme in Wales.

But there was real anxiety as to what wider spiritual responsibilities might – or should be – assumed by its teaching staff. The earnest

Christians of the ESSGS knew perfectly well that most Highlanders lived far away from regular sermon and that there were many indifferent and, worse, potentially hostile ministers. But there was widespread fear of popular revolt and perhaps undue regard for 'order'. It was allowed, then, that the new schoolmasters could read the Scriptures aloud to the people on the Sabbath, and conduct prayer meetings. But it was absolutely decreed that on no account were ESSGS teachers to be 'preachers nor public exhorters of any denomination whatsoever'.

The impact of the new programme, especially on Lewis, was immediate. In December 1811 an Angus MacLeod, from Skye, opened the island's first ESSGS school, at Bayble. He began with just three pupils. He soon had sixty. Soon, each Lord's Day, he had 300 local people gathering to hear him publicly read the Bible. In 1813 – with plenty of folk left behind in Bayble to carry on the work – he was transferred to Gress, where he quickly gathered 150 pupils: these schools of his, notes a correspondent from the time, 'had done more good in spreading knowledge, and in warming the hearts of the common people to true religion, than all the other means which they had enjoyed for the last century'.

Glasgow Christians, not to be outdone, quickly caught on and founded their own Gaelic Schools Society in 1812; in 1817, one was established in Dundee and another, in December 1818, at Inverness. By 1815 there were eight assorted Gaelic Society schools on Lewis – as well as Bayble and Gress, now running happily under their own momentum – and the enthusiasm for the opportunity to learn is still affecting to read. Reporting in 1819, Rev. William MacRae of Barvas tells us that Ness had over a hundred scholars in their Society school, including many married couples; and that their progress since the last examination had been truly astonishing. The eager new students, all over the island, included grandparents and at least one great-grandmother sought a place – and was happily admitted.

Shamed into action, the Church of Scotland began from 1824 to establish similar schools of its own, an endeavour later replicated by the Free Church. By 1844, ESSGS directors calculated that more than 90,000 people in the Highlands had been taught to read Scripture in their own tongue; by 1861, Society schools had been opened in 687 locations. Another striking feature of these schools is that they taught a very high proportion of girls. What is certain is that the debt of Lewis Evangelicalism to these Societies is incalculable – and for nearly fifty years, in a show of gratitude, island churches made a special collection for the ESSGS at the close of every Communion season. Rev. John MacRae, the century's greatest Lewis minister, put it best and most poetically. *'Cho fad'sa bhitheas muir a' bualadh ri lic, agus bainne geal aig bo dhubh, cha bu*

choir do mhuinntir Leodhais na sgoiltean Gaidhlig a dhi-chuimhneachadh,' –
'So long as the sea dashes against a rock, and white milk comes from a
black cow, the people of Lewis should not forget the Gaelic schools.'

Disentangling the skein of how Evangelicalism took hold so rapidly on
Lewis and Harris is far from easy. Christians from Ness have naturally
hailed the endeavours of a schoolmaster at Galson. Most ministers – who
largely write the history – focus on Rev. Alexander MacLeod, installed in
Uig in 1824. And a mid twentieth-century Free Church minister at
Barvas, Rev. John MacLeod, thought John MacKay, *Catriona Thangaidh*
and others of that community the earliest Gospel witnesses.

But the revival on Harris should not be overlooked – especially as it
took place amidst extremely difficult circumstances – nor the wider
context forgotten. This was a century generally of Evangelical awakening
– in the Highlands, in England, in cities like Dundee (where Robert
Murray McCheyne, returning in 1839 to his parish from a jaunt to the
Holy Land, found no fewer than thirty-nine prayer meetings flourishing
in connection with his charge, five of these exclusively got up, organised
and attended by children).

Perhaps the most important instrument, though, was neither a Lewisman nor a minister, but a wandering preacher from Easter Ross, Finlay
Munro,[5] who was finally so overwhelmed by the need about him, and the
general indifference of clergy, that he forsook all to become an itinerant
evangelist. His travels took him through the Highlands and he spent a
great deal of time in the Western Isles and especially on Lewis.

We know surprisingly little biographical detail, save that Finlay Munro
was from Tain (where, not without difficulty, for he died many miles
away, he was taken to be buried); that he was born at some time in the
1790s, and that he was still very young when he was converted. At that
time he was employed as 'glebe-man' by the local minister, Dr Angus
Mackintosh – and after what appears to have been a dramatic conversion,
he did something extremely foolish. Sure that spring of his faith and
certain of a miracle, he gave all the minister's oats to the poor and sowed
instead the previous autumn's chaff. The field bore no oats that year and,
convinced that Munro had sold the grain and pocketed the proceeds,
Mackintosh understandably sacked him. Thus defined as a dangerous,
addle-headed 'enthusiast' by ministers of both Moderate and Evangelical
persuasion, and distrusted all the more when he took up 'irregular' lay
preaching, Munro was loathed by ministers for the rest of his life.

Before 1820, Munro was at Clyth in Caithness as a teacher for the
SSPCK; it was in the huge parish of Latheron and, as was SSPCK
custom, he was allowed to conduct occasional services for folk who lived

far from the church. 'He went from place to place preaching to his fellow-sinners . . .' writes Principal John MacLeod. 'Shortly after 1820, the school of Clyth knew him no more, and he definitely embarked on those labours that engaged him until his death.' So another Gael, many centuries after Columba, went *pro Christo peregrinari volens*, seeking to be a pilgrim for Christ.

The heroism of this lifestyle – which Munro would maintain, with rare respite, for some fifteen years – should not be minimised. He travelled arduously and in all weathers. He was constantly denounced, and on several occasions physically assaulted. His strong sense of vocation he took from a portion of Scripture, in the tenth chapter of Matthew's Gospel, and he can emphatically be cleared of any charge of embarking on this mission for a life of ease, or gain, or prominence, for he took such injunctions as 'Provide neither gold, nor silver, nor brass in your purses, Nor scrip for your journey, neither two coats . . .' with flat seriousness.

He carried little more than his Bible. He owned only the clothes he wore. He refused to carry money, and indignantly refused any offer of it. Though always rejoicing to find a Christian home, or any place where he was made welcome, he refused to sleep under its roof, asking only if he could rest in the byre. That was no doubt partly to allow for his long, earnest and vocal private prayer, without disturbing the wider household; but in all it attests to a man who, like his Saviour, made himself nothing. He was almost comically worried that folk might mistake him for a minister. Once, in Argyllshire – when his bonnet must have looked most disreputable – he timidly asked a fellow-tramper if he had any idea what he did. He was delighted to be told, 'Well, if it wasn't for your hat, I'd take you for a public teacher; but anyone wearing that thing can't be anything so important!'

Finlay had only three vulnerabilities as a West Highland evangelist. For one, his Easter Ross Gaelic – even at that time – lacked the purity and excellent grammar of the Gaelic still vibrant in the Hebrides, and at times he had to be quietly corrected after some howler in a discourse. For another, he could not actually read Gaelic: he read the English Bible, and translated as he spoke; and – despite his brief career as an elementary schoolteacher – he had actually very little education. Nor was he mentally tough. Though, probably, barely forty when he died, there is strong evidence of psychiatric illness in his final years.

Yet he is an outstanding figure. Such of his sayings as survive, too, have their own power and insight. 'How grievous must it be to see the Lord's pigeons biting and pecking one another!' 'Strive you to get into the sea-coast of Emmanuel's blood . . .' and so on. His real spirituality, though, was elicited in 1819 by Lachlan MacKenzie, minister of Lochcarron and very much his own man. 'What kind of godliness is found in the parts that you come from – that of the memory, or of the pocket?' (The reference was to hypocrites, who stored up sayings – and sometimes written notes – of others, to earn a place in Christian circles.) 'Neither,' said Munro instantly, 'what godliness there is is from the hand to the mouth'; that is, grace gathered daily in secret prayer and meditation.

Yet he was an unworldly, impracticable fellow, which no doubt is how, in 1820, he allowed a friendly lobster-smack in 1818 to drop him off at the cove of 'Filio-cleit' – Filiscleitir, on the modern map – between Ness and North Tolsta and as daft a first landing on Lewis as one might choose. But he was quickly welcomed by a young woman from Ness, Marion MacRitchie, who fed him in her *taigh-earraich*, a spring-house by a remote growth to which people might resort with their cattle when early grazing was scarce. It is said that she was converted by means of the grace he asked before they ate, and was later a noted Christian, *Mor Bheag an t-Soisgeul*, 'Little Gospel Marion'. Finlay then made south for Tolsta. A housewife befriended the evangelist and asked him – when her husband was away – to conduct a service in the house. When her man returned, he exploded, seized the youth and threw him out of the house. It is said thereafter that this man's health quickly failed, and that he became a 'broken and subdued man' who deeply regretted this behaviour.

Finlay conducted many services on Lewis – at South Beach Street on Stornoway; in the natural arena of Dalbeag, on the West Side; and at another open-air locality in Gress. In Ballalan, on his way to Harris, there is another striking story, for it demonstrates this remarkable evangelist's humility. Speaking with his usual fervour, and eager to extol the blood of Christ, he declared that 'one drop of that blood was sufficient to wash away the sins of the whole world.' But afterwards, retiring for the night, he told his hosts soberly that a 'man of God' would be the first to open the door the next morning. So it happened, for one Donald Kennedy duly appeared, troubled by Finlay's remarks. Surely the salvation of even one sinner required not just a drop of blood, 'but the Saviour's full sacrifice of Himself unto death'? Rightly corrected, Finlay praised his God on the spot for the privilege of meeting someone there with sufficient Bible knowledge – and pluck – to correct him.

And there are many stories. One woman at Back was an Anne MacFarlane, a Mrs Stewart, whose son became a noted catechist: she was converted by something Munro said to the infant in her arms. On a subsequent visit, the young Stewart boys of another house had taken such a shine to the traveller that, on a wet and miserable night, they scampered outside to retrieve a sail from the shore and lay it over the inadequately roofed byre, lest Munro get wet. Learning of this the following day, he insisted on blessing them: they were all, later, eminent Christians.

He was known everywhere as *am balach leis a' Bhiobull*, 'the boy with the Bible', and must still have been pretty young. But he had remarkable people-skills. Once, staying with a family of Finlaysons in Coll, he had to baby-sit their little boy, James.[6] Finlay decided to teach him something more of prayer. The boy obediently knelt. 'Say your prayer,' said Finlay Munro solemnly. 'Say your prayer,' said wee James. 'You wicked creature,' said the vexed Munro. 'You wicked creature,' lisped the child back. It dawned on Munro that this was how Mrs Finlayson had been teaching her mite its first spiritual exercise – by obedient repetition. James Finlayson grew up to be a noted office-bearer in Ness and, in 1894, would help establish the Free Presbyterian congregation there.

At Dalbeag, Finlay struggled to find a precentor, for few in the district could then read; finally, a young Shawbost boy[7] – only fourteen or so, who had evidently attended the new ESSGS school in that village – offered to lead the praise. This lad, Angus MacLean, wore a brown kilt, and may well have accompanied Finlay elsewhere, for the evangelist prayed for him publicly all over the island, calling him *an gille donn*, the 'brown boy'; he was a great-grandson of that Iain Dubh, the posh MacLean who had fled to Lewis with the Earl of Seaforth after Jacobite reverse at Cromdale. On anther occasion, on the lonely trek between Ness and Tolsta, Munro met another young woman, Margaret Gunn, who gave him a drink of milk. He asked to see her wedding ring. 'How like eternity a ring is!' he said. 'It has neither beginning nor end,' and she too was brought to think of her soul and – a great friend of Little Marion – is still remembered as *Mairead Mhor an t-Soisgeil*, Big Maggie of the Gospel. In Carloway, a self-important tacksman was angry to find Finlay Munro in his kitchen, talking to his servants about Christ. He slapped the evangelist hard across the face, with the flat of his hand. Munro promptly, with level gaze, turned the other cheek to him.

Around 1820, a new ESSGS teacher came to Lewis – John MacLeod, who was born in Kilmaluag, Skye, and had been converted around 1815. He was an earnest Christian and already an experienced teacher, and he is still remembered in Shawbost as the first man openly to challenge Sabbath-breaking in the district. In Galson, a fertile vale in a sort of no-man's-land between Barvas[8] and Ness, the general heathenism weighed on his conscience; there was still no ministry in Ness, and they were ten miles from the Barvas manse and seldom saw the minister, Rev. William MacRae. Despite explicit Society rules, MacLeod could not confine himself simply to reading the Word aloud each Lord's Day. He started to explain what he was reading, to present the Gospel to his hearers and to hold full-blown services.

John MacLeod cannot be credited with bringing Evangelical religion to Lewis – and certainly never claimed that he had – but he was the first Gospel witness in Barvas and Ness, and his activity counterpoints interestingly Finlay Munro's endeavours in the east and south of the island. And his message took hold. People from both districts started flocking to hear him.

Now the Barvas minister of this time, Mr MacRae, has often been damned as a Moderate. At first, though, he genuinely approved of the new endeavour – 'Would that everyone in Barvas, Shader and Galson went to hear John MacLeod! I would fain go myself.' And MacRae is still remembered with remarkable affection on Lewis. A native of the Black Isle, he was presented to Barvas in 1813. A strong believer in universal education, he actively encouraged the ESSGS to establish schools in his district, at Ness, Galson, Shader and Arnol, as well as a later parochial school, and took a keen interest in them. Malcolm MacPhail assures us that, in his day, MacRae 'was the most popular man on Lewis' – a man of high intelligence who stood up ruthlessly to the Seaforth estate and other bullies, a man renowned for his kindliness to people in trouble, and generous with money and provision for the desperate.

He had excellent knowledge both of medicine – maintaining a 'veritable dispensary' in his manse – and of Scots law, and gave his advice freely to all. Catriona Thangaidh, to the end of her days, would not hear a word against 'Good Mr William' and Murdo MacAulay describes him as 'the best friend the Lewis people ever had in civil matters . . . a fine specimen of the cultured, shrewd and manful clergyman'. He fought and won a lawsuit over disputed ground on his glebe, against the laird himself, but later – magnanimously – invited him to a meal. The laird, determined to play the gentleman, manfully agreed, but wondered darkly if the roast had in fact been grazed on the debated acres. 'Aye, Laird,' said MacRae, in his dignified way, 'and has it stuck in your gizzard yet?' When all but one of the local 'Disruption Worthies' had fled Lewis for comforts elsewhere, within a year of the 1843 schism, MacRae remained with his people. He allowed all his servants to attend Free Church services at Barvas, if some pulpit star were conducting them, and was so friendly with the remaining minister – Robert Finlayson of Lochs – and a new Free Church minister at Stornoway, Duncan MacGregor, that they used to stay in his manse when conducting Barvas services.

Nothing, though, can excuse Mr MacRae's antics over Galson. Like most ministers, he was fiercely territorial. His initial approval of John MacLeod's endeavours fanned into alarm, and he moved to destroy him, writing a letter of formal complaint to the ESSGS. When MacLeod refused to stop preaching, the Society dismissed him. But the furious folk of Galson simply built John MacLeod a new schoolhouse and even managed to salary him from their own scant resources. The irate Barvas minister promptly struck every Galson member from his roll, thus permanently alienating the entire community.

Finlay Munro quickly made common cause with John MacLeod, making his way to Galson. They were soon fast friends. Patting the evangelist's knee, MacLeod noticed how worn his trousers were. With no spare pair, he ordered Munro to bed and started darning the garment by firelight. 'How honoured I feel, mending the trousers of a Christian,' mused MacLeod. 'And how honoured I feel,' came back the warm response, 'lying in the bed of a Christian.'

Later, when the Galson meeting was due, MacLeod insisted that Munro take it. There was present a boy from the Dell township of Ness – where many now supported John MacLeod – an Angus Morrison, born in 1805. He had come up to Galson once with his uncle, in little more than idle curiosity, and both were immediately shaken by the powerful preaching and what John MacLeod had to say. They had rationalised it away as they hiked back home, assuring one another they were not the sort of sinners John MacLeod had described and even – daringly – that they would not go to hear him again. But they could not get rid of what they had heard and, in old age, Angus Morrison used to say that he had soon felt 'as if his pillow was stuffed with thorns'. He found peace under Finlay Munro's preaching, and lived to a great age.

For now, the Morrison lad practically adopted Munro, accompanying him everywhere, leading the singing and sitting manfully through the address as an exuberant preacher pounded his shoulders. 'Should there be no witness against me at the last day,' Morrison would say wryly in his final years, as to Gospel privileges, 'but the many blows I got from Finlay's hands, it would be enough.' Mortified by the good man's awful suit, Angus Morrison quietly organised a whip-round and bought a new one. Five shillings were left over, and Morrison slid the coins discreetly into the waistcoat. Shortly afterwards, Munro had to take a ferry – either to Skye or, more likely, to Uist, where his labours saw great success – and as usual asked plainly what was the fare. Having always hitherto been welcomed and given free passage, he was most startled when the boatman announced, in obvious expectation of getting it, that it was five shillings. The alarmed Munro searched his pockets, and found the money; much later, in quiet mirth, he demanded of Angus Morrison how it had got there. 'For had it not been there it would not have been asked for!'

The early decades of the nineteenth century were dreadful for the people of Harris.[9] In 1779 the extravagant and increasingly hard-pressed

MacLeod of Dunvegan had sold his possessions across the Minch to a Berneray cousin, Captain Alexander MacLeod. The Captain tried to build a Harris fishing industry, and not only built great works at Rodel but recruited fishermen from all over Scotland: MacKays from the Orkneys, MacDonalds from North Uist, Cunninghams from the Small Isles, MacSweens and MacKinnons from Skye, and many others besides from Lewis and Wester Ross and elsewhere, whose names are in Harris to this day. He also, as we have seen – and in perhaps a conscious gesture to link all with a great past – renovated St Clement's Church at no small cost.

Harris was materially a happy place, of very different human geography to that we see today. The Bays of the east coast, fine coves shredding rocky and all but useless land, were practically empty. The people of Harris lived on the splendid machair pastures of the west; on the lush offshore islands – Pabbay alone, in 1794, supported around 250 people; in sheltered dales amidst the mountains of the north; and in quite a cluster around the verdant glen of Rodel.

But, not for the first time, Harris was undone by incompetent government and Stornoway greed. A fatuous provision in the tax and excise laws insisted that everything was landed through that town, which all but throttled the nascent Harris industry from the start. Fatefully, in the 1790s, laird and people largely turned their backs on fishing to make the most of a new industry – the harvesting of seaweed, or kelp, which – burned to a slag – could be processed into soap, munitions and even glass, most lucrative when sustained war with France prevented chemical imports.

Kelp transformed the West Highlands, as landlords realised its potential.[10] People everywhere, by encouragement or duress, were pressed into the harvest, and a whole new style of land-use was engineered, with the old clachans and communal or 'run-rig' use of the ground replaced by small rented allotments, just enough to provide minimal subsistence but not so big that the people could live without the wages paid for kelp (which, per ton, were of course only a fraction of its worth.) Rents for this new system – crofting – were of course increased to reflect even that wage, and in Harris the Captain encouraged settlement of the Bays, whose rocks and reefs and inlets were thick with wrack. Fearful of losing cheap labour, lairds successfully lobbied Parliament to achieve a high and minimal fare, by force of law, for passage to the Americas, deliberately putting voluntary emigration beyond the reach of their tenants.

MacLeod's wretched successors saw their inheritance as nothing more than a cash cow. His son, another Alexander, was so determined to be an

Edinburgh gentleman that he dropped the surname all together, and squandered rich revenues in extravagant city living. His own son, Alexander Norman Hume or MacLeod, was an even bigger fool, but by now the Napoleonic Wars were over, and the kelp boom. He savagely raised rents (though the people were equally impoverished by the calamity) and imported a wicked factor – Donald Stewart – with a vague commission to squeeze as much money out of the estate as possible.

The story in detail is agonising. Donald Stewart, a sheep-farmer himself, simply evicted crofters from every piece of remotely worthwhile land and put it under sheep; his own, in many instances, and other pastures under his cousin, Alexander MacRae. The last MacLeod – or Hume – was such a dolt that Stewart ran rings around him, by wholesale trickery and embezzlement, until the last of his line was 'reduced to such a poor condition that he actually obtained his support in Donald Stewart's own house . . . while Donald Stewart was making his hundreds by his cattle on this man's lands.' Bankrupt by 1830, MacLeod sold Harris in 1834 to the Earl of Dunmore; but his desolations were nothing beside those wrought on his tenantry.

Stewart had scarcely got his boots under the desk when thirteen little villages in the North Harris hills were cleared, and their people dumped onto barren Scarp and still more desolate localities. Rodel was cleared. 'There were one hundred and fifty hearths in Rodel,' a witness in 1883 recalled. 'Forty of these paid rent. When young MacLeod came home with his newly married wife to Rodel he went away to show his wife the place, and twenty of the women of Rodel came and met them, and danced a reel before them, so glad were they to see them. By the time the year was out – twelve months from that day – these twenty women were weeping and wailing; their house being unroofed and their fires quenched by the order of the estate . . .'

Soon 'the whole of North Harris, from Husinish to Kinlochresort and Cliasmol was cleared for a farm,' records Bill Lawson, 'then the whole of west Harris from Rodel itself to Luskentyre. Many hundreds were sent away to Cape Breton, and others squeezed into the little fishing villages which Captain Alexander had set up along the Bays coast. . . . The end result of Alexander Norman's period of ownership was that Harris had been ruined, its people either driven to the rocks of the Bays or to the wilds of Canada, while the ownership of the island had passed out of the hands of the MacLeods, the proprietors for so many centuries. The only perceptible benefit had been to the factors, and to a few farmers from the mainland. Where there had been thriving communities there were now only sheep and deer.' Decades of exploitation and tyranny would continue, with large-scale evictions as late as 1867.

It is impossible to exaggerate the devastation of Harris society. No family can trace occupancy of its present land to much before 1843. Some cannot even visit the graves of distant forebears: the ancient burial ground at Seilebost, for instance, did not escape. 'The tide being as ruthless as Stewart who had Loscintir [Luskentyre],' mused Alexander Carmichael decades later, disturbed by coastal erosion on Taransay, 'and who ploughed the *cladh* the people had at Seilebost, the oldest in Harris, till skulls and thigh-bones etc. were rolling about on the surface of the ground like stones in a stony field, the ground being literally covered with them. The crops were so heavy that the place had to be kept from manure for many years. That is when they made the graveyard at Losgaintir itself. These Stewarts were the greatest curse that ever came on Harris.'[11]

By contrast, the 'Lewis Clearances' are largely a myth; of all the Hebrides, it was the least affected by forced evictions, and where they did occur – the worst were in Uig and Pairc – it was overwhelmingly to other parts of the island (rather than compulsory passage overseas) and in response to social crisis.[12] Through the nineteenth century, the population of Lewis climbed steadily, from fewer than 9,000 in 1791 to 25,487 in the official Census ninety years later. The increase in Harris, over that same period, was meagre: from 2,536 to 4,814. As recently as 1900, one could have walked down her west coast, from Tarbert towards the Obbe, passing only a handful of houses.

It was amidst the misery of the early 1820s that Finlay Munro made several visits to Harris. He once held a meeting at Tarbert, a good gathering place for adjacent hamlets and islands, where an official present – perhaps even Stewart himself – made plain his contempt for the evangelist and his message. A strapping lad of ten or eleven, John Morrison is said finally to have seized a great piece of kelp from the shore – some accounts even say it was a length of timber – and clouted the fellow mightily on the head. The boy then prudently fled, amidst the inevitable uproar, and ended up staying with an aunt in Uig; Morrison was later a well-known Stornoway merchant. On another Harris jaunt, Munro stayed with 'godly Mrs MacDiarmid', according to Principal John MacLeod. 'Food was scarce. She had some oatmeal and went and bled the cow to mix the blood with the oatmeal. This food, duly cooked, she gave her guest without a word of comment. When next he came round she had daintier provision for him, which again she gave without making any remark or saying that she now had something better for him in the way of food. She was content with what God's Providence put at her disposal, and she took it that so also would her visitor be. This, he said afterwards, was the finest instance he had ever come across of the refinement of culture that godliness brings in its train.'

But the primary instrument for the spiritual awakening of Harris, amidst all its turmoil and unhappiness, was a native – a blacksmith from Rodel, who also had the excellent name of John Morrison.[13] We know a great deal about *Gobha na Hearadh*, the Harris Blacksmith, because his name is revered there to this day and because, long after his death, he had widespread Highland impact through his verse: he was the greatest poet Harris ever produced, and – even in a crowded field, alongside Dugald Buchanan of Kinloch Rannoch, Peter Grant the Strathspey Baptist and many others – perhaps the outstanding bard of Highland Evangelicalism. He was also, by the way, astonishingly good at his day job; once he even came to the aid of a steamer, stuck uselessly at Tarbert after a mighty component in her engine cracked. Summoned to help, Morrison – who had never seen an engine in his life – studied the part carefully, then forged a perfect replacement.

John Morrison was born around 1796 and his grave, under an impressive and recently refurbished stone, can be readily visited at Rodel churchyard. Though, as we have noted, the Morrisons of Harris are a different clan from those of Ness, he can in fact claim descent from them – a forebear, Roderick Morrison or the 'Blind Harpist', was a son of that genial Bragar tacksman, and a strong dose of Brieve blood may well account for our subject's undoubted gifts of literacy and leadership. For the Harris Blacksmith, though almost entirely self-educated – he seems to have spent just one month at school, in Rodel – could speak and write, fluently, both Gaelic and English, and acquired too some knowledge of Latin. Though he had quite a dark side, he seems generally to have blended winsome charm, and even a playful streak, with a dignity not readily mocked. For high days he could dress most formally: beaver hat, blue breeches and a brown frock-coat, and in attainments, presence and ability he is fully the equal of any of the eminent laymen of this period and, indeed, surpassed not a few ministers.

Around 1820 he married Sarah MacLean, whose very name tells us she was a fairly recent arrival on Harris; her father was a MacLean of Duart, and her mother was a Gillies from Skye. She had borne him four children by her untimely death in 1829. He also came very early under Evangelical influence, and had probably heard Finlay Munro by 1820, for that year he wrote a remarkable hymn, *An Ionndrainn* – 'The Soul's Longing For God' – which has been described as 'one of the gems of the Gaelic language'. Yet he always insisted he was not then a converted man himself – though already anxious, and immersed as his duties permitted in earnest study of the Bible. About this time, Rev. John MacDonald of Ferintosh – who had been asked by the SSPCK to visit St Kilda – was forced to put in at Rodel for a week, his voyage delayed by bad weather. He was naturally prevailed on to conduct a service: John Morrison attended this evening meeting, and had never heard anything like it. He pressed a friend to go to the next one. The man demurred: the place would surely be packed. 'Well, I shall go,' declared *Gobha na Hearadh*, 'should I not get past the door.' When he arrived, there was no precentor, and Morrison was made to lead the praise. Dr MacDonald preached from Paul's first Epistle to Timothy – 'This is a faithful saying, and worthy of all acceptation, that Christ Jesus came into the world to save sinners, of whom I am chief,' – and John Morrison, as we say, was loosed from his bonds. Thereafter – for MacDonald could scarcely linger, and only the dregs of religion were heard at the parish church in Scarista – he was practically the minister of Harris.

At first there was widespread resistance. 'The state of those around him fell heavily on his soul,' Alexander MacLeod of Uig later recorded,[14] 'and his first attempt to spread the light of truth was by conversation. He was regarded as having the natural use of his reason greatly impaired. While some pitied him, others hoped time would cure him. In course of time he began to read publicly the Scriptures in his own house; and as a matter of course the people would flock about him to hear if he should say something strange . . .' At first he read; then, if he saw an important Gospel truth, he would remark on it. Men began to answer him back – even contradict him – and Morrison would enlarge further. Soon there would be vigorous debate. 'The people freely brought forward their objections, and their ideas of things, and John Morrison had thus a fair opportunity of bringing the truth clearly in contact with their notions and conditions.' Men and women began to pack his house each Lord's Day; they began even to gather by his forge. As oppression and eviction increasingly threatened all they had, people were desperate for new certainties in a frightening new Harris.

And, as in Galson, Barvas, Gress and elsewhere, a change came over the place. Open, shameless immorality became furtive. Opponents to the Gospel were sobered into silence. More and more resorted, in dales and behind rocks, to private prayer, and more and more place was given to Scripture. As Rodel became a very different sort of community, Morrison was emboldened to go around the wider island, as MacLeod vividly puts it, attacking 'with the weapons of truth the strongholds of Satan, and the workings of iniquity'. In 1828, he was given the post of SSPCK teacher, and still more liberty to tramp around Harris exhorting and catechising. He also began from 1830 to organise prayer meetings, with the help of the three or four ESSGS teachers on Harris. 'At the first of these prayer meetings, at Tarbert, in the open air, the number present was said to be above 2,000. Family worship was set up in each family, and all, old and young that could lisp, were given to frequent private devotion. All were given to silence and meditation, except when two or three met each other and talked seriously of their state and of the truth.' Within months, Harris was seized in full-blown revival.

At services, Morrison was at times so overcome that, having read the chapter, he could not address the people. Dozens – hundreds, hanging on every word – were likewise overwhelmed by emotion. Some cried out. For evenings on end, save for Saturdays, these diets continued, night upon night, week upon week; on Sabbath itself, three meetings were held. 'After the meetings the people quietly found their way privately to the rocks on the shore where they wrestled alone with God. Vain songs were now replaced by the songs of Sion, and serious conversation took the place of vain talk. Love and good works took the place of backbiting and abuse. Even the children laid aside their youthful amusements, and might now be seen here and there in the furrows of the field, on their little knees lisping their supplications to the Father of mercies.'

Morrison laboured prodigiously. Sometimes, at night, he was so exhausted he nodded off during family worship. With the staunch support of his second wife, Catherine MacLeod – and, indeed, later a third – he threw his own home open to the anxious, squeezing in seven or eight new beds. He genuinely loved the Sabbath rest, and kept it with unusual strictness. No bread was to be cut with a knife. If he caught the servant-girl washing dishes, the crockery was at once set aside, never to be used again. He would not go to bed till after midnight on Saturday, to welcome in the Lord's Day, and would not retire until the early minutes of Monday morning, so he could bid it farewell. That same year, tumultuous 1830, Dr MacDonald found time amidst his determined voyaging to make another call on Harris. Morrison was overjoyed. 'I tried to subdue my emotion and longed for the absence of the messenger. When he had gone I ran to the smithy door and bolted it. I could then when alone give scope to these emotions. I danced for joy – danced round and round the smithy floor; for I felt a load suddenly taken off my spirit. I danced until I felt fatigued; And I then knelt down, and prayed and gave thanks.'

The fervour – one might even say the excesses – of revival in Harris had already swept Lewis, in 1822.[15] That year, the labours of Finlay Munro, the ongoing witness of the increasing pool of converts and rapidly widening access to the Bible, both read and heard, seem – in all reverence – to have reached critical mass. Starting, apparently, in Barvas, and moving out from other centres like Gress and Callanish, an extraordinary movement now swept the countryside. One version relates that a young woman found a page of Scripture, from a crude thatched meeting-house at the obscure hamlet of Tangaidh – of such little account there is today no clear agreement as to where it actually was, though it seems to have been somewhere on the Barvas glebe – and took it home to read to her mother. Murdo MacAulay gives a clearer account.

> A crofter left his wife at home indisposed, and went out to work at his peats. His daughter, who was a young girl, attended the Gaelic school, but was kept at home that day to attend to her sick mother. In the course of the day the mother asked the daughter what she was being taught at school, and made her read her lessons beside her. The lesson happened to be about the crucifixion of our Lord. It was new to the mother, and she was so affected that she began to weep. The girl, thinking her mother's illness had taken a turn for the worse, ran to call a neighbour who, on hearing the cause of the woman's agitation, re-quested the girl to read the lesson to herself. She also was similarly affected. One woman after another came and all had the same experi-ence. When the husband returned and heard the sobbing, he concluded his wife was seriously ill, but on learning the cause of the commotion he desired to hear the lesson read to him. He also was affected in the same manner, and this work continued to spread until a great number in the Barvas district were converted by the Lord. This incident is regarded as the beginning of the revival in Barvas . . .

And 1822 is still remembered as the 'Year of the Swooning' because it was accompanied by still more dramatic human phenomena. People did swoon, by the dozens, in excited gatherings. People screamed and shouted out. Many, too, went into the most alarming trances and a few, in some districts, declared to all they had become 'angels' or 'prophets'. All of this lent powerful ammunition to the ministers increasingly disturbed by the new Evangelical movement.

By 1823, writing to the Chamberlain of the Lews, William MacRae was complaining of 'blind daring fanatics', 'cases of insanity' and – improbably – that the people of Galson had 'signalised themselves more by their idleness, theft and disorderly conduct since John MacLeod went to reside among them, than before his arrival.' Another teacher, at Lionel in the north of Ness, had also been dismissed by the Society, and had likewise been maintained and waged by the community. 'It is easy to see that no good can arise to society from raving effusions of such ignorant men,' scribbled MacRae, imploring the factor to 'take an opportunity of checking this growing evil, for with you alone the remedy remains.' Another and scarcely less temperate letter had already been sent to the

Chamberlain from the Manse of Lochs, Mr Simson denouncing 'that religious phrensy', making the wildest and most improbable allegations of suicide; insanity; 'dreadful doctrines' and 'the most impious rites': Simson calls explicitly for one individual, a lad at 'Carlasnish', to be 'taken into custody', and some decree by the factor that 'no preaching or explaining of the Scriptures take place except by the regular constituted authorities, under pain of dispossession of lands'. These are the rantings of men sensing the irrevocable loss of control.

There is no doubt that extreme, even alarming things were happening. Simson himself had in 1822 been shaken by open disruption of his own Communion service. In his Moderate reign, of course, practically every-one in Lochs who could walk or talk was a communicant, regardless of spirituality, knowledge or lifestyle, and when the elements were ready to be served he called on all present in his usual formula – 'My Christian friends, take your place at the Lord's Table.' Four men – all recent converts, two from Harris, a man from Back and a man from Shawbost – promptly stood up and denounced him as 'a murderer of souls'. There was instant outcry, and the congregation fell at once violently upon them, slapping and pulling and roaring. The zealots had been badly beaten by the time order was restored and an ashen minister announced an incongruous hymn:

> *Failte do 'n la 'san d'eirich Criosd,*
> *le cumhachd a nios o'n uaigh . . .*

> Blest morning! Whose first dawning rays
> beheld the Son of God . . .

Other, similar demonstrations are recorded in Back, Barvas, Bernera and Harris. Most weird goings-on of 1822 were unhelpful, or unedifying, or simply silly. Convulsions and loud, wild wailings were distracting for congregations, annoying to those exhorting them and genuinely frigh-tening for attendant children. It is difficult to see how protracted trances did anyone any good and – especially in reading of the stunts, widely witnessed and well documented, to which many in a trance-state got up to – difficult to regard them as more than attention-seeking entertainment. According to Malcolm MacPhail's nervous account,

There was a very unaccountable thing which those who fell into trances could do in that state. With their eyes closed, they could find out and put their fingers on chapters of the Bible mentioned by themselves as the passage to be read to them in order to recover them out of the trance-state. They could do this while unable to read themselves, and were tested with their eyes bandaged. Moreover, persons in this physically inactive state were known to have been directed to send for persons with whom they were unacquainted, to come to help them out of their trance. . . . Stranger still, the persons sent for were mysteriously warned in a trance to rise and go . . . to relieve persons there in the same state. The person or persons to whom they were coming could tell when they left home, and the different stages of the journey until their arrival. On their arrival, the party in the trance put their fingers on the passage of Scripture, with closed eyes, which the newcomers were to read to them, to help them out of their trance . . .

But MacPhail himself, writing seventy-six years later in October 1898, had not personally witnessed any of this; nor does the apparent 'supernatural' element long withstand careful reflection. An awed audience in a fervent atmosphere who were still, in many instances, illiterate, could not readily have told whether a Scripture passage miraculously found was the one mesmerically quoted; nor, in what was still quite a small community – there were only 12,000 people in all Lewis at that time – is there anything very clever about naming folk of whom one has heard, even if one has never met them; nor, without the aid of telephones and close liaison to witnesses at the other end, could the veracity of departures and journey details have been confirmed.

In any event, there is hard evidence to disprove any positive linkage between such weird goings-on and real spiritual change. Most true converts, like Gobha na Hearadh, Angus Morrison and many, many others, never behaved so bizarrely. By contrast, many who did lapse into screeching, trances and so on never became Christians at all. A woman from Melbost, a Mary MacLeod, could not only give a good show of finding verses with her eyes shut – and what was the point in such displays anyway? – but claimed a 'person' unseen and inaudible to others present, kept her turning the pages until she reached the right one. (It was evidently a most inefficient system.) More strikingly, Mary MacLeod was twice directed in a trance to travel across to Breasclete and reprove certain named individuals for living an 'irregular life' – and indeed, confronted, they admitted their guilt, and promised amendment. But, in times of such religious fervour, people might well have confessed to anything. Much more solemnly, 'This woman gave no evidence in after-life that she had undergone a saving change, but rather the reverse.'

Fools apart, there were charlatans. Bragar and Shawbost each boasted a man greatly given to trances – both of whom were called John MacLeod. Indeed, the Bragar character was so highly thought of by the villagers that, for that summer anyway, he was called the 'Bragar Angel', and they used to carry him shoulder-high from place to place – once, for much of the way at least, as far as Bernera. His career was rudely ended by an irreverent but prudent sea captain there, who said he could prove whether he was an angel or not. He did so simply by offering money, which the Bragar Angel happily accepted. That was the end of his reign.

Future seasons of island revival would occasionally witness such scenes. It is worth stressing certain home truths. For one, as we have seen, they bore no meaningful link to saving grace: real, Christian change of heart and lifestyle. For another, when actively resisted and discouraged by a later generation of Evangelical ministers, they promptly took end, without any evil consequence for Gospel progress. For still another – and this is especially important in our own day, with an established Pente-costal strain of Christianity, the emotional excesses of the charismatic movement and a general desperation to see open signs of 'a move of the Spirit' – they are not in any meaningful sense Christian. The antics of the Dervishes, the heavily stage-managed rallies of Communist China and the exuberance of Muslim pilgrimage (or *Hajj*) produce identical phenomena.

Some Christians would go so far as to suggest that the activities of Mary MacLeod of Melbost were actually the work of an evil spirit. It is much more likely that such antics are simply a product of mass hysteria, and an occasional hazard of any true religious revival. Perhaps the wisest response, when the most ridiculous things force themselves on a believer and cannot be ignored, is simply to laugh at them. Folk all but scurried to the Manse of Barvas to tell William MacRae of Mary MacLeod's latest apocalyptic vision: she declared to all that she had seen him, on his favourite horse besides, cast into the depths of Hell. MacRae listened to this malediction with unruffled composure. 'Well, I'll tell you this,' he said solemnly. 'I can understand well enough why I might be seen there myself. But I certainly can't understand why my good white mare should be.'

But the hills and shores of Uig, its people and townships, remained wholly unaffected either by signs and wonders or by any evidence of this new Evangelicalism. And – a walk-on part by Dr MacDonald of Ferintosh aside – the great new tide of faith had, so far, owed nothing to clergymen. That was about to change. In 1824, word swept Uig that a new minister was coming, so strict 'he would not baptise a single child unless the parents were exemplary in conduct, and stood a searching examination in Scripture teaching.' There was great alarm throughout the parish, and all the parents with new, unbaptised infants promptly trekked as one through the mountains to Harris, where Rev. Alexander Bethune promptly sprinkled the lot in some perfunctory minutes.

Murchadh Mor nan Gràs worried – and hoped – and lay in wait when, in due season, Rev. Alexander MacLeod disembarked at Stornoway. 'Where are you from and where are you going?' Used to deference for the cloth, MacLeod asked icily, 'Who made you my catechiser?' 'The Spirit of God did!' 'Oh, well, if that is so,' said Alexander MacLeod, warming a little to this strange fellow, 'I come from Stoer, in Assynt. There I was born and brought up. I have been a minister in Dundee and Cromarty, and I am on my way to be the minister of Uig, where I hope to preach the Gospel in its glory and wonder.'

'It is sorely needed there,' said Murdo MacDonald quietly, 'for there is not a soul in that parish who knows anything about it, except one herd-laddie – and they think he's stark-mad.'

Finlay Munro, that same year, made what appears to have been his last visit to Lewis; and the new minister would hear him. He conducted his very last service on a spot at Muirneag, the low central hill of northern Lewis, still known as *Tom Fhionnlaidh,* or Finlay's Knoll, before a great congregation who hiked out to hear him from both coasts, and took as his text verses from the twenty-fifth chapter of Isaiah, 'And in this mountain shall the LORD of hosts make unto all people a feast of fat things, a feast of wine on the lees, of fat things full of marrow, of wines on the lees well refined. And he will destroy in this mountain the face of the covering cast over all people, and the veil that is spread over all nations. He will swallow up death in victory: and the Lord God will wipe away tears from off all faces: and the rebuke of his people shall he take away from off all the earth: for the LORD hath spoken it . . .'[16] The name of Muirneag means 'little pleasing woman', and – looking on his great and solemn audience – Munro cried, '*A Mhuirneag, A Mhuirneag,* it is you that may feel well pleased today with your new coat on . . .'

In his final, more disturbed years, Finlay Munro spent more time in Uist, Lochalsh and the glens of Inverness-shire. And, around 1827, Finlay Munro left an undeniably eerie legacy in Glenmoriston, as recorded by Principal MacLeod.

In this glen the tradition is very much alive which tells of a meeting that he held on a hillside near Torgyle. His hearers sat on the rising ground in front of him while he stood on a flat little space of clay ground which doubtless was under grass at the time. Before he was done it bore the marks of his footprints in the clay . . . As he spoke the congregation were disturbed by the behaviour of some Roman Catholics from Glengarry who, by moving about, distracted their attention. The speaker addressed himself to them, and told them that as a proof of the truth of his teaching his footprints would remain there for long. The accounts vary as to the length of time he mentioned; one account being that he said until his hearers should go to judgement, and another, until the Day of Judgement. But the fact is that after a hundred years the footprints can still be made out.

Though deliberately vandalised around 1980 by some infidel with a spade, the 'footprints' remorselessly returned – a patch of bare ground where nothing will grow, and when my friend Duncan MacLean and I visited the spot in June 2008, they were there still, surrounded by the lushest grass, and with no immediate and natural explanation; though there may well be one.[17]

Worn out and increasingly erratic, Finlay Munro died at Aberarder in Strathnairn, after a brief illness, in 1834. Lately installed as minister of the East Church in Inverness, the redoubtable Finlay Cook watched sombrely as Finlay's Strathnairn friends carried the late evangelist's coffin through the town. Many a minister had mocked, miscalled and sought to destroy Finlay Munro. Cook removed his hat, and gave audible thanks to God 'that I was never suffered to cast a stone against Thy faithful servant'.

7

'No Finer Moral Spectacle'

Alexander MacLeod and Evangelical Ministry, 1824–1843

Rev. Alexander MacLeod, who presided over the biggest parochial revival the Long Island has ever seen, is both admirable and peculiar. He was the son of a crofter and was born, in 1786, in the township of Balachladich, in the Assynt parish of Sutherland.

Evangelical religion was rapidly taking hold a little to the north of that district, with a long-established mission at Eriboll and, from 1802, the presence of the senior John Kennedy. In 1802, Kennedy became assistant minister of Assynt itself – his son would later write that the incumbent, William MacKenzie, was 'all that a minister ought not to be', and Norman MacFarlane assures us he was 'devoted to the whisky bottle much more than his Bible'.[1] In perennial debt, MacKenzie once ordered his only boots to be taken to one David, a local tradesman, for repair. But the Sabbath came and there was no word of the boots. He padded pathetically to church and dusted off a sermon about David in the armour of Saul. He began to read. And just as he had declaimed, 'And what did David say?', his manservant ambled in. 'What did David say? Just what I expected, that never another pair of boots would ye get till ye have paid off all those ye owe him.' When MacKenzie died, the people of Assynt were determined that Kennedy succeed him, but the Duke of Sutherland presented a Moderate nonentity instead; it is said the people marched out to meet the Presbytery with sticks and clubs, and drove them and the unwanted minister out of the parish.

This, the older John Kennedy, if less celebrated than his Free Church son, was in his day as high in the estimation of Highland Christians as any, Donald Beaton asserts.[2] Murdo MacAulay adds that many of his converts became catechists and teachers. Yet Kennedy's Assynt labours were tormented from an early stage by the antics of Norman MacLeod, who, having been a 'sharp, clever, irreverent youth', seems to have been converted or, as Kennedy senior slyly puts it, 'joined himself to the people of the Lord'. Today, Norman MacLeod is famous on three continents: he started to train for the ministry, but threw it over – he wanted to preach, not to study – and simply separated from the Church of Scotland, forming a sect of his own and quickly winning ardent support, for he had magnetic speaking abilities. At one point he had won over all but two of the male communicants in the parish.

Efforts to arrest this cult – which, of course, invited astonishing vituperation – nearly killed Kennedy. For his endeavour, Norman Mac-Leod declared that Mr Kennedy 'had no more grace than a horse'; though John MacDonald – 'a bag of sand' – did not escape either. Norman MacLeod is the most notorious and certainly the least Christian of the North Country Separatists. On one occasion he even declared he had combed all the Highlands in search of those who were Christians *indeed*. He found two. The sort of ecclesiastical thug who occasionally appears in the Highland church, in 1817 Norman MacLeod mercifully emigrated to Nova Scotia with a few followers; later still, in his late seventies, he resettled with many more in New Zealand. Norman MacLeod died in 1866, in his eighty-seventh year, leaving Highland communities and memorials in both far-flung lands, to say nothing of a recently erected monument by Clachtoll Bay in Assynt.

But to our tale. Assynt has still a distinctive religious flavour – 'People do not come out here to hear the Gospel,' my father was told when he spent a summer in Balachladich as a divinity student, in 1963, 'but to hear if you have it,' – and the very young, zealous Alexander MacLeod had been briefly caught up in Norman MacLeod's sect. He was converted when he was only thirteen, at Ferintosh Communion, and amidst intense private study – he seems to have been naturally a solitary, withdrawn sort of fellow – he supported himself in crofting and fishing. He was duly received as a student for the ministry and attended University in Aberdeen.[3]

The summer he completed his studies, he was offered a place as tutor in the household of a rather prosperous Skye farmer. Though reluctant at first to go, he was soon much taken with the beautiful sister of the lads he was teaching. Even better, she fell utterly in love with him. Her family, however, did not approve; a penniless divinity student of poor prospects and tedious personality was little catch. But Alexander MacLeod is full of surprises. A plot was framed, friends briefed, a boat arranged, a ladder procured for my lady's window – and he and his sweetheart simply eloped. They dashed for Edinburgh, were wedded before anyone could catch up on them, and after living in the Horse Wynd – he had to send for his sister to train his new bride how to keep house – the young couple set up home in a humble, thatched Assynt cottage.

It took his furious in-laws time to track them down: her brother, Macfarlane insists, even accosted our hero with loaded guns. At length, all involved kissed and made up, but when Alexander MacLeod was at last licensed to preach, in 1818, by the Presbytery of Tongue, he was already thirty-three. To add insult to delay, as a condition of this belated status he was forced publicly to deplore and repudiate – and only after intense interrogation – his past association with 'a certain party or religious sect in the parish of Assynt' and to swear 'firm attachment to the Church of Scotland'. He was duly appointed, the following year, minister of the Gaelic Chapel of Dundee; and in 1821 he was presented to Cromarty. So, before he was even ordained, MacLeod had made formidable enemies. All these trials and uncertainties go a long way to explaining Alexander MacLeod's immensely guarded personality and a very great wariness of 'enthusiasm', not least amidst genuine revival. They also explain his very strange, obsequious letters, from the Manse of Uig, to Lady Elizabeth, especially once his Lewis colleagues had turned on him.

He made his first visit to Uig early in the year, in January 1824, and later wrote the proprietrix in oily terms. 'I have heart-felt satisfaction of giving you good tidings of great joy. Through the whole island there is a great thirst for religious instruction and information.' At length, on 28 April, he was inducted as its first Evangelical minister, and his surviving Diaries begin on 2 June.[4] In this and other instances they are in diverting contrast to his correspondence with the heritor.

> The first month that I laboured amongst this people I observed that they were extremely attentive to the preaching of the Word. But the truth made no visible impression on them . . . Having commenced to examine several of the parents previous to my dispensing the order of baptism to them, I found that they (with very few exceptions) were grossly ignorant of the truths of Christianity in God's Word. In questioning them respecting the covenants of works and grace, they acknowledged that they were perfectly ignorant of the origin, nature, and systems of both. They were but few among them that could tell me the names of our first parents, of Noah, or of any of the patriarchs and prophets, and but few could tell of the nature of our Lord's mission and the names of His disciples and their history. In asking how many sacraments Christ appointed, the answer in general was that He instituted seven. When I enquired their hope of salvation as to its grounds and foundation, good conduct and doing the best we could was the answer, and with regard to their expectation of Heaven, they said it would be a wonderful favour to be somewhere else upon the borders of that happy place, though not admitted to the society of the holy.

MacLeod sighed, and dipped his pen. 'By such interviews I have at once discerned their consummate ignorance of true religion, and that the polluted remains of Popery, since it was the religion in this place, was the only notion they had of Christianity. Swearing, lies, and stealing were very common vices in the island, notwithstanding they were in general kind and obliging, and but few instances of drunkenness and uncleanness among them.' So, he decided 'to begin the very first principles of Christianity with them, and to make it my great care and study how to come to a level with their untutored capacities, so as to render the truths delivered intelligible to them . . .'

His parishioners were not stupid. Uig abounded in skilled tradesmen.[5] But illiteracy and superstition abounded. There was only one true Christian, that 'poor herd-laddie', a boy called Malcolm MacRitchie,[6] whose father was the minister's grieve. When his mind had first turned to religion, in 1818, there were only two Bibles in the entire parish – one in the church and one in the manse. Someone lent him a Gaelic Testament, and his spiritual anxiety only grew. Naturally, he decided to visit the minister, the ageing Rev. Hugh Munro. When the boy got to the manse, he found his pastor indifferent, bemused and faintly hostile. When MacRitchie called a second time, the doors were locked and wild-eyed maids peeped from windows: Mr Munro had declared MacRitchie was insane.

Desperate for his own Bible, the youth walked all the way to Stornoway for one – only to find that, at five shillings, he could not afford it. He trudged home – but subsequently found a cask of palm oil on a Uig beach, and when he reported this prize to the Custom House at Stornoway, he learned the reward was five shillings. So he got his Bible. Soon neighbours crowded the house to hear him reading it. The old minister, Rev. Christopher Munro, then threatened MacRitchie's father with eviction. He replied bluntly, 'You may take the land from me, but you cannot take grace from Murdo!' By 1823, still only twenty, Murdo was teaching at Aline, hard by the Harris border on Loch Seaforth; children, parents and grandparents soon crowded the schoolhouse, and he began to take services. There were many conversions. Malcolm MacRitchie was later a greatly loved minister; but he would always maintain, according to MacAulay, that he would be happy 'if he saw as much fruit of his labours in the three congregations of which he was a minister as he had seen in that small township alone'.

But Alexander MacLeod had been shocked by more than the evidence of catechising, or the 'stupid attention', as John Wesley would call it, evident in his hearers at sermon. He had already learned how many folk in Uig were communicants – there were eight or nine hundred of them, around half the population. On Sabbath, people sold whisky and tobacco outside the church. He was aghast to see folk bowing in homage to the

Sun and Moon. No one, anywhere in Uig, conducted family worship. Mr Munro himself had not even bothered to keep it in the manse. Eager to try his office-bearers, MacLeod held a prayer meeting. The elders bravely attended. One man was duly asked to lead. 'O Lord, Thou knowest that we have come a long way to this meeting. We have put ourselves to a good deal of trouble, and we hope that Thou wilt reward us for it by casting some wreck on the shore on our way home.' Scarcely believing his ears, the minister called on another. This man besought the Most High to grant them a great catch of cod and ling, in return for their faithful service in attending the meeting. The appalled minister then 'put up' a third, who evidently believed the death of Christ on Calvary was the worst thing that had ever happened in history: '*is latha dubh dhuinne an latha bhasaich Criosd*' – 'and it was a black day for man when Christ died'. MacLeod did not even let him finish. '*Suidhe sios!* Sit down, man. You have said enough.'

Alexander MacLeod could be in no doubt of the scale of the problem. And he was remarkably decisive in his response. He simply cancelled the Communion, scheduled for that summer. Indeed, he probably 'purged the Roll', or destroyed it, or hid it, treating everyone henceforth as heathen till proved otherwise. Third, he maintained the new midweek meeting as a Thursday lecture, and instituted assorted prayer meetings; the more these people were taught, the better. Fourth, and to that end, he planned and drew up in detail systematic, intensive education: he would plant schools, and we can imagine the missives flying off to the assorted Societies. All he lacked was manpower. For the first month or so, he was too dispirited to do more than keep services and immerse himself in devotion and study, but then it was brought strongly home to him that he should start systematically visiting his people, 'not to gossip,' says MacAulay, 'but to press home what they had heard.'

It is difficult for us to grasp how unusual, even in Evangelical circles, this was. A minister was in Georgian days a gentleman, who did not usually honour the cotts of the poor. MacLeod also – according to a story retailed by my own grandfather, the late Murdo MacLean of Shawbost – did something no other minister had deigned to do; he went – incognito – to hear Finlay Munro preach,[7] on a visit to Glen Valtos during his last Lewis tour. He wanted to give the evangelist something, but knew the delicacies and so – in what must have been a tense encounter, after the address – asked the young preacher if he might have a pinch of his snuff. Munro readily handed over his snuffbox; MacLeod took his ostentatious fill and had secreted a 'pound-sterling' inside – probably a sovereign – before he closed and returned it. It was a very Highland manoeuvre. But the minister of Uig had now heard the preaching that had seized Lewis, and could not doubt its depth.

It seems a change then took place in MacLeod's own sermons. 'They had always been scriptural but commonplace and unarresting sermons, delivered in a pleasant, silvery, easy voice, but now they became tongues of fire that swept into the inner corners of the soul . . .' It is all the more impressive as, though a new and commodious wing had been added in the year of his induction to the Manse of Balnacille, MacLeod had only an old shack of a church, no longer fit for public worship. He had to exhort his people in the open air, from a 'tent' or preaching-box erected behind the manse below the natural arena formed by the slopes of Cnoc Eothail. On top of all his other concerns, Alexander MacLeod had to lobby both patron and Presbytery for the provision of a new church, and agitated besides for a bigger glebe. On 10 June 1825 – he refers to it in his diary – he narrowly escaped drowning. 'Forget not . . . that tempestuous day you were in a small barque tossed on the mighty and roaring ocean, and when all thought you were destined for a watery grave . . . the mighty god of Jacob rebuked the storm and brought us into safe harbour.' After the death of Rev. Simon Fraser in the Minch the previous year, this must have been a terrifying experience.

MacLeod's preaching may well have improved; significantly, a change took place in the listening. That summer, John MacRae bustled in as parish schoolmaster – 'he was a magnificent asset,' says MacFarlane – and in short order others would follow. Schools were hastily established; there were eventually nine of them. By 1827 some 600 pupils attended the new schools of Uig and, by 1834, there were in addition thirteen Sabbath schools. And for this sustained programme of education, Alexander MacLeod obtained teachers of remarkable calibre. As well as MacRae and MacRitchie, four others – John Finlayson, Alexander MacColl, Peter MacLean and John MacQueen – would be eminent Highland ministers. MacLeod was no longer alone. Only a month after that first bleak analysis in his Diaries, he could write, 'From 2nd June to this period, many people from the neighbouring parishes attend divine service regularly, and many, young and old, seem to be under serious impressions. They now give close attention to what is spoken. Many young and old are in tears every Lord's Day, and several are so affected as not to be able to contain themselves or to retire . . .'

What survives of MacLeod's Diary is best taken in small doses. Yet there are some striking lessons here. The steps he felt guided to take – suspension of Communion; the institution of additional teaching meetings; the perseverance with prayer meetings, even after so unedifying a start; the focus on education and sustained, draining pastoral visitation – all show profound common sense. It is noteworthy besides – for there had still, even after two summers, been no sacramental season on his watch –

that he had men engaged in public prayer who were not at that stage members in full Communion, something that would certainly not happen on Lewis and Harris now and which would have ministers in paroxysms if it did.

By 1829, MacLeod could enjoy a new parish church, erected within sight of the manse and on a commanding spot above Timsgarry. Marking out a new glebe was much more fraught; two 'honest and discreet men' were detailed to mark out a considerable area of land, to afford Alexander MacLeod and his successors a comfortable area for pasture and corn. To his irritation, he could not at first assume it, as it was still under crops sown and tended by his poor neighbours, and there was real local resentment, as MacLeod himself nervously notes in one of his whining letters to the Lady Elizabeth. 'Indeed if it should be agreeable to the proprietor,' he writes, 'I have no wish to have any of the lands in their possession included in my glebe, seeing that some of them are foolishly disposed to blame me for their removal, and fearing that this circumstance may render my gospel ministration unsuccessful among those few of my parishioners. . . .' This, as we shall see, was less than frank.

It is doubtful if there was much vocal protest, amidst the new religious environment. Uig was now an irresistible Evangelical attraction. Crowds now flocked, from all over Lewis, to join even the routine Sabbath worship. 'Men and women travelled from Ness, Back and Knock,' records MacAulay, 'distances of twenty to forty miles, to Uig ferry on Saturday' – that was at Callanish – 'and the distance to be travelled by sea, which cannot be less than ten to twelve miles.'

His own writings cloud the sustained postponing of the Sacrament in great confusion. MacLeod's private Diary, or what survives of it, confirms he personally decided there would be no Communion until the Uig people were fit for it. With his patron, though, he again avoided candour. Lady Elizabeth Stuart-MacKenzie was instead told, in November 1824, 'there is [sic] no sacramental tables or cloth of the things needed on such a solemn occasion in the parish, so that I am much afraid that I will not be able to have the Sacrament here next summer, God willing, which, if I will not have matters arranged for that purpose, will be a great disappointment, and a matter of deep regret to myself and to others.'

It is difficult not to feel that this is dishonest, for in 1825 – when it became known there would be no Uig Communion for the second year in succession – there was an outcry, with unhappiness in Uig and general uproar all over Lewis. Word of what was going on in Uig had thoroughly rattled MacLeod's Moderate colleagues, and the new Stornoway minister – John Cameron – arrogantly despatched a messenger to Uig with a bag of communion tokens, so that its oppressed and persecuted Christian populace might at least be able to enjoy the Sacrament elsewhere. Word of this reached Uig before the tokens. MacLeod did not hesitate: the envoy had to be stopped. But who could do it? For him personally to intervene was unthinkable. John MacRae, the most robust of his new teachers, was keen; but MacLeod would not hear of it – MacRae was parish teacher and a divinity student of the Established Church besides, and there would certainly be grave consequences for him. The day was saved by another of their circle, Francis MacBean,[8] who was now a frequent visitor to the Manse of Balnacille. MacBean, a handsome man from Corpach, was an Inspector of the Edinburgh Gaelic Schools Society and on Lewis, that summer, as a builder of schools and a contractor for new roads. He was a fervent Evangelical of high principle and strict views; better still, the Kirk had no jurisdiction over him, for MacBean had left her fold and joined the Secession Church.

So Francis MacBean headed quickly into the rugged moor and lay in wait for Mr Fraser's agent of mercy, upon whom he sprang with the roar, 'Your tokens or your life, sir!' The terrified fellow dropped them and fled. At the next Presbytery, Alexander MacLeod was harangued by his colleagues, not just for the inexplicable attack on the token-bearer, but for his own 'disturbing' sermons. The minister of Uig refused to budge, declaring that in no circumstances would he hold a Communion in the parish, and Presbytery prepared to sentence him to a year's silence for 'contumacy', or contempt of court. He said quietly that it mattered not what he might do, for *am Ministear Mor* – 'the Great Minister'; the Lord – was on his side. Alexander Simson, that year Moderator of Presbytery and rather out of it, took this as a charming compliment. 'That's right, MacLeod, I am with you!' he burbled. 'And we'll have them at defiance.' He then promptly stood and pronounced the benediction, and Presbytery was over before sentence could be passed.

It would be the fourth year of MacLeod's ministry, on 25 June 1827, before a Communion season was at last celebrated in Uig. It was a dramatic contrast to the sacramental feasts of the older order. For one, Dr MacDonald of Ferintosh, that prince of the Highland pulpit, was the officiating minister. For another, the attendance was prodigious: some 7,000 people were present in a huge open-air gathering. 'This is the first occasion we had the Communion here in my time, and only six individuals have come forward to the Lord's Table. There were no more than twenty communicants in all . . .' It is said that, when all was finally dismantled and the white linen taken up from the communion tables, they were so wet with tears that they had to be wrung out. In 1833, 9,000 are said to have converged on Uig Communion, with visitors from Harris and even further.

Many tales and traditions survive of the two decades through which Alexander MacLeod was minister of Uig. There were astonishing conversions. One, Catherine or *Ceit* Smith, could repeat the Twenty-Third Psalm at the age of three and was in almost constant prayer. Another convert, Malcolm MacLeod, who was ninety-five years old, was infirm, blind and bed-ridden. His daughter told him of sermons and the minister visited him. When the next Communion fell, that year of 1834, four men carried Malcolm MacLeod to the Lord's Table 'with tears of sorrow and graceful love for the grace that saved him, coursing each other over his furrowed cheeks. The whole multitude was moved, every eye glistening with sympathy and love. Mr MacLeod said of him, 'He is a most interesting sight, caught at the eleventh hour. Oh, how wonderful are the ways of sovereign grace.'

Most famous of all, though, is Angus MacLeod, born in Carishader about 1810, but whose father shortly became a shepherd in a 'lonely place among the hills of Uig at the head of Loch Hamanaway', and from this squalid mountain bothy his son got the nickname *Aonghas nam Beann* – Angus of the Hills.[9] *Aonghas Dhomhnaill Mhuirchaidh Mhoir*, to give him his patronymic, was almost fabulously simple-minded – 'he could not count his own fingers, and could be trusted with nothing, so senseless was he.' He used, for fun, to crawl across a tidal dyke – probably a crude fish-trap – regardless of sea and danger, and then come home sodden to sprawl on the earthen floor and dry off by the fire. While the possibility of Down's syndrome cannot be discounted, MacLeod's learning difficulties, to use the modern euphemism, were almost certainly the result of gross inbreeding: two sisters were likewise 'sunk in hopeless idiocy . . . spent their days at the fireside, and did not move from it.' But Angus liked to roam into wider society and, perhaps from curiosity, started attending MacLeod's open-air services. He was so useless even at shepherding, though now a grown man, his father did not miss him in the slightest.

But Angus MacLeod was converted and when 'the light of the Gospel dawned on his dark mind' a change took place in him so remarkable neighbours observed, wondering, that he had gained double wisdom – spiritual and natural. The latter was always limited. Despite heroic attempts, neither Angus Morrison, Alexander MacLeod nor anyone else could teach him to read. ' A B, ab,' cried the lad, 'I see nothing here about God or about Christ or about the soul. I should prefer to be praying behind the hillocks than to be at this. This is as dry as cork to my soul.' Nor could he ever count. He did acquire sufficient wit to herd sheep and cattle, to the point that his absence from home became resented; but his real abilities were spiritual and are recorded by many witnesses. Though Angus MacLeod could not read, 'the word of God dwelt richly in him.'

His head was full of accurate Scripture, heard and memorised. Though he could not maintain sensible conversation, he had one astonishing gift. 'Grace had so elevated and ennobled his mind that one could scarcely discover any traces of a defective intellect when he engaged in prayer. It was remarked by those who knew him well that after his conversion he was wont to acknowledge his want of intellect, a thing which he never did before, and which fools seldom or never do.'

MacLeod's application to sit at the Lord's Table was at first resisted by the stern MacLeod, 'on the ground of diminished responsibility and intellectual capacity, but grace prevailed and he was able to overcome this rebuff.' He was admitted to membership subsequently, for – in an anecdote often and tediously retailed – 'he was sitting at the communion table, and when the elder came where he was for the token Angus had none. "Have you lost your token?" said the elder. "No," said Angus, "I have only lost the bit of lead." He had not lost his "token for good."'

There has been an unfortunate tendency almost to make a cult of *Aonghas nam Beann*, especially as new and fatuous anti-intellectualism has grown fashionable in Lewis Christian circles; and besides, of late, to justify such innovations as, for instance, abandoning communion tokens. But there are many striking stories of him. He always protested when called on to pray – 'I am surprised that you are so pressing me, knowing what I am.' And he often quoted a text, 'I thank thee, O Father, Lord of heaven and earth, because thou hast hid those things from the wise and prudent, and hast revealed them unto babes.' On one occasion, despite intense pressure, he did refuse. He mumbled afterwards that he had felt too uncomfortable to lead. 'Jonah was not too comfortable in the belly of the whale,' expostulated his harasser, 'yet he prayed.' 'If the whale had been in the belly of Jonah,' retorted Angus MacLeod, 'he would make no prayer.'

Though he could not count beyond three, he once strikingly illustrated the Trinity – folding a piece of greasy trouser-leg in three, and then stretching it back out to one. He had the habit of exhorting folk outside after a meeting. Once, by the shores of Loch Roag, MacLeod cried, 'Poor Angus will be a witness against you if you reject the Word of God. You know him and his weakness. You have your natural faculties, and he has not, so this will be your increased guilt if you do not make use of faculties that were never given to him.' Some ministers resented such speeches and once, at Uig Communion, ignoring Alexander MacLeod's chuckled word of warning, one strode over to Angus and his little audience to make them disperse. *Aonghas nam Beann*, in full flow, looked at him sharply. 'I knew we had something good, and that Satan would soon make an effort to disrupt us!' The minister hastily retreated. 'Och, they soon sent me away as an instrument of Satan,' he had to report at the manse.

It was seldom prudent to take on Angus of the Hills. Someone once nastily baited him in Stornoway – 'Are you not the Uig fool?' The simpleton lashed back, 'The Bible says the fool is he who trusteth in his own heart.' Once, Roderick MacLeod – *Maighistir Ruaraidh* himself – entertained him at the Snizort manse, and observed kindly, 'Angus, has not grace greatly honoured you when it brought you to my table?' 'And did not grace greatly honour yourself, minister, when you invited me?' At Snizort, besides, where his dress and visage betrayed his want of intellect, someone sneered, 'There's one that wants something.' 'Yes, I do want something,' said Angus of the Hills, 'I want Jesus Christ, the true bread, that came down from heaven.' A grand sportsman once wagered he could bribe the village idiot to miss the Thursday services of the Communion, accompanying him to the hill instead. But MacLeod could not be tempted. The offer grew and grew, until he snapped. 'No, I will not sell the Communion services for your money. Thy money perish with thee.' After a prayer meeting, the man presiding said, 'Angus, there were three mistakes in your prayer today.' 'Glory be to God that it was not all together a mistake.'

When John MacRae served as Uig parish teacher, Angus MacLeod became most attached to him, and later stayed with him at the new Cross manse. Once, when he should have been herding the cows, he lost himself in private prayer and the beasts wandered into the corn. MacRae rebuked him in some temper, to which Angus meekly submitted. Someone overheard, and tried later to tease him. What a scolding he had got. But, quoted Angus,

> Let him that righteous is me smite,
> it shall a kindness be;
> Let him reprove, I shall it count
> a precious oil to me . . .

Not knowing he was already beaten, the man waded on. 'But why did you not pray that the Lord would keep the cattle from coming into the corn?' Angus MacLeod had an instant response. 'A prayer with cows in it would not be worth much!' At that Snizort Communion, kind ladies gave him a little money. It preyed on his mind – 'Angus, you love your money more than you love Christ,' – and he finally hid it in a turf dyke. 'I can do without you until Monday, but I cannot do without Christ tomorrow.'

But John MacRae was no less attached to the 'Uig fool' than MacLeod was to him. Once, sailing to Callanish from Uig Communion, Angus noticed MacRae on board and sidled affectionately over to him. MacRae naturally asked him how he had enjoyed his last sermon. Angus began instead to speak on the text himself, enlarging till their ferry had reached. 'Angus has taught me things today,' said a bemused MacRae to Kenneth Ross, 'which I never heard of before or thought of in my life.'

There are many versions of these stories, and more tales besides of *Aonghas nam Beann*. Once, as a Christian friend walked with him besides a dried-up river, he asked the simpleton, 'How would you, Angus, describe the way faith acts towards the promises of the Word?' He replied, 'Faith is often comparable to a trout that would be endeavouring to come up this river, and the water so low that its back has become dry, so that it concludes that it will never be able to reach the loch from which the river comes; but bye and bye it sees a pool a little in front of it, and it makes a plunge into it. So does faith when it is almost on the point of giving up for want of the water of life; when it sees the promise, it plunges into it.'

Angus died in Skye around 1859 – probably at another Snizort Communion – and is buried on that island, at Uig cemetery. On 13 October 1877 – the sensation is particularly remembered because many thought it a judgement on the vicious landlord of the Trotternish district, Major William Fraser – torrential rain triggered a flood of the Uig rivers, the Rha and the Conon. They burst their banks and joined in one catastrophic rush of water, dislodging two-ton boulders, smashing through the Uig cemetery and demolishing Major Fraser's lodge, which has never since been rebuilt. Coffins and bones were everywhere; the still more ghastly recent dead bobbed by the shore. The remains of one most recently evicted tenant were found in the wreckage of Fraser's living room. But the grave of *Aonghas nam Beann* was quite untouched.

By the Highland Church Act of 1823, forty-two new religious parishes were sanctioned in the region, and two of these were agreed in Lewis, elegant Telford churches being erected, by government grant, at Cross in the Ness district and at Knock, near Aignish on the Eye peninsula. The situation in Ness was particularly urgent, in view of the needs of Galson – now estranged from Barvas – and a new church and manse at Cross were completed in March 1829, with neatly walled churchyard and garden and a little over six acres for a glebe. That same month, identical buildings – though, in this instance, with only a four-acre glebe – were finished at Knock. Each church cost about £750, and each manse £720, and the new congregations benefited besides from small endowments. Later, on 29 July 1829, Rev. Finlay Cook was inducted as the first minister of Cross.

Born in the south end of Arran, in 1778, Cook came to a strong personal Christian faith at the age of twenty-five and would see a striking revival on his native island. During vacation from his divinity studies, Cook was employed as missionary at the Lanark cotton mills then operated by Robert Owen, best remembered today as a founding-father of British socialism. And, on his licensing in 1817, Cook was stationed at the Achreny Mission in Halkirk, Caithness, which had long been a lighthouse of Evangelicalism.

Finlay Cook was a prim fellow who always wore black gloves to preach and has left no manuscripts whatever of his sermons – simply because he sketched them in outline on a slate, and erased the chalk after due delivery. He was not confronted, in Cross, with quite such heathen desolation as MacLeod had found in Uig – he had Galson and a bridgehead of established Christians – but there was plenty of darkness to fight. There was also an appalling poverty.[10] As a strident young minister, he had 'unsparingly denounced' folk for gaudy dress, taking odd exception to, for instance, ribbons, straw bonnets and even umbrellas. He was aghast to find couples appearing 'bare-footed, bare-headed, and miserably clothed, and in this condition requesting that he should marry them . . . a man and his wife appeared in the church with the view of having their child baptised, the mother bare headed, bare footed, and her body covering almost as scanty in longitude as the famous "cutty sark", the covering of the husband being not much better. The worthy man refused to perform the rite of baptism till the dame and her husband should provide themselves with garments of modest dimensions.'

As folk from the bounds of Barvas began travelling to Cross to hear him, William MacRae started to agitate against the new arrival. Cook had already sufficient experience of church politics to handle the situation with care. Once, when the new Stornoway minister – Rev. John Cameron, an out-and-out Moderate – met Cook in town, he asked unpleasantly if the minister of Cross had called by the Barvas manse on the way in. Told that Mr Cook had not, he reminded him of the commandment, 'Follow peace with all men.' 'And why did you leave the other part out?' asked Finlay Cook, '. . . and holiness, without which no man shall see the Lord . . .' Cook, who had already seen fervent excesses on Arran, stamped on them firmly in Ness. He also deliberately sought to rattle the sermon-tasters from Barvas, challenging their motives from the pulpit. Some were scared off for good. But others, under true spiritual concern, continued to tramp all the way to Cross. 'My neighbour's flock has departed,' Cook would say, 'but those who were heavy with young stayed behind.'

It is said of Cook, too, that Satan once met him on the Ness highway, as the minister walked home; a sinister stranger who said menacing things, but whom the evangelist sternly resisted. Despite real encourage-ment, though, Cook's Lewis ministry was brief. Nor was Robert

Finlayson,[11] a portly and gracious son of Clythe, Latheron, long to serve at Knock. Having assisted for three years at Aberdeen Gaelic Chapel, he was inducted to the new Lewis congregation in 1829 and served there for only two years. But his impact was immediate. For one, he genuinely loved people. Though a warm, original preacher, Finlayson's strength lay in pastoral work and, specifically, in catechising. He could laugh off frightened silence, and turn the most fatuous answer to his advantage, neatly using it to elaborate on the Gospel message and leave the child or hearer feeling important, rather than ridiculous. His new church was soon packed. And the people of Point even piled into the manse every evening – jamming the parlour and the hall, the stairs and the lobby – just to hear their minister conduct family worship.

But Mr Finlayson did not long stay in Knock; he quit in 1831 and his successor, Rev. Duncan Matheson,[12] who to had done service as a schoolmaster in Uig, was ordained to the Point charge later that year. Born in Plockton in 1793, Matheson would join the general flight for greener pastures after the Disruption. A surviving photograph is all scowl and whiskers, though MacAulay timidly suggests 'there are traces of deep kindliness under his frowning eyebrows . . . He was a complete contrast to his predecessor. He tore like a tornado the roots of all attempts at self-righteousness, and often sent an alarming shiver through those anxious as to whether they had truly experienced a saving change or not . . . "There are diversities of gifts, but the same spirit."'

Mr Matheson could certainly be ruthless. Exasperated by the incoherent endeavours of a probationer in his own pulpit, he ordered him to sit down, took command and finished the sermon himself. He had no time for those who felt a sermon could be casually thrown together, speaking darkly of ministers 'so impudent as to preach from a text without looking at the original language in which it was written.'

But these eminent ministers were not the hyper-Calvinists of common caricature, so conscious of predestination and election as to shun the free offer of Christ to sinners. Duncan Matheson was once vexed at a Fellowship Meeting – we shall explain this ordinance in detail later – when a speaker savaged Evangelical ministers. 'They press us to believe,' the man moaned, 'and we cannot believe of ourselves; and if we will not believe they will break our heads.' Closing the meeting, Matheson rebuked him. 'Man, you seem to find fault with preachers for pressing you to do your duty. They press you to believe, you say – well, ought they not to do so? The Lord commands you to believe. You say they will break your head if you will not believe – but I tell you, man, God will break your head if you do not believe.'

As he prepared to leave Cross for the new East Church in Inverness,

Finlay Cook asked one of his young converts what sort of minister they would like as his successor. The reply came in a flash – 'a dead dog at the King's table': an allusion to the story of Mephibosheth, last of the house of Saul, who thought as little of himself as a dead dog, and yet who dined continually at the table of the king.

Moderate ministers still held the Manse of Harris, as they would for decades to come. It was almost inevitable that, even by 1823, at the height of revival, the Disruption had to all intents and purposes occurred. Almost everyone had forsaken the Established Church, to the dismay of John Morrison, who urged people to remember that fault lay not in the Kirk, but in patronage. As an SSPCK teacher, of course, he had a vested interest in the Establishment. But it boded ill for the first Evangelical minister to reach the district – Francis MacBean, now an ordained minister of the Secession Church and who had won her commission as a Highland evangelist.[13] At first he worked on the margins of his native Lochaber, and then by Loch Sunart, and later in the Uists – there is still a *Cnoc Mhic-bheathain*, 'MacBean's Hillock', on North Uist, on which spot he presumably preached.

To John Morrison's surprise, and mounting resentment, MacBean then fetched up on Harris in the early 1830s, and soon built up an impressive Secession congregation, their first in all the Hebrides. It is difficult not to think that *Gobha na Hearadh* felt personally threatened, in his office and importance, and responded with little more than personal spite. Certainly, Francis MacBean miscalculated in organising a Secession Communion on Harris and assuring his new parishioners that *Maighstir Ruaraidh* himself would preach at it, for Rev. Roderick MacLeod was embroiled in war with his own Presbytery of Skye over the question of baptism and most would have shared MacBean's view that he would finally lose the day and secede, if he were not deposed first.

But – on appeal to the General Assembly – MacLeod won. He did not secede and he did not come to Harris. There was acute disappointment, MacBean was left looking silly and the Harris Blacksmith took full advantage, taunting him publicly and writing two satirical songs, *Seisean Shrannda*, 'The Kirk Session of Strond', and *Na Sgiobairean*, 'The Captains', as malicious as they were profane. The Communion was held, and some of the tokens Mr MacBean had prepared for the occasion still survive, with the inscription, *Fraing Macbheathain, Ministeir, 1836* on one side and the usual portion of Scripture on the other.

But neither his confidence, his authority nor the congregation he had so painfully gathered could survive the onslaught, and one has to admire the patience with which MacBean bore the deepest hurt. Later he returned to the Established Church, and in 1843 cast his lot in with the Free, soon becoming the first Free Church minister of Fort Augustus and Glen Moriston, where – despite his extreme views on baptism – he was respected and loved. Francis MacBean had left sufficient of independent spirit in the Harris people, though, to embolden them in the crisis of 1893.

Robert Finlayson, no less principled but much more of what we would now call a 'people-person', is best remembered for his very long pastorate in Lochs, which he took up on 15 June 1831.

The new minister enjoyed a decent church, manse and glebe at Keose; but his charge was no sinecure. Indeed, its vast bounds require, even in the twenty-first century, the combined labours of five Free Church ministers. In 1831, it was bigger than several Scottish counties, including even the villages of Carloway and Shawbost; Finlayson had to preach at least once a quarter in this district, and notes bleakly himself – in the Statistical Account of 1833 – that, save when he was in Carloway, there was no service at all. The new church at Keose, which could hold 700, was the only place of worship in all the bounds of Lochs, which boasted dozens of villages and around 500 families – but not a single road.

Lewis has had greater intellects in its church than Robert Finlayson, and better preachers, but no minister has ever been so loved; certainly, none in the Long Island's history, as MacPhail observed, so fulfilled that potency of which Robert Murray McCheyne spoke – 'it is not great gifts that God blesses, but great likeness to Christ.' Placid, affectionate, unhurried and good-humoured, Finlayson is in striking contrast to the firm manliness of MacRae, the prim piety of Cook or the remote and authoritarian MacLeod.

His sermons, rich in illustration and pithy saying, were as entertaining as they were arresting, and as captivating as they were solemn. He had a diverting way of addressing Bible characters in the pulpit, and MacFarlane records many examples. 'O Paul, Paul. It's yourself that was the grand DD! What small fry, in comparison, our pulpits now offer!' 'Ho, ho, Noah! What a wonderful admiral you, of this Ark! Many an old crock has floated the seas, but yours was the strangest of the ships of the world's fleets, and your cargo the most amazing. . . .' But his sermon on Noah's builders was still more arresting.

When the Ark was finished a group of the carpenters called in for their wages. They knocked and Mrs Noah came to the door. 'Is Noah in?' 'No, he's away at the stormy Butt of Lewis for a hull for the Ark.' A few days afterwards they called again. 'Is Noah at home?' 'No, he's away to hilly Uig for a ram.' They came again and found Noah at home. They asked for their wages, and he paid them. Then they went to Stornoway and called for whisky and brandy, and they drank themselves into wild revelry. They were shouting and singing their songs and dancing their drunken dance when – lo! – a thunderbolt crashed and the rains began. What peal of thunders! The like was never heard before. The heavens poured in torrents. The public house was flooded and a river rushed through it and rose with appalling rapidity. Then did the mocking carpenters cry. But the Ark was closed and Mercy's day was gone. O people of Lochs, God's Ark stands open for you today. But the day of the closed door is coming.'

He had a droll, unthreatening way of addressing awkward moments. The deplorable state of a crude meeting-house at Eishken bothered Robert Finlayson, and he once spoke of it in the Keose pulpit – he had met a big Bible, he said, walking in the Eishken road. 'Oh Bible, why are you sad and where are you going?' 'Oh, I'm leaving Eishken meeting-house. The big drops of sooty rain that fall on me there blacken my pages and waste me badly.' Half-enchanted, half-affronted, the folk of Eishken overhauled the building that very week. Early in his ministry, he visited a local weaver, who assured him he had recently become a Christian. 'Go, go,' carolled Mr Finlayson, as if to an unseen messenger, 'and tell the people of the district the good news that Donald the weaver is converted.' He then asked a few gentle questions, which quickly exposed the darkness of the man's heart and the emptiness of his profession, and called again, 'Run, run, recall the courier, for Donald is not yet converted.' There are many stories of his absent-mindedness – he would lose things in pockets, or put away a sum of money and forget where – but that was inevitable in a conscientious man whose head was stuffed with Scripture and who seemed constantly to be framing sermons. In later years he became a convinced Premillennialist,[14] like McCheyne and the Bonar brothers and others soon affectionately dubbed the 'Evangelical Light Infantry' – but this view, that Christ will return to Jerusalem and reign for a thousand years over an earthly kingdom, has never been part of traditional Reformed theology and never caught on in Lewis or the Highlands.

Finlayson's most abiding work was done in the homes and townships of his people, making his unhurried way about on a little white pony that was soon as beloved as himself. Even church discipline could be admin-istered without self-indulgent bile. 'Fergus, it is not because of your stature the women are so fond of you,' he once affectionately berated a man who had to stand before the congregation for notorious and most fecund immorality, 'Fergus, it is not on account of your beauty that you

are such a favourite with the women', and so on. Years after his induction,
Dr Charles MacRae of Stornoway – a son of the Barvas minister –
playfully asked a lad from Lochs if there were still fairies down there. 'No,'
came the solemn reply, 'they all left when Mr Finlayson came.'

Mr Finlayson had one mortifying difficulty, though it is doubtful how
much he was aware of it. His wife, a MacAulay from Uig, was kindliness
personified; but she was also a cousin of one of the most notorious
criminals in Lewis history, Robert Stronach,[15] who was the son of the
innkeeper at Garve in Wester Ross. A psychopath, a murderer, he ended
up in Lewis, around 1831, skulking the hills of Uig and Park and Harris
as an outlaw and a fugitive, and to this *Mac an t-Sronaich*, who is still a
veritable bogeyman to the children of the Long Island, an improbable
number of killings are credited – most done simply for fun, if the story can
be believed.

Nevertheless, Stronach was a cousin of Mrs Finlayson, and it is said she
took care to leave a lair for him in a barn of the Manse of Keose, where he
could always privily help himself to provisions and kip on a bed of straw
for the night. Though his history is still shrouded in confusion – and it
has no doubt since been politic to credit murders to him rather than to
your next-door neighbour's great-granduncle – the law finally caught up
with Stronach, who was duly hanged on the mainland. He is said to have
declared on the gallows,

> *Seachd bliadhna ghleidh thu tearuint' mi*
> *a mhointich, riabhaich Leodhais;*
> *Agus fhad 's a ghleidh mis' thus*
> *Ghleidh thusa mis' . . .*

> For seven years you safely kept me
> O brindled moors of Lewis;
> And as long as I kept to you
> you preserved me . . .

If Mrs Finlayson had indeed aided and abetted his continued flight
from justice, she got away with it. But dreadful tragedy did befall the
Finlaysons, in 1849, six years after the Disruption. Two of their teenage
sons joined friends for a pleasant fishing trip on Loch Erisort. The boat
capsized and Robert, who was seventeen, and his brother John, who was
only fourteen, drowned in full sight of their father's manse. He wept over
the bodies as they were laid out, cold and lifeless, in his parlour, but
insisted on keeping Sabbath sermon as usual, even before they were
buried, and to have preached that day with singular power. Privately, his

faith was tested in full measure. 'Robert, this is hard on flesh and blood,' remarked a well-meaning friend, braced to unleash a flood of spiritual commonplaces. 'Indeed,' said Robert Finlayson, 'and it is hard on grace itself.' Few Christians, then or today, are so honest and human in the face of horror; whatever faith we are given, as MacAulay has written in another context, will be tried in full measure.

His most celebrated sermon, according to Norman MacFarlane, was on the Prodigal's return: specifically, his father's call for the best robe to be draped about him. ' "What Robe is this?" asked the father. "It is the robe of Unfallen Man's Righteousness." "Ah, it's very beautiful, but that is not the best. In that garb Adam fell." Another, white and more shining, was brought. "What," asked the Father, "is this?" "This is the robe of the Angels that surround the Throne and adore their Lord." "Ah, it's very fine, but there is a better." At length one of exquisite loveliness was brought, and the Father asked, "What is this?" "This was woven amid the awful splendours of Calvary. Its every thread was a pang. It is the choice robe of Thy Son's sufferings. It is the Righteousness of Christ." "Yes," said the Father, "that is the best robe. Put it on this, my lost son, who has come home again . . ." '

Finlayson could on occasion be wry, if never sharp. 'Rise, man, rise,' he said, at a prayer meeting at the height of this Lewis Awakening, when a fellow he had called on to pray showed obvious hesitation, 'for there are people here who would gladly give me a crown were I to ask them to pray.' Towards the end of his life, when he had finally quit so demanding a charge for ministry at Helmsdale, there is something almost wistful in his observation to a man who similarly dithered at a Fellowship Meeting in that Sutherland town. 'Rise, rise, Sir – I saw a day on a green knoll in Lewis, and you would not be asked to rise.' Robert Finlayson 'came out' at the Disruption of 1843, and took every soul in Lochs with him; so did his three Evangelical colleagues on Lewis, but only he stayed on the island, and thus cemented himself in Long Island affections.

Men like John MacRae and Robert Finlayson instinctively appeal to a modern age: robust, tender, of immense humanity and considerable humour. Finlay Cook and Francis MacBean represent really a subtly different, long-established Highland brand of vintage spirituality, which can trace its roots directly to the very Reformation and, in its earnest badinage and profundity and distrust of the modern, is best seen today in the Free Presbyterian Church. But the pattern of Evangelical ministry set for all of them on Lewis was established by Alexander MacLeod.

MacLeod was not all together admirable. It is difficult to square his private observations in some points with his obsequious letters to the

Lady Elizabeth and, while he may privately have deplored parishioners being turfed off long-held lands for his nice new glebe, he certainly did nothing to prevent it. Much moved by word of the dreadful things happening in his native Sutherland, he began so often to refer to the evictions in his preaching, and with such venom, that Mary MacArthur of Breasclete had once to rebuke him for raising his voice like that: he ought, she said, to keep his temper in God's house. Yet he had himself precipitated evictions for his own greed. A cross note unearthed from estate records by Bill Lawson still survives.[16] 'The Timsgarry tenants are not willing to move to make a glebe for Mr MacLeod, and have been told that they are not bound to do so without warning. Mr MacLeod expected much more for pasture than the factor could allow. Only allowed grass for the one horse and two cows they are entitled to after having an arable glebe set apart, and just now MacLeod has twelve large milk cows and a bull and seems to expect as much to continue.'

A kitchen-garden, some land for sheep and a house-cow are one thing, but a minister who already enjoyed an annual stipend of £150 – unfathomable, unimaginable riches to his parishioners – can only have maintained a dairy herd of such proportions to make yet more money. These aspects of *Maighistir Alasdair* are, of course, absent from any Evangelical hagiography. And it had consequences; the crofters 'of course lost the land at the next term day', records Lawson.

Even Murdo MacAulay, not himself noted, in post-war Lewis, for any aversion to the exercise of doughty leadership, concedes that the minister of Uig could be despotic. 'In matters of discipline Mr MacLeod ruled like an autocrat. It is said that when his people went to the Stornoway Communion, thirty miles away, he did not permit them to transact any business, or enter any shop or office, if they were supposed to be there for spiritual purposes only. Even after the service on Monday they were supposed to go back to Uig and, if they had any such business, come back to Stornoway again on Tuesday.' Certainly he was censorious. Once, engaged in that uniquely Presbyterian duty of 'fencing the Tables' – an address just before the communicants come forward, designed to identify who are invited truly to that Table and who should be debarred – he did so with such enthusiasm and rigour that Duncan Matheson himself, no slouch in polemic, later remarked, 'He debarred everyone in the congregation; he debarred me; and in my opinion he debarred himself.'

Yet Professor George Smeaton, a noted Free Church divine after the Disruption, gave it as his opinion that, of all the awakenings he knew, that under Alexander MacLeod's ministry in Uig was the purest revival in the history of the Scottish church, only that on Arran surpassing it 'in freedom from wildfire and fanaticism. It was so free from excesses, and its fruit was so lasting.' MacPhail makes plain how, throughout Lewis, the new faith had not only transformed devotional habits but transformed conduct, to the point when visitors would speak in wonder of a 'street of song' – they had walked through a village just as every household was embarked on family worship – and where, in all the West Side, only two villages – Dalmore and Dalbeag – did *not* hold prayer meetings, so that Alexander MacLeod could refer darkly to *fithich nan Dailean*; the 'ravens of the dells'.

It is of this new island that an eyewitness could write,[17] 'At all hours, from eight p.m. to one a.m., I have heard people at prayer as I passed by.' An anonymous naval captain, whose ship lay off Lewis for months and who had abundant opportunity to explore the place, spoke of what he came across in words still cherished. 'They are an extraordinary people here. One cannot but be struck with their honesty, kindness and sobriety. I think I have never seen a drunk person out of the town. One hears of religion elsewhere, but one sees it here in everything.'

Alexander MacLeod would quit Lewis in 1844, being for three years Free Church minister of Lochalsh before a much longer pastorate in Rogart, where his imprecations against everything from dances, witch-craft and gay apparel to tea-leaf reading soon provoked hate-mail; and where he never again experienced the 'Pentecostal glories' of his Lewis pastorate. He was never, in fact, the pulpit star. John MacRae framed delicately his tribute to an old colleague – that MacLeod's sermons were 'a striking instance of how the foolishness of preaching was made effective by God' – yet had to add, besides, as MacAulay paraphrases, that 'the finest moral spectacle he had ever witnessed during his whole career was that of the congregation of Uig under the pastorate of Alexander MacLeod.'[18]

8

'The Church of Scotland, Free'

Big MacRae and the Disruption, 1843–1876

It was 1842, feelings in the Church of Scotland were running high, and it was a packed meeting in Lochcarron. Tonight, though, John MacRae – past colleague of MacLeod in Uig, now minister of Knockbain – had just given his talk, and now listened to an ally. The Church was in crisis; the Highlands had to be informed. All now knew a great Disruption loomed, under Evangelical leadership. But the Moderates thought otherwise and one blowhard, in Lochcarron this night, began to mock the present speaker. When John MacRae told him to be quiet, the gentleman flushed. 'And I knew you right well too, when you used to be hunting foxes in the hills above us . . .'

'Quite right,' roared the Rev. John MacRae, to the convulsed delight of his audience, 'and I see I did not get them all!'

No Highland minister is as cherished and defining a figure as *MacRath Mor*, Big MacRae.[1] Mighty of build, merry, practical and spiritual, he stood nonsense from no one and embodies ancient Celtic ideals. He and Chalmers were perhaps the greatest Scottish preachers of Victorian Scotland. And MacRae eclipses Alexander MacLeod or anyone else as the quintessential Lewis minister, certainly the greatest the Long Island has ever seen. John MacRae began his ministry on Lewis; won his wife on Lewis; ended his ministry on Lewis; and he did more than anyone else to shape the Free Church we see here today. The common sense, the realism, the wry and knowing humour both of the frailties of human nature and the impossibility of attaining a 'pure church' are an abiding MacRae legacy and go much way to explain, for instance, the very limited Lewis support, decades later, for the Free Presbyterian movement.

Born in 1794, at Achadh nan Gart in Kintail, MacRae was the youngest of but six survivors in a family of twelve. He was still only a baby when they removed to Ardelve, in the Lochalsh district. And, though he grew to be an affable enough youth, John MacRae was of intimidating appearance, tall and muscled, oozing pugnacity. There were two distinct lines of the Clan MacRae – the 'Fair' and the 'Black' – and someone once asked the stockman as to which his own people were. 'The fair,' said John MacRae. 'Then God have mercy on the black.'

It was a troubled childhood. His schooling ended when his father went bankrupt. Grown, MacRae tried his hand at fishing and shepherding. Later, in rather more remote terrain south of Loch Duich, he acquired and with another friend worked a holding on the slopes of Mam Ratagan, which today a precipitous winding road ascends for Kylerhea ferry.

The young bruiser drank, roistered, swore. He once hunted down and hammered men who had mugged his colleague; better still, he recovered the money. He had a booming voice and was a born sailor, warrior, leader, as passionate and robust as Columba himself. Even as a Christian, he retained real Highland spirit. Once, in Aberdeen, a lout knocked a hole in the divinity student's hat. In a moment the aghast man was on his back, with a knee on his chest and huge hands at his throat. 'John . . . John . . . remember grace!' yelped an aghast fellow-student. 'But for grace,' snarled MacRae, 'the beggar would never breathe again.'

Evangelicalism had at last reached the West Highland seaboard, enjoying a bridgehead at Lochcarron under the successive ministries of Aeneas Sage and Lachlan MacKenzie.[2] A notable preacher took it still further. In 1813, John MacDonald became minister of Ferintosh. Born in Reay, Caithness, in 1779, he was baptised in extraordinary circumstances: his parents, carrying him in determined search for their Moderate minister, finally found the man on the frosty moor looking for game. He baptised the mite there and then, smashing an iced pool with the butt of his fowling-piece for the necessary water.

After service at Achreny, a stint as minister of Edinburgh's Gaelic Chapel and now secure on the Black Isle, John MacDonald began increasingly to roam the Highlands. 'The droning "Moderates", who delivered their sermons half-asleep themselves to congregations which they effectively put to sleep Sabbath after Sabbath, were very wide awake when the rousing preacher from Ferintosh appeared among them,' enthuses Beaton. A complaint was brought against him to the General Assembly, and a motion was duly passed forbidding such liberties in future, though, as some angrily observed, those who sought to silence MacDonald had happily protected a colleague who had not preached in his own congregation in seven months.

John MacDonald was so important an evangelist he has been immortalised as 'the Apostle of the North'. Unfortunately, his well-rounded humanity was largely buried in Dr John Kennedy's worshipful biography – publicly disowned by Dr MacDonald's own son, writing angrily to a Highland newspaper in 1865. 'Whilst I most warmly thank the reviewer for his kind observations respecting my father, I cannot condemn the book itself too strongly. It is precisely what I had expected from the author of "The Days of the Fathers in Ross-shire". It smacks strongly of superstition and of whining mock-piety. It is disfigured, too, by blotches of bad taste and arrant bigotry. It is, in fact, nothing short of an attempt to expose to ridicule a departed champion of true religion, and to blacken the memory of one of the most charitable of men.'[3] Though over the top, he had grasped how Highland Evangelicalism had been reinvented by a prim, intimidated new generation of ministers. MacRae fascinates because he resisted this trend – driven by overreaction to the abiding forces of North Country Separatism – to the end of his life. Kennedy, by contrast, had seen Separatism almost destroy his father's career, and was overly anxious for his own.

The Ferintosh manse had been a happy, grounded place. 'Dr Mac-Donald was himself a piper, and local tradition has it that after the preaching there was always dancing for which he would play merrily on the pipes. He would always play, too, after officiating at a wedding, but he would put a strict time limit on the festivities . . . Evander MacIver, factor to Duncan Davidson at Tulloch, says in his memoirs, "I used to see as merry dancing in Dr MacDonald's house as anywhere, when many folks thought that it was a sin to dance."'[4] And on Dr MacDonald's death, in 1849, amidst the Evangelical warmth of that time no one had thought it either unusual or unseemly when his widow – her account-book survives – spent the usual £4 10s. on his oak coffin; but over £9 on whisky for the mourners.[5] He was, besides, a gifted Gaelic bard whose hymns are still sung.

Yet this was a man of meticulously ordered routine, as his diary confirms. 'From 7 to 9 am – Private devotion; 9 to 10 – Family worship and breakfast; 10 to 3 pm – Parochial duties, study etc.; 3 to 4 – Dinner; 4 to 5 – Study; 5 to 6 – Tea and conversation; 6 to 9 – Private devotion and study; 9 to 10 – Family worship and supper; 10 to 11 – Private devotions; 11 to 7 am – Sleep and dressing.'[6] And his preaching tours were protracted and prodigious. We have already noted MacDonald's visits to Lewis and Harris, but we should outline his repeated visits to St Kilda,[7] much later grossly misrepresented. The facts are as follows. Burdened to make his first visit in 1822, at the express behest of the SSPCK, he took the time to make a detailed census and, on return, set busily to work to raise funds for a proper church.

There is a lot of nonsense spoken of St Kilda, which through the nineteenth century became a major tourist attraction, with damaging consequences.[8] It was no Arcadia. Nor were they a lost tribe who had endured for millennia; almost all the islanders died in a smallpox epidemic, around 1728, and only eleven survived. The island was quickly repopulated from Skye. The 'St Kilda Parliament' of popular belief was but a media stunt; obliging menfolk posed by a Victorian photographer. Practically everything still retailed as evidence of a unique St Kildan lifestyle, from their sea-fowling habits to their alarming folk-medicine, was then general in the Hebrides. Their later ministers would certainly be vilified by a succession of gentleman-writers. But John MacKay and Angus Fiddes strongly resented the exploitation of their flock by patronising visitors. Fiddes was so devoted to his people he personally did a course in midwifery, familiarising himself with the new concept of asepsis, in a successful bid to end the infantile tetanus (or 'seven-day sickness') that killed so many babies. Scorned journalists took vindictive revenge, but recent, sober studies have annihilated long-established libels.

Dr MacDonald came in 1822, though, as a troubled missionary to a place utterly neglected by the Church. By the time he left, he thought five or six were truly awakened and that the St Kildans as a whole were now anxious about eternal things. 'When all was got ready, about nine o'clock, and we had been taking leave of the inhabitants, all of them in a body (children not excepted) followed us to the shore, and amidst cries and tears, in which my landlord and I were brought to share, we shook hands with them and bid them a final adieu. . . . After we got under way, they ascended the brow of a steep hill, and sat, following us with their eye, till our little bark, at the distance of fifteen or twenty miles, became no more visible.'

When he returned there was great joy and on his third trip in 1830 – church buildings had now been erected – Dr MacDonald brought their very own minister, Rev. Neil MacKenzie, who would be supported by the SSPCK. An enduring Christian faith was established on St Kilda, which adhered solidly to the Free and later the United Free Church. There is no evidence that their new faith brought to their lives anything but good. St Kilda's final – and requested – evacuation, in 1930, was the consequence of sustained depopulation and their learned dependency on vulnerable mainland supply-lines; and she was not the only island, in the last century, to be deserted.

MacDonald's wider travels took him to South Uist, and he even managed a preaching tour of Ireland, having invested a few weeks in Irish Gaelic study – drawing great crowds and priestly opposition. Wherever he went, he drew multitudes. 'What is that man's secret?' someone once asked Thomas Chalmers. 'I'll tell you John MacDonald's secret,' said he. 'He preaches justification by faith alone.' It was a shrewd insight. Even in the Highland church, and even now, there is an inveterate tendency to one form or another of 'Christianity plus'; to make belief in Christ complicated.

And the Apostle wrote some affectionate verse about St Kilda; his
poetic parting is still quoted in the Hebrides:

> 'S a nis, mur faic mi sibh tuilleadh,
> Mo shoraidh dhuibh uile 's mo ghradh;
> Is, gu'm bu slan dhuibh fa dheireadh,
> Aig am cuir na cruinne na small.[9]

> And now if I don't see you again
> farewell and my love to you all;
> and may you all be well
> when the universe is ablaze . . .

John MacRae's conversion was protracted. The early death of a Christian
sister sobered him. Then – when the wandering preacher joined his road-
gang at Mam Ratagan for a bite to eat – something in Finlay Munro's
grace lodged in his mind. Months later, Dr MacDonald himself was
conducting an open-air service near Lochcarron, when MacRae went by
with a great flock of sheep; he may well have done so deliberately, to
distract the congregation. But he could not help remembering what he
heard. He finally found peace under the preaching of Angus Mackintosh,
minister of Tain, at Ferintosh Communion. MacRae soon determined to
enter the ministry.

He quickly made up lost educational ground and shocked younger
students in Aberdeen by besting them in algebra. In Edinburgh, he
developed an abiding regard for Thomas Chalmers, who now taught
theology and shared his love of mathematics, and Chalmers took greatly
to him. It was a long course, and MacRae spent his summer vacations
teaching. At Arnisdale, south of Glenelg, he took services as well as
school; and a revival broke out there, 'a work of grace . . . as striking and
as satisfactory as he at all saw in his entire career', his son-in-law much
later memorialised. We have noted his adventures in Uig: in 1830, John
MacRae was licensed, spent time as an assistant minister in Gairloch, and
in 1833 was settled as Finlay Cook's successor in Cross.

There his preaching disturbed uneasy consciences, and one local ned
decided to teach the pastor a lesson. He confronted him on the highway
and challenged the minister to a fight. MacRae calmly doffed his coat and
the fellow fled. Later, he got hold of the hide of a recently slaughtered
cow – head, horns and all – and, on a gloomy night waylaid MacRae on
the road as his horse trotted by. After repeated warnings, MacRae
dismounted, and had a good swing at what proved a very corporeal
demon, who was flattened by a single blow. Again, he could only run

away and – in due time – came to apologise. This man was subsequently converted and, when MacRae left in 1836, he was an elder.

Another tale is still more characteristic. The minister of Cross had joined a party of men who sailed on a day from Ness to Stornoway, in an open sailing boat. 'On the return passage a great storm arose. After rounding Tolsta Head, where the great Atlantic leaps and roars against the sea gates of the Lews, the oarsmen, who had toiled until they were bone-weary, were about to give up. The rage of the mounting waves crushed them. MacRae's early sailoring came now to his aid with compound interest. He rallied the men, and threatened them. It was his threatening that roused them. He said he would apply the tiller to the first man who ceased rowing. He was not now their minister, but their skipper. Their experience that day enhanced Mr MacRae in their eyes, and his people feared him with a growing fear.' But he was no less regarded and respected; and his new wife – the beautiful Penelope MacKenzie, from Bayble in Point – was universally loved. There was real distress when, in 1839, MacRae accepted a call to Knockbain, on the Black Isle. He was succeeded by Rev. John Finlayson, a Skyeman, inducted in 1840.

The Disruption of 1843 is the defining event of Victorian Scotland.[10] From the late eighteenth century, mounting demand for Evangelical ministers magnified the outrage of patronage. But other factors hastened the crisis. An ancient Gaelic social order was in advanced collapse. New religion now offered literacy, dignity and meaning. Meanwhile, the Industrial Revolution had swept through the Lowlands and hosts – in only a few decades – forsook rural Scotland for new lives in the central belt. All this brought new, dreadful social division:[11] the wealthy, the burgeoning middle class, the skilled working class and, 'probably largest of all', write Drummond and Bulloch of the miserable unskilled masses in the new slums, 'who lived in an appalling and secluded poverty, without influence in politics and who, so far as the Christian Church was concerned, were heathen, unless when Roman Catholic. This was the silent factor in all the debates and battles of the Church in Victorian Scotland.'

Tensions long building finally took a critical turn in 1834. In that year the Evangelical party gained, and held, control of the General Assembly. Thereafter they fought for reform, renewal and – in a phrase widely used – for the 'crown-rights of Christ', the sole Head of the Church. Under Chalmers' leadership, the Church fought to erect additional parishes and sought support and endowment from the government. Whitehall could not care less and the Secession Church, of course, lobbied ferociously against any State aid for her hated rival. An 1836 Royal Commission decided the Kirk's demands were unjustified – more evidence of London indifference to Presbyterial realities in Scotland; and, indeed, the blame for the Disruption must rest ultimately with a contemptuous Parliament, who knew little of Scottish needs and refused to address them.

Thus the Kirk embarked on the 'Ten Years' Conflict'. Even as Chalmers directed fund-raising for church extension, war was waged on patronage. In 1834 the General Assembly passed the Veto Act, granting in every parish the absolute right of a majority of 'male heads of families' to reject an unpopular presentation by the landlord. From our perspective, the Veto Act seems only fair, preventing an unwanted pastoral settlement. In 1834 the gentry thought it the stuff of bloody revolution. And it was quickly tested in Auchterarder, Perthshire. Of 336 heads of families, 286 expressed their adamant disapproval and only two would sign the call of the laird's nominee, Robert Young. He appealed, but the 1835 Assembly rejected his case. Young sued. In 1838 the Court of Session sensationally found for him, ruling that the Veto Act was illegal.

The Seceders rejoiced; the Evangelicals were humiliated. The General Assembly appealed to the House of Lords who duly found for Young and flatly decreed that the courts of the Church were in all things subordinate to the courts of the land. 'The ignorance and contemptuous slightness of the judgement did great mischief,' sighed Lord Cockburn. 'It irritated and justified the people of Scotland in believing that their Church was sacrificed to English prejudices. . . . We shall soon see what the Church means to do.'

The battle in Auchterarder ground on and it would be after the Disruption before Robert Young was finally inducted. By 1839, thirty-nine other cases of disputed patronage were clogging the Scottish courts. The most celebrated fell in the parish of Marnoch, within the bounds of the Presbytery of Strathbogie. In this instance, the male heads of families had emphatically rejected the first nominee, but approved a second. But the first minister promptly appealed and the Court of Session ruled that the second 'presentation' was not to proceed. Under fantastic pressure from all sides, and by a narrow majority, the Presbytery of Strathbogie decided to obey the civil law. The guilty men were almost immediately suspended by the Kirk, went to law and were upheld by the Court of Session. These suspended ministers then blithely inducted the detested candidate, amidst national outrage.

The lines of battle were now clearly drawn. To the civil authorities, supported enthusiastically by most Moderates, a patron had an absolute and untrammelled right of presentation. To the Evangelicals, the Court of Session was but an agent of tyranny: the Church's internal discipline, her pastoral settlements, were matters in which the civil law of Scotland had absolutely no right to interfere. The Kirk besought politicians and Parliament for reform. There was vague talk, but nothing was done. In 1842 the General Assembly adopted a dramatic, well-argued Claim of Right, detailing the despotism under which she laboured, and sent it to Queen Victoria herself. At the eleventh hour, in February 1843, a petition was laid before the Commons supported by the overwhelming majority of Scottish MPs. It was duly dismissed.

It has become fashionable, even among the Free Presbyterians and in pietistic Free Church circles today, to deplore the Disruption. This is fantastic and absurd. The Church of Scotland had been denied by government, in 1836, the authority and resources properly to do her job. Her people were denied the right to call the ministers they wanted. Her church courts found their authority and their decisions routinely overturned on civil appeal. It was intolerable, and only the Disruption itself and the astonishing success of the new Free Church finally, decades on, secured liberty for the Auld Kirk.

The most eminent Evangelical leaders – men like Thomas Chalmers, Robert Candlish and William Cunningham – prepared prayerfully for the breach. Assessment was made of the spiritual needs of every parish. Plans were drawn up for new buildings. Detailed financial arrangements were laid for a body supported entirely by congregational contributions and on a national scale. The people had to be readied for the division – grounded thoroughly in the principles involved. When the break came, they would leave behind every stick of property. There would be no attempt to occupy church buildings. Otherwise, Chalmers knew, their cause would be morally compromised. Besides, the new arrangements for money – a great Sustentation Fund – would be as egalitarian and levelling as possible. All ministers would be paid the same stipend; all congregations – great or small – would pay in as much as they can afford.

It is also most important to grasp that Evangelicals had no intention at all of splitting the *Church*. By exercise of their General Assembly majority, the Church of Scotland as a whole – and as a body – would break with the State. It failed because of another vindictive Court of Session judgement in 1842, declaring that ministers of parliamentary and *quoad sacra* charges had no right to seats in church courts. At a stroke, the Evangelicals lost their majority in the Assembly; otherwise the Church of Scotland could have officially broken with the State and indeed subjected any who refused to 'come out' with church discipline.[12] Now, Disruption must of necessity be a departure from the Church itself, and many potential supporters drew back. It must be remembered, after all, that any minister who 'came out' would do so at considerable personal cost, losing his home, social status and what was often a very comfortable living.

In the event the breach, on 18 May 1843, at St Andrew's Kirk in Edinburgh, was deftly stage-managed. The retiring Moderator, Dr Welsh read a Protest while he still occupied the chair. He then rose, bowed to the Lord High Commissioner – representing the Queen herself – and led his fellow Evangelicals out into George Street watched by an adoring multitude. All then processed down the hill to Tanfield Hall, and there was duly constituted the first General Assembly of the Church of Scotland, Free.

Out of 1,195 ministers in the Established Church, a full 470 – on the Tuesday after the Disruption – duly signed the 'Act of Separation and Deed of Demission', forfeiting between them an annual revenue of more than £100,000. And the damage to the Kirk was still greater: 'within their ranks', as the biographers of Thomas Guthrie assert, 'was contained beyond controversy a very large proportion of the talent and piety of the Scottish ministry.'[13] Lord Cockburn grasped the gravity of her position:

> The notion that the secession has done positive good to the Church – which is what some sulky railers pretend – is nonsense. Neither is it true that the Establishment cannot survive even the immediate effects of the very peculiar blow by which it has been smote. It is no doubt sorely crippled. What was its soul is gone, and gone to animate a hostile power. But, for the present, it will survive all this. It is for the future that it has to tremble. The charm that was in the very words, "The Church of Scotland", is broken. To a greatly increased extent it has ceased to be the Church of the people. The contrast between the popular zeal of Dissent and the official coldness of Establishment is always against any Church . . .'[14]

A majority of Highland ministers – seventy-nine – 'came out', and the great mass of Highland people. The minister of Harris, Mr Bethune, clung to the Establishment, as did the two Lewis Moderates, William MacRae of Barvas and John Cameron of Stornoway; but John Finlayson of Cross, Duncan Matheson of Knock, Robert Finlayson of Lochs and Alexander MacLeod himself all joined the Free Church of Scotland. Highland strength had little to do with landlords or the Clearances; the big factor was Evangelicalism. Over nine-tenths of Presbyterians in the Highlands flocked to the Free Church, including the mass of folk on the Long Island.[15]

Only about 460 of the 23,000-strong population of Lewis stayed in the

Kirk. In Uig,[16] local tradition assures us that only two women in the entire parish adhered to the Established Church – a young girl and a crone of a hundred. (They were wickedly dubbed 'the hundred and one'.) Alexander MacLeod had, of course, to vacate his manse and take up residence in a Reef cottage, 'unsuitable,' we are darkly told, 'to his circumstance as a minister'. At least he could stay in Uig. Forced to quit their manses, Robert Finlayson and Duncan Matheson moved for the moment to Stornoway with their families, renting accommodation and travelling out of town to tend their respective congregations. In Lochs, only one man had stuck by the Established Church. It was just the same in Cross – as recently as 1920, my late grandmother could remember only two people who attended Established Church services – and Big MacRae himself, still loosed from his Knockbain pulpit, attested in 1844 that on Harris '4,000 of the people are conscientiously attached to the Free Church', which was practically everyone. On Lewis the Lady Elizabeth was a keen supporter – and even attended that first Free Church General Assembly. In 1844, though, Sir James Matheson bought Lewis on the profits of a very dubious past in the China seas – 'a dreadful man, one MacDrug,' lamented Disraeli, 'with a pound of opium in each pocket'. Sir James proved generally benevolent, though his sustained paternalism was not always competent and some of his factors were bad men. But he was tolerant of the Free Church.

Where landlords elsewhere fiercely opposed the Free Church cause, tales of harassment are legion. The minister of North Uist, Norman MacLeod, had built a manse at Truimisgarry and at his own expense. He was now locked out of it, and the MacLeods had to repair to an inferior cottage twenty miles away. A crude Free Church was built from turf and stones by its harried congregation. It was demolished by factors and those involved in its erection – if identified – were evicted from their homes.

On St Kilda, where every single resident had embraced the Free Church, their use of the solitary church and school was forbidden until 1857. On Harris, a new proprietor – the Earl of Dunmore – refused sites for years. Examples of yet nastier persecution are well documented – and Ansdell describes events in Kilmallie and Strontian, for instance: while site-refusal was not, in fact, widespread, it did create a useful narrative of martyrdom, doing much not only to foster Free Church solidarity but a new, real sense of Highland dignity.

Yet there was an acute, national shortage of Gaelic ministers, and Lewis pastors – hitherto unwanted and stranded in a community remote and desperately poor – were quickly courted by prosperous charges elsewhere. And this had fateful consequences. By the end of 1844, Alexander MacLeod, Duncan Matheson and John Finlayson had all fled

Lewis; a betrayal remembered with real bitterness. (Finlayson found no happiness in his new Skye parish. He was shortly killed in a carriage accident.) John Cameron in Stornoway, still an Established minister but with a much reduced congregation, also quit the island. Thus, at a most unsettling point in their history, the people of Lewis were deserted by their ablest leaders. A mild distrust of ministers became, understandably, a festering anticlericalism.

John MacRae had lobbied all over the north in preparation for the Disruption. He was now again loosed from Knockbain to roam the 'destitute districts' as a superintendent pastor. He was not always tactful. Presiding at a Fort William Communion – the crowd was such that services had to be held in the local burial ground – MacRae (himself of ruffian stock) went rather too far. 'People of Lochaber,' he roared, 'seed of the thieves and the murderers, you are there sitting on the graves of your fathers where their bodies are rotting and their souls are roasting in Hell . . .!'[17]

The better to ease his wide-ranging travels, John MacRae and other Gaelic-speaking agents needed a boat – a substantial one. So the Free Church built one: a 30-ton rigged schooner, the *Breadalbane*.[18] She was described as 'safe, fast and excellent', had comfortable accommodation for six – plus her master and four crew – and was perfectly suited for the job. Capable even of voyaging to St Kilda, she bore twenty-two ministers on Free Church business in 1845. The next year, she took forty-six, and carried besides suitable Free Church literature. When potato blight – and famine – ravaged the West Highlands, as it ravaged Ireland, true disaster was widely averted by a Free Church programme of famine relief, using the *Breadalbane* to deliver food. Some fatalities there indeed were, but nothing like the Irish disaster.

The Free Church moved urgently to address the spiritual needs of the region and supply Gaelic ministers. And the specific needs of the Long Island were discussed. As early as 1843, a full-time catechist was appointed for the Back district – the coast west of Broad Bay from Tong to Tolsta, hitherto in the Stornoway parish – and in 1845, by which time 1,700 Free Church adherents had been counted, it was agreed without hesitation that this should be a sanctioned charge with its own minister. It was 1858, though, before a manse was built and the first minister,[19] Donald MacMaster – a native of Lochaber and whose wife, Jane, was John MacRae's daughter – was only ordained and inducted in February 1859. They used to enjoy romantic little drives in their trap, and sometimes cheerfully made their 'man' get out and walk ahead, the better to chat and canoodle in privacy. The MacMasters buried two young children in the Gress cemetery, but even that little lair shows determined witness against a surviving, remnant superstition. In the oldest Lewis burial grounds, the dead lie with their feet to the east, ready to face Christ coming on the Resurrection morning. The small MacMasters, alone in the entire cemetery, lie facing south.

Barvas, too, was granted the status of a sanctioned charge in 1845, with an additional catechist. A church was built in 1850 and, in 1857, Allan MacArthur, from Mull, became its first Free Church minister, serving for thirty years; his successor in 1887, Neil Morrison MacLean, a native of Lochs, would enter the Union of 1900. John Campbell, from Kirkhill, near Beauly, was installed as Free Church minister of Uig in 1846, and stayed – as events would prove – rather too long. Local tradition attests that *Aonghas nam Beann*, that idiot savant – 'It will go here!'[20] – chose the site for the new Free Church, at Ceann Langabhat, at Miavaig. Of all Lewis parishes it was, economically, the most vulnerable; there was sustained anxiety over crops and fishing and, by 1851, Campbell actively encouraged migration. Point, Tolsta and Shawbost would all benefit from *Uigaich* settlement; forlorn ships, too, made for the Americas.

Cross Free Church had a still briefer wait for a pastor. Donald MacRae, another worthy of Kintail, was inducted as minister in 1844, and buildings at South Dell were completed in 1846. Donald Murray – a real live Lewisman, from Melbost and within the bounds of his new charge – had become the first Free Church minister of Knock in 1844, and new buildings were finished the following year. But he is quite eclipsed by his successor, that 'stark-mad herd-laddie'; Malcolm MacRitchie was inducted in 1869, died in the Knock manse in 1885 and is still revered in Point.

Stornoway would not get its minister, Duncan MacGregor – from Lochtayside – until 1849; his manse was completed in 1850, when the recently built Free Church promptly burned down. It was quickly replaced. MacGregor sired a notable dynasty – his son, Rev. W. M. MacGregor, was later Principal of the Free Church divinity school in Glasgow, Trinity College. But Peter MacLean, a Mull man and another of Alexander MacLeod's Uig teachers, spent some years as Stornoway minister too – and was succeeded in 1872 by a Canadian Highlander, James Greenfield, born at Montreal in 1831. MacLean, remote and austere, was greatly feared in Stornoway; the town Sheriff said he could happily leave on his holidays, knowing none would dare misbehave while Peter MacLean was in town.

Harris, in 1845, was unhesitatingly granted a salaried catechist – John Morrison, of course – and, not least for the relative ease of communication, was kept sensibly in a Free Presbytery of Uist. In 1848 it was

conceded that the island really needed two ministries. Meanwhile work
began on a Free Church at Manish, for which funds were energetically
raised by Morrison, at no little sacrifice for himself and a new young
family. The first Free Church minister of Harris, Alexander Davidson –
from Moy – began his very long ministry in 1852 and, until a Free
Church was completed at Tarbert in 1860, and Mackintosh MacKay
inducted as its pastor in 1862 (after an adventurous eight-year detail in
Australia), the busy Mr Davidson had the whole island, and its satellites
from Scarp to Berneray, as his cure. In 1884 Tarbert Free Church was
pressed into service for the local hearings of the Napier Commission.
Through two Unions they are now places of worship for the Church of
Scotland – indeed, these, and the Free Church at Barvas, are the only
Disruption churches on the Long Island still in use, most being replaced
late in Victoria's reign by rather grander buildings.

John Morrison, great and flawed as he was, harried by factors – he was
cleared from Strond to Leacali – had all but burned out. He died in his
sleep, at Leacali, on 6 December 1852, leaving a young widow and six
children. In time, a handsome gravestone was erected for Morrison at
Rodel, and it is still tended; but the best the folk of Harris could do for his
surviving family, and to their abiding shame, was hastily to arrange their
passage to Canada. There, posthumously, the first edition of his spiritual
verse was published.

Lochs Free Church was duly completed at Crossbost – hard by the
shore so that it could be readily accessed from all districts by boat. Such
was Finlayson's stature that few then spoke of dismantling the enormous
parish, but its western wing was another matter: in 1844, the folk of
Carloway petitioned for a settled ministry. A charge of Callanish and
Carloway was duly sanctioned[21] – from Garynahine and Linshader to
Shawbost, some 3,000 souls; and Kenneth Ross – 'by the concurrent
opinion of both the clergy and the godly . . . the most eminent laymen, all
things taken together, for gifts and godliness in Lewis in his day', writes
MacAulay – was that same year settled as resident catechist in this
district. Born at Crobeg, Lochs, in 1800, Ross had been converted under
the preaching of Finlay Cook in 1829, and had already served as a Society
teacher by Loch Sunart and in Lochaber.

Kenneth Ross was the equal of most Highland ministers, but resisted
to the last all suggestion that he submit to licensing and ordination. He is
still remembered. Speaking at a fellowship meeting in Fort William, in
1848, he rightly deplored a cant remark then doing its Evangelical
rounds. 'People speak of the "remainder of sin" being in the saints. It
is not of a remainder of sin that Paul complains, but of an entire body of
sin that does not lack even the little finger.' And those over whom he

laboured on the West Side grew proud of this most gifted layman. Dismissing the pulpit endeavours of some probationer, a Shawbost man – *Calum mac Chaluim*, or Malcolm MacLean, sneered, *' 'S e an coileach againn fhin 's binne ghairmeas na fear ud fhathasd.'* 'Our own cock can crow better than that one yet!' And John MacRae himself recorded that he did 'not know of any congregation in Lewis better organised and managed than Carloway under Kenneth Ross.' By his death in 1862, Carloway had its own minister: John MacLean, a native of Islay, was inducted in 1858.

MacLean had striking blond hair, which grew silver and white as he aged, and he was known as *Am Ministear Bàn*, 'The Fair Minister'. Evidently restless, MacLean had spent only two years in his first and previous charge – Muckairn – and gave Carloway only six. He quit for Stratherrick in 1863, went to Back in 1877, to the Arran charge of Shiskine in 1880 and finally to Tarbert, Harris, in 1885. MacAulay mentions, too, an instance of the strict discipline John MacLean and his Session could exercise – a woman who came before them in December 1858. The circumstances are spared us, but sentence was duly passed – public rebuke before the congregation, one Sabbath a month for six months. Such rigour was typical of the Church at the time.

In 1849, John MacRae accepted a call to the Free Gaelic Church, Greenock – then home to a huge Highland community. For eight years crowds massed to hear him. But Greenock was a filthy, smog-laden town and MacRae's 'excessive toils of the Disruption period had taken a toll which even his massive strength could not afford.' Clean Hebridean air may have reinforced his startling decision to accept a call as Robert Finlayson's successor at Lochs. As he sailed back to Lewis in 1857, MacRae was still a commanding preacher and a few roads had at least begun to thread some timid way among the 5,000 people of his new charge. Better still, in so sea-girt a parish, *MacRath Mor* had a yacht, a gift from Rev. Roderick MacLeod and the Free Church congregation of Snizort. The *Wild Duck*, though not nearly as large as the *Breadalbane*, was a most serviceable craft and so proud was the Snizort pastor of his congregational present to the new Lochs minister that he sailed her across the Minch himself to present it.

MacRae detested hypocrisy. Some fellow, the sort of busybody the Free Church was apt to appoint to the job of local Sustentation Fund collector, tried to impress MacRae on his travels by lamenting the general tight-fistedness and reluctance to give. 'Well, how much do you give yourself?' asked Big MacRae coldly. The man was discomfited. 'Oh, the Lord hasn't given me much of this world's goods.' 'Wasn't the Lord wise?' But there are also abundant tales of his kindliness. And the fresh air, clean

surroundings and great Christian community which he took over enchanted MacRae. He loved sailing and could still cope with hard work.
Once, after a Barvas Communion, MacRae lifted his pen to scribble a
note to his son-in-law, Donald MacMaster, at the Back manse. 'The day
was cold, but the services were short,' he writes. 'Began at quarter to
twelve and finished at quarter past four, with six Tables. There is
concision for you!' Few in Lewis would endure such 'concision' today.

A huge 'awakening' of 1859, which first broke in Lochs under MacRae's
new pastorate, was in some respects even more spectacular than that first
revival of the 1820s and, inevitably, better documented. Indeed, it was a
national movement: the last revival of religion Scotland has seen. Numbers
attending Lewis services were such that many had again to be held in the
open air. Forty young men were added to the Lochs communicant roll,
and still the excitement continued, surging from Lochs and all over Lewis.
At Carloway alone, in September 1860, thirty-three new members were
admitted. As news spread to the mainland, it even fell under attack. At one
Highland fellowship meeting in Easter Ross, one speaker spoke disdain-
fully of this Lewis movement – he evidently thought it little more than 'false
enthusiasm'; but a good Lewis elder, Angus MacIver, was present on that
occasion, and not only put down a few home-truths in his turn but mocked
the 'black crows of Easter Ross' for their loveless and censorious attitude.
MacRae could have laughed off the scorners; the death of his Penelope, in
this same revival year of 1859, was a shattering loss.

But all did not augur well for the Free Church of Scotland. Thomas
Chalmers did not long survive the Disruption: he died in 1847, and much
of his vision died with him. Chalmers had held ferociously to the
'Establishment Principle' – that the State should recognise and indeed
support the cause of Christ – as opposed to 'Voluntaryism', or entire
separation of Church and State, as embodied in the United States
constitution. Though forced by patronage to breach with Establishment,
the Free Church still believed in it, and Chalmers had hammered this
home in 1843. 'We hold by the duty of government to give of their
resources and their means for the maintenance of a gospel ministry in our
land,' he declared. 'We hold that every part and every function of a
commonwealth should be leavened with Christianity, and that every
functionary, from the highest to the lowest, should, in their respective
spheres, do all that in them lies to countenance and uphold it. That is to
say, though we quit the Establishment, we go out on the Establishment
principle: we quit a vitiated Establishment, but would rejoice in returning
to a pure one. To express it otherwise – we are the advocates for a national
recognition and national support of religion – and we are not Voluntaries.'

But principle was one thing; the practicalities were another. An inevitable consequence of the Disruption was abiding, competitive denominationalism, and the very structure and mechanics of the new Free Church of Scotland held the seeds of trouble. Chalmers had dreamed of a vibrant, Evangelical order in every parish. But Free Church support was far too uneven and, in burgeoning cities, parochial bounds became meaningless. Her ablest urban preachers became pulpit stars, enjoying magnificent manses and augmented wages, such as Robert Candlish – 'the minister of a city church thronged with an overflowing middle-class congregation gathered by his preaching.'

Country colleagues meanwhile languished on the minimum stipend. The Free Church rapidly lost interest in the urban poor; and there are early signs of empire-building. On education, the Free Church tried to match the Church of Scotland, school for school. Over the protests of her ablest theologian, William Cunningham – who wanted one centre of excellence – she built three divinity colleges, in Glasgow, Aberdeen and Edinburgh. There was even talk of a Free Church university.

Her achievements were prodigious. Free Church people gave, and gave, raising vast sums for churches, manses, colleges, foreign missions and a host of good works. But there were evil results of a self-sustaining system. A Free Church bureaucracy had to be established, in addition to church courts, and this could be (and was) readily controlled by a clique. Church discipline is always vulnerable when any you might be about to suspend are not merely members, but contributors. The Free Church was an uncomfortable place for the urban poorest – they could barely feed their bairns, let alone place precious coin in the collection ladle, the rattle (or lack of rattle) on bare wood being horribly obvious. It was besides too easy to focus Free Church ire on intemperance, gambling or illiteracy; 'the mark of middle-class censoriousness on working-class vices', Drummond and Bulloch tartly observe.[22] The Established Church held no collection, it asked nothing of the poor, a great many of her ministers – one thinks of such notable Gaels as Norman MacLeod of the Barony kirk in Glasgow – spent themselves in their service, and in time it was to the Auld Kirk that working-class Protestants increasingly turned.

And, increasingly struggling to pay its way, it was inevitable that Free Church leaders would start actively to resent Established Church privilege – their rivals enjoying good buildings and generous endowments and the bounty of the 'teinds', even where the Free Church had the people. Inevitably, men began to mutter of 'disendowment' and, in time, clamour for Disestablishment. By 1900 the Free Church all but spat on State recognition of religion. Even by 1880, she had ceased to be in any sense a church of the masses. Greedy and drifting, she had grown sectarian.

For the Auld Kirk had not been smashed in 1843. Battered as she was, she boasted State support and social respectability, and a great pool of hitherto unemployed 'stickit ministers', or probationers. She rapidly filled her depleted manses and even won recruits from the Secession and Relief churches. Four charges in Lewis had fallen vacant in 1843; and Stornoway too needed a new pastor a year later, when Mr Cameron quit his depleted flock. But they were all settled by the end of the decade. Admittedly, they had hardly any people.

The solitary adherent of the Established Church in Lochs lived on the south side of Loch Erisort: the Manse of Keose was on the north. Each Sabbath, according to Ansdell, the parish minister would peep out to see if his stalwart was waiting on the opposite shore. He would then splash over in his boat, row him back, and hold divine worship. This worked fine until one day some local urchins, who knew their neighbour had no plans for a sermon that Lord's Day, assembled a convincing scarecrow at his usual waiting-place.

David Watson's career as the new Established minister of Uig began in farce and ended in horror.[23] He had no congregation; the Uig people refused even to ferry him over to be inducted. He was finally ordained, in March 1845, in the Callanish schoolhouse. There was no Kirk Session at Uig in his eleven years as its Established minister, for he had no male members. Indeed, from 1847 to 1852, there was no Communion season at all – not that anyone in Uig minded, for apart (presumably) from 'the hundred and one', Mr Watson's wife and household constituted the entire congregation. The minister grew increasingly disturbed. On 11 May 1856, David Watson hanged himself in the shed. Even in death, the Disruption triumphed: the first man on the scene, taking entire charge, was the Free Church minister, John Campbell.

As for Cross, a succession of Auld Kirk ministers enjoyed everything except a flock. The last Auld Kirk minister of Cross, John MacPhail was inducted in 1905.[24] This benevolent, bewhiskered son of Shawbost seldom preached to more than two people, whom he would invite in afterwards for tea. A predecessor, Godfrey William Bosvill, inducted in 1878, had not even bothered to hold services at all. It is said two Free Church lads accosted him on the Lord's Day, for 'Gorraidh' – as he is yet remembered – was chopping firewood, Sabbath or no Sabbath. Why was he not preaching? Well, he said, he had no one to preach to. The children then offered to enter the church, there and then, to hear him. Recording this in his little history, Angus Smith groans, 'The bones of that nonsensical sermon have come down through the ages.' My father, who heard of it as a little boy, assures me it went something like this. 'Can you imagine the biggest rock in the world? And can you imagine the tallest, highest mountain in the world? And can you imagine the biggest, deepest, loch in the world? And can you imagine the biggest rock in the world being rolled down the tallest mountain in the world to the biggest, deepest loch in the world? What a splash!'

In Uig, though, things took a weird turn. By 1874, John Campbell had been Free Church minister for nearly thirty years – too long; he was now unpopular. A serious factor, besides, was economic. In Uig, poorer than ever, the people felt great attraction to a church funded solely by the 'civil magistrate'. But John MacLeod overstates – as have later Free Presbyterian propagandists like William MacLean – the sagacious Uig repudiation of Free Church doctrinal decline. Pastoral alienation, human tensions and – above all – deliverance from the obligation of the Sustentation Fund were what counted when, in short order, in 1874, patronage was abolished and, the following year, Uig parish church fell vacant.

Uig Free Church split. Led by the senior elder, Murdo MacDonald, feelers were put out to the Established Presbytery of Lewis. Over 300 Uig people duly signed a 'Memorial' asking (to compound drama with sheer nerve) that a Free Church minister in Glasgow, Angus MacIver, be settled over them as their Established minister, and added the excuse of 'mounting Voluntaryism' in the Free Church. Though born in Ross-shire in 1832, MacIver's father had been a Uig catechist and he had many local relatives. So an Established cause was resurrected in Uig, and a call was signed by over 600 people. On 11 January 1876, Rev. Angus MacIver was inducted to the charge of Uig, where he laboured happily for thirteen years and then returned to a Free Church charge in Strathconon. His predecessor there was a Uist man, Donald MacFarlane, a retiring character of whom few took much notice.

Campbell's unhappy Uig ministry – as far as the Free Church went – ground to a close and in October 1879 Duncan Morrison was ordained as his 'colleague and successor'. Six hundred and three members and adherents signed the call, suggesting that the 1875 division was a pretty even split.[25] And all this was but the beginning of Uig's adventures. By the mid 1880s, the general, evident recovery of the Auld Kirk in the Highlands no longer vexed Free Church leaders; it incensed them.

The ever fissile Secession Church was, by 1799, in four distinct groups – two 'New Licht' factions of a lighter Calvinist theology who increasingly retreated from old austere principles, and two conservative 'Auld Licht' bodies. In 1852 most of these very orthodox 'Original Seceders' nego-tiated successful union with the Free Church. In 1847, though, the New Licht group – dubbing themselves the United Secession Church, perhaps the most ridiculous denominational label of all time – found union of their own with the still more innovative Relief Church.

These new United Presbyterians[26] were a mercantile, upwardly mobile bunch supporting a few hundred ministers, strongest in west-central Scotland and with only a few, colonial Highland congregations. They produced a great missionary – Mary Slessor of Calabar – but, most self-consciously progressive of all Presbyterian bodies, the United Presbyterians really epitomise the worst of Victorian religion. Rightly demolishing the myth of universal church attendance in the nineteenth century, Drummond and Bulloch warn, 'There was much superficial conformity in Victorian Scotland. Though the jury found it hard to reach a decision, there is every reason to think that Madeleine Smith administered arsenic in his cocoa to her unwanted lover on Sunday night after attending St Vincent Street United Presbyterian Church in the morning and family prayers in the evening . . .' Dripping with cash, one city congregation was so grand that the hand-bill for an annual meeting concluded, 'Carriages at 10 p.m.' Though 'UP' congregations graciously opened mission halls in the slums, they had no sense of parochial responsibility. The wife of a visiting minister once hastily threw on her worst raincoat to hear him preach. As she left, a lofty man said, 'We were glad to have you here tonight, but wouldn't you be more at home in the Mission?' Such snobbery defined the Church and Scotland's poorest detested her.

In 1858 the United Presbyterians acquired a congregation in Stornoway. A few like-minded families had decided to repudiate the Free Church. Gaelic and English tensions and the social baggage bound up in enduring Stornoway disdain for 'the maws' of rural Lewis were largely responsible. A little United Presbyterian church was duly built on James Street, and this 'James Street United Free Church', as it finally became, only shut up shop in 1912. The building has long served as the premises for the town's main supplier of electrical goods and services.

And more division would come. In 1875, no fewer than 300 town communicants separated to form the Stornoway Free English congregation. They erected a very grand church indeed, to which the 'best people' of the town have long adhered and which, through several denominational incarnations, is now Martin's Memorial Church of Scotland, after its very first minister. Donald John Martin,[27] from Arisaig and of liberal Evangelical perspective, was a genial soul, whose passion for temperance was such that he bought out a town pub – the Star Inn – and turned it into a coffee-house; but in his laid-back ways and keen fondness for golf, he was very much a Lewis aberration.

The island now boasted besides an Episcopalian church.[28] Lady Matheson was posh and English and her father – Spencer Perceval, murdered in

1812 and Britain's only assassinated Prime Minister – is still memorialised by a Stornoway street. And she was a staunch Anglican. In 1839, the foundation stone for a little Episcopal church, St Peter's, was laid at Francis Street by the consent, and perhaps even the encouragement, of Sir James Stewart-MacKenzie. The Mathesons, and Mrs Perceval, now succoured the cause, over the decades funding some expensive features – a great stained-glass window in the nave, and a splendid Berrington and Sons organ to commemorate the queen's 1887 Jubilee. (Lady Matheson first offered it to St Columba's Parish Church, who declined the gift.)

A priest, William Oldfield, was settled in 1839. His successor, George Shipton, curate from 1851 to 1856, has an Act of Parliament in his honour: the 'Shipton's Disabilities Removal Bill' was passed in 1856 to allows him to assume a charge in the Church of England. The new Stornoway priest from 1857 to 1869, Hely Hutchison, lived at Soval Lodge in Lochs and was more interested in shooting and angling than religion. Frederick Catcheside, who served from 1886, seems to have been a fine Evangelical man, but tragically drowned in a boating accident off Cuddy Point. The most celebrated incumbent to date was Canon H. Anderson Meaden, who served twice at Stornoway, from 1908 to 1920, and again from 1927 to 1953. He introduced the town's first Christmas services, took keen interest in youth work, founded what are now the Sea Cadet Corps – one 'Old Boy', Donald MacLean, became Commodore of the Cunard Line – and added still more artefacts: the bell of St Lennan's, Stornoway's first parish church, and a prayer book which had belonged to David Livingstone and was donated by the explorer's daughter at the consecration of a restored *Teampall Mholuaidh* for Episcopal worship, in 1913. Between visitors, touring gentry and a few natives who decided that Presbyterianism was a little too common for them, St Peter's has survived, despite some colourful recent incumbents and acrid divisions. There is now a separate Scottish Episcopal congregation on Harris and another worships besides at Tong and Ness, their ranks enriched by English immigration. In light of recent jibes by twenty-first-century Lewis settlers against splintered Calvinism, it is noteworthy that the very first breach in Lewis Christian unity since the Reformation was this 'church of the priest', established by English and anglicised incomers in 1839.

By 1860, though, increasingly anxious to eclipse the Auld Kirk, Free Church leaders opened protracted talks, with a view to union, with the United Presbyterians. John MacRae was at first an enthusiastic supporter though, as real difficulties emerged, increasingly thought better of it.[29]

Big MacRae was fully seventy when, in 1866, sensibly realising that the labours of Lochs were now beyond him, he acceded to a call to Carloway and so began his final ministry. For a year or so, in a last guttering blaze of energy and power, he was as vibrant as he had ever been, though already – a man who belonged in his habits to the Napoleonic age – slightly eccentric. He had long worn an unconvincing wig, usually dark brown. He had, besides, a disconcerting habit of chewing tobacco in the pulpit. MacAulay asserts that he used to take 'two or three cuds in his mouth' during the sermon from his chunk of the 'bogie roll', before throwing the rest on the floor, where the church officer used afterwards to retrieve it and find it 'sufficed to last him for a whole week's smoking at home!' But no Free Church minister, even MacRae, would have wasted perfectly good tobacco, and one suspects MacAulay bowdlerised the truth: Professor Collins told me, in 1986, that it was the chewed and sodden fragments, spat out and abandoned, which the beadle would retrieve, dry out and smoke for himself.[30]

John MacRae retired, in 1871, to Stornoway, and for the next year was able frequently to preach in the Free Church there, gaunt and frail. He finally retired to Greenock. A new Free Church spirit was depressingly evident. The new Lewis-born minister, Murdo MacAskill, was already a Highland pulpit star and windy with it. A dark note of MacRae to his Back son-in-law survives, asserting that 'abundance of sound, and volubility of speech is not all that is necessary for an effective ministry.' But MacRae had better to think on. 'What a meaning there is in that word GRACE for such as I am,' he wrote his daughter, Jane MacMaster, in the last months of his life. 'It contains everything necessary for the salvation of a sinner, leaping over mountains of aggravated rebellion, infinite in its absolute freeness. What I need is to realise this in its power and glory.'

In his final sermon, old and frail, his text echoed his first calling on the braes of Kintail. 'He shall feed his flock like a shepherd; he shall gather the lambs with his arm, and carry them in his bosom, and shall gently lead those that are with young . . .' He died at Greenock on 9 October 1876, at the age of eighty-two, and there he is buried.

In Carloway, they still remember how a man, came to the Session seeking baptism for an infant; but an elder objected strongly to this, asserting that this fellow had been seen brawling. John MacRae, who had seen it all by now, demanded an explanation. 'Well, a number of us fishermen were standing at a dyke and a tramp came along and began to spit on us. So I gave him one and knocked him down.' MacRae beamed. 'Give the man baptism,' he rumbled. ''S e as fhiach 'nuair nach laigheadh e fo na smugaidean!' – 'he deserves it when he would not lie under the spits!'

9

'The Devil's Kitchen'

The Crisis of 1893

On 29 May 1879, Gavin Crawford – a bored Lowlander who was staying, on Hebridean holiday, with a Carloway teacher – penned some sly little lines to his brother John.

> I don't know what interest you would take in the rambling thoughts to which I have given expression in my last letter, but as I have given a faint description of the place, and of our sources of amusement and contemplation, I shall now hurriedly relate a few of the hindrances to my pleasure which originated to the human race at Babel. It is on Sabbaths in church that I feel most of all my want of Gaelic, for then there is nothing else spoken.
>
> The church service commences here in the forenoon at 12. About an hour before the time many have arrived and are to be seen loitering about the walls. People don't know the time very well and as a rule make sure by coming early. But they are not very particular about the time of commencement; if the minister happens to be up early they commence early; if not, late. Last Sabbath we went in 10 minutes before the time and were too late, they were finishing the first psalm. The musical service here is of a very interesting and at the same time, of a very amusing nature, and it required a very great effort on my part to restrain signs of amusement from playing upon my face, when I first heard the quaint strains embodied in their praise . . .
>
> The evening service is the curious one. An old man 'Morrison' often leads off by giving out a psalm. If there should happen to be much running out and in while he is reading it, after he is done reading he gives a stern look over the top of his glasses and shouts, 'Shut the door boys!' Of course, the congregation are quite unmoved by such ejaculations. Then he will call on somebody to pray, and that somebody will object, then he will assume a tone of authority and say 'Go on, you must pray, and see that you pray in the spirit.' The man generally holds out as long as he can and then he succumbs. Then Morrison will give out

another psalm, and then he shouts over to another man to sing it, for the elders here all seem to be a very versatile genius, and can act whenever occasion requires as either minister or precentor. Then the man will reply, 'I can't sing. McArthur will sing!' Then the officiating elder says, 'No, McArthur will not sing, you'll sing, and go on.' Similar somewhat amusing preludes take place before almost every prayer and psalm. The only other point of peculiarity I shall mention is, Morrison, who generally acts as minister, always descends from the pulpit during the service, walks along the passage with an air of dignity, gets outside to the least exposed side of the church where he leaves a little rivulet, then returns in the same unaffected way and takes his seat in the little pulpit. I should mention that just now the pulpit is not occupied at all. For it is the custom here that no unordained man should enter the pulpit; and so they take the precentor's box . . .[1]

All the arrogance, incomprehension and ignorance of the visiting gentleman-writer – already mining what have proved rich seams in 'funny' Hebridean religion – is thus embodied in three turgid paragraphs. That Carloway Free Church had then no minister; that these men, most elderly, were responsible for keeping services in a great district from Shawbost to Garynahine; that nowhere in the locality then boasted plumbing or sewerage and that the aged Morrison probably had prostate trouble is lost on Gavin Crawford; that they might have found his own church order down south, from blaring organs to clergy in frocks, still more comedic probably never flickered over his mind.

But even the self-consciously benevolent, opening a new place of worship some years later, could describe local Christians as they might the 'natives' in some distant, patronised Bongo-Bongo Land. 'A commodious and handsome new church has just been completed at Carloway,'[2] burbled the *Highland News* on 20 October 1884,

of which, it will be remembered, the memorial stone was laid last year by the Rev. Principal Rainy.

The new church was opened for the first time on the fast-day of the Communion, when services appropriate to the occasion were conducted in Gaelic by the Rev. Mr Maclean, and in English by Dr Rainy. The ceremony of opening and consecrating the new building as a place of worship excited much interest among the congregation, while the presence of Principal Rainy and the other esteemed ministers who assisted on the occasion attracted many people from a distance, as was manifest by the large number of strangers present from Stornoway and other parts of the island. The church, large and commodious as it is, was

filled to its utmost capacity. Among the strangers present was Mr
Munro Ferguson of Novar, M.P., who seemed much interested in the
services.

The collection on the happy occasion came to £60, including a
'handsome sum' from Mr Ferguson, evidently not a man to do his good
deeds by stealth; and the Communion season was evidently most demanding, for no fewer than six ministers descended on Carloway for its
duties: their very first minister, John MacLean, joined the present
incumbent, Roderick MacRae; and Alexander Lee of Nairn, James
Greenfield and D.J. Martin of Stornoway, Allan MacArthur of Barvas
and Duncan Morrison of Uig. But the reporter oozes on.

> The congregation of Carloway deserve to be congratulated for the
> substantial and handsome church they have erected at great cost and
> labour. The people themselves undertook to provide all the stone and
> sand, and nothing could be more gratifying than the heartiness with
> which the men quarried the stones and brought them to the site, or the
> cheerful readiness with which the women from time to time carried the
> sand on their backs from the lochs on the moor. The church is seated
> for 1000, and the cost of it, exclusive of the people's own labour in
> providing stone and sand, is about £1500. Of this sum the congregation
> have already paid about £300, while £300 more has been received from
> other sources, so that there is still on the church a debt of £900. If
> friends in the south only knew the amount of labour cheerfully rendered
> by the men and women of Carloway in building a suitable place for the
> worship of God, they would doubtless generously aid them in clearing
> off the residue of the debt. Considering the poor circumstances of the
> congregation and the amount of work they have done in connection
> with the building of the church, as well as the honest efforts they make
> to contribute what they can out of their poverty to meet the debt, it is
> thought no apology is required in making this appeal on their behalf to
> the sympathy and liberality of Christian friends. Donations will be
> thankfully received by Rev. Dr Rainy, Edinburgh, Rev. Mr Lee, Nairn,
> or by Rev. Mr Macrae, Carloway.

And still there was more.

The MacRae Memorial Church at Shawbost – a section of the Carloway congregation – was opened on Tuesday of the communion, when
suitable services were conducted by Principal Rainy and Rev. Mr Lee.
Several gentlemen from Stornoway, interested in the church, were

present at the celebration; and a letter from Novar, enclosing a cheque for five guineas, was read in which he expressed regret at his inability to be present. The need of a suitable place of worship at Shawbost was felt for a long time, but this want is now supplied by the present large and comfortable church built entirely through the kindly interest and benevolent exertions of Principal Rainy at a cost of nearly £1000. It bears the name of the late Rev. John MacRae of Carloway, 'a great and good man and a hero of the Disruption.'

It may be mentioned that some years ago, says our correspondent, an Established Church was erected in this district with the view of enticing the people into its communion, but the neat little edifice, with its empty pews, is is to all intents and purposes little better than an ecclesiastical mockery, and serves only as a monument to commemorate the folly and weakness of the policy of the Established Church in the Highlands. To the credit of the Shawbost people be it said that in spite of such aggressive policy on the part of the Established Church, fomented and encouraged in this instance by the influence of a malcontent Free Church elder, they, with three or four exceptions, have loyally adhered to the Free Church, and repudiated all overtures and promises made to win them over to the State Church. They have now the gratification of seeing their confidence, loyalty and attachment to the Free Church amply rewarded by the erection for their benefit and comfort of a suitable place of worship; and we feel sure the people of Shawbost will ever cherish a deep sense of gratitude and indebtedness to Principal Rainy for the warm interest he took in their welfare, and the noble exertions he put forth on their behalf in raising funds sufficient to build for their use so handsome and comfortable a church.

In these complacent paragraphs, regardless, all the might, standing and growing arrogance of the Free Church in late Victorian Scotland are laid bare. This was then, after all, no mocked Highland rump, but a huge organisation, boasting some 1,100 ministers, active in every parish of the land. The Liberal MP for Ross and Cromarty, Ronald Munro Ferguson, still only twenty-four – he would later be a noted Governor-General of Australia – milked Free Church events for votes. (It availed him nothing: he would lose his Highland seat the following year, on a greatly extended franchise, to the Crofters Party.) And the Auld Kirk, of course, is quite equated with the forces of darkness.

Robert Rainy is a complex figure – clever, deft in his use of words (often of studied ambiguity, a rhetoric detractors used to bewail as his 'golden mist') and cool. But he was really, by temperament, a politician. He actively cultivated the Liberal leadership, and they in turn took care always to carry him, for the mass of the Free Church vote (and that was a very big vote indeed) was Liberal. And his own determined policy in Free Church affairs was to build one great, conglomerate denomination, eclipsing the Established Church and making Robert Rainy great. His only mild concern was those strange, incomprehensible Highlanders.

Born in Glasgow in 1826, the son of a prominent physician and distant kin to William Gladstone himself, Rainy was an outstanding student and, later, a mediocre pastor.[3] He left both his charges – Huntly, and the Free High in Edinburgh – smaller than he found them. But he had powerful friends. In 1862 he was appointed Professor of Church History at New College, Edinburgh, and in 1874 he easily succeeded his late mentor, Robert Candlish, as its Principal, amidst the wreckage of their first, cherished scheme for a union with the United Presbyterians. 'From that time onward,' records Alexander Stewart, 'he ruled the Free Church.'

At first most Free Church leaders, like Big MacRae, had enthused. But real difficulties rapidly emerged. As a matter of fixed principle, the United Presbyterians now opposed the State recognition of religion. They had grown theologically loose, tolerating – and increasingly favouring – a watered-down Calvinism, or 'Amyraldianism', teaching a universal if conditional atonement.[4] And they were innovating in worship, rapidly introducing hymns and organs. As the serious differences grew apparent and formidable opponents to a union – like James Begg and Dr Kennedy – mobilised support, these 'Constitutionalists' made plain they would lead a second Disruption if a union were forced.

Robert Rainy and his 'Advanced Party' had to wait twenty years for the tide to turn – for robust old Disruption leaders to die off, for change in the country and in the Free Church. For now, disturbed by the steady recovery of the 'Auld Kirk', they whipped up a losing campaign for her disestablishment, and, still more preposterously and no more successfully, to prevent the abolition of patronage by the new Conservative govern-ment in 1874. The partisan feeling behind such antics – mocking the very Disruption witness itself – disgusted many. But, as was sharply observed at the time, the Rainy party had 'a vested interest in the abuses of the Establishment'.

The tide did turn. The Free Church was rapidly abandoning core Disruption convictions. The sensational revivalist preaching of an Amer-ican evangelist, D.L. Moody[5] – vast Scottish crowds turned out to hear him in the early 1870s – softened Free Church sentiment in favour both of a less rigorous theology and a jollier worship. By the end of the 1870s there was an official Free Church hymn book. From 1883, by General Assembly sanction, churches rapidly acquired organs. A new sort of theology – 'Higher Criticism' – took root in the Free Church colleges, men now openly teaching (both in a defeatist response to Darwinism and in the confident, progressive spirit of the age) that the Bible was a human book like any other, unreliable and with mistakes.

'For the first time in Scottish church history,'[6] writes Iain Murray, 'a comparative disinterest in doctrinal purity was found in alliance with evangelistic endeavour and this explains why men who were adopting Higher Critical views could be found engaged in evangelism alongside others who still retained the orthodox view of the Bible. The latter were still in the large majority and perhaps their very numbers served to blind them to the danger. They believed that a toleration of different views of Scripture and of a modified Calvinism would do no harm to the evangelical religion of the Free Church.'

There was another significant change. In the 1860s, the robust 'Constitutionalists' were all over the country and maintained an advantage. By the 1890s, Constitutionalism was a Highland phenomenon, as Ansdell emphasises.[7] And these ministers were backed by the overwhelming majority of their people, who had little desire for a shotgun marriage with the United Presbyterians – most had never laid eyes on one – and a very keen, informed grasp of Free Church principles.

But the most formidable opponent, Dr John Kennedy of Dingwall,[8] had been but sixty-five when in 1884 he finally succumbed to diabetes. Though profoundly conservative, Kennedy was of national repute. He is sometimes damned as an obscurantist. But he loved Shakespeare, fiercely supported Highland land reform and had a playful streak. He found time and inclination even on his last bed to call for the necessary materials and fashion a bow and arrow for a little boy, and even Robert Rainy's bigoted biographer concedes Kennedy was 'an authority on English cricket'. Kennedy grew in his last years convinced that division was inevitable and that a stand would have to be made, predicting a new, independent 'Caledonian Church' – one found only north and west of the eponymous canal.

'Perhaps I shall have joined the Church of the First-Born before the crisis comes; but that it will come, within a very few years, seems to me inevitable,' mused Dr Kennedy. Had he lived, there might well have been a united Highland stand in 1893. But he was gone. His Dingwall successor was that noisy populist of Greenock, Murdoch MacAskill, much given to brave words, and who shunned brave deeds.

Of this Rainy, even in September 1884, was already well aware. For that union, in all its pomp and glory, he was firmly determined. But he knew – he himself had penned the figures, as part of a wider, determined bid for the Auld Kirk endowments he coveted – that this Long Island was the most Free Church corner of Scotland. Out of 23,439 people on Lewis, he had pointed out,[9] 22,979 were Free Church adherents, the Established Church – and the little Episcopal Church in Stornoway – accounting for the derisory remainder.

Robert Rainy would get his Union – and, in the process, blow Highland religion apart.

The tragedy began with a continued, determined effort to butter up the Highlands – new churches, more ministers. It was compounded by increasingly officious efforts, through a Highland Committee Rainy made sure to control – Alexander Lee of Nairn, who had joined the Carloway jaunt, served as his eyes in the north – to stifle opposition. And it was secured by the steady, inevitable removal of senior clergy with the principle and the presence to resist Rainy's scheme.

Lewis largesse continued. Carloway and Shawbost were not the only new churches. The Free Church at Lochs had been almost completely rebuilt and two new charges, Park and Kinloch, carved from its vastness. An imposing structure had, besides, just replaced the original, more humble Free Church at Back. Stornoway Free Church had been reconstructed after the 1850 fire and would be further, handsomely enlarged in 1894; and by 1893 the Ness people could boast the biggest place of worship of all, a magnificent new church at Cross.

Thereby hangs a tale. In 1878, after the death of Donald MacRae, Duncan MacBeath[10] – who had been training for the ministry as long as most could remember – was sent to Ness as a resident lay preacher. Though nearly fifty, and with no university degree, his impact was such that the congregation quickly petitioned that MacBeath be ordained and inducted as their minister; in 1879, he duly was. 'He was tall and handsome with a rosy face and golden hair,' enthuses MacFarlane. 'There was an air of stern majesty about him. His preaching was illustrated with many memorable stories and sayings, and I have heard young lads of his church say they could listen from start to finish without losing a word. He held them as if he had the "Arabian Nights" in his portfolio . . .'

It was at MacBeath's initiative that the inadequate, off-centre Free Church at South Dell was duly replaced by the present, rather grand building at Cross. (The reduced Dell premises still survive as a meeting-house.) But he was perhaps abrasive and high-handed in driving the project and he quickly alienated his catechist, Kenneth MacPherson – a clever Gairloch man who had been there much longer than him – and other strong characters at the northern end of his parish, who really wanted a better meeting-house at Lionel.

Feelings grew high, and the muttering on both sides darker, and MacBeath – who had the reputation of being rather a seer – grew exasperated as a disaffected group increasingly absented themselves from his services and plotted in assorted homes. And he made very unguarded, imprudent remarks. When he heard that Helen Lilly MacLeod of Lionel – a conspicuous truant – was saying piously she would certainly go and hear the minister if she had only the proper clothes, MacBeath growled, 'She'll yet have only the clothes she is wearing.' As for his Catechist, the Catechist's gracious but perhaps opinionated wife, and other awkward office-bearers, he declared, 'None of those people will die in their beds.'

And, indeed, none of them did. In June 1884 Murdo MacKay and Malcolm MacDonald, most prominent in opposition to the minister – though MacKay was fifty-nine and MacDonald sixty-six – sailed huffily out to North Rona as summer shepherds in splendid isolation. On 25 October 1884, Anne MacPherson – the Catechist's wife, sixty-five, from Valtos in Uig – was found dead in a ditch near their Lionel home. No one had seen the two shepherds since August, when some men had dropped briefly by North Rona – to learn how frightened the old men had been by a raiding party of armed fishermen, who had coolly taken sheep and tobacco – but the island was now cut off by winter storms. There are eerie stories. Fionnaghal Bheag, a godly woman in Barvas, grew certain in the early spring of 1885 that something awful had happened and sent word to Dr Rhoderick Ross in Borve, the local physician, that a party be sent immediately to North Rona. A man in Tolsta, Donald MacKenzie – who knew both men and prayed regularly for them – had a very similar experience, exclaiming, 'The stream of prayer dried up two days ago,' and announced they were no longer in the land of the living. And a ghostly figure is said to have knocked on a Habost door and vanished as soon as the son of the house opened it.

Rumours ran about. A boat made for Rona on 22 April 1885. Anxiety grew when neither man appeared as they approached, nor could smoke be seen from the bothy. Malcolm MacDonald was found dead – very dead, dead for weeks – on the ground outside the house. Murdo MacKay was found inside, on the floor, even deader, sewn within a plaid and a shirt covering his face.

The visitors panicked. They sewed the bodies in canvas, buried them in Rona's little graveyard and returned to Ness with the news. Within days the *Daily Mail* had sensational reports. Questions were even asked in Parliament. The Crown Office directed Stornoway's procurator fiscal to investigate. On 26 May a party returned to the island – the depute fiscal, a policeman, two doctors and Donald MacDonald, Malcolm's son, who had brought two coffins. The bodies were exhumed for autopsies, and the house was examined. It held an abundance of food and a small, crude calendar. The last notches were faint, and the final one cut on

17 February. The doctors reported that MacKay and MacDonald had both died of natural causes, and the remains were coffined and reburied. Later a gravestone was erected.

We can only speculate, but it is most likely that, when Murdo MacKay fell ill and died, Malcolm MacDonald – though able to dress the body – was himself too weak to take the remains outside for burial. Horror finally drove him outside, where he succumbed to exposure. Fionnaghal Bheag, in Barvas, had a dream, which she later described to a friend of Alexander Carmichael. 'Murdo MacKay stood before me and repeated the first two verses of the 73rd Psalm . . . and then vanished. I saw no more of them since.'

> But as for me, my steps near slipp'd;
> my feet were almost gone . . .

Resistance to MacBeath's construction plans became very subdued. In Skigersta, James Finlayson – that same little boy from Coll whose prayers had thrown Finlay Munro – still held the line, but Kenneth MacPherson was an old, broken man. He retired to his daughter's house in Galson.

On 28 July 1886, MacPherson disappeared. He had been seen outside earlier – varied reports suggest he had been padding towards the loch or the shore – and his body was never found, despite dragging of the water and exhaustive searches. 'A search was made and every footprint was scanned but not one foot told of him,' lamented Norman MacFarlane, who knew MacPherson well. 'The news spread throughout the Island, but never an eye had seen him and no one could cast one ray of light on the mystery. It seemed as if another "Enoch was not, for God took him." It is years ago, many years, and not one ray has been shed on the strange disappearance of this man of God.'

Duncan MacBeath saw his big new church roofed and insisted on teetering in the internal scaffolding to lead in prayer. He pronounced himself unhappy with the acoustics. He died in his manse on 9 October 1891, only months before the church was ready. His pulpit is still in the little church at Dell, with a little recess for 'his snuff-box', they say, though it is more likely to have been for his pocket-watch. He is buried in the Swainbost cemetery within a high and – oddly – gateless *cabail*, an enclosing stone wall, as if – even then – folk were frightened he might get out.

What is really remarkable about the Free Church climate of the 1890s, even as it all but doled out strings of beads, is the palpable anti-Highland racism. It was appalling, it was widespread – even in the highest reaches of the Free Church – and it is amply documented.[11] Rainy and his intimates

seem to have been genuinely incapable of grasping that their Highland
brethren were not only well informed, theologically acute and perfectly
capable of grasping the precise issues at stake, but that they were endowed
even with normal intelligence. Their critical miscalculation, however, was
their conviction that Teuchters were extremely biddable – that if their
Free Church ministers could be carried along, the rest would follow – and
that their opposition to innovation was of little account in the direction of
Free Church policy.

James Lachlan MacLeod – with copious quotation – roots this prejudice
in long-established Lowland thought, evident (as we have seen) from the
fourteenth century; the explicit racial theories of Robert Knox, a noted
Edinburgh medical lecturer, best known to a wider world for buying corpses
off Burke and Hare – and getting away with it; and a general tendency to
equate the Highlanders with the Irish as one childlike, undisciplined rabble
in need of paternal Anglo-Saxon guidance. And he neatly boils all the
patronising nonsense down to three central prejudices. Rainy and his clique
thought Highlanders a fabulously remote people, cut off from wisdom and
affairs both by their strange language and pathless geography; they were
readily swayed by irresponsible local demagogues; and – as a breed – they
could be relied on to oppose any sort of progress, standing against
'ecclesiastical changes for the simple reason that they were changes'.

Pathetically, even ministers could spout this piffle, like Kenneth N.
MacDonald of Applecross, whose *Social and Religious Life in the Highlands* is of course from a most partisan and rattled United Free perspective.[12] 'We find that assertions of the wildest kind', MacDonald would
write, 'make impressions on some minds with whom the clearest reason-
ing in sober language go for nothing. Our Highland people are very
credulous and very excitable, and consequently they are easily alarmed and
roused by religious questions whether they understand them or not.' But
all will be well, he trills, for the 'schoolmaster is now abroad, and it is to be
hoped that the rising generation will not be so easily imposed upon by
priestcraft as their grandmothers were. I have no doubt the day is coming
when native intelligence will be more fully developed, and when our
Highland people in general will resist all attempts to befool them.'

This is, as James Lachlan MacLeod properly observes, 'quite staggering' from a man who was not only a Highland minister but of Highland
birth. But they are precisely the views of Principal Rainy and they are
made explicit in the fawning biography of the great man duly produced by
P. Carnegie Simpson.

Behind the ramparts of the Grampians and in the distant Hebrides a
people of different race and different tongue heard of all these changes

from afar. They were constitutionally prejudiced against all changes, for their lives, physically and intellectually, knew little variety and, in many things, traditional usage had become to them sacred. Besides, they had been poisoned in their minds with suspicion and hostility against all changes promoted by the Church in the south. Moreover, these movements were extraordinarily rapid; and the whole environment of these people made their thoughts move slowly, because their character was moulded, not by the novelties of the outer world and amid the excitement of the hour, but by undisturbed introspections on an eternal world within, and under the solemn influences of the slow-moving round of nature and the unaltering hills and the overarching sky and the great sea. Their whole mental being became thus something that was set. And being set, how easily was it found set against such changes as these that touched things so near and sacred. They fastened – naturally, inevitably – on the familiar things these movements were taking away or losing. And with wounded hearts, as men who were being robbed of the very treasure of their homes, they stood on the defensive. Of course, the result was that they confounded essentials and non-essentials: in a time of transition, only education delivers from that.[13]

MacDonald of Applecross is a long-forgotten fool; Simpson was highly educated, and MacLeod has every right to declare that his 'racism is not only consequential but censurable.' But these attitudes prevailed; and – now that conservative resistance was identified with the Highlands – they informed Free Church policy.

At the General Assembly of 1889, matters came to a head, with no fewer than thirty-three separate overtures calling for review of the Confession of Faith: about a third demanded retention of the present strict allegiance, but two-thirds were manifestly hostile, inspired both by recent United Presbyterian legislation and a widespread urge to jettison old, increasingly despised doctrine. The motion finally passed, by Rainy's leadership, only set up a committee 'to consider carefully what action it is advisable for the Church to take, so as to meet the difficulties and relieve the scruples referred to . . . it being always understood that this Church can contemplate the adoption of no change which shall not be consistent with a cordial and steadfast adherence to the great doctrines of the Confession.'

That was masterly 'golden mist' from Robert Rainy, most accomplished architect of ambivalence. By the Assembly of May 1891, he had a plan of his own, presented to the General Assembly as 'the mildest, the least startling, the least offensive way . . . of taking in hand the duty which was committed to them,' and served only to bring the Free Church into line with 'those sister Churches' who had lately amended their creeds, insisted Robert Rainy and the relevant Committee. It was a proposed Declaratory Act.

Some important qualifications are required here. The Westminster Confession of Faith is not holy writ and prudent ministers stress it is but a 'subordinate standard', subordinate to Scripture. We ought also to remember that, even without a Declaratory Act or similar measures of relief, any church can slide into indolence, heterodoxy and spiritual death. The Original Secession Church is a recent example. But it is one thing for a church to grow careless. It is quite another for her to overthrow her own constitution and to grant licence for all sorts of error. And, hyperbolic as he might have been, anyone with a grasp of Reformed theology could understand why Dugald MacLachlan, Free Church minister of Portree would be driven to exclaim – in 1894, on the floor of the General Assembly, when all was lost – that the measure was 'the blackest Act ever cooked in the Devil's kitchen'. A Declaratory Act is meant only to explain or clarify church principle; the Free Church had passed one, for instance, in 1847 to make plain her repudiation of 'all intolerant or persecuting principles'. Rainy's measure did not clarify Free Church teaching: it demolished it, not merely establishing what have proved most elastic terms of ministerial Communion, but repudiating Calvinism and arro-gating final authority over truth from the Bible to the General Assembly. But such was his skill as a wordsmith it is not immediately apparent.

WHEREAS, it is expedient to remove difficulties and scruples which have been felt by some in reference to the declaration of belief required from persons who receive licence or are admitted to office in this Church, the General Assembly, with consent of Presbyteries, declare as follows:–

(1) That in holding and teaching, according to the Confession of Faith, the divine purpose of grace toward those who are saved, and the execution of that purpose in time, this Church most earnestly proclaims, as standing in the forefront of the revelation of grace, the love of God, Father, Son, and Holy Spirit, to sinners of mankind, manifested especially in the Father's gift of His Son to be the Saviour of the world, in the coming of the Son to offer Himself a propitiation for sin, and in the striving of the Holy Spirit with men to bring them to repentance.

(2) That this Church also holds that all who hear the gospel are warranted and required to believe to the saving of their souls; and that in the case of such as do not believe, but perish in their sins,

the issue is due to their own rejection of the gospel call. That this Church does not teach, and does not regard the Confession as teaching, the foreordination of men to death irrespective of their own sin.

(3) That it is the duty of those who believe, and one end of their calling by God, to make known the gospel to all men everywhere for the obedience of faith. And that while the gospel is the ordinary means of salvation for those to whom it is made known, yet it does not follow, nor is the Confession of Faith to be held as teaching, that any who die in infancy are lost, or that God may not extend His mercy, for Christ's sake, and by His Holy Spirit, to those who are beyond the reach of these means, as it may seem good to Him, according to the riches of His grace.

(4) That in holding and teaching, according to the Confession of Faith, the corruption of man's whole nature as fallen, this Church also maintains that there remain tokens of his greatness as created in the image of God; that he possesses a knowledge of God and of duty; that he is responsible to comply with the moral law and with the gospel; and that, although unable without the aid of the Holy Spirit to return to God, he is yet capable of affections and actions which in themselves are virtuous and praiseworthy.

(5) That this Church disclaims intolerant and persecuting principles, and does not consider her office-bearers in signing the Confession, committed to any principles inconsistent with liberty of conscience and the right of private judgement.

(6) That, while diversity of opinion is recognised in this Church on such points in the Confession as do not enter into the substance of the Reformed Faith therein set forth, the Church retains full authority to determine, in any case which may arise, what points fall within this description, and thus to guard against any abuse of this liberty to the detriment of sound doctrine, or to the injury of her unity and peace.[14]

One can immediately share the unease of the man who declared that the only word of the Declaratory Act that did *not* require amendment was that opening 'whereas'. The Act was thick with ambiguity.[15] This was of course to accommodate the Amyraldianism of the United Presbyterians. In fact, it can accommodate practically anything. The second problem is in the last paragraph, 'the substance of the Reformed Faith therein set forth'. What was that substance? What is the irreducible minimum the Church would accept? What did men have to believe to become, or to stay, Free Church ministers, elders, deacons? It was never defined. It never has been in the United Free Church, nor in the much larger descendant of Rainy's brethren, the present Church of Scotland.

The third problem, also in the last paragraph, was more dangerous still: the General Assembly now arrogated to herself the role of supreme authority as to doctrine. No Reformed church in the world had ever before dared – not even the United Presbyterians, in 1879 – to declare that the majority of a gathering of mere men, rather than the Bible, the Word of God, was the final rule on faith and doctrine, 'the judgement of the Assembly,' anguishes Stewart, 'or rather of a majority of the members of Assembly in any given year.'

And it is impossible substantially to disagree with Rev. James S. Sinclair, a son of Wick who became an early Free Presbyterian minister in Glasgow and in 1900 took the detestable measure apart. 'In 1892 the Free Church passed a Declaratory Act, which tells us what "the Church holds" on very important points. According to this Act, "the Church holds" Arminian views about the love of God, the Atonement and the work of the Holy Spirit, Pelagian views about our relation to Adam and state by nature, Voluntary views about the Establishment Principle and Popish views about the authority of the Church.'

The Declaratory Act is today generally viewed, outwith the Free Presbyterian fold, as little more than a 'relieving' Act; a measure granting formal tolerance to error, and licence even to serious error. It was far worse: an explicit repudiation of Calvinism and of historic Scottish theology and biblical teaching, and the casting aside of the authority of Scripture for the arbitrary and entire authority of the Church, binding – on final adoption – on the whole Free Church and everyone associated with it. And the uproar was such, at first, there seemed every prospect of united Highland revolt.

For opposition was incandescent. Clear leaders emerged: Murdo Mac-Askill of Dingwall, Murdo MacKenzie, minister of the Free North church in Inverness, William Balfour of Holyrood Free Church in Edinburgh, the decent Henry Anderson of Partick and Kenneth Moody-Stewart of Moffat, by Dumfries. These were the princes of protest: there were many other ministers, a few young, determined divinity students and, of course, the mass of ordinary Highlanders.

The leading clergy canvassed, agitated and argued, and by February 1892 were holding great public rallies lambasting the Declaratory Act and all its iniquities, even as it became plain the Act would be endorsed overwhelmingly at the General Assembly. It would then indeed go down to Presbyteries and, if passed by a majority, would – finally ratified in 1893 – become a 'binding law and constitution', by any sensible under-standing of Free Church procedure.

As the 1892 General Assembly began, Murdo MacAskill took care at the start of the renewed Declaratory Act debate first to present a protest, that neither he, his fellow commissioners nor those who adhered to them admitted 'the lawfulness of altering the relations of this Church to any part of its received doctrines.' This was plainly on legal advice – lest MacAskill and party at length separate, and then sue for title, churches and manses – and was signed by eighteen ministers and twelve elders.

Dr John MacEwan led for the Constitutionalists, but the Declaratory Act was passed by 346 votes to 195. Another motion led by MacAskill, demanding more explicit commitment to the authority of Holy Scripture by the Free Church, won only 47 votes, and his speeches that day were interrupted by howls of protest and derision and were 'heard with so little sympathy,' record the unfeeling Drummond and Bulloch, 'that more than once his voice was drowned out by the noise of members going out for a smoke . . . Thus, after an astonishingly rowdy debate which still provides good reading for those with a taste in such matters,' the Declaratory Act was adopted. It had, though, still to be affirmed by a majority of Presbyteries and carried again at the 1893 Assembly – by an ancient mechanism called the Barrier Act, to guard the Kirk against radical change – before becoming a 'binding law and constitution'.

Until the spring of 1893 no one in Lewis or anywhere else could have been blamed for confidently expecting widespread and decisive action, so ferociously did so many ministers inveigh against the Declaratory Act, most publicly and in the strongest language. At Dornoch, a young probationer, James MacDonald, insisted at his ordination and induction by writing, as he subscribed to the Formula, 'I am to sign the Confession of Faith *simpliciter*, and wholly irrespective of the Declaratory Act passed by last Assembly, as signed at my licence, and by the other members of this Presbytery.' Murdo MacAskill had thundered, 'This movement on the part of our opponents means – Bible or no Bible, Confession of Faith or no Confession of Faith. Let Dr Rainy and his party put their fingers on the Confession, and the whole thing is done.' Dr William Balfour 'had no hesitation in saying that the present body of men who constituted the Free Church of Scotland would cease and determine to be the Free Church of Scotland the moment that Act was passed.'

Near year's end, the minister of Kilmallie Free Church in Lochaber, Donald MacFarlane[16] – a quiet, even timid fellow, born at Vallay, North Uist, in 1834, and who had been fully forty-one when ordained to his first charge at Strathconon – directed his kirk session in engrossing a formal Protest against the Act in their minutes, in January 1893; and MacFarlane had weeks earlier told friends that, if the Declaratory Act were not repealed, he would separate from the Free Church. In the general din, hardly anyone noticed.

There were, besides, divinity students. In March 1872, John MacLeod, from Fort William, led a determined resistance in New College, Edinburgh. Though still only twenty – photographs show he was boyish at that – he drew up a remarkable Bond, on 2 November 1892, where he and eight classmates attested that 'seeing the Declaratory Act is now an integral part of the Constitution of the Free Church of Scotland we the undersigned have ceased to prosecute our studies with a view to the ministry of that church as presently constituted.' Repairing variously to the Original Secession divinity halls and Queen's College, Belfast, nine became Free Presbyterian ministers, though only four – Neil Cameron, James Sinclair, Donald Beaton and Neil MacIntyre – would die in her embrace.

John MacLeod – he would crown his career as Principal of the Free Church College – would by 1893 be urging Free Church members to 'cut their connection with an apostate church.' For now, he made for Lewis, lodging in Back with a very old stalwart of the faith, Angus Morrison from Dell. MacLeod found employment as a classics master in the Nicolson Institute – Stornoway's grammar school – and worked hard besides to master Gaelic. He also learned as much as he could, from Morrison, about the earliest days of Gospel power on Lewis. Almost ninety, this eminent tradition-bearer, weary of Duncan MacBeath's whims and maledictions, had quit Ness to live with his daughter and enjoy the preaching of the Reverend Hector Cameron.

We have already met Mr Cameron, another son of Lochaber, born around 1835 or 1836 at Guiseachan – a lonely farmhouse, rather than a hamlet, to the east of Loch Shiel.[17] His father, as we saw, was a staunch Roman Catholic. But he had married a Protestant woman and about 1842 Donald Cameron was converted, under the witness of Neil MacLean, SSPCK teacher at Corriebeg, when little Hector was around seven years old. Thereafter, and with much arduous tramping, the family worshipped in Strontian. John MacQueen, from Skye, was settled there in 1853, and there was great spiritual blessing. Young Hector was one convert and, after training in Glasgow, he spent two years preaching at Strathconon before, in 1871, being settled in Kilfinnan on the Kyles of Bute, which then included Tighnabruaich. The following year, Hector Cameron married Miss Margaret Stuart MacQueen, a daughter of his old minister. In 1876, he accepted a call to that most demanding Lewis charge – Lochs – and, demitting what was left of it in June 1881, he succeeded John MacLean, *Am Ministear Bàn*, as the third minister of Back Free Church.

That was touching in itself: MacLean's father was that same Neil, SSPCK teacher at Corriebeg, whose words had been blessed to Cameron's father. But Hector Cameron's life intersects still more strikingly with that of Donald MacFarlane – the Lochaber connection; in divinity training – they were fellow students in Glasgow; that early service as 'resident supply' at Strathconon – MacFarlane would be its first settled minister; and at the Kyles of Bute: days after the final triumph of the Declaratory Act, MacFarlane would oversee the formation, at Kames and Tighnabruaich, of the very first Free Presbyterian congregation anywhere. And they were real and life-long personal friends; when Cameron finally died, retired in Dingwall, in May 1908, MacFarlane paid generous words of tribute to him from the town's Free Presbyterian pulpit.

The irony is overwhelming. In June 1892, at Inverness, Cameron had all but led the charge against the Declaratory Act and the *Northern Chronicle* indeed reported that there were 'three parties in the meeting, the most extreme of them being led by Mr Cameron, Back . . .' The Lewis minister, notes Ansdell, made plain he thought the resolutions finally adopted were totally inadequate. Hector Cameron even orated that 'it deeply concerns everyone to know whether he is really found fighting for or against God and His truth by remaining in a church which seems so fast and speedily to be gravitating towards socinianism.' (He used an archaic term for 'rationalism', or liberal, materialistic theology.) A week later, the Inverness newspaper had still more explosive reports. Hector Cameron had now pronounced that the 'function of every church is to witness for the truth of God and when she ceases to discharge that function she is no longer a church of Christ but a synagogue of Satan.'

There have been rather desperate attempts to argue that Hector Cameron saved Lewis for the Free Church. It would be a good deal more accurate to assert that he denied Lewis to the Free Presbyterians and thus cheated the Long Island of a surviving, united Evangelicalism. The more one discovers, the less heroic Hector Cameron becomes. Even the determined efforts of Murdo MacAulay, in 1982, cannot bury the reality: a pompous, noisy, really rather stupid man, whose antics on at least two occasions – and neither had anything to do with the Declaratory Act – would unhesitatingly provoke decisive church discipline today; a man easily outmanoeuvred in debate, as defter minds ran rings around him; a man who left division wherever he went. His long-suffering wife, Margaret, did much to minimise the worst pastoral damage, and a son and grandson – both outstanding Free Church ministers – were of very different stamp.

Cameron was certainly a man of piety and courage. And he was no stranger to sorrow, for the Camerons lost several small children. Old

Angus Morrison seems genuinely to have appreciated his ministry. But there is little to suggest true greatness and much to suggest an insufferable boor. Indeed, the worst instances feature even in MacAulay's little tribute.

Mr Cameron proved quickly so unpopular as a Lewis pastor that both the South Lochs and Kinloch districts petitioned – and in the case of South Lochs, at least, fought hard against his sustained opposition – to win recognition as recognised preaching stations and, in time, as sanctioned charges; by the end of 1885, both Park and Kinloch were separate congregations with their own ministers. When a man quite properly refused to answer questions at a Lemreway meeting on a recent fishing tragedy, having already been examined in court, Cameron shoved him so violently that, but for the press of people, the fellow would have been on the floor. Cameron's ministry in Lochs effectively ended when a man he had falsely accused from the pulpit simply sued him – and won.

A couple once tramped the seven miles from Tolsta, with their witnesses, to be married at the Back manse; Cameron smelt drink off one witness, and announced he would not perform the ceremony. Had his own wife not frantically interceded, the humiliated couple would have had to trail home, unwed, to a village all set for festivities. Even after MacAulay himself was inducted to Back, in 1956, ladies would still not sit in the front row of the gallery, for Cameron had once publicly pronounced that only a 'brazen-faced woman' would place herself so prominently.

One wonders if Cameron ever really shook off the sacerdotalism and baggage of his Roman Catholic childhood and early community. Intimated to preach at Barvas Communion, he was riding over the moor when he met a Barvas man coming in the opposite direction, as if to boycott his endeavours. 'How dare you go to Stornoway on the Fast Day when I am preaching in Barvas today,' he roared, deaf to the protests that the hapless crofter sought only to lay in provisions for Communion hospitality. Cameron capped that by later relating the encounter in the Barvas pulpit and adding, 'It is not you I should blame, but the hornless minister sitting beside me,' – but the term MacAulay translates, *caora mhaol*, has a still coarser meaning, a 'wedder' or castrated ram.

Tempted over his Roman Catholic baptism, the young Cameron had been anguishing over the possible duty to be sprinkled a second time when he happened on the sensible writings of Charles Hodge, an American theologian, who rightly argues that any baptism is valid when dispensed by one ordained in the name of Christ, performing the rite with water, in the name of the Triune God. Thereafter, Cameron was an ardent student of Hodge, even adopting some of his habits, such as the reading of elegant novels. Yet an old woman who could remember her pastor told MacAulay that Mr Cameron had been in the habit, whatever the context, of wearing his frock-coat, and on one occasion sallied forth from the manse to supervise the man shearing sheep on his glebe. With characteristic tact, he criticised the shepherd's efforts, until the shearer cheerfully invited him to have a go himself. Hector Cameron bristled. *'Cha chuirinn smal air mo dhreuchd le mo lamh a chuir ri leithid sin'* – 'I would not besmirch my office by putting my hand to the likes of that!'

Such arrogance scarcely becomes anyone one who professes to serve the one 'who made himself of no reputation,' and whose preaching was marked too often by vituperation – 'red-hot exhortations which ran down the hill like lava,' snorts Norman MacFarlane, who heard him often. And yet he records besides that Cameron 'was a warm-hearted soul, and more impulsive than the Apostle Peter. His language had high colour and his sermons were thoughtful and impressive. He wrote out every word and slavishly committed to memory . . . He often scolded in the pulpit in measured terms but carried no ill feeling. He went through . . . Lewis abusing his own church, which always lends interest to a minister.'

But the ministers who had made the most noise against the Declaratory Act were the first to duck out. 'The questions today are these,' Murdo MacAskill had roared, 'Bible or no Bible, atonement or no atonement, salvation for a perishing world on the basis of the finished work of Christ, or salvation by works . . . we are only getting our weapons in order.' He declared, besides, the Declaratory Act was a 'most defective piece of legislation, and most dangerous . . .', and still more ferociously, 'if the Declaratory Act becomes part of our constitution, what remains of our former principles is wholly obliterated, and anyone who pleases may pronounce the funeral oration of the once noble Free Church of Scotland; she is no longer the Free Church of our earthly love and loyal adherence.'

William Balfour wobbled hours after the Act was adopted by the 1892 General Assembly, musing there were but two alternatives if the Act were ultimately confirmed – to separate immediately, or continue to fight for their creed and 'be kicked out one by one'. Unease grew evident. One minister warned that their people might not follow and recalled the great, enduring Highland hardships after the Disruption, and for many years. Murdo MacAskill then rose and carolled, 'I never thought or dreamt of a disruption.' He had openly threatened one. Students, though, demanded to speak: three made plain they had no intention of staying in a Declaratory Act Free Church.

Further meetings were held, in Glasgow and Edinburgh, but a crack, however faint, had appeared, and as events unfolded and the reluctance of ministers actually to act – especially in any way that entailed the loss of churches, manses and stipends – grew depressingly evident. For one thing, ministers were now oddly eager to agree that the Declaratory Act, while undoubtedly a *relieving* measure – allowing error to flourish – was not an *imposing* one, binding the consciences of all the Free Church.

This quite contradicted what the likes of Murdo MacAskill had earlier and most publicly said; but it is at the heart of the imminent, enduring division between the Free Presbyterians and the Free Church minority. All who saw the Declaratory Act as an imposing Act were, as Ansdell points out, Constitutionalists; but not all Constitutionalists viewed it as an imposing Act (or, at least, decided not to see it that way now). Even a keen Free Church student, John R. MacKay – who did in fact go at last with the Free Presbyterian cause – speculated, to the horror of friends like Neil Cameron and Allan MacKenzie, that they might honourably stay in the Free Church until the 'Questions and Formula' were altered. Neil Cameron – depressed, beset with atheistic doubts – grew even more alarmed to learn that Donald MacFarlane was leaving Kilmallie for Raasay. He would surely be compromised by signing the Questions and Formula in the present extraordinary circumstances, and he was the only minister Cameron believed would make a stand. (MacFarlane had covered himself with the Kilmallie kirk session protest, but Neil Cameron did not know that.)

And Lewis was not the only place boasting fine new churches. In Moffat, Kenneth Moody-Stewart had just taken triumphant possession of a grand new place of worship; his manse had been enlarged a year before. Murdo MacKenzie, in Inverness, now preached in a new and grandilo-quent Free North – it had cost £11,000 and was shortly to open – and, the year before, he and his lady had moved into a palatial new manse. He would, as one dryly points out, 'have been an exceptional man to have contemplated secession in such a situation.'

If there were a single, defining moment in this tragedy, it fell at Inverness in February 1893. A great Constitutionalist conference had been advertised and ministers and elders converged in the town from all over the Highlands and Islands. The poorest had walked, and even sailed, some for very many miles, in grim conditions. But the ministers – in an act as arrogant as it was unfathomably stupid – took immediate command and resolved it be a meeting of clergymen only. The elders were ordered out. The ministers then solemnly resolved that separation was not necessary or commendable and, further, that the Declaratory Act was only a relieving Act; that did not impose beliefs on anyone and all could stay in the Free Church with a clear conscience. One undeniably partisan history can scarcely be blamed for exclaiming, 'This unexpected wheel-round was viewed with amazement by many who had listened to the soul-stirring and denunciatory speeches against the Declaratory Act by these modern sons of Ephraim.'

Apart from the volte-face, such closed-shop clericalism was an insult to Highland laymen, a slap in the face of an essential Presbyterial principle – the parity in church courts of the teaching and ruling elder – and a gross tactical blunder. It was already a very long shot, on the evidence of previous votes, that the General Assembly would repeal the Declaratory Act. Now that Robert Rainy had been so emphatically reassured there would be no large-scale departure of ministers, its confirmation was sealed.

Meanwhile, office-bearers all over the Highlands were in open revolt. At successive meetings – most notably at Flashadder in Skye – men explicitly declared 'they would shake from off their feet the dust of a Free Church grown decadent and unworthy of its founders.' And the Flashadder meeting made plain their feelings, declaring that 'the Constitutionalist ministers were evidently afraid to lead the people out of a church which has so manifestly backslided from the truth. They were to be greatly blamed for the way in which they had acted at the Inverness conference in not allowing the elders, who came from different parts, to take part in the proceedings.' Things were beyond bitterness now: they were poisonous, with the consistent and remaining few now the target of focused anger, in correspondence columns and elsewhere, by embarrassed but defiant Constitutionalists. 'The "Cons" hate us more than the Act itself,' wrote a distressed Allan MacKenzie this February of 1893.

The General Assembly that May met, of course, on the Jubilee of the Disruption. There were delegations, nobility and statesmen from all over the world; an atmosphere of exultancy and jubilation; one great society of mutual admiration. So marginalised was the Constitutionalist party by now – and so discredited its leadership – that what we are now apt to imagine as high drama, the final Declaratory Act show-down, was little more than an administrative detail. On Thursday 25 May, the Assembly took up ten separate overtures for the repeal of the Act. After windy debate, Dr Rainy moved that the court 'pass from the overtures', which it did, by 415 votes to 120. Inevitably, there was a dissent, lodged by twenty-one ministers and twenty-one elders. Then the quiet little minister of Raasay stepped forward, and read out a very detailed and emphatic Protest, signed and dated. It dawned on Murdo MacAskill and the rest that Donald MacFarlane had just formally separated from the Free Church.

At the end of the Assembly, still in Edinburgh, MacFarlane showed face at a Constitutionalist meeting and was asked what he would do. Well, he said, he hoped to form a Presbytery, and that they would then proceed to license those students who followed them and had finished their training. Still not taking it in, MacAskill blurted out, 'You will compromise us.'

Mr MacFarlane entrained for Glasgow and met the supportive students there. He then made his way to preach that weekend at Millhouse, Kames,[18] and on the Monday the congregation voted to quit the Free Church there and then. Back on Raasay, on the Monday of his own Communion, all but six of his own parishioners likewise agreed to back him. The following Tuesday, 13 June 1893, at an advertised rally in the Inverness Music Hall – the attendance was huge – he was backed firmly by another minister, his boyhood teacher and another son of North Uist, Donald MacDonald, nearly seventy years old and Free Church minister of Shieldaig, Wester Ross. There were besides good men from all over the region – from Argyll, from Sutherland and from Caithness, from the glens of Inverness-shire, the firths of the east and the inlets of the west, from Skye and from Lewis. There was, besides, a telegram from Free Church people in Harris – 'Deputation wanted to enlighten Harris on Declaratory Act.' Men spoke of feelings running high on Lewis, of positive uproar in Ness.

On 28 July 1893 at Raasay, with local elder Alexander MacFarlane – he was the schoolmaster, but no relation; and, born in Lochs in 1842, had been baptised by Robert Finlayson – the ministers constituted what they called the 'Free Church Presbytery of Scotland'. And they licensed John R. MacKay to preach the Gospel. On 14 August, at Portree, they drew up what Drummond and Bulloch call 'a remarkable Deed of Separation', and even lodged a copy with the Register of Sasines. It gives four grounds for their stand: abandonment of the Establishment Principle is the first; the sanctioning of uninspired hymns and instrumental music the second; toleration and support of office-bearers who denied divine authorship and entire perfection of the Scriptures the third; and the Declaratory Act, destroying 'the integrity of the Confession of Faith as understood by the Disruption Fathers and their predecessors', was the fourth. 'They had neither the money nor the inclination for a lawsuit,' observe Drummond and Bulloch, 'otherwise they might have anticipated the decision of 1904 and been awarded the whole property of the Free Church.'[19]

John R. MacKay and Allan MacKenzie witnessed this Deed, and Presbytery besides licensed MacKenzie. By the end of November, MacKay was the ordained minister of Gairloch and MacKenzie of Inverness. By the end of 1896 they had seven settled ministers, two Presbyteries, a ruling Synod and an official, monthly publication. And in September 1894 they had settled on their name, the Free Presbyterian Church of Scotland.

10

'Israel and Judah'

The Crisis of 1900

Most Scots, Drummond and Bulloch cheerfully point out, have never met a Free Presbyterian.[1] Though widely thought a Free Presbyterian stronghold, Lewis has remarkably few of them and, save for two or three villages, the Church is only strong in South Harris. It is doubtful if 350 people now fill Free Presbyterian pews on the Long Island each Lord's Day. In the wake of the 1893 Assembly, though, the Free Presbytery of Lewis viewed the 'Seceders' with great unease. (The tag, which has survived, is profoundly unfair: they had not 'seceded' and argued, with some justice, that the Free Church had left them.)

The Free Presbyterians were not a definitive, immediate split, but a movement, radiating through the Highlands from the summer of 1893 and continuing to grow till at least October 1900.[2] It was massively hampered, though, by an acute shortage of ministers. If several of the Highland eminences had 'come out' in 1893 – or even one, like Gustavus Aird in Creich or John Noble in Lairg – there would have been a Free Presbyterian landslide. Though the Free Presbyterian Church continues globally to grow – the last decade alone has seen new congregations in England, Kenya, Ukraine, Singapore and even the USA – its ministerial strength peaked in the mid 1970s in the low forties and, since the Lord Mackay affair and the secession of 1989, when they lost fourteen ministers and perhaps a quarter of their people, their British ministerial ranks have never got out of the teens. They have not had a full complement of Western Isles ministers since 1981, and have been most prone everywhere to an odd mix of inordinately long pastorates and inordinately long vacancies.

The Free Presbyterian Church was besides, from the start, 'more lay than clerical', and in some striking respects has a more democratic character than its rivals.[3] Laymen take services, adherents often precent and Free Presbyterian women have always been obituarised in their magazine. Though born in protest against the declension of doctrine formalised in the Declaratory Act – and, on the ground, detestation of

Darwinism was a very strong motive – the new body was heavily shaped in the tradition and emphases of 'North Country' Separatism[4] – her very high view of the Communion table, the relative paucity of communicants (there are now fewer than a hundred male members in Scotland) and marked lack of interest in the Disruption testimony. Indeed, in several localities – Wick, Oban, Greenock, Stratherrick – Separatist groups had long already met and now became quickly Free Presbyterian congregations. She alone, these days, remains vigorously and frankly Protestant, though never beyond the bounds of courtesy, and openly deplores such ugly things as the Orange Order. She has also been determined not to be defined as a Gaelic church of exclusively Highland identity.

From the first the Free Presbyterian Church of Scotland was the church of a poorer class of Highlanders, a church especially of geographical extremities – the remote glen, the lonely promontory, the far bay, the township at the end of a road; and has, accordingly, suffered disproportionately from twentieth-century depopulation. Preferring clarity to compromise, on several occasions her order has broken down in vehement division and uproar. Yet she has been marked from the start by a spirituality that, at its best, is profoundly Christ-centred; she has held staunchly to the free offer of the Gospel; and, as even one who deserted her ranks left on record, she 'was rich, within the limits of her sway, in those things which form the true glory of any church – men and women of believing hearts and godly lives.' Archibald MacNeilage, a Free Church stalwart in 1900 and the first editor of the *Monthly Record*, declared 'the flower of the Church' had been provoked into departure by the Declaratory Act; the minister of Plockton, William Sinclair, frankly told the 1894 Assembly that it had cost 'hundreds, if not thousands, of the Church's most loyal adherents,' and that he felt his own hands greatly weakened.

We should remember besides that, almost from the start, Free Presbyterians have been persecuted. MacFarlane and MacDonald were hounded from their manses and buildings, and MacDonald even robbed of money in a Lochcarron bank account – including some of his own – he and his congregation had laboriously raised for a new meeting-house. Neither attempted to resist these legal actions. MacFarlane was not even paid the balance of stipend the Free Church owed him. Everywhere, Free Presbyterians were harassed. One child in Lochcarron never forgot mud being flung – real mud, literally flung – as 'the Seceders' went to service. Raasay's nasty proprietrix, the widow of Herbert Wood – they had tormented and driven about the people for years – denied the Free Presbyterians sites for a church or for even a manse, and for seven years MacFarlane had to lodge in Broadford and sail across, in an open boat, in all weathers – when possible. MacDonald, who was nearly seventy, had not even had a church building when inducted to Shieldaig in 1872, and had for years to preach in the open – at times brushing the snowflakes off the Bible to see his text. He and his people were reduced once again to the wastes of Torridon: in striking contrast to the United Free majority in 1904, MacDonald nevertheless 'consented to the spoiling of his goods without making any noise or attempting the least resistance.'

And vituperation everywhere followed Free Presbyterians. Robert Rainy himself spoke contemptuously of the two ministers as practically non-entities who had been 'exploded into space' by forces they neither controlled nor understood. Robert Balfour, their recent Constitutionalist ally, reduced the same Assembly to laughter by open mockery of Highlanders, 'very strange people', whose real problem was that they could not understand English.

Murdo MacAskill not only failed, after all, to stand in 1893, but in 1896 collapsed with remarkable lack of resistance into the purposes of the 'Advanced Party' and went into the Union of 1900 like a lamb. He was swift to revile the Free Presbyterians – a 'mischievous movement . . . calculated to do immense damage among our beloved Highlands,' for actually doing what he himself had failed, after all the threats and blow, to do. Still more unwisely, he actually taunted Donald MacFarlane – 'Where would you be if I had come out?' Someone very properly replied that Mr MacFarlane would stand exactly where he stood now – high in the estimation of the Lord's people. James MacDonald of Dornoch, who had publicly repudiated the Declaratory Act at his 1892 ordination, not only ended up himself in the United Frees but entered the great union of 1929, dying as a minister of the Church of Scotland.

For now, Free Presbyterians were taunted, pelted and ridiculed. They were of course in a Highland, Constitutionalist country; those who made their lives miserable were former Constitutionalist allies, and a good many of them – including not a few ministers – ended up in the Free Church minority. The Free Presbyterians have often been condemned for refusing to return to a purified Free Church. Even by 1900, this was in human terms asking rather a lot.

Free Presbyterians enjoy near-absolute uniformity in worship, from Achmore to Auckland, hold steadfastly to the Authorised Version of 1611 and have a weakness for strident encyclicals. While the zest of her discipline is much exaggerated, the communal nature of assorted courts and committees – and the inevitable 'de-individuation' of kindly men in the process – results occasionally in decisions that are loveless and cruel. (That is of course no less true of the Free Church.) From her principled insistence that not merely individuals but the whole Scottish community are under the law of God to the white-tie garb favoured by many of her ministers, she really echoes the pre-1843 Established Church, with an assured mindset and a retention of some very old Scots customs.

Yet a great Free Presbyterian cause has now for over a hundred years prospered in Zimbabwe, with schools and a hospital and, in recent years, focused care for the victims of Aids. By Neil Cameron's early endeavours, too, the Church has long tended congregations in Canada, Australia and New Zealand, and in recent years her overseas outposts have increased – Singapore, Ukraine, the USA. The Free Presbyterian Church is marked by stability in her leadership (all members of Presbytery are members of Synod), transparency in her finances, and an abiding culture of Edwardian etiquette, generous hospitality and dry, delicious good humour.

The *Free Presbyterian Magazine* savaged apartheid even before Malan and the National Party won power in South Africa and, in 1962, it was unequivocally denounced by the Synod. (By contrast, some Free Church ministers – she had an extensive mission in the country – defended it shamelessly to the end.) Twice, in 1965 and 1988, a black African pastor has served as Moderator of Synod. Shortly after the Second World War, her ministers refused to admit Ian Paisley as a student – he went back to Ulster, and of course, stole the Free Presbyterian name for his sect. Unlike the Free Church, the Free Presbyterians have maintained social mission at home in Scotland, with two excellent care-homes for the elderly.

Lewis was much stirred by the 1893 division. By September, Ansdell reports,[5] a correspondent cried that islanders were 'anything but satisfied with the explanations offered' for the Declaratory Act. A Presbytery report that autumn damned it as a source of 'irritation and alienation . . . the obnoxious Act' and in January 1894 ministers spoke of dissatisfaction, dispeace and division 'almost universally within the bounds of the Presbytery'. They sent an alarmed overture to the Assembly begging, in vain, for the Act's repeal. There can be little doubt that, but for scant human resources, the Free Presbyterians could have swept the island. But her leaders were as yet few and grossly overworked. John R. MacKay was so viciously slandered in Highland newspapers he wrote home to his worried parents assuring them he was 'never calmer in all the days of my life'. Yet he did his best, with others, to carry forward the cause, in just one month of 1894 visiting 'Ullapool, Lochinver, Coigach, Lochcarron, North and South Harris, Inverness, Tighnabruaich and Glasgow.' 'I have

Na Tursachan, the Standing Stones of Callanish. From certain angles they are eerily humanoid. *Ann Bowker*

Above. Teampall Mholuaidh. John MacLean Photography

Left. Teampall Mholuaidh – St Moluag's Church, Eoropie, near the Butt of Lewis. Restored by the Scottish Episcopal Church shortly before the Great War, it is the oldest place of present-day worship on the Long Island.
Nathanael Smith

St Columba's Church, Aignish – ancient Christian site and sepulchre of the MacLeods of Lewis.
John MacLean Photography

A delicate Harris evening, from the tower of St Clement's, Rodel. *Nathanael Smith*

'We were obligated to go in by a window.'

Above. A Roman Catholic interior, with central altar and imagery. Assorted maritime touches lend a grounding charm to this noted Western Isles example, St Michael's on Eriskay. *www.undiscoveredscotland.com*

Left. The imposition of 'patronage' on the Established Church from 1712 was hugely unpopular; at times, lairds had to resort even to military force to install a new minister in an outraged parish. This engaging illustration is from a Victorian edition of John Galt's wry 1821 satire, *Annals of the Parish*

Gress, on the Broad Bay coast, much as it would have appeared when Finlay Munro began his remarkable 1820 mission to Lewis – with special success in this area. From *Lewisiana*, W. Anderson Smith, 1875.

A pre-war photograph of Finlay Munro's footprints, by Torgyle, Glen Moriston. They can still be seen today but there is almost certainly a natural explanation – which by no means negates his assertion they would remain in the sod till the Day of Judgement. *Knox Press, Edinburgh*

Rev. Alexander MacLeod, a complex, fearful, high-handed and faintly greedy man whose ministry in Uig nevertheless saw astounding revival.

The church built for Alexander MacLeod at Balnacille, Uig. Closed in 2002, its future is uncertain and one of increasingly bitter dispute between the Church of Scotland and the local community. *John MacLean Photography*

Perhaps the most famous convert of the Uig revival – Angus MacLeod, *Aonghas nam Beann*, an idiot-savant of noted sanctity whose name is still invoked on Lewis today, too often as a weapon in smug anti-intellectualism.

Rev. John MacRae, *MacRath Mor*. 'Big MacRae' is a vast personality – one of the greatest preachers of Victorian Scotland and whose emphases and humour define the Free Church on Lewis to this day.

A classic of Disruption iconography – this is a steelcut of a treacly sub-Landseer painting, *Leaving The Manse*.

Another iconic Disruption scene – preaching at the seaside to a dispossessed congregation, in this sentimentalised instance probably at Kilmallie.

The new harbour at Carloway, as Big MacRae would have known it during his final pastorate. From *Lewisiana*, W. Anderson Smith, 1875.

Above left. My late great-grandmother, Mrs Mary MacLean – *Banntrach Calum Mor* – of New Shawbost, who died in 1946 at the great age of ninety-four. There is something quite timeless in this 1930s snapshot of warm, unaffected Lewis piety. *Mrs Christine Montgomery*

Above right. Principal Robert Rainy, commanding and handsome, dreamed of a new 'super-church' by means of a controversial Union between the Free Church and the United Presbyterians. He ended up wrecking Highland Christian unity and is still bleakly remembered as 'Black Rainy.'

Left. A dramatic bond drawn up by Free Church divinity students at Glasgow, in 1892, avowing their intention to repudiate her training if the Declaratory Act was adopted. It was, and they all joined the Free Presbyterian movement. *Knox Press, Edinburgh.*

A meeting of Divinity & Arts Students of boots to the Declaratory Act was held in Glasgow on the evening of Wednesday Nov: 2 The finding of the meeting was as follows –

Seeing the Declaratory Act is now an integral part of the Constitution of the Free Church of Scotland we the undersigned have ceased to prosecute our studies with a view to the ministry of that church as now constituted

Allan MacKenzie, Divinity Student
James S. Sinclair, " "
Alex: Macrae D.
Neil Cameron " "
Roderick MacKenzie " "
John Macleod
George Mackay Arts student
Donald Beaton " "
Neil McIntyre " "

Right. Rev. Donald MacFarlane (1834–1926), father of the Free Presbyterian Church of Scotland.

Below. There is some disagreement over this dramatic image, but most agree it shows a vast (and still homeless) Free Presbyterian congregation worshipping in the open air at Garden Road, Stornoway, in the 1890s. *Stornoway Gazette Ltd*

'Locked Out!' The Free Church minority in October 1900, denied access to their own Assembly Hall by a stern policeman and a foul-mouthed janitor. The 'Wee Frees' duly appealed to Caesar – and won their case in the House of Lords, only to be stitched up by press and politicians. *Knox Press, Edinburgh*

Rev. Kenneth A. MacRae (1883–1964) His published *Diary* is a memorable record of twentieth-century Christian ministry, but the austere pastor of Stornoway Free Church is remembered with curious ambivalence. *William G. Tulloch, Balerno*

A minister and a 'missionary', or resident lay-preacher – Rev. Malcolm Gillies and Angus MacKinnon, in stolid Free Presbyterian partnership. Gillies was a much jollier personality than this earnest study reflects.

Right. Rev. William MacLean (1907–1985). He twice served as highly respected Free Presbyterian minister of Ness: intense, earnest and kindly.

Below. Two Free Presbyterian doctors – Peter A. MacLeod and Hugh Gillies.

A splendid study of Free Church ministers at a Scalpay induction, 21 June 1950. Back row – Revs. Murdo Murray (Carloway); Murdo Gillies (Canada); William Campbell (Knock); John MacLeod (Bernera) and Murdo MacRae (Kinloch.) Front row – Angus Finlayson (North Tolsta), Malcolm Morrison (Scalpay), Kenneth MacRae (Stornoway) and John Morrison (Cross.) *Angus M MacDonald ARPS*

Rev. Duncan Campbell, United Free minister and Faith Mission evangelist at the centre of the grossly overblown 'Lewis Awakening' of 1949 to 1952. He dined out on it for the rest of his life and his manipulative methods, untruths and exaggerations did abiding harm.

In his eighties, Rev. Murdo MacAulay (1907–2001) was still an imposing figure – seen here on 11 November 1989 at the dedication of the new Carloway war memorial. Though robust and bossy, MacAulay was probably the most influential minister in post-war Lewis, and much revered.
John MacLean Photography

Rev. Murdo MacRitchie (1919–1983), minister of Stornoway. In June 1977, as a boy of eleven, I had my first cruise on the paddle-steamer *Waverley*. Mr MacRitchie was staying with us that night; he spoke to me of Dunkirk, and how he had witnessed the 1899 *Waverley* succumb to German fire in that desperate evacuation, how he had helplessly watched so many men die. It was a moment when history became alive; personal holiness most real.

A timeless scene of harvest: my uncle, Malcolm MacLean (b. 1931) and my grandfather, Murdo MacLean (1891–1974), reaping the New Shawbost corn.

A timeless scene of fellowship, perhaps later that same week: an informal Shawbost Communion gathering in my grandfather's house, with the stooks drying outside.

Above. A family business: Clan MacLean at my uncle's induction as minister of Tolsta Free Church in the summer of 1973, supported by his brother, his sisters and their reverend husbands. Back row – Mrs Joan and Rev. Angus Smith (Cross); Rev. Alastair Montgomery (Scalpay); Mrs Mary and Rev. Donald Macleod (Partick Highland); Mrs Alexandra and Rev. Malcolm MacLean (Tolsta). Front row – Mrs Christine Montgomery, Mr M. D. and Mrs Annie MacLean.
Mrs Christina M. MacIver

Left. Murdo and Marilyn MacRitchie about to fly from Stornoway to the South Africa mission in 1979, the year he served as Moderator of the Free Church General Assembly.
W G Lucas – Hebridean Press Service

Rev. Murdo Alex MacLeod, minister of Stornoway. In 1995, 'Murdo Alick' – best man at my parent's wedding – had to serve as Moderator of a gruelling General Assembly. My mother and I met him at church the Sabbath night before; he spoke at length to her, and all the time clenched and pumped my hand in a grip he would not, as one preacher's kid to another, relinquish. At Assembly's end, he breezed forth to speak to waiting press. The statement done, he caught my eye at the door, winked broadly, and vanished. I never saw him again.

Rev. Donald MacRae (1918–2005), from Miavaig in Uig, was for many years the cherished Church of Scotland minister of Tarbert and exemplified the best of the old United Free tradition – tolerant, urbane and evangelical.

Twenty-five years in the Free Church ministry: Rev. Donald and Maryetta MacDonald celebrate in Carloway with close friends and a vast cake. *W.G. Lucas, Hebridean Press Service*

That abiding, faintly Edwardian dignity of Free Presbyterians: after the Communions, Tarbert, September 1998. *Author*

Free Presbyterian ministers at Stornoway Communion, August 2002 – Revs John MacLeod; Keith Watkins; David Campbell and Barry Whear. *Author*

A typical Presbyterian interior – Rev. Iain D. Campbell and office-bearers, Back Free Church, 2002, inside the 'latron' and below the central pulpit. *John MacLean Photography*

In the spring of 2008 these footballing girls of Back School fought their way to the final of the national Coca-Cola Sevens, beating several older, bigger teams and conceding not one goal. Then it emerged the final was to be held on the Sabbath. Despite the best efforts of the Club, their school, the islands Council, and even the lobbying of the MP and MSP, the organisers refused to budge. The girls unanimously refused to play and forfeited a real chance of the trophy. *John MacLean, Head Teacher, Back School*

been here only three Sabbaths for the past three months,' he wrote John MacLeod from Gairloch, 'and the battle is fought here quite as keenly as it can be anywhere else . . .'

Neil Cameron, finally ordained to a huge congregation in Glasgow in 1896, was one of nature's born leaders. A tough fellow of steely good looks, lately a hill-shepherd, he was born at Kilninver, Argyll, in 1854, and (significantly) was brought up in the Established Church. He had no natural ties with the Free Church, in 1893 or subsequently, and no one has more defined the Free Presbyterians than Cameron, who rapidly eclipsed MacFarlane or anyone else as its most assertive and determined leader. In 1893, he fell upon Lewis, amidst a great tour of the north-west in advocacy of his cause. At Stornoway, over 400 people gathered to hear him in the Drill Hall; in the discourtesy that marks such rallies in this period, Rev. James Greenfield – the town's Free Church minister – attended this occasion and orated volubly at its close, to general displeasure. The Presbytery had confidently expected two mainland pulpit stars – Angus Galbraith and Murdo MacKenzie – to visit the island and persuade everyone to stay in the Declaratory Act Free Church, but they failed to show up.

In September 1893, Mr Greenfield and Hector Cameron held their own rally. Over 500 attended and Cameron, determined to throttle the Free Presbyterians at birth, announced 'he had given himself to the study of history and as a result had found 'the good old path which brought rest to his soul. "As a consequence," the press report of the meeting tells us, "he was there to express the belief and tell his hearers that the Secessionist party stood with one foot planted on ignorance and the other on deception and falsehood. In such a foundation of sand, assuredly their footing would soon be swept away, and great must be the fall of the Secessionists."' Imminent Free Presbyterian collapse has been foretold ever since.

Weeks later, on 11 October 1893, John R. MacKay held a Stornoway meeting of his own, arguing fluently otherwise and pointing out that the Declaratory Act but legalised backslidings now long established. Yet it was in 1894 that actual bodies took shape. A 'vigorous congregation' formed in Stornoway, and at its first Communion season, at the end of August, a good many more joined it: they had some outstanding laymen to take services and kept three weekly prayer meetings. At first they kept services in the Drill Hall, but that first Communion – and the crowds anticipated – was a great worry. At short notice they secured a builder's yard; the men set to with a will, and it was quickly covered over and fitted out for the occasion: the minister of Shieldaig, old MacDonald, presided, and afterwards related he had never known such blessing. At least one sacramental season was held outdoors, for a photograph survives. In December 1895, Lady Matheson granted a site at the top of Scotland Street, and in 1899 a 'neat, compact church' was completed and, beauti- fully furnished and proportioned, is perhaps the loveliest place of worship on Lewis. It was planned and overseen by George MacLeod, a gracious man – and the governor of the little Stornoway prison.

In December 1894, John R. MacKay returned, by invitation, to address the anxious people of North Tolsta. A great crowd had gathered, but it was a cold raw day and someone had deliberately locked the church and made off with the key. It took time (and, one suspects, strong words) to secure and, in the cold, a good many had dispersed by the time MacKay could speak. Otherwise, some maintain, all Tolsta might have gone Free Presbyterian. Half of them certainly did. Local factors counted for much. Donald MacDonald, a later village historian, blamed the pastoral 'mis- management' of Hector Cameron. 'This split had little to do with the Declaratory Act. Young office-bearers were elected and older men were overlooked.'[6]

On the West Side, several families turned Free Presbyterian at Breasclete and Tolsta Chaolais. Services are still held. There was con- siderable support in Point and a little church was erected in Swordale; but generally, Free Presbyterians braved the considerable walk to Stornoway. There was also strong support in North Lochs, with services held regularly at Leurbost for some decades. Few care to be reminded that two Free Church ministers of the last century, Rev. John Morrison of Bernera and Cross and Malcolm MacIver of Lochs, were baptised as Free Presbyterians. A congregation also arose at Achmore, supported by most of the community, though its roots are hard to identify and some anonymous (and abusive) letters in the *Highland News* attacking its leaders are best ignored. For months, the local Board denied the Achmore people the use of the school for services and it was only won after agitation and angry appeals. This congregation also survives.

In Ness, a real opportunity was lost. The congregation was vacant; they had just completed a new church that belonged outright to the people; and they hated the Declaratory Act. Indeed, office-bearers tried to secure a Free Presbyterian minister for Cross. But the local Presbytery moved fast. As early as August 1893 it held a special diet in Ness 'to consider the state of matters in our island as regards the action of the secessionists and the steps that should be taken to secure the peace and unity of our congregations'. Presbytery insisted besides on meeting the congregation, threatened that any office-bearers with thoughts of separation would be 'summarily dealt with' and wrung out a declaration of loyalty to the Free Church from the elders. One, Murdo MacFarlane, had apparently signed the 'Bond of Union' at Inverness, and refused to attend: he was suspended *in absentia*. And, late in 1894, two elders – Malcolm MacLeod of Swainbost and James Finlayson of Skigersta – did separate.

There is little evidence to suggest their action had anything to do with continued argument over buildings, though the Free Presbyterian congregation was very much one of northern Ness, including almost every family in Skigersta. James Finlayson's involvement should certainly bury mythology that the Free Presbyterians in Ness were launched by the most ardent admirers of MacBeath. And he, too, did not die in his bed. One account of his passing, in 1902, asserts that he had an outside haunt for private prayer, and was found there one day, gone to his rest: another relates that, during his last illness, he suddenly – despite efforts to prevent him – struggled from bed, tottered outside and collapsed. Free Presbyterians later completed churches at Lionel and Skigersta and, though now much reduced, are still a respected body of believers in Ness.

Assorted practical disadvantages, aggressive action by Presbytery and a cultural aversion to 'secession' greatly limited Free Presbyterian prospects on Lewis. Harris was a different matter. It was in the Presbytery of Uist and much more readily reached from Skye, where support was considerable and men abounded. There was a huge exodus, especially in the south: around a third of Free Church people and almost everyone of strong Constitutionalist sympathy – reflecting, perhaps, both MacBean's early endeavours for the Secession Church and the weakness of the local ministry.

By 1895 there were seven Free Presbyterian groups in Harris with at least 1,400 adults adhering to the cause; and over 1,000 attended an early Communion season. (A large tent erected for the occasion was so badly slashed they had to make other shift.) They were particularly strong in Tarbert – where they met at first in a big salt-store, on the site of what is now the MacLeod Motel – in Kyles Scalpay and Stockinish to the north and at Finsbay and Strond to the south. The failure of the Free Church minority to win any Harris following after October 1900 reflects the totality of Free Presbyterian success in Harris.

It is difficult now to assess the total strength of the Free Presbyterian movement, but it is not difficult to reconcile Donald MacFarlane's own claim in July 1895 – some 20,000 people, 5 serving ministers, 18 students and 40 missionaries – with the statistics rigorously collated by the Free Church in 1896, putting the 'secession' at 6,756 elders, deacons, communicants and adherents over eighteen, once one factors in children. The Free Presbyterian Church continued to expand until the Union of 1900.

The last rites of this bleak narrative are acutely depressing. Robert Rainy moved quickly to tighten his grip on the Highlands, but his decision to appoint Rev. Alexander Lee – released from his charge at Nairn – as 'visiting agent' of the Highland Committee, at the prodigious salary of £500 and in charge of new and rigorously trained lay preachers, was a dreadful own-goal. For one, as an obvious general of the 'Advanced Party', Lee was immediately distrusted. For another, he was a fool, who grossly misled Rainy as to popular support for Union in the Highlands.

Rainy besides moved to limit further flight. Plans to introduce, in 1894, a new 'Questions and Formula' were aborted. Diverted by the new Constitutionalist line, he slyly had a motion passed at the same Assembly which solemnly stressed that, yes, the Declaratory Act was only a relieving measure. In 1896 he turned Murdo MacAskill, and fought to the last – almost succeeding – to subvert Murdo MacKenzie.

Most Constitutionalists ministers would at last trudge miserably into the Union. About two dozen were of sterner stuff, loathing of the Free Presbyterians being exceeded by a belief – on what proved sound legal advice – that if they simply stood where they were at the last battle, they could continue a purged Free Church with good hopes of securing both her name and assets in law. But the mass of ordinary people were restive. 'Deeply unhappy, they felt in their hearts that the Free Presbyterians had been right,' say Drummond and Bulloch, 'and that they had allowed themselves to remain in a Free Church which had slipped its moorings and was adrift in uncharted seas. . . . To use a contemporary phrase, they had been conned, and they knew it.'

The dwindling band of determined Constitutionalist ministers, tabling dissents and protests at every turn and relying constantly on the advice of their solicitors, were as much the prisoners of these Highlanders as their leaders. They held meetings on Lewis, several of which were invaded by pro-Union ministers and which grew on occasion most noisy. There is evidence that Free Church colleagues deliberately lured Hector Cameron into noisy Presbytery debate, with a provocation here and a red rag there, knowing that the angrier he became the less sense he generally made and the more damage he did to the anti-Union cause. At his nadir – when Peter MacDonald, minister of Stornoway Free English, asked him coolly to give just one text of Scripture in proof of the State's duty to recognise the Christian Church, Cameron could think of none, blustering pathetically, 'But I know I am right . . .' This actually did him good. The Hector Cameron of 1900 is a much more chastened, tender figure than the wind-bag of 1893.

The Union was effected at last on 30 October 1900, when – despite torrential rain – the massed General Assembly trooped down the Mound to converge with a no less determinedly jolly United Presbyterian Synod, and then processed to the covered Waverley Market, the only hall in Edinburgh big enough to host the gathering. There the General Assembly of the United Free Church was constituted, and Robert Rainy enthroned as its first Moderator.

The day before, at the close of business, the minority had retired to a committee room and endeavoured to carry on as the Free Church General Assembly, despite some nasty heckling. This morning they now turned up at the Assembly Hall. They found it locked and guarded by policemen. The United Free 'had been the first to appeal to Caesar'. The janitor refused insolently to admit them, claiming the hall was being cleaned. Rev. John Kennedy Cameron, minister of Brodick, snapped, 'We could have done without it being cleaned.' 'I believe that quite well,' sneered the janitor, 'you are among dirt anyway.' (One suspects he used a much cruder word.)

Yet twenty-seven Free Church ministers and tens of thousands of Free Church people, mostly in the Highlands, refused to enter the Union. And on Lewis, though Hector Cameron alone of the ministers refused to join the United Free Church, the vast majority of Free Church people declined to enter it either.

What was left of the Free Church on Harris 'went in', but only two congregations on Lewis – Uig and Stornoway English. The people of Bernera, though, adhered to the Free Church – and later, fairly reliable Free Church figures suggest that otherwise only 600 folk on Lewis had gone United Free: 100 in Lochs (out of 4,000), 60 in Carloway (out of 2,000), 80 in Barvas (out of 1,800), perhaps 120 in Ness (out of 1,800) and 100 in Knock (out of 2,000). United Free support in Shawbost and Back was derisory. After a few weeks in the United Free, trying desperately to haul his congregation with him, Hector Kennedy of Park gave up and crawled back to the Free Church. 'On the fateful day of 31st October 1900,' gushes Murdo MacAulay, 'Hector Cameron stood alone of all the Free Church ministers in Lewis. The splendid cohesion of the Free Church people, who so faithfully followed him, was the finest tribute that could have been paid to a minister of Christ.' This is untenable. Cameron was borne before the multitude like a corpse.

But the Free Church minority was reviled in the newspapers, and there was wholesale United Free persecution throughout Highland districts. Pensions were even stopped from retired, feeble old lay agents who refused to endorse the Union. One – who was bed-ridden – had dared to make plain his Free Church sympathies. Servants who might have thought of standing by the Free Church decided otherwise, on pain of dismissal. All over the Highlands, the Free Church majority in most districts was denied the use of its own building, and there were once again open-air assemblies, all the grimmer in this winter of 1900–1901. In some places local authorities were lobbied to deny Free Church groups the use of halls. Money everywhere – endowments, bank accounts – was seized and withheld, even in places where 'the United Church was not represented by a single man, woman or child in the community.'

One striking aspect of the Lewis division is that in rural districts, especially, the self-styled gentry joined the United Free Church.[7] These were people of power: doctors, like Rhoderick Ross in Borve; teachers with power to win bursaries and university admission for their ablest pupils; tweed-merchants and grocers, who might have dozens in their debt. In Carloway, especially, these joined forces to prevail on certain families to enter the Union. Ranald MacDonald, the schoolmaster, coerced several away from the Free Church, asserts Murdo MacAulay. And there was noisy dispute over buildings.

The most notorious row was at Ness, though its details are disputed to this day, both sides claiming they had offered reasonable terms for sharing the building – to be frustrated by the intemperate blackguards on the other. What is certain is that the church at Cross belonged to the community and the vast majority had not followed their minister, Donald MacDonald, into the United Free Church. At one point a desperate knot of Free Church lads broke into the building and occupied it; a smashed panel can still be seen on the vestry door.

MacDonald then foolishly involved the police, and raised a Sheriff Court action to secure the keys. They were not produced. A deputation led by the Sheriff Officer came in their pomp to Ness, to change the locks; the found their access to the church blocked by a 100-strong crowd and the official was jostled. Alexander Stewart admits delicately to 'unfortunate acts of violence'. Seven men from Ness were duly charged and fined £10, and feelings ran all the higher, for the local Sheriff of the county, C.J. Guthrie, was of open United Free sympathies – indeed, the Church's official legal adviser.

Police duly arrived to change the locks at Cross in December 1901 – and 'had to take refuge in the church until they managed to negotiate a safe departure,' enthuses Ansdell. At this point, threatening to make entire drama out of parochial dispute, the Secretary of State for Scotland, Lord Balfour of Burleigh, sent a great troop of police all the way to Lewis in a Royal Navy cruiser, and – lest they be overwhelmed by a thousand hand-bagging ladies – put a regiment at Fort George on stand-by, speaking even of an armed march on Ness as the ship hove off to Port to cover His Majesty's soldiers with her guns.

Only too mindful of what could happen, John Kennedy Cameron dashed to Lewis, met the Free Church leaders of Ness, and stressed on them the importance of calm and order, and of ceding possession of the building for now, lest all end in disrepute and even bloodshed. According to James Shaw Grant, writing in the 1980s, John Kennedy Cameron had a signal tactical advantage – his brother, a Deputy Chief Constable, was in charge of the Ross-shire detachment of policemen on this determined expedition, and the two men almost certainly liaised. The other divisions were from Inverness-shire and Lanarkshire and, once they found all peacable and the United Frees again in unmolested possession of the Cross church, there was an affecting sequel. The Highland policemen joined the Free Church congregation in their Sabbath worship; their Lanarkshire colleagues, on the initiative of their commander – Superintendent Gracie of Hamilton – heard sermon in the Established Church on the machair. (An exhausted, starving Gracie had met the minister the previous day – all the policemen had been horribly sea-sick on the Friday crossing – and been fed delicious scones, his first food in over twenty-four hours. 'He felt he should repay the minister's hospitality by giving him a good congregation for once,' concludes Grant, though cannot resist adding, 'I think, on the whole, the police come out of the affair with more credit than the churches!')

So – to evident journalistic chagrin – there was no confrontation, resistance, or anything but quiet, amused courtesy. The Chief Constable of Ross and Cromarty had opposed this absurd action from the start and expressly blamed the United Free minister at Cross for his intransigence. 'The United Free Church showed an eagerness to resort to the methods of physical force which is not easily reconciled with her vaunted repudiation of "compulsory measures in religion",' says Stewart, who rightly points out besides that Lord Balfour's decision could have had 'disastrous results'.

The Free Church, locally, was deftly organised and could draw on mainland support. In 1901 Hector Cameron made one of two tours of the West Side that year, escorted by Rev. John MacLeod of Duke Street, Glasgow. In February they held explanatory meetings and in June returned, as promised, for an open-air lecturing tour. A great tent was fashioned from boat-sails between Carloway and Tolsta Chaolais for a spectacular rally that June. A reporter describes the singing as 'transporting' and the scene 'beyond description'. Cameron, it seems, spoke ably and well as folk sat for hours 'without the slightest inclination to move.' The Carloway kirk session was afterwards constituted on the hillside as Mr MacLeod busily baptised a great many children in the tent. The people of Bernera sent a boat over to Garynahine, where the ministers stayed that night, bore them back, and 'unanimously resolved to stand by the Free Church', though it cannot have been that unanimous as a little United

Free group survived to the 1920s. There were more meetings on this scale at Shawbost and by the Barvas river. And 1902 brought a welcome surprise: Nicol Nicolson, one of the 1900 stalwarts, accepted a call to Shawbost from Garve.

Ness was not the only scene of building dispute. Two young men from the Borrowston township locked themselves in the Carloway church all night, hoping somehow to secure it for the Free Church; but two wiser young men forced their way in later (breaking a pane of glass in the process) and found the revolutionaries hiding under the pulpit. Someone had to be sent hastily to Bragar to secure new glass. This all sounds almost civilised, but the United Free group – having demanded, and secured, exclusive use of the church for their Communion – then asked the majority to pay half the expenses. They were denied, but there was much chuckling.

In Shawbost, after final Free Church victory, Rev. George Campbell left quietly. A little corrugated-iron UF church was built and the boundary-wall and gate-pillars still identify it, over a ditch to the south of the Free Church car-park and now enclosing a private house. Other, much larger corrugated-iron buildings were earlier erected by the Free Church as the case dragged on. The one at Lochs, opened as early as 25 February 1901, could hold 1,000 people; and the concrete founds of another can be seen at Barvas to this day, below the main road. At Lochs and, besides, at Garrabost, the Free Church had sensibly sought the advice of the police superintendent in Stornoway, who discouraged thoughts of forcible possession.

It would be silly to pretend that harassment and oppression were one-sided. A Church of Scotland minister told me in 1991 of a vicious little plot against Mr MacDonald, United Free minister at Cross; a party of men would waylay him on the road, cripple his horse with scythe-blades, and then give the parson a good seeing-to. However, said he solemnly, a 'great blinding light' blazed behind Donald MacDonald as he came, and the attackers fled. Whatever the truth of this early appearance by the Angels of Mons, there are claims besides of the corn-stacks of United Free elders in Ness being fired, windows in MacDonald's manse being smashed and great stones landing on the bed where he was sleeping. (*An Domhnallach*, as he is still remembered – of such august presence that I knew an old lady who, as a little girl, hid behind a peat-stack if she saw him coming[8] – was either of robust stuff, or such assassins of very bad aim, for he survived until 1938.)

The United Free minister of Lochs, John MacDougall, said there was 'intimidation' of his cause in the district. Communicants who had adhered to him were threatened with loss of credit. Mr Morrison at Barvas talked of two men who refused to hear him for fear of their neighbours. In some districts, it was alleged, the doors of United Free folk were daubed with red paint. In Knock, at first, things were quite amicable.[9] The United Free minister, George MacLeod, though no doubt aghast so few had followed him, even allowed the Free Church majority use of the new, 1882 Garrabost building for their first Communion. Then he fell out with them over peat-banks. It is not clear if continued exile was because he denied them the building or because they would not ask for it. Free Church services were held in a deep gully, *Allt na Muilne*, a stream flowing down to the shore. They then erected a 'tin church'; by the time Garrabost Free Church was at last recovered, it was in such disrepair that it fell into entire disuse, and it was only in 1922 the Free Church at Knock finally restored what is still their place of worship. The *eaglais-shinc* stood for many more years and the concrete founds were still to be seen into the 1990s; the site is now occupied by a community war memorial.

Douglas Ansdell – relying too much on a 1987 newspaper article from a partisan source – claims that, after the House of Lords judgement, Knock Free Church refused flatly to rent their lately erected corrugated-iron place of worship to the United Free, only yards from the original building. So MacLeod's little congregation had to erect a wooden one; and then, later, a permanent building beside that, so that by 1912 four churches stood cheek-by-jowl in the middle of Garrabost. But, even if there were four church buildings – which is unlikely – that does not equate to four *churches*, and all the evidence we have from the 1930s, at least, is that by then relations between the two denominations in Knock were singularly cordial.

In all of this, it should not be forgotten, neither Robert Rainy nor the United Free Church of Scotland offered the least compromise. They refused to part with a stick of property, to dole out a penny of funds or offer access to colleges, libraries and the records vital for church order. They extended no charity whatever to the two dozen colleagues and tens of thousands of Highlanders who had the temerity to resist the Union. All invitations to talk were rebuffed; every suggestion of equitable division was scorned; legal actions raised to evict and to secure.

The sheer disparity of the two denominations must be born in mind. One was – it is no exaggeration – as entrenched and powerful in national life as, in much of post-war Scotland, the Scottish Labour Party: a church with over 1,500 ministers, tens of thousands of schoolmasters, the backing of the press, the backing of the professions, the backing of politicians and the backing of local authorities. The other was a Highland rump, with no friends in high places, who sought merely to stand where they had always stood and – as far as the ministers were concerned – on the principles clearly contracted when they were ordained. For this they were to be stripped of everything belonging to the body to which they alone were *adhering*.

The Free Church of Scotland has never in some quarters been forgiven for raising what is still studied as a historic and important law case. Pietists mock their 'worldliness' and the United Free majority, in final humiliation, desperately invoked the principal of spiritual independence, asserting it and it alone stood for the 'Crown Rights of the Redeemer'. This is specious nonsense. The Free Church had not been the first to invoke the law. And the matter was not about spiritual rights, but civil ones. The 'Free Church Case' – Bannatyne versus Overtoun – specifically centres on trust-law as understood in Scotland, the duty to devote funds and use facilities for the purpose for which they were given, and not to subvert them to other doctrines, another religion, and other ends.

On 9 August 1901, Lord Low and the Second Division of the Court of Session found for the United Free majority. The Free Church appealed. On 4 July 1902, the Second Division of the Court of Session found against them once more, and United Free delight did abound. Increasingly desperate, still more determined, the Free Church appealed to the House of Lords. A verdict there was imminent when one law-lord died, and the case had to be heard again. Marcus Dods, a rather radical theologian who delighted in controversial sermons (the 1890 Free Church General Assembly had weakly acquitted him after he asserted, in a St Giles sermon, that 'one must not too hastily conclude that even a belief in Christ's divinity is essential to the true Christian'), worried about the House of Lords and inveighed darkly, in his United Free pomp, at the very idea of the State being granted authority 'to prevent a church from revising her belief'.

Archibald MacNeilage replied robustly in the *Monthly Record*. 'No one hinders Dr Dods from changing his creed; the one thing which the law of the land happily prevents is that Dr Dods will appropriate the funds destined for the promotion of the doctrines of the Westminster Confession of Faith and use them for the promotion of doctrines of an opposite character. It is a pity secular judges should need to teach doctors of divinity elementary morality.'[10]

On 1 August 1904, the House of Lords declared that the United Free Church was not the Free Church; that it had no right or title to any of the property held by the Free Church prior to 31 October 1900; and that the present, beleaguered Free Church of Scotland was the lawful owner of every last brick, document, pound and chattle.

With astonishing ease – and simultaneously rousing all her allies and all her massed forces to a great, howling outcry – the United Free Church reinvented herself as one great, innocent, wounded martyr, bringing all the pressure she could to bear on Scotland's politicians and the London government and demanding defence and redress, while simultaneously doubling her vilification of the 'legal Free Church' or (a name that has stuck, to the unbounded joy of sub-editors) the 'Wee Frees'. They besides belaboured the judges of the House of Lords. 'The reproach of ignorance, indeed, was one that was freely heaped upon the whole company who formed the majority. If proof of the assertion were sought, it was deemed sufficient to point out that, with one exception, they were Englishmen. If this fact was not considered altogether conclusive, there was the additional enormity that they were Episcopalians. Then they had made a radical mistake in applying the principles of the law of Trusts. This was degrading the Church to the level of a mercantile company . . .' But the House of Lords decision was, of course, final; and has set an abiding precedent: that even a tiny minority, if a church chooses wholesale to change her doctrine and constitution, can rightfully claim all assets held in trust. The judgement in detail focused on the Establishment Principle, which the United Frees had plainly repudiated; and expressly on the Declaratory Act.

Right was one thing. Possession was quite another and, as Scotland's press took up the outcry, the Conservative government of Arthur Balfour – acutely aware that the United Free Church commanded very many votes – weakly gave way. A Royal Commission was appointed to confirm – what the Free Church herself openly granted – that she could not possibly administer all the assets to which she had entire legal title. There followed an unprecedented 1905 Act of Parliament setting aside the Lords' decision and placing all the disputed property in the hands of an Executive Commission. This, crudely and in the teeth of United Free hysterics, apportioned the goods.

The Free Church minority won some meagre funds and many Highland buildings (all the churches and manses on Lewis, for instance, save those of Uig and Stornoway Free English), the records of the six northern Synods and of seventeen Highland presbyteries. But she lost the great Free Church libraries, the Assembly Hall and all the colleges, retaining only the former Free Church Offices for a college and a nearby church for her General Assembly. The terms reached in Scotland's cities were particularly unjust and – attesting just how despised the 'Wee Frees' were – not a single Member of Parliament from the Highlands spoke out on her behalf.

Yet folk here and there drifted back. One young man, born in Dingwall in 1883, had spent recent months in spiritual anguish. In the summer of

1909, he found Christ, and then trudged Edinburgh in search of a church where his soul would be fed, braving organs and hymns, sermons read and platitudinous. In November, he tried St Columba's Free Church, a newly welded Highland congregation at the top of the Royal Mile, whose building – the former Free St John's – served also as the new Assembly Hall. Kenneth MacRae was overwhelmed by the worship and the preaching. He joined the following year, and shortly applied for the Free Church ministry.

'When the Lord in mercy opened my eyes,' he wrote many years later, 'I was an adherent of the United Free Church. Very shortly afterwards I came in contact with Free Church preaching and studied the position of those whom I had been taught to believe were a small body of ignorant Highlanders. On the one side I had the preaching of Christ crucified which was as honey to my soul, on the other I had that hateful and soul-destroying thing called Higher Criticism. Which was I to choose? I did not hesitate for a single moment. For ever I turned my back upon a Church which so dishonoured my Lord.'[11]

The Free Church of Scotland was left – and remains – overwhelmingly the church of Lewis Christians – and, before the Second World War, would recover some ground in Harris – but no longer as a great national Church. She would on the Long Island long struggle against a catalogue of abiding bitternesses, dreadful tragedy and protracted economic recession, licking her scars until the last years before the Second World War.

One might well wonder why, in October 1900, the minority did not immediately make common cause with the Free Presbyterians. Certainly the *Free Presbyterian Magazine* was at first friendly and supportive, though – understandably in the chaotic circumstances – declined 1902 overtures for union as 'premature'. Even so, and the hurts of the 1890s notwithstanding, the rift might well have been healed but for calculated Free Church decisions, especially after the House of Lords judgement and amid the protracted, painful scrap for congregational properties. First, the Declaratory Act was in May 1905 repealed by the Free Church in terms explicitly offensive to the men of 1893 – 'this Church adheres, as she has always adhered, to her subordinate standards'. A mortified Donald Munro, now Free Church minister at Ferintosh and a New College contemporary of John MacLeod, had been out-gunned on the relevant committee. He dashed off a note of apology. 'I am afraid it will be regarded as quite objectionable, by some of your men . . . The older ministers . . . will insist on some such phrase, and will carry the day.' They did. It stood. Many Free Presbyterians then eager for reunion thus had the ground cut from under them before their own brethren. A motion to begin conference with the Free Church was decisively defeated at the July 1905 Synod.

Such Free Church language reflected an ambivalence already reflected in action. From the winter of 1900–1901, even as the United Free bade to wipe out her, she seems in many districts to have done her utmost to undermine Free Presbyterian congregations and to poach her best ministers. After 1904, these efforts were redoubled. In December 1905 John MacLeod – then of Kames – and his Stornoway colleague, George MacKay, jumped to the Free Church. MacLeod became Professor of Greek and New Testament Theology; MacKay was cynically inducted as Stornoway's Free Church minister, in a calculated bid to win his original flock besides. The following year, Alexander Stewart took most of the Edinburgh congregation into the Free Church, and the building besides,[12] leaving only a remnant nastily dismissed as 'five silly girls'. Finally, Dugald Cameron abandoned his Free Presbyterian pastorate in Tain and Fearn, became minister of Croy Free Church and was never heard of again. The Free Presbyterians lost besides many divinity students to the resurrected Free Church and, when the last serious bid for union was thrown out by Synod in 1917, four more ministers, including John R. MacKay. Edinburgh apart, between 1900 and 1910 many other congregations – Alness, Latheron, Barra, Garve, Keiss, Lybster and Glenelg and more – were gobbled up by the Free Church.

Their flight, and Free Presbyterian anger, cemented the leadership of Neil Cameron,[13] who adroitly outwitted these undoubted intellects and cemented his Church on a base of absolute, unwavering conservatism, 'the absolute infallibility of the Scriptures of the Old and New Testaments, and the whole doctrine contained in the Confession of Faith, both in her profession and practice.' Cameron is one of those paradoxically anticlerical ministers the Highlands throw up from time to time, and certainly fashioned the Free Presbyterians into what is to all intents and purposes a 'closed shop'. Only her ministers may preach in her pulpits. They cannot preach in any other. While officially eschewing closed Communion, she observes it in practice, declaring that 'none are to be received to the Lord's Table in this Church but such as are known as God-fearing persons'. She also and with some rigour dealt with communicants who on occasion chose to join Free Church services, Cameron himself often dashing about to seize command of any convenient kirk session for the purpose. In most instances, though, he bluntly offered a disjunction certificate on pain of suspension. And, when few Free Presbyterian congregations had then even permanent buildings, he was consciously fighting for his Church's life.

The Free Church would long try to vindicate her position between

1893 and 1900, as her leaders huddled in Highland manses on the pay-roll of the Declaratory Act Free Church, and mock the Free Presbyterian stand – asserting their departure was premature; that the Declaratory Act was *ultra vires* and, accordingly, non-binding and inoperative; that the Questions and Formula were not changed and that, in any event, the House of Lords recognised her at the last as the true Free Church. These are deep waters. But Free Presbyterian claims were never heard, or even heard of, by the House of Lords. Her leaders had walked into consider-able hardship in 1893 because they could not conscientiously do other-wise. Dr Rainy's decision in 1894 to postpone alteration of the Questions and Formula was a direct consequence of the 'secession'. And, while undoubtedly *ultra vires*, the Declaratory Act was real law with real consequences. James MacDonald's declaration at Dornoch, in 1892, was stricken from the record by the orders of higher Free Church courts; in his speech arguing for repeal in 1893, Angus Galbraith – one of the 1900 Free Church leaders – openly declared that the Act 'regulated their creed and public testimony as a Church'; Dr Rainy likewise asserted that 'as long as it lasts, no doubt it is authoritative'.

But the Christian history of Lewis over the last century is largely the history of the Free Church. And the Free Church of Scotland should not be despised. For one, every man's hand is against her: she is attacked from both left and right. For another, she has striven conscientiously to build a far-flung evangelical witness in Scotland, opening many new congrega-tions. In the Free Church College she has maintained the most orthodox and academically rigorous theological seminary in the British Isles; by contrast, the colleges of which she was robbed in 1905 were quickly given away to the State. And she has been a force for Highland betterment. Of special importance in Long Island history was Murdo MacRae, minister of Kinloch from 1927 to 1961; he fought long, hard and tirelessly for the Harris Tweed industry,[14] securing parliamentary legislation and inter-national agreement to protect its brand and safeguard the livelihoods of island weavers.

The Free Church has one most striking virtue: she is profoundly self-critical. From General Assemblies through decades of the *Monthly Record* to almost any gathering of Free Church people, voices invariably bleat just how awful a failure the Free Church is and what must be done to improve her. The failings of the Free Church have been generally those of charity, as have her most notable successes, and if she lacks the consistency of the Free Presbyterians she has been free of their frequent complacency. She has really been a coalition of different emphases and of Highland and Lowland elements. After the House of Lords vindication she belatedly restored her traditional form of worship – prohibiting instruments and 'uninspired materials of praise' in public worship, though pressure mounts in the new century for its overthrow.

In time, both the Free Church and the Free Presbyterians would accomplish much good and the United Free and, later, Church of Scotland in Lewis and Harris have also seen some notable and gracious ministries. But the immediate consequences of the Declaratory Act division were abiding.

The Highlands, as my father once observed, can probably supply an outstanding minister, a competent session-clerk and a tuneful precentor for every parish. But they cannot do so in triplicate. And for many years only the largest, most central districts would enjoy a minister of every denomination. In most, there was marked asymmetry, with one or two dominant denominations and a much smaller, marginalised one – to say nothing, until 1929, of the Established Church besides. There were accordingly immediate and serious consequences of the disastrous failure to make one, united Highland stand in 1893.

It became much harder to impose church discipline, particularly in the careful administration of infant baptism, and the worst abuses on the island all fall in this twentieth-century period. And, in such a desperate shortage of Gaelic talent, the calibre of the ministry itself fell. Desperate to fill Gaelic pulpits and prevent further seepage to the Free Church, the United Free Church actively recruited very young Highland schoolboys, offering bursaries and other inducements, even lads who were Free Church or Free Presbyterian and, more seriously, lads who were not converted – so aggressively that the *Free Presbyterian Magazine* warned parents against it.

There were gifted ministers, even in this period. Nicol Nicolson was a highly respected pastor in Shawbost. Yet another John MacLeod, inducted to Barvas Free Church in 1922, was a conscientious minister; we have noted Murdo MacRae of Kinloch, and might note besides Malcolm MacIver of Lochs, ordained in 1924, and Murdo MacLeod of Park, settled in 1920. These men had very long and influential pastorates, as did their colleague William Campbell, inducted to Knock in 1926. We will take a closer look at John MacIver, also ordained in 1924 at Carloway Free Church. But several other Free Church ministries in this period were unmemorable, unavailing and short.

George MacKay's successor as Free Presbyterian minister of Stornoway, Neil MacIntyre – translated from Duirinish in 1908 – was a fine Lochaber man; indeed, that congregation has always had solid pastors. Harris was not easily settled. The colourful Ewen MacQueen was ordained and inducted as Free Presbyterian minister in July 1901, but

the charge was huge and demanding, and his manse at Tarbert decidedly
off-centre, and he left after only two years. A new pastor, from North Uist
– Donald N. MacLeod – was ordained at last in 1911, and his name is still
most cherished, but Harris really needed two ministers. Nor were the
United Free Church lacking in eminent talent: several of the 1900 men
were of genuine stature, and Duncan MacLeod – ordained to Carloway in
1903 – was a beloved man, who had later a notable pastorate in Tarbert.

Sectarianism should not be exaggerated. Two later Carloway ministers,
Donald MacLeod (Free Church) and Neil Morrison (United Free) served
there during the First World War and were great personal friends, often
seen ambling about 'arm in arm when their parishioners were at logger-
heads.' Relations between the Free and Free Presbyterian Church were
cordial until well after the Second World War. The Free Presbyterians
happily lent out their Tolsta church for an overflow service at the
induction of Angus Finlayson, the first Free Church minister, in
1948. Boatloads used to sail from Bernera – Free Church and Church
of Scotland people – to hear Free Presbyterian ministers at Breasclete
Communion. Free Presbyterian meeting-houses, even in the 1960s,
closed in South Harris so that people could enjoy the weekday services
of the Free Church Communion at Leverburgh. More recent and
sustained chill reflects, as much as anything, spiritual decline.

All the churches had after 1900 to resort, for the first time and on a
very large scale, to the use of lay agents or 'missionaries'. In order to tempt
men to especially difficult situations, the United Free Church offered the
prospect of later fast-track promotion to the ordained ministry; Donald
Cameron of Shawbost is one example, and the late Alexander Morrison –
from Maraig in Harris, who ended his career as Church of Scotland
minister of Barvas – was another. The Free Church, equally pressed for
men, created a curious class of 'ordained missionaries', ministers who
could preach and dispense the sacraments like any minister, but who were
appointed rather than inducted to a charge and could not be called out of
it save by the express permission of the church courts. Some of these men,
like Murdo MacIver of Shawbost, were eminent; others were amiable
mediocrities. A bad missionary, stationed for years in one place, could do
great harm.

An unfortunate and enduring legacy of 'black Rainy' is abiding distrust
of Lowland leadership and especially of Edinburgh. It is notable that the
Free Presbyterian Synod has only once met in that city, to commemorate
the Reformation in 1960, and the annual diet alternates between Inverness and Glasgow. The Free Church College and its professors have long
been viewed with Highland and especially Lewis ambivalence and, even
half a century ago, was subject to open attack as a potential bridgehead of

declension. This fed easily into a lazy pietistic anti-intellectualism, only reinforced by so much bad lay preaching, marked not by clear and doctrinal teaching but by 'spiritualising' – allegorical preaching on, usually, Old Testament themes and, at its worst, little more than careless play on words.

Like a small boy who has been treated to rather too many doughnuts before his tea, congregations too often lost a taste for good sermons. When a minister delivered a sacrificially wrought, worthwhile expository discourse, Christians did not like it, and this is still a real problem in the larger island denominations. Depopulation has emptied many former stations, and the private car has eased shuttling 'pulpit supply'. There are no resident lay agents on the Long Island now. Yet, the odd bad egg apart, there were conscientious men who for pitiable pay and little support worked long, unsung and largely forgotten, to advance the Kingdom and to maintain the cause.

But amidst all this drama, more people turned to Christ. There are reports of modest revival, amidst the Union strife, in Ness and at Uig, and there is no reason to doubt their authenticity. Murdo MacAulay relates a good story about the curious circumstances in which another awakening began in the Callanish, Breasclete and Tolsta Chaolais districts.[15] George MacKay was then Free Presbyterian minister of Stornoway and had to preach in Breasclete on 21 January 1904, and besides to perform the marriage of a Free Presbyterian man and a Free Church woman, both from Tolsta Chaolais. On the day – as was then customary – a procession, led by a piper, tramped from that township to the crossroads at Breasclete. MacKay pointedly told the wedding party after the ceremony 'that unless they were circumspect in their behaviour he would call upon them again that evening.'

That night, George MacKay duly kept his word. He burst in full, clerical might into the wedding-dance in a Tolsta Chaolais barn, seizing a melodeon with such force that the musician struggled to extricate his thumb from the strap. But another started up on his instrument – whereupon that box, too, was seized by George MacKay, who sat decisively down with one on each knee. Revellers fled into the night from the Free Presbyterian minister, but MacKay was swift to run down Plan B: another dance, in another Tolsta Chaolais barn, with no fewer than three pipers. This time, the revellers had appointed a guard to keep the door, but perhaps he had been paid in whisky, for MacKay somehow eluded his watch. He marched at once to the piper on duty and demanded he hand over his instrument. The man said politely they were not his own pipes, but those of another, *Iain Amhlaidh*. George MacKay – the evening has an extraordinarily mannered air about it – wheeled on this *Iain Amhlaidh* and demanded the pipes. But this Iain had been a soldier and had been presented with the pipes by his company in the Army, after continuing to play his previous set during an action even as he was wounded. And he replied splendidly to the Free Presbyterian minister, '*Le fuil a fhuair mi iad, agus le fuil a chailleas mi iad*' – 'by blood I obtained them, and by blood I shall surrender them!'

MacKay wisely retreated and called at the bride's home, where he observed that 'there would be two or three there who would be anxious to see him soon.' When he returned two days later, it was to preach a 'powerful and impressive sermon in Tolsta Chaolais . . . that no greater curse or judgement could come upon a parish than a crippled piper (*Iain Amhlaidh*), a drunken schoolmaster (Finlay Smith, the Doune schoolmaster) and a graceless minister (Rev. Duncan MacLeod, Carloway minister of the United Free Church).' MacAulay rightly points out that Mr MacLeod was an able minister of the Gospel, and adds that *Iain Amhlaidh* 'was later a good man'. His silence on Smith is delicious. A revival began. Two young people came later to see George MacKay and apologise, now actively seeking their Saviour; and in time a number of young men came forward who were later fine office-bearers of the various churches in that district. Later an eminent Free Church minister at Fearn, MacKay is affectionately chronicled in the jolly memoir, *My Uncle George*, by the noted journalist Alasdair Phillips. And Phillips inherited a desk which bore a warm inscription – *Presented to the Rev. George MacKay by the Young People of Tolsta Chaolais, Lewis, 1910.*[16]

In September 1922, travelling to Lochs Communion, Kenneth MacRae – now Free Church minister of Kilmuir, in Skye – made his way to catch the MacBrayne steamer. 'At Kyle I found the Revs. MacIntyre (Stornoway), MacLeod (Harris) and MacDonald (Portree), all Free Presbyterian ministers, in the hotel at breakfast and they kindly took me up to a bedroom to have worship with them. I enjoyed it very much. My soul longs for those men to come in among us. How long will Israel and Judah be divided?'[17]

III

'The Shore of Trouble is Hidden'

Spring Tide

Uair is uair agus mi briste
thig mi smuain ort is tu òg,
is lìonadh an cuan do-thuigsinn
le làn-mara 's mìle seòl.

Falaichear cladach na trioblaid
le bhodhannan is tiùrr a' bhròin,
is buailidh an tonn gun bhristeadh
mu m'chasan le suathadh sròil.

Ciamar nach do mhair an reothairt,
bu bhuidhe dhomh na do na h-eòin,
agus a chaill mi a cobhair,
's i tràghadh boinn' air bhoinne bròin?

Again and again when I am broken
my thought comes on you when you were young,
and the incomprehensible ocean fills
with floodtide and a thousand sails.

The shore of trouble is hidden
with its reefs and the wrack of grief,
and the unbreaking wave strikes
about my feet with a silken rubbing.

How did the springtide not last,
the springtide more golden to me than to the birds,
and how did I lose its succour,
ebbing drop by drop of grief?

Somhairle Mac Gill-Eain
Sorley MacLean (1911–1996)
from *Reothairt is Contraigh*, Edinburgh, 1977.

11

'That's What I Thought Too, When I Heard the Bell'

1914–1934

Few have ever grasped that the defining tragedy in Gaeldom was not Culloden, or even the Clearances, but the Great War.[1] Its casualties have been exaggerated by rather too many English teachers – most who served in the conflict survived it and most, contrary to myth, recalled it as a positive experience – but the absence of so many men for four or five years destroyed Highland communities and left abiding damage in local agriculture.

The real problem was not that so many men were killed, but that a very high proportion were loathe afterwards to settle in their native glens; they had been away too long, seen rather too much and had lost too many childhood friends. They swelled, instead, Scotland's cities, or emigrated abroad. The scale of that depopulation is grimly attested in Highland induction statistics. Over 800 Free Presbyterians in Assynt signed the call to Murdo Morrison, their first minister, in 1913. When his successor, Alexander MacAskill, was inducted in 1937, only 400 signed it. Church attendance was still the done thing, but in twenty years half the people of the parish had vanished. In 1987, *his* successor – Archibald MacPhail, inducted in 1985 – reported he had nine communicant members, seventy adult adherents and eleven children; his Sabbath attendance ranged between forty and forty-eight. In 2008, Free Presbyterian attendance in Assynt is in single figures.

But Lewis had a fearful blow in the first weeks of hard-won peace. When millions of Royal Naval Reserve veterans were demobilised in the last day of 1918, the Admiralty quite failed to organise adequate transport home and were confronted, on New Year's Eve, with a very large and restless throng of Lewis and Harris sailors at Kyle of Lochalsh – far too many for the inadequate MacBrayne mail-boat. An Admiralty steam-yacht, the *Iolaire*, was hastily sent from Stornoway and, in the small hours, jammed to the gunnels with happy lads, made back for Lewis in increasingly fresh conditions. She had neither the lifeboat capacity nor anything like enough life jackets for all on board; her commander had never made a night-voyage to Stornoway in his life and there is some real anecdotal evidence – it was after all New Year – that he or at least some of the officers were drinking.

The *Iolaire* never made it.[2] In the small hours of New Year's Day, hopelessly off course, she hit a notorious reef – the Beasts of Holm – by the mouth of Stornoway harbour; the saloon door jammed and most on board could not even get on deck. Two hundred and five men were drowned, 188 natives of Lewis and Harris. The body of the ship's commander was one of many washed up; he was wearing two life jackets. There were but seventy-nine survivors. The disaster was never satisfactorily explained and the subsequent, brisk Admiralty inquiry smells suspiciously of a cover-up. Though still Britain's worst peacetime tragedy at sea since the foundering of the *Titanic*, few beyond the Highlands have ever heard of the *Iolaire*.

The tragedy devastated the island and left its mark on all old enough to remember it. Scarcely a family on Lewis was untouched (and eleven from Harris were lost besides). Nine men were lost from Shawbost; eleven from Leurbost; eleven from Tolsta. My grandparents in Ness, small children in 1919, remembered seeing the carts trundle back from Stornoway – one, or four, or six coffins on a cart.

Another child in that parish, Peggy Murray, later the vibrant and clever wife of Rev. Donald Gillies, never forgot the excited night she waited up, late, and still later, in her Lionel home – she was only four years old – for her father at last to return from the war.[3] Finally, puzzled, they retired. Next day there was an ominous air about the household, and then they saw a party of elders approaching their house. But ahead scurried a small boy – he had a terrible stutter, especially when he was excited, and he burst into the kitchen crying, 'They say that the b-b-boat went on the rocks and that Iain is d-d-drowned!' Mrs Murray went white – she clung to the dresser – and, as the men came silently in, she said, 'Is it true what he said?' It was true. That night, Peggy related many years later, her mother had a dream. She dreamt that her man came to her, and she said, 'Oh, Iain, how am I going to manage?' and he said, 'Well, that's what I thought too, when I heard the bell.'

Not without agitation – one very recent bride was nearly denied it, because she had no child, until her father demanded that the Admiralty produce hard evidence that she was *not* with child – a modest cash-pension was wrung for *Iolaire* widows. But it was only the start of terrible years for the Long Island – the failure of Lord Leverhulme's grandiloquent schemes; wholesale emigration; widespread unemployment, hardship and even hunger, rampant tuberculosis and the throbbing wounds of the Great War and the *Iolaire*. The Free Presbyterians had even to open a 'Lewis Destitution Fund', so bad were island conditions. Desperate people grew avaricious and manipulative: a mean, clutching spirit seized villages.

In the grim 1920s, struggling people could behave ruthlessly. Anyone with any cash income, however modest, was envied. 'We had that pension,' said Peggy, 'but we had no chickens. We had no eggs. We had no cow.' Yet, strapped as she was, Mrs Murray took in two very old Free Presbyterian ladies from Skigersta, no longer capable otherwise of walking the long distance to service at Lionel. (This sort of selflessness typified many Great War widows. 'It wasn't only our own family that my mother's widow's pension brought up,' a Point woman, Mary Crane, told Calum Ferguson.)

Peggy watched her mother – dressed now and for always, like so many other women, in black from head to toe – toil all day for neighbours, and count herself fortunate to get a pail of potatoes for her pains. Nor were Mrs Murray's sorrows done. One beloved son suffered so horribly from spinal tuberculosis that she afterwards confessed she had prayed – the youth was a fine Christian – that the Lord would call him home. He duly did. Another son was lost off Malta, in the Second World War. Finally, when – after an extraordinary and, as Peggy inimitably described it, a hilarious courtship – she and Donald Gillies were married, and he was at last trained and ordained, Mrs Murray joined them in the manse, first at Lochcarron and, from 1960, in Lochs, in final security and with doting grandchildren. She observed, in the last months of her life, in 1967, 'You know, my dear, the Lord has been very good to me.' And the final jolt came before they closed the coffin, when Peggy looked once more on her mother – the extraordinary shock, after half a century of widow's weeds, of beholding her clothed in white.

Two boys from Swainbost were lost on the *Iolaire* – brothers, Donald MacDonald, twenty-seven, and his brother Murdo, who was twenty-one. Donald, a strong swimmer, fought his way to shore, and searched desperately for his brother, staggering about the other shocked stragglers: '*Am faca sibh Murchadh; am faca sibh Murchadh?*' – 'have you seen Murdo?' Then he plunged back into the sea, making for the stricken ship in search of him, and so he too was drowned. Their father was a gracious man – an elder in the United Free Church – and, months later, a visiting preacher made reference in prayer to the men of the place who, in the late tragedy, had been taken 'before their time'. The old man asked afterwards, in all courtesy but most firmly, to see this minister, and declared quietly, 'My sons were called by the Lord at the time He had ordained for them from all eternity, not a moment longer and not a moment before.'

It was very many years before a simple monument was erected on the low cliff above the Beasts of Holm, and it has no answers; only a verse from Psalm 77.

> *Do cheuman tha 's an doimhneachd mhòir,*
> *do shlighe tha 's a' chuan:*
> *Ach luirg do chos cha-n aithnich sinn,*
> *tha sud 'am folach uainn.*

> Thy way is in the sea, and in
> the waters great thy path;
> Yet are thy footsteps hid, O Lord;
> none knowledge thereof hath.

The Great War and the *Iolaire* did not, in the bleak aftermath of the 1920s and amidst unrest, land-raids and emigration, provoke more spiritual renewal. If anything, these years are the nadir of island Evangelicalism – of lovelessness and legalism, of palpable spiritual decline.

Better days were looming. And one denomination, at least, was already on the way out as far as the West Highlands were concerned. The United Free Church had, by the 1920s, increasingly lost the will to live and was in open negotiation for wedlock with the Auld Kirk. The Established Church had been in steady recovery for half a century and we have noted the dark impact of this reality within the Victorian politics of the Free Church, as a partisan denominationalism displaced the great vision of the Disruption. And the Auld Kirk had taken full advantage, in 1905, of her rival's woes, cleverly seizing on the Churches (Scotland) Act – rushed through Parliament by the Balfour government to rob the Free Church minority of most of its lawful goods – to win the insertion of a clause wherein Parliament granted the Kirk the liberty to alter her own relationship with the Confession of Faith. Robert Rainy's fury can be imagined – he loathed anything that might improve the Established Church's freedom or appeal to a new age – but he desperately needed this legislation and he could do nothing. By the Great War, the ardent Evangelicalism of his United Free creation was already sliding with remarkable speed into quasi-Pelagian modernism. By the 1920s, the old 'Voluntary' passions were a minority; most United Free ministers, and most United Free people, now thought return to a national church rather attractive. One Lewis congregation – Bernera – was even in the vanguard; her United Free and Established bodies married a year early, in 1928, to much publicity and satisfaction.

Scottish churchmen had learned their legal lesson. In 1906 the Kirk altered her Questions and Formula, and in 1920 the Church of Scotland Enabling Act went through Parliament, loosening the terms of State recognition still further and allowing the Established Church to adopt assorted Articles Declaratory without losing title – either now or in the Union to come – to the old endowments. When it became evident that a minority of United Frees – led by the Reverend James Barr and mostly, as one would expect, of the old United Presbyterian background – were determined not to return to the Auld Kirk, terms of divorce were most amicably agreed, with an equitable division of properties. The Great Union was at last celebrated, with much self-congratulation and in the benevolent presence of the Duke and Duchess of York, at Edinburgh on 3 October 1929, and thus the modern Church of Scotland was born.[4]

Against all these manoeuvres towards Union, of course, the Free Presbyterians waged vigorous witness, but the real danger – as Dr John White and other leaders of the Kirk well knew – came from the Free Church, which could genuinely claim in many Highland districts to be the de facto parish church and could cause great trouble, especially with regard to the endowments of Highland charges – the parliamentary *quoad sacra* parishes, for instance, benefiting even in the 1920s by some £17,000 in direct grants from the Exchequer. Indeed, this issue was explicitly asserted in the 1842 Claim of Right. Her silence had to be bought.

White, with astonishing ease,[5] persuaded Principal Donald MacLean, J. Kennedy Cameron and the Free Church leadership to withdraw their opposition to the Enabling Act, while smoothly denying their demand that a specific clause be inserted to grant the Free Church a share of endowments. He pointed out darkly – a potent argument in these days – that 'other claimants, especially Roman Catholics, might come forward.' He promised instead a later committee with regard to the Highlands and a share of endowments after the Union, assurances expressly confirmed on the floor of the House of Commons by the Secretary of State for Scotland. So the Free Church shut up, in exchange for fair words. The Church of Scotland (Enabling) Act sailed through Parliament – and the Free Church afterwards got absolutely nothing, failed by her greedy, credulous leaders.

Save for Orkney and Shetland, where congregations survive in 2008, almost every Highland congregation of the United Free Church entered the Great Union. Surviving congregations at Fort William and Balintore (near Fearn) are now her only northern outposts.[6] In certain localities, the position was a good deal muddier. Substantial United Free bodies in Fort William and Portree, for instance, returned to the Free Church – reviving her representation in the Skye capital and granting her the first viable congregation at the Fort since 1900. And things were still more fluid on the Long Island.

For one, an extraordinary cynicism prevailed on Harris: as Finlay J. MacDonald rightly asserts, in the turbulent waters after 1900 – when the island boasted two United Free congregations, a huge Free Presbyterian body, and a parish church at Scarista with around twenty in weekly attendance – most in some districts would have signed up happily to any that promised them a settled local ministry. The Free Church were the first beneficiaries of a silly and eminently avoidable Free Presbyterian dispute in South Harris, probably a signal factor in Donald N. MacLeod's 1924 departure for Lochbroom and in no way his fault. The church courts had sensibly dissuaded the Strond and Northton villages – both Free Presbyterian strongholds – from building separate meeting-houses, agreeing instead that one central place of worship be erected at Obbe (recently renamed Leverburgh, when the kindly if stubborn soap-magnate settled on it as his sphere of Harris enterprise[7]). But a superstitious element in Strond had an obsession with the ruins of John Morrison's forge, and unilaterally began building a place of worship on those sacred precincts. The Northton folk, angry and discomfited, then set about building one of their own and, faced with a fait accompli and resigned to the alienation of many whatever they did, the Church had to accept the situation.[8] Plans for a Leverburgh church were abandoned and local feeling was, understandably, such that a good many families seceded to the Free Church, who received them with striking graciousness. 'Harris' was duly declared a sanctioned charge and the first pastor settled in 1923. With the outstanding exception of Rev. John MacKenzie – minister at Leverburgh from 1946 to 1968 – there have been singularly unfortunate ministries. It was 1988, decades after it was demonstrably needed, before a rather magnificent Free Presbyterian building (though with awful acoustics) was opened in Leverburgh.

The Free Presbyterians had another distraction during the War: the antics of a brilliant but unstable divinity student from Gravir, in the Pairc district. Peter Chisholm – who, before his conversion, had been no less industrious in extreme socialist politics – started to agitate both against lay preaching (he took the odd position, for an unordained student who himself complacently kept services, that elders should not speak from the Word) and, besides, against communicant members who kept pictures ('graven images') and any sort of musical instrument in their homes.[9]

The church courts in 1913 had very properly stopped Chisholm from preaching until he came to another mind. He flounced away in dudgeon and, improbably, ended up in the Free Church, being ordained to Coll in

the Inner Hebrides in 1921 and subsequently holding charges in Glasgow
– he was the first minister of Partick Highland, launched initially as a
mission to Gaelic-speaking girls in West End domestic service – and
Lochalsh. But a few Lewis supporters – mostly in Achmore – separated
from the Free Presbyterians in his support and spent the rest of their lives
as a righteous little sect; one that did not even trouble to hold services, but
merely dressed up in their best at the appointed hours of divine worship
and sat silently in their chairs. The very last Chisholmite endured till the
early 1980s: sweet, eccentric and implacable.[10]

Now, on the Long Island, two very different congregations – in different
denominations – decided to eschew the imminent Union and from opposite
ends. As if Uig were not sufficiently broken, the Established folk at
Balnacille decided the new reworked, revised, reinvented Church of Scotland was not good enough for them.[11] This was a great congregation,
remembered both for the outstanding godliness of many members and their
magnificent singing, practising four-part harmony even in Gaelic praise.
(Peggy Gillies, in 2002, vividly recalled sneaking down with her brothers to
the Cross machair on a Communion Sabbath, where a multitude – most
of them Uig people – partook of the sacrament in a natural, open arena
by the Atlantic billows, their voices rising in praise in what, eighty years
later, would still be the most celestial praise she had ever heard.)
    Led by their minister, Roderick MacInnes – admitted as pastor only
in 1928 – a majority of the Balnacille folk left in December 1930 for the
Free Presbyterian Church. He himself had been a student for the Free
Presbyterian ministry. With South Harris now belatedly erected as a
sanctioned charge – Donald John MacAskill was ordained and inducted
in 1934 – and with two Lewis ministries at last, as well as a regular
ministry in North Uist since 1916, the Free Presbyterians were, besides,
finally able to erect a separate Outer Isles Presbytery. But the fracturing of
Uig, barely a century after the extraordinary events there, must give pause
for thought. Delaying in 1929 what did finally have to happen, fifty years
later, the Church of Scotland stubbornly maintained two ministries – for
an adhering Balnacille minority, and at Miavaig – and, besides, another
on Bernera. The Free Church finally inducted a Bernera minister in 1929.
And the Free Presbyterians kept a ministry in Uig, and may yet – even in
2008 – settle another. Thus, where Alexander MacLeod had once ruled
all, the parish of Uig now supported five different pastorates.
    But MacInnes did not last long in his new Communion; in 1936, he
resigned from the Free Presbyterian ministry, though pathetically failed
to win readmission to the Kirk. To a man, his people stayed where they
were, though the Church of Scotland 'gave him his pension', a son of

Miavaig would wryly recall. Even relatives admit MacInnes was 'undeniably eccentric', and some have averred that in 1930 the Balnacille folk
were seduced from the Kirk by a secret drunkard – relating, for instance,
that after his departure for the Free Presbyterian Church dozens and
dozens of empty whisky bottles were found in the Balnacille manse
stables. But milk was then (and for decades afterwards in rural Lewis)
routinely supplied to manses in all sorts of bottles, and Mr MacInnes died
in 1971 at a hale old age, remembered to the last with high respect even
by former Free Presbyterian parishioners, some of whom kept in touch to
the end. Roderick MacInnes retired to Raasay; his son, John, is an
outstanding Gaelic scholar and was an early, important leader in the
School of Scottish Studies.

In 1939, John Angus MacDonald – a winsome fellow from Drinishader,
in Harris, who had been converted very young and is still remembered
walking to the Stockinish prayer meeting, over rock and heath, in his bare
feet – was ordained and inducted as Free Presbyterian minister of Uig
and thus began a popular career in pastoral ministry. Warm piety,
irrepressible good humour and remarkable people-skills more than compensated for limited academic gifts. The death of a twin brother and a
beloved older sister – both Christians – from wasting tuberculosis was a
witness he had never forgotten. He visited tirelessly, prayed continually,
delivered fervent, heavily anecdotal sermons so plain a child could follow
them, and left a succession of charges – Applecross, Raasay, Fort William,
bigger than he had found them. Once called, in emergency and at the
height of the Blitz, to make the very difficult journey from the west of
Lewis to London Communion (the city now boasted a great Free
Presbyterian congregation), John Angus fought his way through all the
restricted zones of the West Highlands and finally, in full clerical raiment,
onto a departing troop-train at Inverness. It was full of Americans and an
officer angrily accosted him. 'Do you not know that this train is reserved for
the forces?' John Angus stood tall and said graciously, 'Sir, I am going to
London, as an envoy of the Most High King.' He was immediately granted
a seat and, through the protracted rattling journey, enchanted an audience
of young lads from New England, from the Deep South, from Iowa, far
from their own homes and their own plain Christian tradition. He arrived
at London laden with gifts and chocolate. But my memory of John Angus –
retired in Inverness, in his eighties, with decades of Christian ministry
behind him, a Gaelic Bible beside him and a well-thumbed volume of
Thomas Brooks on his knee – is of an old man who said constantly and
earnestly, 'Well, I am praying, as always, that I am kept; that the Lord will
keep me from falling, and from bringing reproach on His cause.'

His successor at Uig, Lachlan MacLeod – ordained there in 1953 – was also an excellent minister and Donald R. MacDonald, minister for many years at Tarbert, was as witty as he was kindly.

Once an embarrassed gamekeeper came to arrange his marriage, hoping the Free Presbyterian minister had not yet learned of circumstances that made the nuptials somewhat urgent. But MacDonald, a shrewd fellow from Shieldaig, was ahead of him. 'Indeed I will,' he said mildly, 'but I hear you've been shooting before the Twelfth.' A bachelor for most of his life, he kept a large and rather grubby dog, inexplicably called 'In' – or 'Juan'; accounts vary – who accompanied D.R. MacDonald on pastoral visitation; the minister's first cheery greeting was always, 'Is the cat in?' He used, when a son or daughter of the community was heading to the mainland for study – and irrespective of denomination – to summon them to the manse for a warm word, and the parting gift of a ten-shilling note. One day, to the mingled delight and twittering of Tarbert folk, he and his housekeeper went by bus to Stornoway, and returned man and wife.

MacDonald is often accused of having lost the Free Presbyterian Church a congregation. As the Balnacille folk retreated righteously, from an Auld Kirk vantage, from the Union, so did the United Free masses of Scalpay.[12] Sailing each Sabbath to Tarbert, week upon week, year upon year, they had long been clamouring – to no avail – for their own minister, repeatedly petitioning the United Free Assembly. In 1929 they sensed new possibilities. Their first approach was to the Free Presbyterian minister of Tarbert. MacDonald received them coolly and, without even reference to Presbytery, gave them no encouragement whatever. This later vexed some of his colleagues; but MacDonald was a principled Free Presbyterian and everything else one hears suggests he was a very shrewd man. He did not trust the Scalpay people and disliked their palpable shopping-about for assurances of a resident minister.

Repulsed by him, they got up a congregational meeting where a deacon, Calum Morrison, successfully moved that they approach the Free Church: they duly wooed, and the Free Church Offices sent honeyed tones back. Almost the entire island duly decamped – save for three elders and two deacons, who seem conscientiously to have felt bound by their ordination vows and led thereafter a tiny Church of Scotland group – and Scalpay became a Free Church stronghold. Her people are resourceful, bustling and articulate and prodigiously good fishermen: by the 1950s, Scalpay was not only still most heavily populated but remarkably, visibly rich. It has never, though, been an easy pastorate. Between 1930 and 1997, Scalpay burned through nine ministers: Kinloch Free Church, in the same period, had two.

D.J. MacAskill, first Free Presbyterian minister of South Harris, was an extraordinary fellow.[13] He was prodigiously intelligent – in his old age I used to see him in the Harris pews reading (as the intimated text required) from a Hebrew or Greek Testament – but of wondrous, guileless eccentricity. After subsequent charges at North Uist, Raasay and Lochcarron he ended his ministry at Uig and, in 1988, stepped majestically into the new Free Presbyterian care-home in Leverburgh, where he was able, morning and evening, to conduct family worship to the end of his life, marching down to the lounge in frock-coat and carpet slippers.

To the end of his course D.J. MacAskill could scarcely see a pulpit, at least at a Communion season, without wanting to sit in it, and would squeeze himself earnestly in beside his affectionate colleagues before drifting off to sleep. Once, as a younger minister preached earnestly in Tarbert, he was disconcerted when a button suddenly ricocheted off the lectern – the old man, unearthing this from his pocket in the natural misapprehension it was a sweet, had instantly realised his mistake and spat it vehemently out. He had been a Nicolson schoolfellow of that great Free Church warrior, Murdo MacAulay – and besides a later Church of Scotland minister, Duncan MacKenzie – and, in his last book, published in 1993, MacAulay chose an affecting frontispiece: pictures of the three of them, over measured words. 'Three old Nicolsonian classmates patiently waiting for God's chariots to ferry them over to the Promised Land, when all denominational strife will be dropped in Jordan.'

About 1990, MacAulay – still active on the Communion circuit – was assisting at Leverburgh Free Church, and MacAskill was duly borne to the Free Church Manse for an afternoon of joyous fellowship. A year or two later, when MacAulay was briefly hospitalised, the old man said wistfully, 'Oh, how I wish I was in need of going myself, so that we might be together.' In his last months, MacAskill had what must be a rare and extraordinary privilege for any minister – sharing the Diamond Wedding joy of a couple he himself had married. His prayers in the Home could be both sweet and memorable. 'Oh, happy Daniel,' he once meditated, 'with a lion for his pillow, and a lion for his electric blanket, and a lion for his hot-water bottle . . .' One month in March 1995, Mr MacAskill was taken out as usual for his morning paper; they found him later, dead in his armchair, with its sheets on the floor and no sign of pain or struggle in his features.

This is the sort of thing that puts a lie to the talk of 'fragmented Calvinist sects' and the widespread belief that the Long Island is one protracted battlefield of loveless ecclesiastical warfare. Ours is an increasingly effeminate age, unable to understand how people could simultaneously conduct the most heated public argument while retaining very real and personal ties of friendship. From their desperate struggle to survive in the early 1900s, the Free Presbyterians had instituted the custom of an annual lecture on church principles (usually at New Year) and – less appropriately – fastened on the Monday of Communion season as the occasion for what was little more than an ugly, protracted denominational rant. Sorley MacLean, the most famous member of a noted Free Presbyterian family on Raasay, never forgot the tirades of what was officially a day of thanksgiving. 'Yes, the Monday service was called *Latha a' Chainidh* [the Day of Scolding] in which there was a denunciation of . . . Well, it didn't mention the Catholic Church, that was beyond mention. The Episcopalians weren't worth mentioning. The Church of Scotland was hardly worth mentioning. The concentration was on the backsliding "so-called Free Church of Scotland". And they wound up with scientists, spiritualists and socialists . . .'[14]

The custom, sustained latterly only by the oldest Free Presbyterian ministers, happily died out in the 1990s. Its most notorious practitioner was the Reverend James MacLeod,[15] from South Rona, of massive build and thick silver hair and a mighty preacher who, though he never served in the Outer Isles – his charges were those of Glendale and, later, Greenock – was a most frequent visitor at Lewis, Harris and Uist Communion seasons.

This MacLeod embodied Free Presbyterian paradox. He was a delightful Christian with a love of people and a great hunger for souls. People still remember him weeping in the pulpit as he called on the lost, the careless, the defiant to come to Christ. Stories follow *MacLeoid Ghleann Dail* like gulls after a trawler. He once solemnly jigged and reeled in the pulpit, to demonstrate the iniquity of dancing. Irritated by the restlessness of a young Englishman in church, he paused, and told him firmly to 'Sit still or go out.' Increasingly troubled on the propriety of clerical dress, he had warned one Sabbath morning that a minister's collar was not a mere Popish vanity and, to drive the point home, took the service that night in a flaming red tie. But his Monday morning tirades were notorious. In fact, they were an entertainment. Free Church and Church of Scotland adherents used to flock eagerly to hear them. On one occasion, at North Uist, MacLeod declared that 'there are three churches on this island: two of them are going to Hell, and one by express train!' On another, slating the Pope, he cried, 'That old bastard, what does he know about women?' – though the phrase is less vulgar in Gaelic.

Yet the paradox was evident and is reinforced by other stories. Around 1926, keeping Tarbert services during the vacancy between D.N. MacLeod and D.R. MacDonald, the new Stornoway minister – Malcolm Gillies[16] – mentioned in public prayer the recent death in North Harris of an eminent United Free elder, a Christian greatly regarded in the community, mourning such a breach in the cause of Christ and commending the bereaved family to the Lord's grace and care. At this time a wretched young man was a communicant in the Tarbert Free Presbyterian

congregation – he is certainly remembered with neither respect nor
affection – and took profound, bigoted outrage. He pursued Gillies all
the way to the Synod in Glasgow, with a scabrous petition. Great was his
joy to see James MacLeod on the steps of St Jude's, and he scuttled up.
'Oh, Mr MacLeod, you will support my cause today.' *MacLeoid Ghleann
Dail* turned and roared – before quietly rejoicing onlookers and in words
still more terrible in their Gaelic, 'Away home to Stockinish, you son of
the devil, and plant potatoes with your father in the *feannagan* of Leacali!'

Malcolm Gillies appreciated such support, and it is no offence to others to
say that he and a later minister of the Free Presbyterian congregation in
Stornoway, James Tallach, were perhaps its most cherished pastors. Both
were Gaelic learners, both had fine ministerial gifts, both were outstanding parents and both hated clerical pretension. Caught out at a
Communion – he had run out of the necessary linen – Gillies happily
knocked up a bow and shirt-front from the white cardboard of a shoe-
box, and was in full and joyous oratory when a colleague had to tug on his
coat, for the assemblage had come loose and fallen to the floor. Once,
when he had to keep a service at Sandwick, Gillies happily accepted a lift
from his brother in law – by a horse-drawn herring-float. A woman was
most disconcerted when he thus arrived and made her feeling plain.
Gillies smiled and said nothing, and next Sabbath preached from
Matthew – 'Tell ye the daughter of Sion, Behold thy King cometh unto
thee, meek, and sitting upon an ass, and a colt the foal of an ass.' 'That
was for me,' she had to say. On another occasion he had to walk all the
way from his James Street manse to take the prayer meeting at Swordale –
a full five miles – and arrived soaked. A kindly lady dried off his footwear
and said he should have sent word: they could easily have hired a car.
'What,' said Malcolm Gillies, 'and arrive in Swordale with no sermon?'
There are many related incidents. When a new young doctor, Peter
Aulay MacLeod,[17] took up his Carloway practice before the war – a casual
Free Presbyterian adherent and immersed in a louche Stornoway demi-
monde – he went one evening to sermon at Breasclete and was shaken by
Mr Gillies' text, 'They that be whole need not a physician, but they that
are sick.' It was at a service at Shawbost Free Church – its minister,
Murdo MacIver, was the instrument – that Dr MacLeod seems first to
have been truly awakened; after months of anguish, he found peace while
reading a sermon by C.H. Spurgeon.
Dr MacLeod became a greatly loved Christian, putting from him a
seedy lifestyle – though never his prodigious smoking of Passing Cloud
cigarettes – and is remembered both as a gifted lay preacher and, like his
father and grandfather before him, a splendid precentor, a 'beautiful

precentor'. He was exceptionally fond of ministers, doing his best to encourage them and to share their burdens. He sparkled in fellowship, but excelled in correspondence, taking time to pen warm, supportive spiritual letters to the burdened, the seeking and the isolated. 'Like other Christians on this side of eternity he claimed no perfection for himself,' wrote Hugh Gillies in 1972. 'If he had a fault it was, no doubt, bound up, as is often the case, with the area in which his usefulness was greatest. Sometimes he would speak hastily and be very sorry for it afterwards. Oftentimes at family worship, and also in public, this petition was used by him: "Set thou a watch before my mouth, keep of my lips the door." If there were occasions when he hurt others we believe he hurt himself more.'

In the last weeks of Dr MacLeod's life, when the cigarettes had finally caught up with him, he padded about the hospital ward in his dressing gown, urging others to seek Christ. He adored Gillies and once remembered, as he watched the minister march up to the Breasclete pulpit with an oilskin over his arm, 'I felt the witness of that man so strongly that I just put my head below the seat and wept.' A Communion there is also remembered, when Malcolm Gillies joined the bus back to Stornoway and refused any offer of a seat – 'The old man [his pride] is very big today, so I will just sit here,' and plonked himself down on the step beside the driver, and from that position precented Psalm 118 from beginning to end.

Mr Gillies took his pastoral responsibilities seriously, both locally and nationally. He had promised his father – a venerable elder – that on no account would he abandon any preaching duties on the mainland, even if the ailing old man should pass away in his absence. That was duly tested, when Malcolm Gillies was assisting at Wick; but the funeral was delayed for six days until the weekend of preaching was over. The gifts of this Stornoway minister must have been remarkable: few clergymen, indeed, can have had such a tribute indirectly paid as his Assynt colleague, Alexander MacAskill, observed after hearing one of Gillies' opening prayers at a Question Meeting – 'I got so much in the prayer that I would have been quite satisfied if he had pronounced the benediction and we had gone home.'

Yet his own children – and this is exceptional; there was an unfortunate and well-attested tradition of the offspring of island ministers repudiating the Gospel, not least in response to the quiet and too readily authoritarian little hypocrisies that have marked too many island manses – were raised with tender wisdom. One, Hugh, had even to cope with a schoolfellow's endeavours at extortion – and never forgot how his father finally resolved his turmoil. Hugh Gillies, later a respected Stornoway doctor and a good man, described it vividly to a nursing colleague, Anna MacAulay, many years later.

> I remember, Anna, when the picture-house – the cinema – first opened in Stornoway. My father, of course, was very much against it. But for the opening day they were very keen to fill the place with children, and it was made known that everyone who went would get a badge and an apple and an orange. But I thought, 'I'm going along to the new picture-house'. So I went, and I got my badge and my apple and my orange. Then of course I was afraid of my father finding out. I remember being sent to the shop once, and the lady there knew. And she gave me a long lecture on children being disobedient to their parents. So I stood there petrified and I stood there so long while she talked that the packet of butter I had under my arm just melted. And when I made for the door she called me back and gave me another packet.
>
> There was a boy and he said, 'I want your pet rabbit.' 'You're not getting my pet rabbit,' I said. 'If you don't give me your pet rabbit,' he said, 'I'm going to tell your father that you were at the picture-house.' 'Well, I don't know how my father found out at last. But he did. And one night after tea he said, 'Now, Hugh, let's go up to my study.' And wasn't I petrified? But when we got there we knelt, and he prayed. Now, Anna, I went very far in sin. I was long in darkness. I'm sure if my father had just leathered me, I would have forgotten it entirely. I'm sure that if he had torn a strip off me – lectured me – I would have no memory of that at all. But he prayed – it was full of love – and, far as I went in sin, I could never forget that prayer: how my father asked the Lord to change me – to give me a new heart and to change me spiritually.[18]

Hugh Gillies was changed and, like his great friend in Carloway, became another eminent Free Presbyterian doctor. Anna MacAulay never forgot his kindness:

> I remember one night, working in the old Lewis Hospital, I was very disheartened and downcast. And Dr Gillies knew all about it. So he came along and took me aside and said, 'Now, Anna, let's go and visit the children of Israel on the night of the Passover.
>
> 'We'll go into the first house. And they're all looking very, very worried. 'What are you so distressed about?' we ask. 'Oh, do you not know that the Angel of Death is passing over tonight, to slay the firstborn?' 'But surely you have taken the Lord's provision?' 'Oh, yes, we have obeyed His word, and slain the lamb, and sprinkled the blood on

the doorposts. But we can't see the blood; we're inside. And – well, you know, it's terribly solemn.

'So, Anna, we'll leave the sad house and go next door. And here they are very bright and happy. 'Do you not know,' we'll ask, 'that the Angel of Death is coming over tonight, and isn't that solemn?' 'But the Lord has made provision for us, and we have slain the lamb and sprinkled the blood on the doorposts, and we're resting on that and trusting in Him.

'So at length the Angel of Death comes. And do you know this? He passes over the sad household, and he passes over the happy household, because all he sees is the blood, and it is written, 'When I see the blood, I shall pass over you.'

It was an important spiritual lesson, that faith is not founded on inward frames and feelings, but the work of Christ. 'I remember the last time I met Dr Gillies,' says Miss MacAulay. 'He was preaching in Achmore, on the mercy-seat and the angels looking down in wonder on the blood sprinkled on the mercy-seat. And afterwards I told him how much I appreciated what he had to say about the mercy-seat. "Oh," said Dr Gillies, "I feel I took very little out of it, but I'll soon know it all." It was the next Monday that he passed suddenly away.'

Malcolm Gillies did not let gratitude stand in the way of pastoral obligation. When, on the Monday of a Stornoway Communion, James MacLeod began quite to surpass himself in unprofitable invective, Gillies acted decisively: he simply stood up and pronounced the benediction.[19] In the late 1950s, mindful of the hazard, James Tallach took equal care to protect his flock. James MacLeod was momentarily relaxing in Stornoway, and had called at the Free Presbyterian Manse. He was of course most warmly welcomed. Tea was duly served. An invitation to conduct the prayer meeting that evening was accepted without hesitation. The two men sat together, the pipes were filled and refilled, the conversation flowed. Tallach noted, with mild concern, that time was drawing on and MacLeod still showed no sign of retiring, nor the flow of comment any cease. 'Mr MacLeod,' he said, 'hadn't you better prepare your address now.' 'Ach!' said MacLeod happily, reaching again to charge his pipe, 'I'll just give them a harangue.'

This Mr Tallach had rather dreaded. 'No,' he said firmly, 'you'll not give my poor people a harangue: Christian people, working all week and who need food for their souls. You'll go now and make ready and prepare a proper address.' And off MacLeod went, 'meek as a lamb', and in due course delivered an excellent meditation.

Mr Gillies had also to contend with the phenomenon of A.W. Pink, a figure whose importance is hugely overblown in post-war Reformed mythology.[20] Born in Nottingham in 1886, Arthur Walkington Pink became a clever, obsessive, sort of free-range preacher, an early harbinger in Highland Christian circles of a breed now dubbed, with rather less patience, as the 'English nutter'. Though raised in a Christian home, the rebellious adult Pink joined a Theosophy group – this Gnostic, distinctly occult movement was fashionable in the early twentieth century – and, despite his conversion to Christ around 1910, seems always to be have been a restless, rootless fellow whose precise doctrinal stances have been determinedly obscured by admirers.

Eager to grow in knowledge of Scripture, Pink went to America, studied at the Moody Bible Institute, adopted (though later discarded) Pentecostal views, married Vera E. Russell of Kentucky in 1916 – a woman as saintly, level-headed and universally adored as he was bizarre – and within months hauled her about Colorado and California before taking her home to Britain. Her adventures continued – from 1925 to 1928, Pink pastored two congregations in Australia; and served as a minister besides, with his patient lady, in four different American states. It is a reasonable deduction that a man who pastored six congregations, on two continents, in just eight years may have had, as we say, issues; and certainly a want of people-skills.

In 1922, though, he had started a little monthly magazine, *Studies in the Scriptures*, and – though its circulation seldom crept over a thousand or so – it won him a devoted following, especially in England. In 1934 the Pinks returned permanently to the British Isles and, bumbling about in search of a base, for a time floated on the margins of the Free Presbyterian congregation in Glasgow, attending warm house-fellowships in the home of two sprightly old sisters, the 'Misses Morton', hearing the preaching of the gifted Glasgow pastor, Roderick MacKenzie, and mixing with lively young converts, three of whom – Donald MacLean, William MacLean and Alexander McPherson – were later ordained to the Free Presbyterian ministry.

Rev. Donald MacLean, still most alert and active in his ninety-fourth year – he professed faith in November 1937 – recalls darkly that A.W. Pink was 'a very eccentric man. Strange. His wife was quite different – a real lady; everyone loved her. But they became most friendly with a couple from Ness, and that is how they ended up on Lewis.' A more cynical explanation is that Pink, now a full-time writer – bashing out his periodical and assorted books and pamphlets – wanted to find somewhere as cheap as possible to live. Despatched to Stornoway with a letter of introduction to Malcolm Gillies, he found them quarters with a fine lady on Lewis Street, Mary MacIver, still affectionately remembered as *Mairi Ghaol*, 'Mary of Love'. She bravely put the Pinks up in her attic.

Cracks, though, had already appeared in this courtship with the Free Presbyterians. For one, Pink was desperate to conduct services, and Rev. Donald Beaton carefully interviewed him to ascertain his doctrine. 'Well, he found that Pink didn't believe in the eternal sonship of Christ,' Mr MacLean recalls. 'It's a common error – he believed in the office, but not the person. So Mr Beaton, of course, reported that he wasn't "true blue"; of proper, Reformed theology. And, of course, he was, as I said, *very* eccentric . . .' Though Pink certainly believed in the eternal deity of Christ – a different issue – his denial of the eternal sonship, a serious error with some traction in certain Reformed sects, would certainly have precluded a Free Presbyterian role.

Though on occasion perhaps granted open Communion – a rare concession – A.W. Pink never sought full membership in the Free Presbyterian Church. He was most offended, though, to be denied any place in her pulpits, and the breach quickly came about in Stornoway, where it emerged he was hysterically opposed to infant baptism – though he disliked the Strict Baptists and their *Gospel Standard* periodical almost as much as he had come to despise the Free Presbyterians.

When Mr Gillies began the sprinkling of an infant, Pink stormed out of the building, his long-suffering wife trailing patiently behind him. He never worshipped in the Free Presbyterian Church again – indeed, thereafter, he determinedly traduced her as unreasonable, loveless and legal – and, more shamefully still, never again worshipped in any island congregation. He never bothered to hear Kenneth MacRae, and is said never to have even met him. The Pinks hunkered down in their lodgings, toiled on *Studies in the Scriptures*, sent forth all the booklets and the tracts; of a Stornoway evening, when the trawlers and drift-netters chugged laden into harbour, Pink would mooch down to the quayside to scrounge free fish. Of a Sabbath, he sat piously indoors with his wife, quite content by now to have excommunicated all Christendom.

A.W. Pink died in Stornoway in July 1952 and lies in an unmarked Sandwick grave. His reputation has since been puffed by the Banner of Truth Trust, who republished many of his writings; Iain Murray, too, has produced a biography, repeating some most unfair aspersions on the Free Presbyterian Church. 'The widespread circulation of his writings after his death made him one of the most influential evangelical authors in the second half of the twentieth century,' insists Murray; but that is manifestly absurd: most Christians have never even heard of Pink. The reality was that his writings were prized by Jack Cullum – co-founder, with Murray, in 1957 of the Banner of Truth Trust, a Reformed publishing charity heavily funded by the considerable Cullum fortune; he had inherited the family acoustics-technology company, and money talks.

The Trust duly ignored all Free Presbyterian protest. On Lewis, few remember Pink with affection; he contributed nothing to her worship or fellowship and he has no part in local Evangelical consciousness. But Pink had some admirers, in his day, on the hyper-Calvinistic margins of the local church; and my late Shawbost grandfather liked his meditations.

The last weeks of Malcolm Gillies were wretchedly sad; through much of the Second World War, the Free Presbyterian Church was in increasing uproar in what is remembered as the 'Protest Controversy',[21] over an arcane detail in Presbyterial procedure of limited interest to most Free Presbyterians and maximally incomprehensible to anyone else. The chief agitator was the Glasgow minister, Roderick MacKenzie – a Lewisman, born in Laxdale, of iridescent gifts but thrawn, obsessive nature: as his old enemy, Robert R. Sinclair, told me darkly a half-century later in March 1989, Roddy MacKenzie 'was one of those clever Lewismen'. He was certainly highly strung. He never married. MacKenzie sought relaxation in repairing clocks and watches; once, having invested in a new car, he took it apart to every last nut and bolt, before painstakingly reassembling it. He was a gifted amateur artist and even composed melodies: one, the common-metre Psalm tune 'Gairloch', is now widely sung and in all denominations, especially on his native island. His preaching was, as we say, signally owned of the Lord, and there were very many conversions.

From 1938 and in the train of some untoward happenings, MacKenzie – whose mind had a weakness for the ordered and the tidy – fell upon a rather muddled Free Presbyterian statement on 'Protest' like a leopard on a goat. He argued and he pamphleteered. He begot quickly an entire uproar, not merely within the great St Jude's congregation but in the wider Church and especially on Lewis, with two Lewis-born colleagues (a Ness man, Wallace Bruce Nicolson, minister of North Uist, and Stornoway-born Alexander D. MacLeod, minister of Lochcarron and Shieldaig) yapping happily behind him. By 1945 – when Free Presbyterians, like everyone else, were exhausted and hungry, battered and grieving, it reached a mighty showdown at Synod. It was the ugliest, most vindictive row in Free Presbyterian history and Roderick MacKenzie, with these two pastors and hundreds of followers, was 'declared separate'. MacLeod ended up, after various adventures, as a Church of Scotland minister, dying in 1993; Nicolson joined the Free Church, passing away in 1984.

MacKenzie and his host acquired a little church on Glasgow's Renfrew Street and sat there for the next forty years. One who grew up in this pathetic breakaway Glasgow group remembers around 350 to 400 people at first worshipping in the 'St Jude's Free Presbyterian Relief Congregation', but – more wistfully – that 'it was a church people never joined; only a church that people left.' Though MacKenzie would conduct marriages – that, he argued, was a civil function – he refused at first to preach from the pulpit; and, having no properly constituted kirk session, there was neither baptism nor the Lord's Supper. There was not even very much light, for the 'Split Ps' – as they are still unkindly remembered – plastered the windows in brown paper, to hide idolatrous stained-glass. Roderick MacKenzie died in August 1972, though Relief groups survived at Glasgow and Waternish into the 1980s.

The affair badly damaged Free Presbyterian morale on Lewis, where MacKenzie had – naturally – widespread support. And it killed Malcolm Gillies. Assistant Clerk of Synod, he worked far into the night banging out documents on a manual typewriter. John Angus MacDonald never forgot waiting in the parlour as the toil continued upstairs; 'just tick-tock, tick-tock on the typewriter he had, and then snort-snort, as he would be taking his snuff' – and, to cap it all, Gillies was vilified, even in his own congregation, for his supposed part in the treatment of that great man of God, a son of Laxdale, down in Glasgow – beset with hate-mail and taunted to his face. These troubles 'were of a heart-breaking nature,' his son wrote quietly in 1987. 'Suffice to say that his own reaction to them was, "This is of the Lord." One person did pay a great tribute to him, after his death, when he said, "We threw plenty of mud at him, but it did not stick."' Malcolm Gillies spent much of 1945 in dreadful pain – he had sustained a thrombosis on his leg – and died suddenly on 14 September.

But the most famous Lewis minister of the last century – and who could count his thousands as Gillies and Tallach tended their hundreds – was inducted to Stornoway Free Church in August 1931. We have already met Kenneth A. MacRae. He was then forty-eight years old. Ordained to Lochgilphead in 1915,[22] he had painstakingly mastered his trade before assuming his Skye pastorate in 1919. There he saw great blessing, especially in the Kilmoluag and Staffin districts – the hardness of Kilmuir distressed him – and, in 1929, led with great intelligence a 'Skye Sabbath Defence League', expressly to stop plans of the London, Midland and Scottish Railway to run Sabbath excursions to Kyle, with a view to 'Misty Isle' day-trips. MacRae organised petitions and a boycott. Many ministers did little to help, and he noted of one such in exasperation, 'Had he as much zeal for the Sabbath as he has dislike for the Free Presbyterians, he would be a most useful man.'

'The truth is that he did not relish controversy,' writes Iain Murray. 'His zeal sprang from the conviction that the fourth commandment is as much the law of God for every individual as every other commandment and that Christians have therefore as plain a duty to resist Sabbath desecration as they have to resist the desecration of marriage or the unjust taking of life. If the Sunday excursions succeeded they would provide a constant temptation to the disregard of God's law in Skye, and he believed it was a sin for anyone not to resist the introduction of such a change in the Island. For himself he could write, "I cannot bear to see the Sabbath murdered in it."'

Kenneth MacRae is a significant figure. He would spend the rest of his life in Stornoway; my father's first public appearance as a newly licensed minister, in homburg and stripes and collar, would be his own pastor's funeral, in May 1964. And he was genuinely feared in the town, by businessmen and politicians and eminences generally who knew the likely consequences of a pulpit rebuke. MacRae, it must be remembered, never quite shook off his United Free past; it left him both a dread of spurious 'revivalism' – he had been badly shaken by the experience of false conversion in the 1903 Scottish campaign of R.A. Torrey, an American evangelist no less manipulative and mechanical than the generality are today – and (temperance being a United Free obsession) a loathing of alcohol atypical in Highland Evangelicalism. He was utterly teetotal and explicitly threatened any communicants in Stornoway who 'had it in the house' with church discipline.

The tough old fellow abominated Remembrance Day services – though an old soldier himself, with part-time service in the Royal Scots Territorials, and the son of a recruiting-officer of the Seaforth Highlanders – because he felt they tended to prayers for the dead. He disapproved strongly of youth associations in the church, bawling babies at sermon and special 'children's addresses' in public worship. In other respects too he seems, on superficial assessment, almost the beyond-caricature 'Wee Free' minister. His splendid portrait, taken in 1961, blazes from the page with the certainty of Knox and the majesty of a Rembrandt. He fought for the Lord's Day. He fought for sobriety. He laid down rigid rules, agreeing to conduct a wedding 'on condition that celebrations ceased at a decent hour and there would be no dancing or suchlike frivolity.' Kenneth MacRae could privately be scathing about colleagues. 'On Friday evening went over to _____ and heard _____ on Exodus 13 21–22. His matter was quite good, but felt angry with him for spoiling his discourse with a most abominable delivery and enunciation. Such a delivery would ruin the finest discourse. What makes it so annoying is that his extraordinary style is not natural to him. At times the noise he made in the pulpit made me think of the lazy droning of a bluebottle upon a windowpane on a hot summer afternoon.'

This was, of course, recorded in MacRae's private journal. He began keeping this extraordinary diary on 25 April 1912, when he was a prodigiously burdened divinity student: he took his MA degree and his Free Church College courses simultaneously and had besides, in these straitened Free Church times, to preach midweek and each Lord's Day, often travelling prodigious distances by bicycle. (On one occasion, during the summer break, he travelled from Dornoch to Edinburgh; it took him five days.) MacRae wrote his last entry on Sabbath 27 October 1963, when he was already weakening before the cancer that killed him. It remains an enthralling record of a Christian ministry in the twentieth century. Edited and with excellent notes and explanatory material by Iain Murray, it was published in 1980 and is still readily obtainable.

Still, any man will on occasion express himself in a diary in terms he might not readily use even to intimates. Besides, for much of his life – after a serious illness in 1934, brought on in large measure by conscientious and grinding pastoral visitation, MacRae began keeping the journal weekly – he wrote it up late at night, when he was tired and often indeed exhausted. The diary itself was published – as those involved were acutely aware – when very many of his colleagues were still living and, inevitably, it reflects in some measure the emphases and prejudices of its editor. Iain Murray was then, for a few brief years, a minister of the Free Church of Scotland and in the hope of a call to some congregation that never came. His later part, from afar, in Free Church affairs has not been entirely happy. And those who knew MacRae best and have been able to peruse the original notebooks and diaries assure me that much earthy, lighter material has been omitted and that his humanity was much more rounded than these querulous notes often suggest.[23]

Nor is Kenneth MacRae held that high in the pantheon of Long Island ministers. If anything, he is today best remembered by the Free Presbyterians, for whom he had a tacit regard and who, today, now and again even quote him in their pulpits. He was hugely respected. Everyone who knew him attests to his holiness, industry and integrity. But, Victorian by birth and Edwardian in their attitudes, Kenneth and Catherine MacRae lived in august, splendid isolation. Reclining in the manse like a duchess, to the last she 'sent down' to Stornoway shops for her messages; no lady of the manse, anywhere, in 1915, could be seen queuing at the grocer. He learned Gaelic, and could preach acceptably in it, but not by the standards or ease of natives, like Murdo MacIver or Angus Finlayson, and could never really converse in it. MacRae had besides that very bad habit of haranguing the congregation in some pre-benediction postscript, always stern and usually negative – the perils of Jehovah's Witnesses, their giving to the cause, the carelessness of unspecified members, the failings of the

National Bible Society. My grandparents heard him, honoured him, walked miles from Newmarket and back – in all weathers and frequently sodden – to hear him at Kenneth Street and had prominently hung that striking photograph, which I have inherited (though it was retired into a cupboard, almost in a gesture of Free Church de-Stalinisation, after his death.) But – 'ach, that man,' my grandmother sighed in November 1989, 'he was always against something!'[24]

Yet the minister of Stornoway is not so readily pigeonholed. For one, he had a real gift of poetry; if some verse in the *Diary* tends to the kailyard, others are sublime and one specimen of comic-verse is both skilled and hilarious. An anthem to his own people, *The Scattered Children of Kintail*, was adopted by the Clan MacRae Association, set to music and published. He loved, utterly and with passion, the landscape of his native country. He was stirred profoundly by her history. He worried about the social and economic needs of Highlanders, cross that potatoes were imported from the Black Isle and furious to see splendid Skye marble being crushed as foundation for a road. He resented pressure on islanders for, for instance, bed-and-breakfast. 'All this cry about the development of the tourist industry is simply an insult to every Highlander who loves his country. We don't wish to become a nation of flunkeys, to await the pleasure of our masters from the south.'

MacRae quietly disliked the Royal Family, noting on 11 December 1936, 'The abdication of King Edward is the topic of conversation everywhere and I feel quite tired of it. It is a great blessing and a merciful deliverance!' He was a tacit republican. In 1956 – when the Throne and its new, shy incumbent were universally venerated in a way that is hard now for us to understand – MacRae refused point-blank to be presented to his Sovereign during her official visit to the Long Island. 'Since the Queen has persistently violated the Fourth Commandment of the moral law of God by attending polo matches upon various Sabbath afternoons; since she has given the sanction of the Crown to the destruction of the Sabbath within her realm, in loyalty to my vows as a Christian, I cannot with a clear conscience accept any honour from Her Majesty's hands.' There was an outcry, with national newspapers recoiling in disbelief and outrage, and much opprobrium was heaped upon this 'sheer pompous bigotry and rudeness'. Yet the *News Chronicle*, at least, saw something to respect. 'Real conviction is so rare those days that it commands attention. . . . Here at least is a man prepared to stand by his beliefs – and the world can think what it likes.'

Yet, if feared, he was loved, not least by children. An uncle remembers what would happen in the playground at Laxdale school when MacRae's well-known car trundled by in the early 1960s. 'We would dash to the wall – every one of us – and lean over, and wave, and he would wave back. Where would you see that on the island today?'[25]

The 1920s had been a wretched time for Lewis and Harris: years of dreadful hardship and hard, cold religion. But flickers were appearing. There was a noted awakening in North Harris – in Tarbert, Maraig and Rhenigidale; in Scalpay, and the Bays. Several eminent Harris converts were later well-known ministers. James Morrison, a Scalpay man ordained to North Uist in 1942, served for four decades. He had some extraordinary attitudes and at times a nasty streak, but Morrison has the unique tribute of a Runrig song to his honour – *An T-Iasgair*, 'The Fisherman' – for Calum and Rory MacDonald greatly esteemed him. 'He was a strict fundamentalist with a big heart and a powerful intellect,' Calum remembers. 'He relished the argument, he thrived on the debate . . . "Give me an atheist any day, rather than a smug Christian," he would proclaim, "at least I can do business with him." And a big smile would crack across his face.'[26]

In 1920, besides, a new minister was inducted to Cross Free Church. Roderick John MacLeod was the son of a Free Church missionary, born in Harris in 1892. At Cross, a memorable though sadly undocumented revival flamed under his seven-year cure. It had two very interesting aspects. For one, 'Roddy John' was unhesitatingly innovative.[27] He encouraged youngsters to come to church and started a children's address, which he made them come down to the front to hear. He also began special evangelistic services, in midwinter and between Communion seasons, with visiting preachers and to which the unconverted were actively encouraged to come. These were at first criticised in other congregations, then avidly copied, but – though *na h-orduighean beagan*, the 'little Communions', still survive – they have all but lost their original relevance, with very few unconverted folk attending them.

My formidable great-great-grandfather, Angus Thomson – who held strong views on Sabbath shaving, for instance – was not at all sure what to make of MacLeod, and once took him staunchly to task, after he saw his pastor climbing nimbly over a fence. Was this way for God's herald to disport himself? MacLeod smiled, and quoted a Psalm of David:

> *Le neart mo Dhia thar balla leum,*
> *'us chaidh mi fèin gun stad –*

> And, by my God assisting me,
> I overleap a wall . . .

The other feature of *dusgadh Roddy John* was that some of the converts were extremely young. One lad from Cross, Donald MacDonald, was only fourteen. Isabella Morrison was even younger. And, when they got a mind to 'go forward' and seek Communion, they were horribly treated. The elders MacDonald faced were openly hostile. He was but a child – a novice – it was nothing but false enthusiasm. He might fall, and bring disgrace upon the church. Vile, insinuating questions were flung at the increasingly bewildered boy about the sins of the flesh. The minister, himself under fire, only carried the day because of the intervention of a Swainbost elder, John Murray. He had had enough. He raised his voice and said, 'Well, you men tell me this. How old was David when he fell with Bathsheba?' He had, as they knew, been well in his fifties.[28]

So MacDonald got the token. Yet from that day he was watched constantly for any sign of worldliness. He had to eschew old companions and anything remotely resembling sport. Once he passed youths playing football with a stone on the road – it was kicked in his direction and he toed it politely back. Someone had had an eye on him, for they tried to raise it at the Session. MacDonald, who had the full and earnest faith of most who find Christ very young, was troubled too by the constant atmosphere of doubts – people who maintained no real Christian had strong assurance, who said lugubriously, 'Ah, but you wait . . .' Attaining manhood in difficult times, he had besides to endure prolonged un-employment. But all those things later, at Urray and in Inverness, made him a memorable Free Church pastor.

North Harris and Ness were harbingers, perhaps. In Carloway, bur-dened and miserable, John MacIver had laboured as Free Church minister for a decade. Things trickled on – there were three or four or five professions a year – but he buried as many believers, and more. His close friend at Lochs, Malcolm MacIver – they were college contemporaries – grew increasingly concerned, as he heard the first talk of resignation.

Then, one night in 1934, the minister at Crossbost had an extra-ordinary dream. He and John were both sitting together in the pews of the great Free Church at Carloway – alone; and John MacIver's pre-decessor there – Donald MacLeod, from Shawbost, one of the heroes of 1900 and who had served at Carloway from 1915 to his death five years later – was preaching. In this dream, Rev. John noticed something. 'That's the seventh time he's preached on that text,' he said to Rev. Malcolm. 'Seven!' said the Rev. Malcolm. 'That's the perfect number.' And then he noticed, still dreaming, that lights – 'cloudy, bluish lights' – were flitting about, alighting on empty pews about them, and on and over particular seats, where this individual and that lady and those brothers and certain families sat.

Malcolm MacIver woke up. It was morning. He thought for a while, and then – wolfing breakfast – announced to his wife that he was going out. 'He had a two-seater car, a tourer,' boomed Duncan John MacLeod, telling me this story seventy-three years later, 'and she asked, "Where are you going?" And he said, "I am going to see John; I am going to tell him that revival is coming to Carloway."'[29]

12

'Give the Swooners No Latitude'

Revival and Change, 1934–1999

The awakening at Carloway began later in 1934 and Murdo MacAulay, one of its most noted converts, relates how more and more young people began to attend the midweek meeting; and how both Rev. John MacIver and men called on to lead in public prayer enjoyed a remarkable new fluency, or 'liberty', in such exercise. There was also a steady increase in professions of faith, peaking in 1938, with thirteen at the March Communion and sixteen in September. The movement had no denominational bounds – the Church of Scotland and the small Free Presbyterian congregation were also refreshed and renewed – and, what was more, it was not confined to Carloway, as MacAulay details – and it is worth giving him the space to do so, recalling poignantly in 1984 how young converts would gather outside church after sermon and

you could observe them in groups either discussing what they had heard or else enquiring where they would gather that evening . . . During the revival itself visiting ministers were greatly uplifted, and older Christians were on the top of Pisgah. Adherents, too, were nonplussed as to what all this would come to, since football, badminton, concerts and dances had lost their most ardent supporters.

As the movement had spread to other congregations such as Bernera, Park, Kinloch, Lochs, Knock, Barvas and Cross the number of visitors gathering at the Communion season was enormous. The churches were full, and the solemnity at those services was awe-inspiring as the Word of God went as fiery darts to the consciences and hearts of the unconverted. Wherever the people met, whether in a house or on the road, at peats or in the field, at fanks or on buses, the subject of conversation was the work of the Lord in our district and those who had been converted. *'Bha'n t-aite air ghoil . . .'* (The place was agog.) Some families had four or five converted, others two or one, and a few none at all. It is remarkable how dark some families remain even in the midst of a revival.

At worship where a death had occurred, the names of two people were called on to pray between singings, and it was not unusual to hear twelve to fifteen prayers during worship. I remember one house prayer meeting where seventeen, almost all recent converts, were called upon . . . Today I would feel two or three longer than the seventeen. Whenever young converts visited homes, tea was immediately prepared, mainly with a view to hearing the young converts asking a blessing or returning thanks. Of this tea recent converts were quite apprehensive.

By the end of the revival there were unusual prostrations, which came mainly as a result of a visit by a busload of young converts and a few old Christians from Shader, Barvas, where raising of hands and praying aloud, almost shouting, had become the custom. Some of us felt as if we were being severely rebuked for having come to spy on these prostrations and activities. As far as I can remember, there were no new converts at Carloway during or after these prostrations, and when the revival ended the prostrations ended too, and the subjects affected became excellent witnesses for their Master . . .

During church services both the minister and the congregation were so visibly affected that the services were veritable Bochims. Some showed signs of great concern and some signs of distress as the Law of God pricked the conscience, constraining them to say as at Pentecost, 'Men and brethren, what shall we do?' (Acts 2:37) They were thus very reluctant to depart from the church after the service, and often sang some verses of their favourite psalms outside the main door of the church, so that the sound of their uplifted praise echoed throughout the surrounding villages. What joy was experienced by the Lord's people when these new converts appeared in the prayer meeting!

The whole counsel of God was declared from the pulpits, and no attempt was made to cater for the stirred feelings of the listeners. The effects on their life were a deep conviction of sin; concern for their eternal state; a sense of their own unworthiness; earnest prayer for mercy; a careful walk and conversation in their daily life; a thirst for more and more knowledge of the Word – together with endless questions as to the deep spiritual meaning of certain verses of Scripture which they had either read or heard, but did not fully understand. As they cried for mercy and grace to help in time of need, some felt as if they were groping in the dark to find true peace in Christ. Some were in this state for a considerable time so that, if they heard any speaker at a fellowship giving marks which they could not follow, they were ready to conclude that there was little hope for their salvation. Others were carried as if on the crest of a wave into the haven of peace, comfort and felicity as they closed in with Christ in full assurance of faith. Many felt

like the father of the epileptic boy, crying, 'Lord, I believe; help thou my
unbelief.' (Mark 9:24) They could well understand the apparent contra-
diction in his request through their own experiences, as they felt more
conscious of their unbelief than their faith.

The effect on the life and conversation of the young converts was
remarkable – a hatred of sin, an abandonment of their former lifestyle,
a longing for holiness, with a dread of bringing any blemish on the
cause of Christ. They often brought truths they did not understand
to their elders, and very often had clear answers to their problems
from the pulpit, so that they felt sure someone had informed the
minister.

The revival did not touch the very young, though some converts were
in their mid teens. Neither did it appear to touch many of the hard
and aged adherents, but it certainly strengthened many who were
semi-lapsed, and those 'following afar off'. This was the case in both
denominations in the district.[1]

MacAulay stresses the role played by informal house meetings – where
new converts could first, in an unthreatening atmosphere, discuss the
sermons and make their first, stumbling efforts in public prayer; the
involved, pastoral role of John MacIver; and – an aspect often overlooked
– that, conversions apart, old and in some cases rather backslidden
Christians were greatly strengthened. And, as storm clouds gathered
over Europe, it spread over Lewis, and with particular force into Point
and Lochs. In Stornoway, Kenneth MacRae was at first sceptical, but by
1939 – with the new complication of mounting press interest, after a
speech at the Church of Scotland General Assembly – all agreed with
Rev. Murdo MacRae 'that there is a deep and profound spiritual movement in the island,' – and, more grimly, that in 1938, as Iain Murray
notes, 'certain features had become evident which were not beneficial to
the work. Prior to that date, solemnity and spiritual concern, brought
about by an uncommon consciousness of the presence of God, were the
most prominent characteristics of the revival.'[2]

We have noted Murdo MacAulay's note of 'unusual prostrations' –
which significantly, as we shall see, were especially associated with Shader
in the Barvas district – and it was these which attracted the unwelcome
attention of journalists, the *Scottish Daily Express* even sending a reporter
to Lewis in May 1939 – an intrepid fellow who covered seventy miles of
the island.

At evening church meetings attended by ministers, which start at 10,
there are few abnormal emotional experiences. At midnight, worshippers

adjourn to private houses where prayer meetings go on for two or thee hours. There may be forty or fifty people present.

Each rises spontaneously and prays. Psalms are interrupted. As hour succeeds hour the 'atmosphere', I am informed, changes.

Sometimes a woman will collapse, others will rise simultaneously, weeping, call in Gaelic on their relatives. Some lose all power of their limbs, have to be carried into an adjoining room and laid on a couch until they recover.

It is expected that renewed manifestations of the revival will be shown this weekend, especially at Sunday's services.

Such reporters naturally focused on the sensational. And the phenomena, which appeared late in the whole awakening – in the last eighteen months before the outbreak of the war – divided Christians and divided ministers. There was even a Gaelic word – *cliobadaich*,[3] defined as 'slipping, stumbling or, in Lewis, wagging like a cow does with its tail' – quickly applied, around the Second World War, to the supposed manifestations of the Holy Spirit. Initially it was 'in reference to the excited jumping and agitated movements which people would manifest in worship, both public and private, at times of revival. The word came to include the weird wailing in which some people would indulge . . . It seems the word gained such currency that in some districts on the island it became synonymous with the word *curam*[4] . . . eg, "*Thainig an cliobadaich air*," "He was converted."'

Some confidently identified these features with true, Heaven-sent revival and the presence of the living God. Others were most troubled and Kenneth MacRae had no doubts at all. In 1939 he gave a long, detailed public lecture on 'Unusual Features of the Present Religious Movement in Lewis'. He stressed that he was now sure a 'really sound religious movement had taken place . . . and was testified to by its fruits.' He then focused firmly on the oddities: convulsive fits in Park, tremblings and cryings-out in Grimshader; women openly praying and exhorting in Point and Shader 'and a good deal of disorder' – and laid particular stress on aspects we have already noted from 1822, 'The Year of the Swooning'. Both believers and unbelievers were affected – so they were evidently not saving in nature; they were not accompanied by any sense of sin; and they bore no relation to the preaching of the Word. People should, then, hesitate before 'ascribing these manifestations to the agency of the Spirit.'

'My opinion is,' declared Kenneth MacRae, 'that these singular manifestations are not of the Spirit, neither yet are they of the Evil One, but they are simply what is medically known as mass-hysteria.' He had brought a medical textbook with him and built a compelling case:

four-fifths of those affected were young women; it was infectious; it came on only in public and with an audience; 'old, mature Christians of sound and strong judgement seemed to be unaffected.' And, while stressing again that a genuine work of God was under way in the community, he gave as his firm opinion that 'late prayer meetings, protracted into the early hours of the morning, and repeated night after night, definitely did induce hysteria': Robert Murray McCheyne, he pointed out, who returned to the great revival scenes in Dundee, had 'resolutely refused to have any religious meeting continued after eleven p.m.'

And he prophetically concluded by deploring sustained newspaper coverage, 'because it might lead outsiders to come amongst them to exploit to their own advantage the very features which were causing uneasiness.'

In his own pastoral practice, MacRae proved no less robust. 'A number of country people were present and for a time felt afraid that we might be troubled with some outbursts of the hysteria present still in parts of the island, but fortunately we were preserved from any such disturbance,' he recorded in January 1940. But, conducting a prayer meeting on 2 May, in Stornoway, things took a ludicrous and potentially dangerous turn. He became conscious of that 'peculiar gasping sound . . . which has caused so much controversy and division.' MacRae indulged himself, at close of sermon, expressing 'my hope that we as a congregation were not to be troubled by what had caused such dispeace elsewhere. When the disturber discerned the gist of my remarks she completely abandoned herself to this strange influence, until at last she was bawling in such a stentorian voice that I had forthwith to pronounce the benediction. There was almost a panic in the crowded hall and at least two other females subject to these attacks became similarly affected. One old woman, in her efforts to escape from the Hall, climbed over the back of her seat . . . If any think that this is the evidence of a revival among us, then all the other, ordinary evidences are absent.'

'It troubles me very much,' MacRae concluded valiantly, 'but I shall give the "swooners" no latitude.' Colleagues generally found it best to ignore them. In Carloway, MacAulay remembered MacIver preaching serenely on, 'when there were such prostrations among the people that some were carried out shoulder high to the slope above the church to recover.'[5] MacIver continued the sermon without pause or comment, and 'neither encouraged nor discouraged these emotional outbursts.'

MacRae was determined. 'There was no "swooning",' he recorded in May 1940. 'I think that matter has been effectively scotched in this congregation. I shall be surprised if it gives us any more trouble. Spoke from Psalm 27:1.' In February 1941, 'Was told today concerning one who is subject to these strange attacks that she stated, when questioned, that she herself neither knew what the preacher said nor what she herself said, although in these fits she would lay off most vehemently. My informant told me that no softening could be observed after these turns, no appearance of heavenliness, but rather hardening.' And, a month later, at Gravir Communion, 'On Friday, when two of the missionaries who favour the "jerks" were speaking, hands were up in the customary style, but there was no more of it, and on that day I was not in the pulpit. I am inclined, therefore, to think that a great deal of this business is just a put-on. I believe that there would have been plenty of it at this Communion had I been one of those ministers who favoured it.'

By this time, of course, men had more desperate things to think on, as Britain stood alone and the Second World War raged on. The revival damped down, but earnest church attendance continued and people – including two teenage aunts of my own – continued, late in and shortly after the Second World War, to profess faith. The first summer of peace saw some prodigious gatherings. One of the most affecting, still remembered in Harris, was the vast attendance at the Free Presbyterian Communion in Finsbay, in the late summer of 1945. On Sabbath evening, so many crowded to the church – including hundreds of children and young people – that, the night being most fine, it was readily agreed all should repair outside; there, seated in rocks and slopes, huddled by the road, perched on dykes, Rev. James Tallach preached on 'Watchman, what of the night?' to some 2,000 people, most not from South Harris and many not even Free Presbyterians. This was one of the last open-air services on the Long Island.

As we near the end of our history, we have established – and amply documented – the great surge of Evangelicalism through Lewis, beginning with great revival from around 1820, through another in 1859, through lesser movements in the first decade of the twentieth century, through more stirrings in the 1920s to a remarkable and sustained time of Christian awakening in the 1930s. Any living church must, from time to time, regenerate. And the Second World War was but an interruption to further, evident times of renewal even to the present century.

It is therefore infuriating that, if one types the words 'Lewis Revival' into Google, all the references that come up on screen are to one localised movement and to one carpet-bagging mainland evangelist, Duncan Campbell, who descended on the island in 1949.[6] It is known all over the world as the 'Lewis Awakening' or the 'Lewis Revival', and described generally in terms that are both extraordinarily extravagant – 'the last great regional revival in the western world' – and suggest explicitly that

Campbell brought the Gospel to souls hitherto benighted in heathen darkness. Today, many persist in believing that the present, relative strength of the Gospel in Lewis is his abiding legacy and that he is the father of its Evangelical religion. The most ridiculous claims are still peddled on assorted Christian websites, many in America. It is asserted confidently that, on a later Campbell mission to North Uist, 'Uist had never known revival'; that in the Hebrides 'not a single young person attended Sunday services'; that the islands 'were now becoming a spiritual wasteland'; that 'most of the bars were put out of existence'; that 'revival went on for the next thirty years', and so on.

And John White's garbled version in a 1986 study of Nehemiah confirms the abiding power of the Campbell mythology. Addressing spiritual renewal, White claims,

> The revival in the Hebrides off north-west Scotland during the 1940s is a good example. Following a fairly standard opening address in a church by Donald Campbell [sic], a visiting evangelist, a teenage boy rose to utter a lengthy prayer. As he prayed, staid Presbyterian men and women fell to the ground under terrible conviction of sin. It was the beginning of weeks and months of conviction, conversion, and renewal among the Hebridean islanders. Fishermen passing the islands in their boats would be overcome by a sense of sin so that they were constrained to pull into the harbour to find relief there. Whole shifts of below the ground miners would be too distressed to continue their work until they had resolved their relationship with God. Events of this sort can only be explained supernaturally . . .[7]

Actually, events of this sort are best explained by taking the trouble to check one's facts, not least that there have never been any 'below the ground' mines nearer the Outer Hebrides than Raasay.

Duncan Campbell,[8] from the parish of Ardchattan in Argyll, was born in 1898, ordained to the United Free ministry in 1930 – after a spell as missionary in Ardvasar, Skye – and, in January 1949, quit his charge to return to full-time service with an outfit called the Faith Mission, a vaguely evangelical[9] organisation founded in 1886 and, with uniforms and many women preachers or 'pilgrims', some superficial similarities to the Salvation Army. In December 1949, at the invitation of Rev. James Murray MacKay, minister of the little Church of Scotland congregation of Barvas, Duncan Campbell visited Lewis. As he himself on at least one occasion let slip, revival was already apparent in the district when he arrived. He spent most of the next three years on Lewis and Harris, preaching in assorted Church of Scotland congregations and, additionally, preaching far into the night in house-meetings, many of which continued till dawn. There was much sensation and busloads converged from all over the island. Some remarks in recently published extracts from Duncan Campbell's diary are unintentionally hilarious. 'All our meetings are crowded with Free Church people. The enemy is at work; pray that he may be defeated.' There was much hysteria (which Campbell encouraged); rapid 'decisions' for Christ (which he also encouraged); some allegations of paranormal incidents (houses shaking, people falling down), which he unhesitatingly ascribed to the agency of the Holy Spirit; and many professions of faith, which included some genuine conversions.

The goings-on were in 1951 explicitly condemned by the Free Presbyterians and were attacked from an early point by Free Church ministers, who deplored Campbell's methods.[10] In a recent 2004 account, Colin and Mary Peckham outline such 'Opposition to the Revival' and suggest that it was no more than bigoted denominationalism. They give details of 'opposition that was vicious at times', assert that 'some who had come to the Lord in the revival were not accepted at the Lord's table'; that Free Church ministers 'stated that the devil had sent Mr Campbell to the island' and 'he had come to steal members from the Free Church for the Church of Scotland.' Not a shred of documentation is offered for these tales.

And some explicit Peckham statements are less than candid. They twice assert that 'all the Church of Scotland ministers on the island at that time were thoroughly Evangelical, and preached the word clearly.' That is not true. Two of its three Stornoway ministers, at least, were unabashed Moderates. Roderick MacDonald, of St Columba's Parish, who translated the complete works of Burns into immaculate Gaelic, would have been positively insulted to be called an Evangelical; another, John de Lingen, in retirement converted to Roman Catholicism.

The Peckhams retail too an anecdote of how Rev. John MacLeod, Free Church minister of Barvas, locked the church building there to prevent informal meetings being held in it in his absence. 'Margaret MacDonald says that one of his elders, Sandy Alex's father, cried out, "I built this church with my own hands, and now it is locked to me!"' He must have been a very remarkable old man. Barvas Free Church was erected in 1850. And MacLeod, like any minister in any denomination, had an absolute right to veto the use of his building, one which could only have been overridden by his Presbytery. He was naturally aghast that, in a community where something in excess of 80 per cent of the people were Free Church, ministers of a minority denomination had not only invited this adventurer to campaign but actively encouraged Free Church people to attend these meetings.

And the Free Church had legitimate grounds for concern. For one, by the creed MacLeod and others were sworn to assert, declare and defend, Duncan Campbell preached false doctrine. The Faith Mission, Murray asserts,[11] clearly teaches a universal atonement. Campbell declares in a sermon on 'Steadfastness in Conviction' – still available on the Internet[12] – that 'repentance must ever precede salvation'; that is unbiblical and, if one thinks about it, absurd. Only a man who is born again (and therefore saved) can repent; and faith and salvation necessarily precede repentance. Campbell taught besides 'heart purity' or perfectionism, the still dafter notion that a good Christian can be entirely sinless in this life, and openly attacks Shorter Catechism teaching to the contrary in another sermon on this theme, also on the Web. His own 1954 booklet, *The Lewis Awakening*, indeed advertises 'A Study in the Doctrine of Entire Sanctification as a Definite Experience'. And Campbell asserted in a 1952 address[13] that 'in one area of the district there was bitter opposition to the movement because I preached the baptism of the Holy Ghost as a separate and distinct occurrence following conversion'.

But this notion of 'spirit baptism' – completely un-Scriptural and another subtle form of Christianity-plus – has discouraged Christians all over the world and caused bitter church division, between Christians who merely have Christ, so to speak, and those who boast of their superior Spirit baptism. Any responsible pastor would warn his flock against it. (It is of course a central tenet of Pentecostalism and the modern 'Charismatic Renewal', which has split Christian churches everywhere and is associated with fatuous, undisciplined and sometimes hysterical public worship of the hands-down-for-coffee variety.)

Secondly, Duncan Campbell told lies. It is no exaggeration to say that he spent the rest of his life – he died in Switzerland in 1972 – dining out on his 'Lewis Awakening', receiving preaching invitations and conference dates throughout Christendom on the strength of it, and peddling the same tired melodramatic yarns wherever he went. Even his biographer, Andrew Woolsey, concedes that his accounts 'sometimes left him open to the charge of exaggeration.'[14] This is far too lenient. In his 1960 account, Duncan Campbell declared, 'At that time [1949] there was not a single young person attending public worship, a fact which cannot be disputed.' It could be disputed by my own mother – thirteen in 1949 and regularly attending both Sabbath services – and hundreds of others, such as the youngsters who listened to James Tallach at Finsbay. Campbell claimed – even quoting the local press – that 'more were now attending the prayer meetings than had attended public worship before the revival'. That is preposterous: church attendance on Lewis and Harris, of a Sabbath, in the 1940s probably exceeded 50 per cent of the entire able-bodied population. Campbell also seized on a proclamation issued by the Free Church of Scotland – nationally – on the low moral and spiritual state of the whole country, read from island pulpits in 1949, and repeatedly passed off such assertions as 'the low state of vital religion . . . growing carelessness toward public worship' as a 1949 description of conditions on *Lewis*.

He told still more fibs in 1952, asserting that in Arnol 'the Sabbath was given over to drinking and poaching', which is dubious, and by contrast, after his own endeavours, 'there is not a single young man between the age of eighteen and thirty-five who is not praying in the prayer meeting', which was laughable; and still more Campbell's claim that the prayer meeting had died out in some districts because of lack of interest. Stornoway, by contrast to all this awakening, was a 'black spot'. Claims that a 'drinking house . . . closed that night and has never reopened since' are untrue. These illicit drinking-dens, or bothans, prospered all over the West Side,[15] continually and for many years after the Second World War – Shawbost, alone, could boast two – and only went into decline with the advent of licensed public houses. Not a single bar closed in Stornoway – where they were all then confined – as a consequence of the Campbell campaign.

Campbell certainly exaggerated. He talks of 'hundreds that came to know Christ' and 'an island in the grip of God', but gives only most limited documentation of a few localities. 'The most prominent feature in the accounts is the phenomena,' notes Iain Murray, 'visions, prostrations, outcries etc – which Campbell constantly tends to treat as proof of the supernatural: Donald "is not praying more than five minutes when God sweeps into the church, and there is the congregation falling almost on the top of each other; others throw themselves back and become rigid as in death."'

The Peckhams use phrases like 'move of the Spirit' or, on occasion, 'a great move of the Spirit' to describe what sounds like a religious Beatlemania; they also, in describing conversions, repeatedly use the phrase 'broke through to God', as wretched people finally found faith, or at least some experience of psychological release , after weeks of misery, and as if their quest were sadistically resisted and salvation had to be earned by prayer and anguish.

This flagellating stuff is not the religion of Lewis and Harris. In fact, the Peckham book is profoundly misleading. Though entitled *Sounds From Heaven – The Revival on the Isle of Lewis, 1949–1952*, and dedicating two-thirds of the book to 'Testimonies of Those Who Experienced the Revivals', close study is instructive. Of the twenty-four conversion narratives, twelve are not from this 1949–1952 'Awakening' at all. Several are from the pre-war movements whose authenticity are undoubted. Of the twelve that are, in five Duncan Campbell was not the means. Of the seven who were, several were 'under concern' and seeking salvation before they heard him. The accounts of two who later became ministers – Alasdair MacDonald and Jack MacArthur – are extraordinarily and, one suspects, deliberately vague.

That there were some genuine conversions is certain. Two – William MacLeod and John Murdo Smith – were later great Church of Scotland ministers. The late Duncan MacKenzie of Tolsta Chaolais – who announced proudly, in my hearing, on the Friday of a 2005 Shawbost Communion that he had first spoken to the Question exactly fifty years before – seems to have been another, who had evidently not the least difficulty attaining Free Church membership and became a hugely loved elder. But the damage done in Lewis was serious. It divided congregations and provoked conflict between pastors and people. There was also widespread recidivism, much beyond the scale of that associated with other revivals. Many early Campbell converts eventually turned their backs on religion. It is sobering that the two localities most associated with Campbell's Faith Mission campaign – Arnol and Bernera – and where hysterics and phenomena are claimed by him – are, today, among the least religious on Lewis. Bernera fishermen, for instance, work even on the Lord's Day. And a still sillier strain of pietism – the obsession with 'testimony' and experiences generally, the more exciting the better – was thus imported, and has yet to leave.

The memories of one West Side lady – in 1949, an Arnol girl of seventeen – are interesting.[16] A humble and intelligent Christian, for many years a Free Church communicant, she remembers Mr Campbell with affection and 'that was when I was brought in.' But she was bothered how 'sometimes he would be at it till three in the morning. And it was just the nice houses he would hold meetings in, the new ones. And – you know – the *cliobadaich* would start. A lad would jump up suddenly and shout, "I will follow the Lamb!" And they would be wailing, and stamping their feet on the floor. I was frightened. I think they were doing it deliberately to frighten us.' John Murray,[17] born in Barvas in 1938, saw sensational things at these house-meetings – 'men levitating on the stairs' – and told my father bluntly, many years later, it had put him off religion for life. He became a noted Gaelic writer and was for some years head of BBC Gaelic radio.

Hysterics apart, there was Campbell's serious misrepresentation of the island's spiritual state on his arrival. Kenneth MacRae had every right both to point out that in Stornoway, a supposed 'black spot', 200 to 250 people attended his weekly prayer meeting; that there were no fewer than eleven held each week in connection with his congregation; that he had over sixty men he could call on to engage publicly in prayer; and that, on the Saturday evening prayer meeting of his Communion, 800 to 1,000 people attended. And that was regardless of the other churches in town. 'Do these figures indicate a low state of religion? Where else in Scotland outside Lewis can they be obtained? I do not give them in any boastful spirit, but if these figures reflect the religious life of the "black spot" of the island, surely they show more vividly than anything else can how utterly untrue is the Faith Mission story as to the materialistic condition of the island prior to 1949. And Stornoway only reflects the state of the island as a whole. In my opinion, religion in Lewis is in a much worse condition than it was prior to the advent of the Faith Mission, for Arminian teachings have been propagated and ill-feeling and unkindly heat generated among congregations and churches, which hitherto had enjoyed peace and were able to live together in harmony.'[18]

In this unfortunate pamphlet, *The Resurgence of Arminianism*, MacRae could not hide his anguish at the 'gross exaggerations, unscrupulous distortion and absolute falsehood', which, he very properly pointed out, were scarcely the fruits of the Spirit. And he had one unanswerable question. 'According to their own profession, the Faith Mission exists principally for the purpose of labouring in rural districts indifferently supplied with Gospel ordinances and the field open to them today is very wide. Why, therefore, come to Skye and Lewis, out of all Scotland the area best supplied with Gospel ordinances and preachers?'

Nevertheless Duncan Campbell's untruths have triumphed; established and viral. MacRae has his *Diary*; but Campbell has Google.

The advent of new sects was one unwelcome twentieth-century development on Lewis. A good man from Lionel, John Nicolson, *Am Fiosaiche*, had emigrated to America,[19] and returned to Ness about 1900 not only as a proselyte of the Plymouth Brethren – a group who resisted any suggestion of a separate trained ministry and who practised adult believer's baptism, by immersion – but with a very rich, pious American wife, Nora Cushing. They held services at first in their home, and started a Sabbath School, which was soon attended by a hundred children. Later they built a remarkable chapel, Edgemoor Hall, and a house for themselves, atop by a terrifying cliff, at Filiscleitir, several miles south of Skigersta and anything that could be dignified as a road. It might seem a ridiculous place for a church, but it was close to both the Ness and Tolsta summer shielings – and, as Nicolson certainly knew, just where Finlay Munro had landed a century before. Here the doughty couple conducted services for many years. Very often, the crews of Buchan trawlers – already

and quite illegally emptying the famous haddock fishery of Broad Bay –
who were themselves Brethren would hove to for Sabbath services. Peggy
Gillies remembered going to occasional services and a Sunday school at
this church, with its 'altar' or lectern draped in a brilliant-hued cloth, and
the robust hymn-singing of the fishermen, and Mrs Nicolson on the
harmonium, a huge novelty to island children. The Nicolsons also
selflessly spent a considerable fortune in the aid of the poorest around
them. They were a highly respected couple, but no Brethren cause long
survived them in Ness. A colleague, though, John Morrison from Habost
– who had been converted to Brethren views in America – became
eminent in their little Stornoway congregation, which still worships in a
wee church at Bayhead, erected in 1952.

The Salvation Army set up base in Stornoway in 1983 and in 1986
opened their own building at Bayhead, but are of little account. The
Jehovah's Witnesses seem to have won a tiny following in the years after
the Second World War and, in 1958, built a 'Kingdom Hall' on Church
Street. The Mormons gained a toehold in the 1970s, and a little church
(with striking steeple) was completed on Newton Street in 1999: former
Free Church adherents were prominent in both and these cults do seem
able to appeal in some way to a certain sort of alienated Presbyterian. A
Pentecostal group, the 'Church of the True Vine', took root in the 1990s,
at first using the old spinning-school on Keith Street; and in the present
century a little charismatic group, the 'House of Peace' have taken over
the old Church of Scotland meeting-house at Arnol. There are no doubt
other such groups, composed almost entirely from incomers who have
been flooding through recent years onto the Long Island (and most of
whom have no time for any religion of any kind). The Episcopalians
gained most, of course, from such settlement – the present exuberant
Stornoway priest, Stanley Bennie, was installed in 1984. But the Metho-
dists – who established a real grip on Orkney and Shetland in Victorian
times – have never had a presence in the Outer Hebrides, and it was 2005
before Stornoway, the last place in the Commonwealth that needed yet
another church, saw a Baptist congregation founded.

But the most striking new arrival is a revived Roman Catholic
Church.[20] Early in the 1900s, the Roman Catholic Bishop of Aberdeen
founded a chapel at Matheson Road in Stornoway for seasonal use by,
presumably, fishermen and herring-girls of the faith – herring shoaled
around Britain, and the industry followed them en bloc – and, it seems,
during one period of inactivity this was 'desecrated in a revolting manner
by a local minority', to widespread disgust. It was not used again, though
the building survives as a private house. Very occasionally a visiting priest
from the Southern Isles – Fr James MacNeil of Benbecula was a frequent

visitor – would celebrate Mass at such venues as the Caledonian Hotel, the Rendezvous Cafe and in the Town House Restaurant.

Those two last are significant; they – and another institution, The Coffee Pot, which still survives – were founded between the wars by certain Italian immigrant families.[21] They were soon part of the fabric and were very much liked, offering cheerful facilities, delicious coffee and ice-cream worthy of celebration in verse. They also made a great deal of money. (In the post-war years when the amount of cash one could remove from Britain was heavily restricted – £50 was typical – my grandfather, a joiner, was once commissioned by an Italian friend in town to fashion a false-bottomed case, so that precious funds could be taken to relatives back home and in desperate poverty.) Mother Church did not overlook this Little Italy and – the official account becomes oddly vague here – by the 1960s Fr J. Ryland Whitaker was appointed as the first resident priest of Stornoway since the Reformation. He became very active in Stornoway Youth Club and this, it is said, 'created a general acceptance of the Catholic presence in the town.' By 1961 they had erected a little church on Kenneth Street, only yards from MacRae's Free Church – a recycled Second World War NAAFI canteen-hut; and indeed very recycled indeed, for it did subsequent service as a printshop and offices for the *Stornoway Gazette*, which was then a fine local newspaper. It was fashioned into quite a neat little place of worship and the Church of the Holy Redeemer finally hosted its first Mass on 11 June 1961 and, damp and inadequate as it was, sufficed for thirty more years.

In 1963, Fr Isaias Gerard Capaldi, SJ, took over and served for twenty-nine years as priest of Stornoway. He was closely related to one support-ing family and was a likable if oddly sepulchral figure about town. The congregation grew very slowly, with Roman Catholic families moving in, and enjoyed support from holidaymakers and especially, from 1974, senior secondary schoolchildren of the old faith from the Uists and Barra, now hostelled in Stornoway rather than Lochaber with the advent of Comhairle nan Eilean, the Western Isles Islands Council.

Fr Capaldi always wanted a proper church and, largely by his en-deavours, an attractive permanent building was opened on Scotland Street in 1991. By now the official Roman Catholic population of the Long Island was assessed at over three hundred, rather than fifty – these are always estimates of baptised adherents, and are no doubt generous. He retired in 1992 to Edinburgh, dying a decade later; his successor, Fr Paul Hackett, from Bournemouth, spent thirteen years on Lewis and, already fluent in German, French and Welsh, made an excellent fist of Gaelic. He relaxed by collecting and tending assorted alpine plants.

Stornoway was momentarily shaken when, in November 2004, the

Roman Catholic church burned to the ground. The cause was quickly identified, though, as dodgy wiring, not sectarian arson. Fr Thomas Kearns, an Irishman ordained late in life after years in accountancy, became priest in 2005 and was granted opportunity to enlarge on Roman Catholic doctrine in the short-lived *Hebridean* newspaper, above the 'Edited Sermon Notes of Rev. MacAulay', another popular feature. A handsome new church of very similar external appearance, though with some inner improvements, was consecrated in May 2007. The congregation has of late been augmented by the arrival of so many migrant workers from Lithuania and Poland.

The post-war years saw some localised Presbyterian dispute. Protracted trouble at Lemreway from 1950 ended in the exodus of all but a handful of villagers from Park Free Church and their subsequent admission as a congregation of the Church of Scotland. Their latter minister, Donald MacAulay, is best remembered for his enthusiasm in politics; he served as first Convener of the new Western Isles Islands Council, Comhairle nan Eilean, with a Barra priest as his capable deputy. In 1963, disputes in the Free Church of Knock ended in its split. The General Assembly sanctioned a new charge, Point Free Church, for hundreds of disaffected 'Rebels', as they are still known.

There is no profit in detailing either that or other post-war rows, and new Presbyterian splinters of limited local impact. The Associated Presbyterian Churches, for instance, who split from the Free Presbyterian Church in 1989,[22] have only two Long Island congregations – at Stornoway, and Seilebost on Harris – and one minister, George Macaskill, inducted to town in 1993. In January 2000, a few hundred Lewis and Harris people, though only one serving minister (who was under suspension) joined the new 'Free Church of Scotland Continuing'.[23] They formed a congregation in Stornoway and others besides, in North Uist, Leverburgh, Scalpay, Knock, Bragar and Cross, with assorted commuters here and there from other districts. The FCC won only some 8 per cent of Free Church communicants nationally, and a still lower proportion, probably, on Lewis and Harris. In April 2010 they maintained five settled ministers in the Western Isles. Carloway Free Church alone, it should be recorded, lost no members whatsoever to this secession.

Not all twentieth-century division was acrimonious. Both the Free Church and the Free Presbyterians, after the Second World War, elevated their Tolsta outposts to a sanctioned charge. A new Free Church congregation at Callanish, which was, in most amicable circumstances, disjoined from Carloway in 1971, has proved a most successful, youthful congregation. There were lost opportunities. Inter-village rivalries prevented a consolidated Free Presbyterian ministry of Breasclete and Achmore – which was seriously mooted[24] – and a new Free Church charge of Borve with Galson, which was also briefly floated in the 1950s. Bragar and Tong, too, could have supported their own pastorates. The behemoth that is Stornoway Free Church might sensibly besides have been partitioned, but for this – even in Laxdale, where a substantial congregation could have been formed – there was no local appetite whatever.

Kenneth MacRae died in the Stornoway manse on 6 May 1964. He was buried at Sandwick two days later. The crowd was so enormous that two separate services had simultaneously to be held – one in the jammed Free Church, and another in the equally packed Seminary on Francis Street – and at least a thousand men took part in the funeral procession. 'Hundreds of women lined the streets,' reported a newspaper, 'many of them weeping.'[25] Both his successors, too, would die in office. Murdo MacRitchie, inducted in 1966, was a handsome man from Back, with an endearing lisp and a special affinity for young people, ordained in Detroit in 1952. Though by the late 1970s largely overwhelmed by an impossible pastoral burden – MacRitchie never had an ordained assistant – he had a commanding ministry, and in the 1970s there was significant awakening in his congregation. In the summer of 1981, he spent some months in America and returned an ill man. Still only sixty-three, he died in April 1983 after considerable suffering, leaving a desolate family and a bereft congregation.[26]

MacRitchie was just one star in a veritable galaxy of Long Island preaching talent in these post-war decades. Through the 1950s, North Tolsta enjoyed two sparkling ministers, Angus Finlayson in the Free Church and a young Oban-born pastor, Fraser MacDonald, in the Free Presbyterians. Though they often disputed one another publicly – often with startling ferocity – they were great personal friends. Another Tolsta man, Murdo Murray, was ordained to Carloway in 1947, and from 1963 exercised a hugely appreciated ministry at Knock.

William MacLean,[27] a Lochcarron man who had been brought up in the Free Church, has a unique claim – he served the people of Ness not merely as their schoolmaster (at Lionel, from 1929) but, from 1941, as its Free Presbyterian missionary, being at length ordained as minister in 1947. He served until 1962, when – startling many – he accepted a call to New Zealand and, later, to Australia, returning as Free Presbyterian minister for a second, surely unprecedented pastorate at Ness in 1976. How MacLean had parted from the Free Church is not entirely clear. He had selflessly started a youth club for local boys, where draughts and ping-pong were supplemented with spiritual talks: this seems to have been resented by the Free Church minister of the time, Alexander MacLeod, and in any event MacLean's schoolhouse was beside the Free Presbyterian Church and he grew increasingly fond of their fellowship.

MacLean has sometimes been blamed for a distinct chill in Free Church and Free Presbyterian relations on Lewis after the Second World War. Having been a Cross Free Church adherent, it is understandable if real tensions developed and he was certainly a very ardent, convinced Free Presbyterian. But he was a sweet-natured, winsome Christian, at once nervous, fast spoken and hugely affectionate, who played an important part in re-energising island Free Presbyterians after the desolation of the Protest controversy.

MacLean, naive as he might at times seem, could show considerable self-possession. On his first voyage to New Zealand – before he was inducted to Gisborne – Mr MacLean lodged in an Aukland home. Inabell Christensen was a good woman, a communicant, and delighted to have him. But her husband, of completely unchurched background, was a hard, godless man with entire contempt for the clergy. Ted Christensen had only one religion: the All Blacks. He never went to church. He did not appreciate this house-guest and quickly resolved to disconcert William MacLean.

'Will you take a beer?' he sneered, opening the refrigerator. MacLean neither winced nor blushed. 'Certainly,' he said, 'but we will ask a blessing first.' Discomfited, Christensen popped bottles and filled their glasses. MacLean said grace, and he quoted two lines from Psalm 73:

> So rude was I, and ignorant
> And in thy sight a beast . . .

They quietly enjoyed the beer. But these words stuck in Christensen's mind. Soon he had gone to hear this composed Highlander preaching. And he became an eminent Christian and Free Presbyterian elder.

William MacLean never married, never learned to drive, and in his New Zealand days – for he could not cook, and local prudery forbade a resident housekeeper – routinely ate out, once confessing to his sister that his best efforts otherwise at making a meal were 'switching two eggs quickly in a glass.' He was so unworldly that any gift of money ended up back in the collection plate. Packing him off with difficulty for a desperately needed holiday, New Zealand friends waited till he was on the very steps of the plane before stuffing a wad of notes into his pocket. Both at Ness and in the Antipodes, there were very many converts under MacLean's warm preaching, and in his final pastorate he was the most mellow, undenominational of men, swift to visit any home where grief had struck, whose door was always open for anyone struggling, for instance, to complete an involved official form.

First ordained in 1941, John MacSween was in 1966 inducted as minister of the new Point Free Church congregation, and was another outstanding island pastor – in most sober opinion, the ablest theologian of the post-war Long Island pulpit, his only weakness being a tendency to hyper-Calvinism. His successor, a Shawbost man – John N. MacLeod, known to all as 'Jack' – boasted scarcely less keen an intellect and offered genuine leadership at a time when, from the mid 1970s, the general calibre of the Lewis ministry was in some decline.

Murdo Alex MacLeod, a son of the manse and of exuberant humour and who was utterly unafraid of anyone, was ordained to Drumchapel in 1966. After pastorates in Dingwall and Inverness, he succeeded Murdo MacRitchie as minister of Stornoway in 1984. 'Murdo Alick' is a most complicated figure. Though he was full of true tenderness – he was, for instance, an outstanding parent to his exuberant children – and took enthusiastic interest both in military history and Premier League football, he served Stornoway in peculiarly difficult times. His fascination with warfare was apt; he was by temperament a general, capable of 'parking' tender emotion. Behind the wringing handshake, the bubbling banter, lay a warm heart and, besides, a cold, calculating mind. Nor was he a well man, surviving his first heart attack early in his Inverness ministry, and surviving a second soon after going to Stornoway. He recovered quickly from the first, bought a bicycle for exercise, and – in shorts and cap – could not resist the temptation to bowl by the other Free Church manse of Inverness and wind up a good but starchy colleague. It was a grand house, at the top of a sweeping gravel drive. MacLeod pedalled to the very doorstep. Still in the saddle, he rang the bell. The lady of the manse could not believe her eyes. 'Hello,' chirped Murdo Alick. 'Can Hugh come out to play?'

From his earliest preaching days, MacLeod had kept a pulpit journal, writing in the text, occasion and headings of each sermon. In October 1995 – he had served that year as Moderator of a very difficult General Assembly – he died suddenly in Aberdeen, only sixty years old. The very last page of that original volume had just been filled with details of his final sermon.[28]

There were other notable Free Church pastorates, such as Callum Matheson's 1980s service in Shawbost – with some manifest revival[29] – or Norman MacLeod's success in building a substantial Callanish congregation. Nor can one ignore a rejuvenated Church of Scotland, which from the 1960s saw much more disciplined ministry in Lewis and Harris and whose ministers, in the 1980s, threatened briefly to eclipse the Free

Church – and from a far smaller base – for Evangelical zeal. Notable post-war ministers include Donald MacRae,[30] born at Miavaig, Uig in 1918 and who exemplified the best of the old United Free tradition – a luminous Christian man who, after ordination to Sleat and subsequent service on Benbecula, was from 1961 to 1988 the beloved minister of Tarbert.

A few days before his death, in July 2004, a good man from Stornoway called to see Mr MacRae. Though very weak, he was awake and alert. He seized the friendly hand. 'And what will you have to say to the Lord,' he whispered, 'on the day of Judgement?' The elder was quite disconcerted. 'Well, you are the minister, and on the good way many years: what will you say yourself?' 'Oh,' said Donald MacRae warmly, 'Mercy, mercy, mercy . . .' Though sometimes mocked for what might be tactfully described as rather optimistic prayers at the funerals of certain notorious sinners – 'Mr MacRae consigned that wretched fellow to Abraham's bosom, whether Abraham wanted him or not!' – such apparent unguard-edness reflected a pastor's heart, and the keen awareness of a manifestly saintly man that grace can, as the proverb says, claim a man even between the stirrup and the ground.

But the outstanding post-war figure – gifted, sturdy and of prodigious industry – was a Carloway convert, Murdo MacAulay,[31] who outlived almost all the others. Born in February 1907, he passed over the chance of university – almost certainly because his folk could not afford it – for service in the Army. Though offered an officer's commission, he could not afford its expected lifestyle either, and his uncle – a Carloway grocer – soon bought MacAulay out. He joined the business and contented himself with a part-time role in the Ross Mountain Battery Territorials, in Stornoway. And then, like many others, he was swept up in the Carloway revival, leaving this delicious account of early ordeals at the Fellowship Meeting.

> Once, on a Monday evening of the Bernera Communion – there being no evening service in Bernera then – Mr MacIver kept a fellowship meeting in Tolsta Chaolais, and many of the young converts were there, probably unaware that they would be called upon to speak to the Question. Even some of the first converts came out in a sweat when they heard their names being called, and whatever thoughts they had of saying something quickly vanished when they attempted to speak, and so they did not get very far. One of those called upon was Norman MacLeod . . . who shot up suddenly when he heard his name, and blurted out, 'The people here . . .' and stopped suddenly, getting no further with what he intended to say. As soon as they came out from the

meeting his cousin Calum Chiribhig began teasing him, 'You going to speak to the Question! No one was to compare with you, but you did not get very far!' This, of course, was all taken in a friendly spirit, and such criticism was not unusual amongst us. Mr Maciver called on Aonghas Iain Ghraidhean, who spoke of his own extraordinary experiences, flying high, until he had to say to the Lord to withhold His hand as he could not stand any more of His presence. Turning to his friend Neil MacLeod, 23 Doune Carloway, he said, placing his hand on Neil's shoulder, 'I saw Christ as clear as Neil's face here . . .'

Shortly after this, Mr MacIver held another Fellowship Meeting, again in Tolsta Chaolais, and this time called on Malcolm MacLeod, Upper Carloway (Calum Chiribhig). Calum did not get on too well. He told two 'notes' [edifying anecdotes] he had heard, mixed them up, and in his excitement made a real 'brochan' (porridge) of them. So when he came out, Norman, ready to get his own back, looked at him and said, 'Is that speaking to the Question?' Later, Norman told Donald Mac-Leod . . . when they would be in Calum's house, to ask him to tell those 'notes' to those present . . . When the opportune time came, Calum's house was full and in the midst of the discussion, Donald asked him about the 'notes' he told in Tolsta Chaolais. Calum replied . . . 'I told them two very good "notes", but they were not good there.' Later on, at a Question Meeting in Carloway, when Calum Chiribhig was called upon, the first thing he said was that the people were telling him that, even if he had something to say, he did not know how to say it!

Donald MacLeod was also called upon at the same Tolsta Chaolais meeting and those who knew him were most anxious as he could hardly remember the text of the sermon when he got outside the church door. But 'Dolligan' surprised them all, and it was clearly manifested that the Holy Spirit had come to his aid in his infirmity, enabling him to declare in an orderly manner those things he had personally experienced in being translated from the Kingdom of Darkness to the Kingdom of His Dear Son. When Duncan MacLeod, 20 Garenin, was called upon he said that he did not experience any strong strivings of the Law [i.e. conviction of sin] as he heard others mentioning, and this worried him. Mr MacIver in closing said that one got sufficient of the Law if one knew one was a sinner, and saw the need of the mercy of God in Christ.

At that time a large Bernera fishing-boat used to ferry visitors from Carloway to the Bernera Communion on Friday, Sabbath and Monday. One of the loveliest scenes we can recall was this boat in the early autumn full of visitors coming in the Loch to Carloway Pier with those on board singing Psalm 122:6–9 . . .

> Pray that Jerusalem may have
> peace and felicity:
> Let them that love Thee, and Thy peace
> Have still prosperity.
>
> Therefore I wish that peace may still
> within Thy walls remain,
> And ever may Thy palaces
> prosperity retain.
>
> Now, for my friends' and brethren's sakes,
> Peace be in Thee, I'll say.
> And for the house of God our Lord,
> I'll seek thy good alway . . .[32]

Murdo MacAulay and this Norman MacLeod would both be Free Church ministers. When war broke out in 1939, MacLeod put off thoughts of going in for the ministry and at once volunteered, genuinely believing that was his first duty when so many contemporaries were in peril. MacAulay, being a Territorial, had of course no choice. He was given a Lieutenant's commission and made a company commander – and, when the 51st (Highland) Division was blithely deployed at St Valery to buy time for the rest to reach Dunkirk he was, like thousands of others, captured by the Germans. It was in these grim years, in the sapping world of a POW camp, that he felt a desire to preach the Gospel. Being an officer, he was allowed to study – and by the time he was liberated, MacAulay had mastered not only Greek but excellent German, and made a good start on Hebrew besides.

At home, that said, his subsequent course was no sinecure: like Kenneth MacRae, MacAulay bravely took a University degree and his Free Church College training at the same time, contending besides with a new baby and a wife, Dolina, who was fortunate to survive serious illness. In 1949 he was ordained to Govan – one of several Gaelic charges in Glasgow – and in 1956 he succeeded his Govan predecessor, Alexander MacLeod, as minister of Back.

'Mr MacAulay was a big man in every sense of the word,' writes Donald MacDonald. 'He possessed a strong physique, a strong commanding voice and held strong convictions. Such a combination inevitably made him a strong personality. He did not suffer fools gladly. . . . He was a man of initiative and a born leader of men.' Of forceful opinion, no one fought harder to stamp out the wretched public discipline of shamed newly married couples and single mothers; and – very much by his direction, for he believed nothing was as solemn as the preaching of the Gospel – the intimation, 'We will now proceed to the more solemn part of the service,' was discarded from the Free Church Communion order. He was formidably practical, supervising in detail the construction of what remains the best manse of any congregation of any church on the Long Island. And he was of great intellect. Though profoundly conservative, he had real theological talent and was not afraid – in German, of course – to familiarise himself with such radical divines as Karl Barth. MacAulay was in 1965 nominated for the Systematic Theology chair in the Free Church College, and should have won it; he lost by the barest margin in the General Assembly, almost certainly from anti-Lewis spite. (This may well explain why, despite several later approaches, he refused firmly ever to serve as Moderator, though he gave important service on the Foreign Missions Board.)

Yet he was a holy man. He read the Bible constantly, for personal diversion – not just daily in Gaelic and English, but daily besides in Greek and German. And he had a pastor's heart, enthused by his experience of revival, often illustrating sermons from his own observation of sheep and lambs on the Back glebe. MacAulay once let something very striking slip in a rare reference to his inner spiritual life. 'During my evening prayers I visit every home in the congregation,' he said, 'and I pray for those in those homes and especially for those in homes where I think there is no witness. From Back I go to other parts of the island and to other parts of the world.' A supremely disciplined preacher, who made full use of an extensive library, his central emphasis was on the person and offices of Christ and, especially, the divine and human natures in relation to the work of atonement. He gave evening, winter lectures besides on weighty themes. In 1963, he seemed a formidable and surprising choice of speaker for a Free Church Youth Conference in Perthshire. But MacAulay proved a huge hit and himself declared it one of his 'most exhilarating experiences since the Carloway Revival'.

His early ministry at Back was not easy. He saw very little response to his preaching and was further discouraged when many office-bearers died in rather rapid succession. Sometimes MacAulay was tempted to wonder if he had been right to accept the call. But he toiled on. In 1971, a real awakening came. In just two years, over fifty new faces appeared at the prayer meeting; in 1973, alone, there were thirty-seven new communicants, and the Back congregation was enormously refreshed.

Murdo MacAulay's decision in 1975 to retire startled many. He was not yet seventy and in excellent health. But his wife was far from well and he had borne a punishing workload from the day of his ordination. The decision was prudent and showed enormous wisdom. Nor did he retire into lazy oblivion. For one, he continued until well into the 1990s to preach, at Communion seasons and elsewhere, with great energy and acceptance. Besides, he wrote prodigiously, leaving behind him some genuinely important little books. They sold strongly, but he accepted no royalties. The profits from his early works went to support Sabbath Schools in Back and Carloway, and from later ones to the new Bethesda care-home in Stornoway.

In his last years, Murdo MacAulay reluctantly, if sensibly, quit his Carloway cottage for a care-home in town himself. The old spark never quite vanished. A nervous young office-bearer – part of a group calling, some Sabbath afternoon, to lead worship – was asked to pray and, not sure quite how to bear himself outwith a church building, simply bent his head and remained seated as he orated. The growl echoed loudly from a corner – 'Air do chasan! On your feet!'[33]

As a new century loomed, the old man grew more and more burdened for island schoolchildren. Murdo MacAulay longed to see a revival among them before he died. He prayed for it constantly, and grew more and more convinced one would come. 'But,' he mused, 'they will be different Christians to us; they will not be like ourselves . . .'[34]

13

The Table of the Lord

Aspects of Evangelical Worship

On Friday 13 June 1913, a very old lady, Mrs Malcolm MacAulay, passed quietly to her rest in the township of Aird Uig. Born as Catherine MacLeod – *Catriona 'ic Mhurchadh Chaluim* – at 17 Kneep in what was then, as we have seen, to all intents and purposes a heathen parish, Catriona had by the time of her marriage seen the securing of a massively Christian one. But, born, besides, when only one Established Church claimed the allegiance of the Lewis people, Mrs MacAulay lived to see it thoroughly, pathetically riven – what remained of the Church of Scotland eclipsed by a battered but finally vindicated Free Church of Scotland, to say nothing of a new United Free rump and her own small but vigorous Free Presbyterian order.

And her formal obituary[1] is as neat a realisation as any of that first Evangelical century, as known in the life of one individual – and, besides, allows us a rare glimpse of the new religious order from the perspective of a woman.

> Many will regret to learn the death of Mrs Malcolm MacAulay, late of Stornoway, which took place at Aird Uig, on Friday, 13th June, at the ripe age of ninety-three years. She was brought to a saving knowledge of the truth when very young. About the age of twelve, she went along with other children to play on Sabbath at the seashore, and in the evening her mother took her to the prayer meeting, which was that evening conducted by the late Donald MacLeod, Erisda. Donald read the fifty-third chapter of Isaiah and in commenting on the chapter said, 'that those who refused Christ in the Gospel were as guilty of crucifying Him as those who actually put him to death on Calvary.' This went like a dagger to her conscience, and she was for some time in great mental agony. We are not in a position to say definitely when, or through whom, relief came, but from her great regard in after life to the late Rev. Alexander MacLeod, Uig (afterwards of Rogart) we may safely conclude that he was the instrument used by the Lord for this gracious purpose.

About the age of sixteen she was pressed to come forward to make a
public profession of Christ. Before going to Mr MacLeod, she laid the
matter before the Lord, and was strengthened by the following passages,
which came with much force and unction – 'He [Ephraim] is an unwise
son; for he should not stay long in the place of the breaking forth of
children'; also, 'If ye love me, keep my commandments.' In the strength
of these words, she went with much fear and trembling to Mr
MacLeod, who was considered very severe in admitting applicants to
the Lord's Table. She, however, found him, not as she expected, severe,
but 'as mild as a lamb.' He asked her but one question, which was,
'Would you suffer for Christ?' to which she replied, 'I am afraid I
wouldn't.' Concluding that her answer was sufficient to debar her from
being admitted, she returned home much downcast, but to her surprise
the following Sabbath, which was the Sabbath before the Communion,
Mr MacLeod's text was, 'If ye love me, keep my commandments.' He
spoke of the different ways in which God's people were to obey His
commandments, and his remarks gave her great encouragement, and in
the strength of this, she came before the Session which readily received
her.

It was a common practice in those days in many places with the pious
women to keep private prayer meetings to which no male member was
admitted. Such meetings were held at Uig, and to these Mrs MacAulay
regularly went. She evidently benefited much by them, for to the end of
her days she spoke of those meetings with great delight, and often
related how they spent whole nights in prayer and meditation. She had a
profound admiration for the late Rev. Peter MacLean of Stornoway.
When Mr MacLean was teacher at Uig she would, when he passed the
way, hide herself behind a knoll to get a glimpse of him, but her natural
shyness prevented her making herself known to him.

At the age of twenty-one she married Mr Malcolm MacAulay,
Islivig, who also feared the Lord, and to whom she had ten of a family,
of whom six are still living. To show the great regard Mr and Mrs
MacLeod had for her, it may be related that ten days before her
marriage they sent for her to the manse, where she stayed until her
marriage-day, during which time she received many wise and valuable
advices in view of her future life.

At the Disruption of 1843, she and her husband, along with the
whole parish, had no hesitation in casting in their lot with the Free
Church. But during the first Union negotiations, when the late Rev.
John Campbell, who favoured the Union, was their minister, she and
the majority of the people returned to the Established Church on the
understanding that they would be supplied by an Evangelical minister.

About the year 1890 she came to Stornoway to keep house with her son, Mr Alick MacAulay, who is now one of our deacons. For the first few years, she attended the Free Church in the town, but when the Free Presbyterian Church in 1893 began to hold separate meetings, she was one of the first to join our congregation, to which she adhered as a loyal member until her death. In taking this step of becoming a Free Presbyterian, she was not a mere follower of men, however much she might admire them, but sought to have the mind of the Lord revealed to her. Her duty was made clear by the following passage: 'By whom? And he said, Thus saith the Lord even by the young men of the princes of the provinces.' It might be observed here that this was the same passage which led the late Alexander MacIver, Lochs, to cast in his lot with us. When he and Mrs MacAulay met and learned that it was the same passage which led them both in the path of duty, their attachment which before was strong, afterwards developed into something similar to that which existed between David and Jonathan.

She was of a most loving and kind disposition, and those of our ministers and people, who visited her home at Kenneth Street, will not readily forget the warm and hearty reception she would give. She seemed to be in her element when surrounded by the Lord's people. As she advanced in years, her strength failed so much that she was unable to attend the public means of grace, and thinking her end was near, she expressed the desire of returning to her native place to be with her daughter. After returning to Aird Uig, she lingered for ten years, in great weakness, but without pain. The Bible was her constant companion, and she could read it without the help of spectacles until the end.

She was no stranger to the 'fiery darts of the wicked one', by whom she was often harassed, as also often cast down by the corruption of her nature, but her defence was the shield of faith and the sword of the Spirit, by which she was enabled to gain the victory. During her last days her memory completely failed her regarding temporal things; even the affairs of her own children were lost to her, yet her intellect and memory were quite clear upon the Scriptures. The night before she died she wished her daughter to leave the lamp lit all night so that she might read her Bible, but this was wisely refused her. In the morning when she awoke she said that the night had been the sweetest night of communion with Christ she ever had on earth, and that Satan 'had no more' in her. After calling her favourite grandchild to her bedside, she kissed him and passed peacefully away to be forever with the Lord. The Free Presbyterian Church has lost a true friend who often wrestled at the throne of grace for its prosperity, and we have reason to tremble when

we think of the many breaches that are made on the walls of Sion and to
pray that the Lord would yet build up the walls of Jerusalem.

On Lewis and Harris, a church building is not the house of God. It is a
place for public worship and, specifically, a place for preaching. In the
common idiom of Lewis, one does not go 'to church'. One goes, or has
been 'to sermon'. And all the Presbyterian churches are remarkably similar
internally. Pews are grouped facing and around a central pulpit, with a
lower lectern or 'desk' before it for the man leading the praise (or, at least
till very recent years, a man leading public worship who was not a
minister).

In the enclosure built around this area, the latron, *suidheachan mor* or
'high seat', the elders sit during public worship and are thus immediately
identifiable. The custom is, besides, a helpful reminder that they, as a kirk
session, have true authority over the congregation; an element, as J.A.
Fraser MacDonald suggests, of greater oversight – '. . . that elders need to
defend the pulpit from false teaching and heresy and must, symbolically at
least, be ready to intervene'.[2]

The praise at Presbyterian worship – outside some congregations of the
Church of Scotland which have now yielded to the organ – is led by a
'precentor', from the Latin *prae cantore* – literally, 'to sing before'. In the
larger denominations the precentor is invariably a male member in full
communion, who will sit in the desk beneath the pulpit; it has been
general Long Island custom that he remain seated in it, facing the
congregation, during the entire sermon, though many precentors now
voluntarily retire to a less exposed location. Precenting myself at one
island Communion in 2005, I grew aware of an odd, fine moistness
landing on my head. I glanced at my suit: it, too, was gently anointed with
fine flecks of froth. Half-amused and half-nauseated, I realised that the
pulpit star above our heads was happily sprinkling us with his own spit.

Visitors, too, long noticed disconcerting reminders that islanders did
not really regard their churches as sacred precincts. For one, it was
acceptable well into living memory for men – and, indeed, office-bearers –
to take snuff during sermon. Worse, Big MacRae was not alone in
chewing tobacco. The practice endured generally among elders until after
the First World War. My grandfather never forgot the disgusting chore
with which he had to help his father[3] – church officer at Cross – on a
typical Monday, washing coconut-matting thick with horror. And, of
course, worshippers still suck sweets. Indeed, it was once so associated
with Highland religion that a certain brand of pan-drops is still cheerfully
described, by older Scots newsagents, as 'big Free Kirkers' – suited, of
course, to very long sermons. The inordinately protracted crackle of

cellophane – especially at the start of sermon – has long exasperated ministers.

There is one other bizarre evidence of casual island affection for church buildings – graffiti. Island churches are still immune from vandalism (with some notable lapses in 1900) but there is a venerable tradition of scrawling initials, dates and even little pictures on the church pew, a diversion all the more readily accomplished in the days before electric lighting. The pews of Shawbost Free Church are replete with such memorials from the 1920s and beyond, though the odds of ever identifying an 'M M 1934' or a 'J McL' are passingly remote. I had not long occupied my present pew in Stornoway when I noticed the immaculate sketch of an Imperial German officer, over the neatly printed, 'BOSCH 1918'. But who drew it we cannot now know, and it is unlikely he survives.

MacDonald's take on this is interesting. 'These graffiti are not very controversial. They do not "adorn in order to desecrate" . . . rather they are a powerful reminder that the space of worship belongs to the congregation, purchased by their tithes and, in some cases, actually built with their labour. Graffiti must be interpreted as proprietorial statements: *this is our space.* Accordingly, these are very Presbyterian transgressions, breaches of etiquette which affirm the ultimate authority of pew over pulpit.'[4]

But even the Disruption parishes were big places and, as well as one central place of worship, local preaching-stations were established and village meeting-houses – miniature churches, complete in time with pulpit, desk and pews – were built. (Pews were always fitted, even to the smallest, lest the premises ever be used for dancing.) At Ness, for instance, these little buildings were erected at Lionel in the north and Galson to the south. Barvas Free Church soon had its own: Borve, Shader, Arnol and Bragar. In time the United Free Church would duplicate them and, where the Free Presbyterians were finally in strength – Harris and Uig – they, too, built district churches. They were typically used for a midweek prayer meeting and for some sort of Sabbath evening service, and the settled minister was expected to tour these stations in turn.

Until after the Second World War, when charges were extensive and hardly anyone had private motor-transport, the need for such satellites was evident. By the 1980s, when everyone had cars, they were an embarrassment. Only in the last decade – when new legislation imposed costly disabled-access requirements on all places of public worship – has it become politic to shut village stations. Only a few actually belonging to a village (and a large, self-important village at that), rather than the denomination, have endured. It is doubtful if there was ever a case for separate evening services at Bragar, a half-hour's brisk walk from the Free Church at Shawbost; now that the buildings are barely two minutes apart by car, there is none.

There is a very interesting difference in Long Island Gaelic. In Lewis, a little village church is known as a *taigh-coinneamh* – a meeting-house; but, in Harris, it is called a *taigh-leughaidh*, or reading house, a surviving folk-memory of the long-closed Gaelic schools. Not that any dedicated place of worship was necessary for a service. Ministers often preached in schools, and have resorted to that even in recent schism. There was also the occasional 'cottage meeting', where a public service was held in someone's home, especially if a communicant was confined therein by infirmity. There are still very occasional such meetings – I attended a Free Presbyterian cottage-service, at Leacali in Harris, in June 2002 – but they have sadly gone out of fashion.

Communion seasons apart, open-air preaching was often necessitated by division and the loss of buildings. But one can readily imagine the physical toll a minister's labour generally – including much travel, often over untracked moor – took on him. Clergymen had to be tough to survive, tramping many miles and often soaked to the skin. Even in the twentieth century, it is sobering how many ministers buckled. The first post-1900 Free Church minister at Carloway, for instance, Angus MacLeod – nearly sixty and who had put in many years as a missionary in Harris and South Lochs – was inducted in June 1913, and died only ten weeks later. Malcolm MacLeod, of Kinloch, collapsed in 1908 in his own pulpit, and lived but two hours more. A Scalpay minister, Murdo MacPhail, died in the vestry in 1964. Roderick J. MacLeod, who had seen such awakening in Ness, died in 1929 in his new charge in Dumbarton, still only thirty-seven years old.

Evangelical preaching was no light matter. For one thing, sermons were not brief – islanders would still feel short-changed if someone preached for much less than forty minutes. For another, reading a sermon is unthinkable; a discourse had to be delivered with but the support of minimal notes. Some men wrote out their sermons in full, and then destroyed them before delivery. Finlay Cook, as we noted, sketched an outline on a slate. A story is still retailed of Dr John MacDonald: once, falling asleep amidst his usual study, he awoke in the morning not only to find that a magnificent sermon had come in his dreams but that he had even written it out. He promptly burned it, quoting the portion, 'beaten oil for the lamps of the sanctuary', and refusing to offer to the Lord 'that which had cost me nothing'.

Many ministers find the composition of sermons best accomplished by meditation on a text, with a certain subconscious aid all the more forthcoming if one were somehow diverted by physical activity. Kenneth MacRae used to roam the woods near his manse. Duncan MacLean, Tolsta Free Presbyterian minister, used to love driving to Harris, maintaining he always had a good sermon by his return. Malcolm Gillies once gave a remarkable discourse on a verse from Joshua, 'And the manna ceased.' An elder observed that he must have spent many hours in the study on so notable a sermon. Gillies explained cheerfully it had come to him on the evening before – when he had been resoling the shoes of his lively young sons.[5]

And few who have never done it appreciate the sheer physical labour of preaching, all the harder before pulpit microphones, when a minister had forcefully to project his voice. Indeed, the Highland pulpit developed a most effective stratagem of its own – the *seis*, or distinctive sing-song chant. 'The great advantage of the *seis* in the old days was that by its judicious use a hard, strong voice could be rendered pleasing and often very affecting,'[6] wrote Murdoch Campbell. 'A musical ear was necessary for its use. In the large open-air gatherings of other days this pleasant enunciation of the Gospel message was never considered an affectation, but as something irresistible and spontaneous, and which also added dignity and unction to the preacher's theme.' Recent masters of this rhetorical device included Murdo MacAulay and Duncan MacLean, but it has largely lapsed.

Highland ministers became coiled springs of energy, bouncing on their toes, roaming the pulpit, pounding the lectern, emphasising points with sweeping gestures. Angus Finlayson, born in Marivig, South Lochs, in 1897, pastored Bracadale and Scalpay before, after the Second World War, becoming the first and hugely respected Free Church minister of North Tolsta, and my father's 1975 sketch of his late colleague's gifts is as good a description as any of the best of the Long Island pulpit.

Mr Finlayson's preaching may be described as typically Highland. It was in the tradition of John MacDonald, John Kennedy, John MacRae and the Cook brothers. In his early years, the delivery was vehement and it was not unknown for such furnishings as the pulpit-lamps to be sent tumbling by the sweep of his hand. He used to tell with obvious relish the story of one church where the beadle from past experience had deemed it wise to remove them! Latterly, the delivery, though forthright and manly, was calm and dignified.

The message itself, like the best Highland preaching, was marked by three great emphases. First, he was a preacher of the Law, proclaiming the exalted nature of its demands and the inviolability of its sanctions. The unbeliever was left in no doubt as to the certainty and the imminence of retribution, while the Christian had to endure the searching criticism of the Law as applied to his own daily life. Secondly, there was a strong Christological emphasis. He proclaimed as the things of first importance that Christ was Lord, that He had died for our sins and that He had risen again according to the Scriptures. The glory of the person of Christ and even more the deep mysteries of priesthood and atonement were the joy of his heart and the focal point of his testimony. But then, thirdly, Mr Finlayson's preaching was experimental. This does not mean that he preached his own experience, although he undoubtedly preached from it. But he recognised that the Lord's people had experiences and that the pulpit must take cognisance of them. This was especially true in two areas – the problem of assurance (or the lack of it) and the sufferings of the present time . . .[7]

Other masters of the pulpit were less consistent. Peter Chisholm, that character from Gravir, had various adventures before winning ordination as a Free Church minister. On Skye, in 1924, Kenneth MacRae was enthralled by Chisholm's preaching. 'I was amazed at such a sermon. I never heard such originality, such flashes of doctrine, such depth of experience, and such power. A number in the congregation were overcome, and he was overcome himself. I had to struggle my hardest to keep from betraying my feelings also.' A decade later, hearing Chisholm at Knock, MacRae was appalled – 'pretty much as he was in Kinloch, full of denunciations, stripping poor struggling souls of every comfort, banging and kicking the pulpit in a ridiculous fashion, and continuing inordinately long. Felt that it was a waste of time to go down to Point to hear such a diatribe.'[8]

And, on occasion, the dramatic oratory could have hilarious consequences. Angus Cattanach,[9] gifted Free Presbyterian minister of South Harris, was once inadvertently assaulted in the Stornoway pulpit. His Tolsta colleague, Duncan MacLean, was preaching with gesticulating energy. All went well until MacLean's arm windmilled to emphasise a point, and a cufflink snagged in Cattanach's elaborate pinned, gripped, secured, combed-over hair. The Harris minister yelped and jumped, MacLean was momentarily thrown off balance, and for a minute or two many worshippers could only choke agonising giggles behind their pews.

At this stage it is worth mentioning the clerical collar. It is in fact remarkably difficult to prove that ministers ever wore distinctive clothing in the Reformed Kirk, though a 1575 Act of Assembly does require that ministers 'be clothed gravely and soberly, not in light apparel in regard of colour, their wives and children to be subject to the same order.' By the eighteenth century there is no doubt Scottish ministers generally wore a white stock or cravat, but this marked two things – a University degree, and the status of a gentleman. In fact, the traditional dress of a Scottish minister is very similar to the traditional dress of an advocate in court. A minister was distinguished as much by context as by white cloth girt about his throat; by the nineteenth century, clergymen – Anglican, Non-Conformist and Presbyterian – invariably wore a white bow-tie, as readily ascertained from Victorian photographs.

The truly distinctive clerical collar – the 'dog-collar' or, more pejoratively, the Roman collar – is actually a Presbyterian invention; a Rev. Donald MacLeod of Glasgow, elected as Moderator of the Established Church in 1894, devised it in the 1860s. 'Personally I have only one claim to immortality,' he told his Presbytery that year, 'and I am afraid it rests on a fact known only to myself and that is: I was the first to introduce what is now known as the dog-collar in my youth thirty-nine years ago. I did it. It is now recognised as the ecclesiastical collar. I hope that my claim to immortality on that account will be taken notice of by the historians.'[10] The Roman collar was not, though, quickly adopted in the Highland church; the 'white front' survived until the 1980s in the Free Church and is still widely sported in the Free Presbyterians.[11] Their ministers besides still usually wear a frock-coat for sermon, rarely sighted elsewhere these days.

There are good arguments for the clerical collar. It makes the church visible, in an age of rampant secularism, and can invite engagement with strangers. It certainly facilitates hospital and prison visiting. Unlike a business-suit and tie, clerical dress is classless; it serves to depersonalise – emphasising the message rather than the man – and, on the street, it is a badge of a public service, as the uniforms of policemen and so on are the mark of theirs. There are also vexing stories of misunderstandings that could readily have been avoided had a minister been identifiable as such.

No doubt sacerdotal attitudes prevailed here and there. My father has a diverting tale of what befell the late Kenneth MacLeay – for many years Free Church minister at Beauly – when left alone to preside over a Communion service in Drumchapel.

Mr MacLeay duly arrived, and then grew anxious.

'Is there no other minister here?'

'No.'

'So who will serve me at the Table?'

'Och, we will serve you at the Table.'

'That is not proper at all. Another minister should give me the elements.'

'Eh?'

At this point the wee church-officer came scurrying into the vestry.

'Ah jist came to tell youse some minister is here, wearin' his collar.'

Mr MacLeay was delighted. 'Away with you then, and see who it is.'

Shortly, the wee church officer trotted back.

'It's yon Reverend James Morrison, frae North Uist.'

Mr MacLeay was thoroughly delighted – they were the best of pals.

'Well, that is just wonderful provision. Go you and explain things to him; tell Mr Morrison that he is to serve me at the Table, and to come to the vestry.'

The wee church officer hurried away.

He was soon back, manifestly crestfallen.

'He'll nae dae it. He's nae frock-coat.'

Gaelic psalmody cannot be ignored in any discussion of Long Island religion, the last corner of Scotland where Gaelic services are still regularly held. In fact – like the Communion system – it was long established on Lewis and Harris before the dawn of Evangelicalism; and it bewilders the stranger. For one, the precentor 'gives out the line'; the first two lines of a psalm are sung in unison, having first been read aloud by the minister; but thereafter the precentor chants a line – there are distinctive chants for each line and indeed each melody – and the congregation then sing it back to him. For another, many think it sounds weird. 'Among those accustomed to orthodox Western music,' concedes Cedric Thorpe Davie, 'the first reaction is usually shock and distaste . . . failure to understand the musical structure and the nasal (and harsh) tone quality.'[12]

Recent years have seen mounting international interest in Gaelic psalm-singing and so emotive are its tones in the ears of anyone born within the island culture that many bereaved families find the first notes of Gaelic praise almost unbearable. Yet, save the language itself, there is nothing distinctively Highland at all about it. The custom of 'giving out the line' was prevalent in the Lowland church, and in English praise, until very late in the eighteenth century, and clung on stubbornly in some quarters for many years. Indeed, as Norman Campbell ascertained in his fascinating study of the question,[13] one Edinburgh congregation – an Original Secession fragment who latterly worshipped on South Clerk Street – only abandoned the practice in 1912. And the custom had come from England to Scotland, and thence from the early Reformed or Huguenot church in France, as Donald Beaton details in an important 1939 essay on Gaelic psalmody. It endured as long as it did because psalm-books were scarce and so many could not read. It was 1746 before the Kirk's General Assembly timidly suggested that, at least in family worship, those 'singing the praises of God go on without the intermission of reading the line.' The issue became a battleground in the Secession churches and even the Scottish regiments, when a chaplain in the Scots Brigade at Holland forbade 'lining out' and a colonel tried to overrule him. And in Gaelic psalmody, established with the translation of the Psalter by 1694, it was essential from the start.

There was, though, a central musical problem: 'common metre' dictates a regular patterning of stresses of a sort quite unknown in traditional Gaelic song. Accordingly, with one beautiful exception, all the melodies adopted in Gaelic psalmody are Lowland, English and even Genevan. In the northern Highlands, such distinctive versions or 'Long Tunes' were devised as to become to all intents and purposes different melodies, and some quaint theories were touted as to their origin – that they were relics of the Columban Church; or had been brought over the North Sea by Highlanders who had fought for Gustavus Adolphus – but they were already in decline by the Disruption.

The tunes sung in the Gaelic psalmody of Lewis and Harris, then, are heavily ornamented versions of airs popular generally in Scottish psalm-singing, whose very names often betray an alien genesis – Kilmarnock, Coleshill, Dundee, Torwood, London New, Moravia, Bangor, Montrose and so on. But they are sung rather differently. The ornamentation and distinctive lines of precenting vary from region to region – the precenting of Sutherland, for instance, was very different from that of Wester Ross, and that again from Skye. A Lewis congregation sings the third line of Walsall quite differently from people in Harris; both, though, sing the last line of London New to very different notes from those favoured in North Uist. But I mentioned one native exception to these imports – the air Stornoway, composed by John Matheson, born at Bragar around 1810. His granddaughter was married to Rev. Kenneth MacRae.

Gaelic psalm-singing is heavily ornamented; analysis by the School of Scottish Studies found that some use fourteen different notes in singing a single syllable. There is accordingly great scope for self-expression and, in a huge congregation, this grants the cascading, spine-tingling effect of the greatest Gaelic psalmody. And there is a vocal and emotional depth that seems quite impossible to match in English. I have over the years seen many an old island lady, her eyes shut and her head thrown back, utterly lost in the psalm, her voice soaring in the sort of fervour we otherwise associate with Charismatic worship.

The skill required of a Gaelic precentor, in memorising tunes and the distinctive chants beside for 'lining out', is evident, to say nothing of another difficulty – he has very little decent opportunity to draw breath or to swallow. The best counsel I was ever given in my own determined endeavours was to leave the last syllable of each line to the congregation as you quickly gathered breath to elide into the chanting-forth of the next one; but while one can with application become an adequate leader of Gaelic praise, only a few become good. Few recordings pre-date the 1960s, but the precenting of Alasdair Graham and especially Angus MacLeod – who lived just long enough to be filmed in his element by Scottish Television – was outstanding. It is unfortunate that politic considerations in some modern recordings of Gaelic psalmody have seen rather too many ministers lay down a track; only Neil Shaw, latterly of Callanish Free Church, has been truly in the top rank – but, by the sober assessment of most, the greatest precentor ever taped was one John MacLeod, known affectionately as 'The Professor', who for many years led the praise at Gaelic services in the High Church congregation of the Church of Scotland in Stornoway.

The practice of giving out the line in English still survives in one quarter – the Free Presbyterian Church. In 1939, Donald Beaton notes it was then still heard 'in some congregations in Caithness and Sutherland to this day, especially in those connected with the Free Presbyterian Church.' And the Free Presbyterians still 'line out' in English at the Communion table in most of their Highland congregations. In the Western Isles, besides, it is still occasionally heard at Free Presbyterian funerals.

Yet the standard of psalm-singing generally in Lewis and Harris has in recent years rather deteriorated. This is all the sadder because, even in Victorian times, there was sustained effort to improve praise and the Long Island saw systematically organised psalmody classes, an especially welcome diversion in the winter months. Presbyteries and Synods encouraged these in a sustained, proactive strategy and there are many references to such classes, in Ness for instance, in early numbers of the *Free Presbyterian Magazine*. My great-grandfather's sister, born in Shawbost around 1853, once in the 1870s walked all the way home from her married sister's house at Crulivig in Uig, especially to make the village psalmody class – she had heard they were to learn a new tune. Photographs are on display at the Garenin visitors' centre of the hugely popular psalmody classes in that village before the Second World War – dozens of young people beaming from the sepia frames. A 93-year-old cousin remembers Rev. John Morrison, newly inducted minister of Uig Free Church in 1929, conducting lessons with a sol-fa 'modulator' hung on the wall, teaching them tune by tune as he tapped each note out with a pointer.[14] Even thirty years ago the people of South Bragar, for instance, were celebrated for the beauty of their praise; so much so that, during the prayer meeting, people would pause on the road to listen to it.

We might in conclusion knock most firmly on the head an idea of late eagerly touted, following speculation by a Yale professor, William Ruff, 'that American Gospel music was influenced by Gaelic psalmody, via slaves owned by Scottish Highland settlers in North Carolina.' There is in fact no proof whatever. The distinct refrains of 'gospel', while superficially similar to 'giving out the line', are almost certainly indigenous and likewise arose as a stratagem for coping with illiteracy. And island enthusiasm for the theory is less than sensitive to abiding African-American bitterness. They naturally resent any suggestion of 'benefit' from slavery, understandably loathe the insinuation that they themselves could not of their own resources beget a rich new musical *oeuvre*, and are only too aware of how, already, the extreme and segregationist forces of white supremacy have pillaged assorted props, such as the 'Fiery Cross', from Scottish Highland culture.

Now we see besides – surely the mark of a culture in serious trouble – the rise of Gaelic psalmody as a self-conscious performance art, a trend that became evident after William Ruff's speculation. A squad of 'Lewis Psalm Singers', resplendent in tartan, has now visited the Deep South of America, performed at a Celtic music festival in Ireland, sung in Paris and – most notably – took the stage in October 2004 at the official opening, by the Queen, of the new Scottish Parliament building in Edinburgh, which at least lent the occasion its only notes of either Gaelic or Christianity. Surely believers should worry when the praises of Zion are reduced to a concert turn?

The traditional Communion season, too, was already established in the days of the Lewis and Harris Moderates. People furth of Scotland, especially Anglicans, have often criticised the church for the infrequency of the Lord's Supper within the Scottish tradition – historically observed only once in a calendar year. But Reformed worship in Scotland is centred not on the Communion table, but the pulpit. For another, in the order of Presbyterian community, the Lord's Supper is observed on successive weekends at different churches within Presbytery bounds, and one can quite easily take Communion within, for instance, the Lewis Free Church a dozen times a year; especially as adjacent congregations normally close on the Sabbath of the neighbouring Communion to permit attendance.

But John Knox and John Calvin advocated frequent celebration of the Sacrament and, as my father noted in 1991, 'Infrequent Communion was forced on the Church by circumstances. There simply weren't enough ministers.' Nevertheless the old Scottish Communion season, in all its pomp, was established by the early seventeenth century and survives in its essential elements on Lewis and Harris and throughout the Free Presbyterian Church. These protracted, warm occasions are in direct descent from the Reformation. When Robert Bruce was banished to Inverness, folk flocked from as far as Sutherland to hear him officiate at the Lord's Supper. And the Communion seasons described in Thomas Boston's *Memoirs* of his Borders ministry in the early eighteenth century are almost identical to those still enjoyed today on Lewis and Harris.

A traditional Communion season lasts five days inclusive, from Thursday to Monday, and each day has its different emphasis. Thursday was the 'Fast Day', *Latha na Traisg*, with the focus on human sinfulness and the desperate need for grace. Friday, *Latha na Ceist* – 'the day of the question', was one of self-examination. Saturday, *Latha an Ullachaidh*, is a 'day of preparation' and, by old Scottish custom, still prevalent on Lewis and Harris at least – though not now universal – special tokens are given out to intending communicants after the main preaching service.[15]

The Sacrament itself is dispensed on Sabbath morning, *Latha Sabaid nan Orduighean* – a complex service. The 'Action Sermon' – the origin of this term is obscure but is probably rooted in the Vulgate translation of 1 Corinthians 11:24, *gratis actis*; an ablative absolute of *gratiarium actio*, or 'thanksgiving' – in the original Greek, *eucharistesas*. The 'Action Sermon' is the sermon of Eucharist: preaching that perpetuates remembrance, remembrance that evokes thanksgiving, for the saving work of Christ on the Cross. It is followed – the traditional intimation is, 'We will now proceed to the more solemn part of this service' – by the exercise of 'fencing the tables', when the minister gives forth signs or 'marks' of outward lifestyle, specifying who should sit at the Lord's Table and who are barred. The word 'fencing' is now generally taken to imply some sort of barrier around the Communion Table, a notion unfortunately encouraged these days by some ill-informed preaching, but to 'fence' is an old Scots legal term, meaning simply to constitute a court. The address is always begun by the reading of Pauline verses from 1 Corinthians 11, and concluded by the reading of more verses – on the 'fruits of the spirit', from Paul's Epistle to the Galatians, and the Beatitudes, from the fifth chapter of Matthew's Gospel.

It was – and, in the Free Presbyterians, still is – a doughty address. 'I debar in the Lord's name . . . All such are completely debarred . . .' and so on: infidels, atheists, idolaters, people who live in open sin, heads of households who do not conduct family worship in the home, those 'at ease in Sion', resting on 'vain denominationalism', and so on. They are 'invited to come' who see beauty in Christ; who can see no good in themselves; who hunger and thirst after righteousness; who would give the world to be free of sin; etc., etc. In other denominations on the island, where communicants now sit at the Table from the start of the service, the Fencing has grown ever more perfunctory.

Verses of a suitable psalm – usually Psalm 116, 118 or occasionally Psalm 40, to a tune traditional in the locality – are then given out and sung, while the elders bring in 'the elements' in what my father once unkindly described as a 'quasi-Episcopal procession'. Once these are on the Table – port is the usual choice of wine, though many Church of Scotland congregations have adopted a syrupy non-alcoholic substitute; the bread is a normal, yeasted loaf – the minister then gives out further verses to be sung and invites communicants to take their seats at the Table of the Lord.

Again, by venerable Scottish tradition, only at this point do Free Presbyterian communicants leave the body of the congregation to sit at the Table – and, in most old Scottish churches, it really was a table (the Reformers were quite emphatic on this point), often running down the central aisle. A fine example still survives in the parish church at Howmore, South Uist. Real tables, too, were deployed when Communion had to be administered in the open air. These days, now that outdoor Communion is a thing of the past, the front pews of the church serve as tables, being marked off by drapes of white cloth. Once the communicants have come forward the presiding minister then says grace. (For this all remain seated; a striking feature, as long Scottish custom was – and in the conservative denominations, on the Long Island, remains – to stand for public prayer and sit during praise, another novelty to the visitor.) In the Free Church, tokens are usually collected as one proceeds to the Table; in the Free Presbyterian order, they are collected after believers have sat down and as the first 'Table Address' is given.

The minister then gives a brief, special and most tender talk to the communicants, and proceeds to follow Christ's example, repeating appropriate verses of the Gospel as he takes and breaks some bread (the rite of 'fraction') and hands it to the first communicant, and then in like manner takes the chalice. He does not touch or in any sense 'bless' the vessels in front of him; and lifting them ostentatiously would be deplored in Lewis, though one wishes more care were taken to ensure the minister's actions are clearly visible. The elements are then served by the elders. Some feel it is more Scriptural if the communicants themselves pass the elements to one another; some wonder if, by specific New Testament injunction, it should be the deacons who serve the Table, and not the elders; and – *pace* Kenneth MacLeay – only the Free Presbyterians still maintain what is undoubtedly Scriptural, that the ministers sit at the same Table as everyone else, rather than being served on high, within the latron, as some sort of priestly caste. There has also been absurd fuss on the Long Island as to the form of the bread. Traditionally, it was served in great thick slices, but since the Second World War the practice of reducing it practically to crumbs has become widespread and in at least one congregation the duty (or privilege) of chopping it up late on the Saturday appears to be hereditary.

But it can be already seen that the traditional Presbyterian Communion service was ordered, stately and reverent. The minutes as the believers actually chew bread and swallow wine are, in fact, the only point anywhere in Presbyterian worship where absolute silence is preserved, and are most solemn.

For, when all have partaken, a second Table address must be given – usually centred on renewed Christian service from the refreshed believers – and they then leave the Table, returning to their pews, as verses of praise – usually from Psalm 103 – are sung. In some congregations the local minister may deliver still another address, this time to non-communicants – Christians who have not 'done their duty', the unconverted and, of course, children. The service is at last concluded with prayer, praise and the benediction.

It can already be grasped that, even when only one Communion Table is served – we have already noted a Victorian occasion in Lewis when there were six – the Sabbath morning service is long. Ronald Blakey mentions an 1841 Communion, at Grandtully in Perthshire, that lasted five hours, and alludes to other Lowland services, earlier in that same century, when 'beginning at 11, they should drag their slow length along until 6 or 7 in the evening.'

It will be evident, besides, that the duties of a Communion season were quite beyond the energies, physical or otherwise, of the local minister. Two ministers usually 'assist' at a Free Presbyterian Communion – a diverting word, as they do all the preaching – and a third usually helps on the Thursday of a Free Church weekend.

The Sabbath evening service of a Communion is addressed particularly to the unconverted and – traditionally – often with a text related to the Second Coming, anticipated by Jesus' own words 'on the night in which he was betrayed.' Monday, the 'day of thanksgiving' – *Latha Taingealachd*; in Ness, *Diluain nan Orduighean* – sees the closing services. There are, besides, all weekend, morning prayer meetings, many sessions of informal fellowship in people's homes, and untold and generous hospitality. This, too, reflects centuries of Scottish tradition – 'It was a credible crood,' an old Rosneath minister is quoted in Blakey's book, *The Man in the Manse*, 'there was fourteen stane o' saumon eaten in the village,' but fare in the tight subsistence economy of nineteenth-century Lewis must have been spartan. In our age, of course, the food is prodigious, even on a Communion Thursday, which Francis MacBean, at least, did keep rather literally, according to Principal John MacLeod:

It used to be the case that on Fast Days Mr MacBean was wont to fast, and he would see to it that his household fasted too. Once his friend George MacLeod was to drive from Lochbroom to Fort Augustus Communion, and he said to his lad, George, 'Now, George, see that you put a piece in your pocket, for when you get to Fort Augustus you will not get a bite to eat on the Fast Day.' This was the case at least until the day services were over. He used to fast at other times too. He was known on a Communion Saturday when he rose from the dinner table in manses where he assisted to ask for some oatmeal and a little sugar in a saucer. With this he retired to his room, and no one saw him again until he appeared in the pulpit the following day to conduct services that would last for about six hours. Quite a number of the men of his generation who shared his intense spirit were careful like him to observe a Fast Day with great strictness. His old comrade, Alexander MacIntyre of Sunart, was one of them. He trained his Australian followers to walk in his own steps in this matter, and among the old-fashioned Free Churchmen on the rivers to the north of Sydney it is still the practice to abstain wholly from meat when the Fast Day comes . . .[16]

Francis MacBean has one more notable place in the religious history of Lewis and Harris, for – in alliance with John MacRae – he held the first Fellowship Meeting in connection with a Long Island Communion season,[17] at Stornoway, though John MacLeod could not ascertain the exact year – it was in either 1825 or 1826, when MacBean was the Inspector of Schools salaried by the ESSGS and MacRae was parish teacher in Uig, under Alexander MacLeod. The Fellowship or Question Meeting became quickly the noon exercise of a Communion Friday – in Lewis, it is still called *Latha na Ceist*, the 'day of the question' – and has survived in Lewis and Harris to this day and in the Free Presbyterian Church generally throughout her bounds.

The form of the Fellowship Meeting has been established for centuries: a professing man present proposes a verse of Scripture, and men then take it in turns to 'speak to the question', in terms of spiritual experience and with illustration from their own. Its precise origins are still a matter of debate, but it almost certainly began with Thomas Hog of Kiltearn. He 'arranged a regular meeting to which he invited enquirers in his parish. He himself presided and the discussion usually centred on some aspect of evangelical religion. When Hog was banished for his anti-episcopal views after the Restoration, in 1666, the supervision of this meeting fell into the hands of the elders: notably, in the case of Kiltearn, into the hands of John Munro ("the Caird"), usually regarded as the first of "the Men".'[18]

Similar fellowships grew up elsewhere, and Alexander MacLeod introduced one two years after his presentation to Uig; he called it a 'private meeting', and this is the probable origin of the *coinneamh uaigneach* or 'secret meeting' which later became a part of Lewis con-gregational life. The secret meeting – so covert that only communicant members are admitted – still survives in the Free Church at Back and in both congregations, Free and Free Presbyterian, in North Tolsta, and was maintained in some other districts till quite recently. It has long ceased, though, to be a fellowship meeting, being conducted generally as a prayer meeting with the *omerta* of its terms permitting firm – if strictly private – resolution both of congregational and local disputes between professing Christians. One reason why most of them have been abandoned is a sad reflection of spiritual decline; its confidence, not least after the advent of the telephone, was increasingly broken.

The 'Fellowship Meeting' as first conceived by Alexander MacLeod had plain parallels elsewhere – in Wales, and in early Methodism. But in the eastern Highlands, it had taken a very distinct character, and for obvious reasons – the removal of Covenanting ministers, and then the blight of Moderatism. As a result, vibrant lay leadership took charge. 'Soon,' my father notes, 'there emerged an order known as "the Men," not, as one wit put it, because they weren't women, but because they weren't ministers.' It began in Easter Ross and soon spread through the north, throwing up in time the full-blown Separatists, men whose lively religion (to say nothing of their militancy) flourished best in the polemical context of Moderate ministry. They were never at ease with Evangelical clergy and the Free Church.

Well before those famous stalwarts, however, 'the Men' of Sutherland had begun to hold meetings on the Friday of the Communion season. Precisely when we do not know, but it had evidently been well launched by 1737, because in that year – according to John MacInnes – the Synod of Caithness and Sutherland tried to suppress them. The format was essentially as it is now: a verse given out and the brethren present invited in turn (and usually by seniority) to speak on it, 'particularly,' as my father observes, 'insofar as it suggests the marks of a true Christian and offers comfort to those of weak faith'.

Unable to eliminate it, ministers reluctantly incorporated the *Ceist* into the Communion exercises, the only alteration being that one minister 'opened the Question', speaking as best he might on a verse given out there and then from anywhere in Scripture between Genesis and Revela-tion, and that another duly 'closed the Question', correcting – and not always diplomatically – anything said by the assorted laymen (and, at the biggest Communion gatherings, there could be dozens) who had successively been called on to speak. The minister – usually the junior one – who opens the exercise has the right to refuse the portion offered, but it is generally considered bad form to dare.

One minister who badly wanted to dare was another Rev. Donald MacDonald, ordained and inducted to Carloway Free Church in July 1964. The portion should really be a verse relating directly to conversion, redemption, change or the 'marks' of these. But once, when he had to open the Question at a Communion and the man who duly rose gave out Isaiah 7:11 – 'Ask thee a sign of the Lord thy God; ask it either in the depth, or in the height above. But Ahaz said, I will not ask, neither will I tempt the Lord . . .' In the context of the Friday exercises, it seems both irrelevant and incomprehensible, but MacDonald took it, and did his best. 'I could hardly turn it down,' he sensibly observes. 'Wasn't the man's son a minister and in the pulpit beside me?'[19]

The Fellowship Meeting was – and in some measure remains – pregnant with tension. On the Highland mainland, there were plain abuses – men taking advantage of their opportunity for digs at each other or, more likely, at the ministers. Stories of such unseemly (if often very funny) episodes in the Highland counties abound. Remarkably, there is very little anecdotal evidence of this sort of thing on Lewis or Harris, partly because Evangelicalism arrived here so late. It also reflects island character; the Fellowship Meeting in the Outer Hebrides is notable both for its general courtesy and occasional touches of humour.

There can still be incident; at a Fellowship Meeting in one Lewis district, in the 1990s, one individual spoke so ill advisedly that his pastor finally stood and shut him up. The man meekly obeyed. Big MacRae, too, is remembered for once sharply announcing, 'That will do; you may sit down.' But he thought so highly of one eminent island believer, Donald Morrison, of Fivepenny in Ness – converted, as a boy of fifteen, under the preaching of Finlay Munro – that MacRae, later his pastor, would in time pay him a unique compliment, rising from his seat in the pulpit to stand as long as Donald Morrison took his turn to speak at the Fellowship Meeting.[20]

This Donald Morrison may have been an important influence in securing the *Ceist* against the sort of loveless little games that brought it into disrepute elsewhere. In Sutherland, for instance, older men had the deplorable habit of criticising – sometimes savagely – the efforts of men who had spoken before them. One, Donald Duff – who, in all fairness, was an eminent and humble Christian – was so apt to 'review the experimental quality and doctrinal soundness' of earlier speakers, according to Murdoch Campbell, that Big MacRae once deliberately put him up first, as soon as the Question had been opened. Momentarily thrown, the old war-horse asked to have the rest up first, which MacRae firmly refused. Accordingly, Duff duly spoke 'with calm power and sweetness, and no personalities were introduced.' Afterwards, someone unwisely suggested to MacRae that he should have given the veteran more time to gather his thoughts. 'It was good for you I did not call him first,' boomed *MacRath Mor*, 'and that he did not speak after you. It was a mercy also that I escaped out of his hands!'

But there were efforts to introduce similar jibes into the Lewis Question Meeting. At one, this Donald Morrison was called on immediately after a grim old fellow had thoroughly attacked the stumbling efforts of a young convert. Morrison was furious, but delivered himself sagely. 'When I was coming to Stornoway the other day, I heard the bleating of a little lamb, which was unable to find its mother. It ran from sheep to sheep, only to be boxed away. At last seeing one it thought was its own mother, it rushed expectantly under it. Unfortunately, this was a wedder, which had no milk for it, but rather boxed it, knocking the poor lamb into the ditch.' A typically coded, rather involved metaphor of the sort aired on those occasions, the rebuke nevertheless stung. And the anecdote was revived still more pointedly at a Crossbost Communion shortly before the First World War. On this occasion young Duncan Morrison – later Free Church minister of Duirinish in Skye – had been trounced for his remarks by a member of the Park congregation across Loch Erisort. The Park minister, Rev. Angus MacLeod, did not approve, and in closing the Question he related the story, turned sharply on his own man and declared, 'Although you had no milk for him, why did you box him?'

Ministers bristled – and still bristle – when what are meant to be flowing, unrehearsed remarks take on any appearance of a prepared sermon. But the 'Ceist' is no easy exercise. It is evidently demanding for the junior minister (who is never tipped off, or should not be, as to the portion, which can be given out by any professing man present, even a mere communicant, belonging to the local congregation.) It is demanding on those called on to speak. 'Where else in the world can men be expected to get up and speak coherently to a large congregation on a text announced only a few minutes previously?' asked my father. Many laymen declare they would sooner preach than speak to the Question. It seems especially to be dreaded by men who cannot point to a specific, clear period in their own lives when they were converted. 'This is the day, Neil,' commented Malcolm Gillies of Stornoway as he travelled with his son to officiate at a Fellowship Meeting. 'We have our backs to the wall . . .' There is but one safety-valve; it is quite in order for a man called on to speak to rise, read the portion, and resume his seat without speaking at all.

The minister opening the exercise has but one nuclear option: to refuse the verse and demand another.

The Fellowship Meeting on Lewis and Harris has never been confined to the Communion season. A quarterly Fellowship Meeting, under presbytery auspices, began in the nineteenth century, being hosted by different congregations in turn outwith normal Communion occasions, and still survives, though now held only twice a year – the *Coinneamh-Raithe*, the 'seasonal meeting'. Congregational Fellowship Meetings, too, have been conducted; Callum Matheson was rather given to them in his notable 1980s' ministry at Shawbost, and the present Free Church minister there still occasionally springs one, without prior intimation, upon his men – with the added twist that, for once, he chooses the verse.

But this distinctive Highland ordinance has come under increasing pressure. For one, a changing economy now precludes the attendance of most professing Christian men; it has always, in a Highland context, been a morning exercise, and local ministers resist transferring it to a Friday evening. For another, it became – particularly in Lewis – the habit not to address the verse and give out 'marks', but simply to give a narrative of one's own conversion: but the same story, told over and over again through years and even decades by the same men, can grow very wearying.

Another factor is Gaelic. The Free Presbyterian Church, pragmatic as always, has long conducted a bilingual Question Meeting and in fact it is now most unusual in Lewis and Harris to hear a man speak in Gaelic. In the Free Church, it remains overwhelmingly a Gaelic exercise and as a result is now attended only by the old and the middle-aged, to the point where it may already be beyond recovery.

The *Ceist* has always been resented by some ministers. 'But it is good for the church to hear voices other than those of the clergy,' my father warns, 'and good to hear men give their testimony not only to their conversion but to the way things have gone with them since . . .' A wider problem may be the mounting and increasingly aggressive anti-Highland sentiment in the present Free Church, mounted on a general enthusiasm for change.

Of that very first Fellowship Meeting, on the Friday of a Stornoway Communion in the mid 1820s, some detail has survived. It was evidently a lay exercise, with no ministers present. Francis MacBean presided and the text was a solemn one, 'The hope of the hypocrite shall perish.' MacBean duly opened the verse, speaking – no doubt at length – on the hope of the self-deceived or 'false professor'. The Christian men present were asked expressly to distinguish between that hope of the hypocrite and the hope of the true child of God and, in closing the Question, John MacRae enlarged on the hope of the believer.

And Angus Morrison of Eoropie, who was present and gave these
details to John MacLeod nearly seventy years later, could still remember a
sober observation of MacBean on that occasion. 'When the hypocrite is in
a company and hears something that pleases them, he says to himself, "I'll
put that in my pocket," and when he hears the next thing that pleases
them he will say again, "I will put that, too, in my pocket, and when I
shall myself be called on to take part in a service, I'll take these fine things
out of my pocket, and the people will say, 'Isn't that the godly man?'"'

14

The Household of Faith

Aspects of Evangelical Community

In 1970 a bubbly young woman from America, Susan Parman, arrived in Shawbost to begin 'fourteen months of anthropological fieldwork in a crofting community . . . on the west side of the island of Lewis in the Outer Hebrides.'[1] She had many interesting misadventures as she at first struggled to make sense of community life and villagers, in their turn, wondered whatever to make of her.

Susan Parman could not help herself colouring the social order she did her best to witness and record. 'Probably my greatest coin of exchange, my contribution to village life while I was there, was my unpredictability; I was better than TV. Was I *curamach*? Was I a hippie? I visited with drinkers but didn't drink; I went to church and psalmody class but didn't take communion . . . The tidal waves of gossip that spread out . . . marked my entree into the cognitive fibre of village interpretation.' She was cheerfully told she was now part of the mythology of the village. Yet her charm, and remarkably good grasp of Gaelic, duly won her an abiding place in the hearts of villagers and she still periodically visits Shawbost.

In 1990, she published her thesis as a book, with a revised edition in 2003, giving the village a pseudonym (by anthropological convention) to emphasise that it is a study in people and not a local history. *Scottish Crofters* is not only the best analysis of a West Highland, Gaelic-speaking community ever written, but wonderfully accessible and easy to read. And Shawbost, where the Free Church remains effectively the parish church to this day – her minister, for instance, has regular and untrammelled access to the village school, holding assemblies and conducting RE classes – is as good a field as any to explore the sociology of Evangelicalism.

The church history of Shawbost is . . . involved. For one thing, the village has been long on the cusp of floating parochial boundaries. At the Reformation, Shawbost fell – just – in the parish of Stornoway. After 1722 and the division of Lewis into four parishes, Shawbost was consigned to a pendicle of Lochs, and can have enjoyed no meaningful ministry until the presentation of Robert Finlayson in 1831. Even then, as we saw, he himself admitted he could only preach four times a year in the Carloway side of his charge.

It took the Disruption – and the settlement of Kenneth Ross as the Free Church catechist at Carloway – to secure any regular Gospel ordinances, though Shawbost had a Gaelic school by 1820 and one of the men who demonstrated so spectacularly at the Lochs Communion around 1822 (and ended up in Dingwall prison) was a Shawbost man, *Alasdair Og* – Alexander MacLean. Pressure mounted besides on Free Church authorities when a little Established Church was built at Shawbost in the 1860s, known locally as *An Eaglais Mhodaireat*, or 'the Moderate church'. Its origins are now hard to ascertain – there seems to have been division among Free Church people locally – and never boasted much of a congregation. Yet it was eventually granted a 'missionary' – a resident, salaried lay preacher, John MacLean,[2] born in the village of Brue in 1859 and who took up his post in Shawbost around the turn of the century, retiring about 1930 and dying in 1936. He had perhaps half a dozen families in his cure and about fifteen to thirty of a congregation.

MacLean was an enormously respected man in the village, even though the vast majority clung to the Free Church and a tiny United Free faction maintained services besides from 1900 to 1929. He ran a Sabbath School, which most children in the village attended; a similar Free Church effort did not begin until after the Second World War. At the great Union a Church of Scotland congregation was amicably amalgamated, using the Established building and its adjacent mission-house, and the little group even won a settled ministry: the Reverend Donald Cameron had spent seven years as a missionary on St Kilda after the Great War.

But he was the first and last Church of Scotland minister in Shawbost; its services ceased in the 1960s, and its adherents happily joined the Free Church. In 1969, under the energetic direction of their headmaster, Charles MacLeod, the children of Shawbost School utilised the old church for an award-winning village museum, begging up and down the West Side and building a remarkable collection of crofting artefacts. Its recent 2005 closure, and the hijacking of their display to much less accessible new premises across the road, is deeply to be regretted.

The spiritual history of Shawbost, though, is the history of the Free Church. She would probably have made a sanctioned charge of Shawbost as early as 1860 had the villagers been able to win the co-operation of their neighbours in Bragar; but this has always been a fraught relationship and the matter was agonisingly protracted, though Murdo MacAulay records that villagers petitioned:

on 25th April 1878 for a catechist for Shawbost, and that, meantime, a probationer be appointed for Shawbost. On 24th September, 1879, a petition for a church to be built at Shawbost was favourably recommended to the Presbytery and to the Highland Committee. Shawbost promised £62 13/- plus labour. Fixing the site was delayed until the Bragar people were consulted, but Bragar did not at first wish to join with Shawbost. On April 28th, 1880, the site at Shawbost was approved. . . . On January 12th, 1881, the Presbytery approved a place of worship being built at Bernera, and a new church at Shawbost. On October 18th, 1882, the Presbytery finally approved the building of a church between Shawbost and Bragar.[3]

As the Free Church descended increasingly into an aggressive denominationalism, the Established endeavour in Shawbost must have been a strong stimulus. The new 'MacRae Memorial Church' – though the name has sadly lapsed – opened in 1884, but it attests to the tangled inter-village politics that pastoral oversight was shared between the ministers of Carloway and Barvas – though Shawbost was officially a preaching-station of Carloway. There are varying accounts of the parting of the ways, which can probably be reconciled. One daughter of the village recalls hearing that 'the men' gathered at the shore to discuss their position, one damning the Established Church in a Gaelic phrase she translates delicately as a 'church of filth'[4]. In another version, two men from Shawbost took their turn as usual to tend the Carloway minister's glebe; a hard day of unpaid labour. When the time came momentarily to rest and eat, one went to the manse and asked politely for some boiling water, so they could make brose. Roderick MacRae was then Carloway minister and Mrs MacRae rudely denied the request. The workers promptly downed tools and left, with the murmur, 'It is time we were away from this place.'

And on 27 March 1893 a petition from Shawbost was presented to the Free Presbytery of Lewis, signed by 378 people and requesting disjunction from Carloway. Only seven families had refused to sign. So Shawbost at last became a sanctioned charge, and a charming newspaper report survives of the very first Communion that October.

SHAWBOST COMMUNION – for the first time in the history of Shawbost, the Sacrament of the Lord's Supper was dispensed within the Free Church there, on Sabbath 29th ultimo [29 October 1893]. Talk of a crowd. Why, in church and schoolhouse, the people were literally crammed like herrings into a barrel. So great, indeed, was the crush, that the 'plate' was too often forgotten, in the anxiety to obtain access to the

church or school. Shawbost Free Church was erected in 1883, as a
Mission Church, for the convenience of the people of Shawbost and
Bragar, under the supervision of the Free Church ministers of Carloway
and Barvas. In May last, however, the presbytery resolved the church
into a separate preaching station, the Rev. Mr Martin, Stornoway [Free
English, but a capable Gaelic preacher] consenting to act as moderator.
Mr Martin has been untiring in his efforts to secure 'supply' for his new
charge, and we understand that a licensed clergyman is to officiate
during the winter months. At the recent Communion, Rev. Martin was
ably assisted by the Rev. Messrs Campbell, Uig; MacRae, Carloway;
and Morrison, Barvas. An English Service was held in the Schoolhouse
on Saturday by Mr Campbell, and on Sunday by Mr MacRae. There
being no manse, the officiating clergymen were entertained during the
Communion by Mrs Ross, the Schoolhouse.[5]

On 17 April 1895 the Presbytery approved plans for a manse and on 10
July George L. Campbell was inducted as the first minister. Born at Port
Bannatyne, Bute, in 1833, he was already in his sixties; ordained and
inducted to North Knapdale in 1863, Campbell had served only two years
there before translation as Big MacRae's successor to Lochs. In 1875 he
removed again to the Argyll Church, Glasgow, and from 1884 had been
employed as a roaming preacher by the Highland Committee. He was an
able man, a colleague would later recall, 'but I remember little about him
except his anathemas on unbeliefs, and misbeliefs of those other days,
foreign and evil things, but with very fine names in -ism. He used to
round off the catalogue with "every other ism, and the Pope of Rome." '[6]
Norman MacFarlane is warmer, recalling George Campbell as 'a man of
unusual preaching abilities, and I have heard him with rare pleasure'.[7]

Though he entered the Union of 1900 – followed by only one family –
and duly lost both church and manse, George Campbell is still remembered with affection. He retreated meekly into a thatched blackhouse, by
the Shawbost crossroads, and, a skilled herbalist, continued to serve as the
local medicine-man till his death in 1911.[8] Indeed, Shawbost has been
remarkably fortunate in her ministers: all have been conscientious and
hard-working and the congregation has never suffered a protracted
vacancy. And, when Dr Parman came to study village life, the Free
Church was still an all-pervading and embracing influence, as she to some
extent remains.

We should grasp that the Free Church in Shawbost – and in this it is
typical of all Presbyterian congregations on Lewis and Harris – is much
more than a building; much more than a kirk session with a presiding
minister; and much bigger even than the roll of communicants. Most

Shawbost people are *adherents* of the Free Church – that is, people who are associated with it to greater or lesser degree but are not communicant members. Adherents can fall anywhere on a scale from those plainly converted people who live an upright careful life and attend the midweek prayer meeting, to those who will never cross the threshold of the building but will, nevertheless, be buried by a Free Church minister after a Free Church worship.

The gradations are striking – adherents who do not come out midweek but attend both Sabbath services; rather more who only attend the evening one (which, by long Highland custom, tends to be especially addressed to the unconverted, though there is a real chicken-and-the-egg factor in this); some who attend occasionally – some are only ever seen on the Sabbath evening service of the Communion season – and those who never come at all. Yet most in the group, if over fourteen years of age, will sign a 'minute of adherents' appended to the formal Call to a new minister, which is signed only by members. Most will pay regularly to the funds of the church, as their means and disposition permit; many will seek baptism for their infants and practically everyone will expect the local minister to marry them, if they want him or a local service at all. He will preside at every funeral worship in the district, and the Session that he chairs interviews all candidates for baptism and the Lord's Supper.

Leaving the sacraments aside for the moment, we may examine other rites of passage. Until well after the Second World War it was still unusual for an island couple to marry in a church building. Yet church weddings became increasingly the norm from the 1940s, part of a creeping 'Westernisation' of Hebridean life.

Traditionally islanders enjoyed 'house weddings', which could last two or even three nights and were supremely happy, inclusive occasions.[9] The whole locality contributed fowl for the feast and things kicked off the night before, when village women gathered in the bride's home to pluck the chickens, and visitors generally dropped by with a wedding gift and to partake of a 'small refreshment'. The wedding ceremony itself might be conducted in the bride's home or, more usually, at the manse; only immediate relatives attended and, though informal and pleasant, it was by today's standard perfunctory. All then repaired to the bride's home where, after serious eating, the young folk would arrive for music and dancing – usually taking advantage of a barn – and the jollification could continue the following day, with more catering in the home for the elderly of the village and, besides, some sort of party for children. The last act was the formal appearance of the married couple, together, in the pew, the following Lord's Day. Even in the 1980s, it was considered most unseemly in Lewis for a courting couple to sit together in church.

'House weddings' of this sort survived in Shawbost into the 1960s – the very last, rather sweetly, was for the nuptials of a cousin of my mother to a cousin of my father. One was held in South Harris as recently as 1974. Traditional, affordable, communal and the most enormous fun, their demise is a very great pity. Presbyterian island churches are simply not designed for wedding rites – few boast a central aisle and the enclosure around the pulpit is a real nuisance.

Island funerals, too, have changed. Even in the 1970s, most in Shawbost still died at home; bodies were routinely laid out by relatives, were 'coffined' at home, and remained at home until the moment they were removed for burial. By ancient Celtic tradition, Highlanders kept a 'wake'; people stayed up in the house all night, folk came in and out, and things got very convivial, as in a different Celtic and religious tradition they remain. The word 'wake' is still used on Lewis – the Gaelic term is *taigh-aire* or 'house of watching' – but never heard on Harris, though they did the same thing. The origins of the custom are not superstitious, but practical: people maintained a watch on the body – the stipulated period between death and burial was three sunrises – to guard the remains against rats, for instance; but, much more importantly, in a day when few trained medical practitioners were about, to make absolutely sure the person was dead. Without going into detail, two or three days is sufficient without becoming unpleasant. Funerals remain rapid on Lewis; someone dying on a Monday morning will usually be buried on Wednesday – but neither funerals nor weddings are ever conducted on the Lord's Day.

The wake was not abolished by Evangelicalism; it was Christianised. Family worship was conducted in the home by the village elders at a regular point each evening, usually 9 p.m. (In Tolsta and Ness, a morning family worship is additionally kept by 'the Men' and in Tong, just to be different from Back, the evening worship is at 8 p.m.) Only the last worship – around or shortly before noon on the day of burial – was kept by the minister, if he were available, and even this is really a very modern, post-war development. When my grandmother lost her first, infant daughter in Ness, in May 1940, no minister showed up at all, and the final worship was conducted by the child's grand-uncle. Neighbours would crowd into the home for these occasions – latterly, stacking-chairs would be supplied from the church – and afterwards tea would be served and opportunity given to 'view the remains'.

After the final funeral worship, the remains would be borne on a bier in a remarkably formal procession of village menfolk, each taking their turn to carry it. There are variations in the precise form of this 'lift' between Lewis, Harris and Skye, and of course a hearse is now used for most of the journey to the burial ground, but if the crowd is considerable and the weather clement, the coffin may be carried for twenty minutes to half an hour. In Harris, too, most would attend the funeral but not the burial; in Lewis, the 'lift' is the main event and many appear for it – and duly travel to the cemetery – who shun the worship.

Within living memory, in some areas, the grave would only be dug when mourners reached the burial ground. Nowadays, it is 'opened' the day before. Most island burial grounds are supervised by a local committee and belong to the community, who wage a part-time attendant; there are no attendants, though, at Bragar or Gravir, and graves are dug by relatives and neighbours of the deceased.

In recent decades, island funeral customs have rapidly changed – there is more use of the church building and ministers are now expected to conduct wakes. This is widely blamed on the late Rev. Donald Gillies, a native of Ness and a fine man, but when he became minister of Lochs Free Church in 1960 he started the very bad habit of attending wakes all over the island, hitherto left entirely to 'the Men'. Discomfited office-bearers naturally felt obliged to ask him to conduct the evening worship, and pressure most rapidly built on all ministers to do likewise, or be denounced as 'heartless' by contrast to good Mr Gillies. A minister, as my father points out, should visit the bereaved as soon as he can; and in most cases should conduct the final funeral worship. For a minister besides to conduct evening worship – as all island ministers presently do – sends out very bad messages; that his 'men' cannot be trusted to conduct such worship and that he himself has no more important things to do, such as study for the pulpit. The practice should be firmly abandoned and the bereaved should desist from demanding it.[10]

From the mid 1980s funerals and wakes were held increasingly, and now almost exclusively, in the church building. This reflects social change. Before the Second World War, all but a few of fortunate prosperity – village merchants, schoolmasters and the like – lived in the same modest houses; as wealth and social division increased, the poorest became stigmatised and the poorest homes became an embarrassment, not least as every community boasted one or two ladies who might well have been described as 'professional funeral-goers', only too eager to see the inside of folk's houses – especially as wakes spilled increasingly upstairs and into bedrooms. One shameless woman in Ness was even known to check for dust on a surface with a wet finger, while reverent eyes were shut for prayer; in March 2000, when a friend's father died suddenly on Scalpay, the wholesale and remorseless invasion of village women – within the hour, taking charge, making tea, shooing folk about, opening cupboards – was disconcerting.

In any event, the 'ceilidh culture', too – general social interaction, the frequent visiting of neighbours and all the old warmth of a close-knit order – had begun rapidly to retreat with the advent of television in most rural communities from the mid 1970s. Another factor was the private car. Once only near neighbours could readily attend a wake; from the 1950s, they drew increasingly huge crowds. The press of bodies could be such that some are said even openly to have feared that the floor could give way. I have not seen a house funeral in Lewis since the spring of 1998 – that of a great-aunt, in Habost; nor in Harris since the death of a friend's sister in February 2006 – and that was the first Harris house-funeral I had heard of in a decade. Only special and poignant circum-stances, such as a stillbirth, would generally occasion a house-funeral today, though the first wake after bereavement is usually held in the home and for immediate family only.

Today, the minister invariably presides at funerals and in the larger denominations will conclude with the benediction. The remains are generally brought to the church as soon as practicable after death, and seldom lie in the home. The funeral service itself has become increasingly dominated by ministers – one presiding, two praying, another even precenting. In the larger denominations, a wake usually features three prayers – my father can remember five – and, as a rule, only eminent Christians will be called on to 'engage', by long custom from outwith the local congregation. It is considered unseemly, besides, if near relatives of the deceased take any part in worship, such as leading the praise. There is mounting unease about wakes in Lewis – ministers increasingly suspect they have become a widespread substitute for churchgoing; the custom, founded on universal, morning and evening family worship in the home, has less and less support in a new reality; and in the new century there is anecdotal evidence, here and there, of families refusing to have them and office-bearers being turned away at the door.

The Free Presbyterians, even before the war, had to inveigh in their official *Magazine* against the demands of some that a minister should always officiate at a funeral – their general circumstances have often made it very difficult – and when Rev. Murdo MacRitchie of Stornoway had fixed holiday plans and had to leave conduct of a last funeral worship to a divinity student, the family took great umbrage, a daughter greeting Mr MacRitchie on his return with the strident claim that she could not sleep at night 'thinking my father hasn't been legally buried.' In emotive circumstances it is hard to reason against such sacerdotalism.

It seems also only to have been in the twentieth century – and in most rural districts after the Second World War – that it became general for the minister, besides, to attend the cemetery. There is no formal rite of committal in the Westminster Standards, and the *Directory of Public*

Worship expressly forbids 'praying, reading and singing, both in going to and at the grave'. The Free Presbyterians seized on this after 1900 as a useful and in their circumstances politic distinction from the continuing Free Church, but the *Directory* is only a guide – it is not binding as the Confession of Faith is binding – and in any event it ordains practices (such as a minister beginning Sabbath service with immediate public prayer) which the Free Presbyterians have not adopted and would not tolerate. The *Directory* does however splendidly stipulate 'that the Christian friends, which accompany the dead body to the place appointed for publick burial, do apply themselves to meditations and conferences suitable to the occasion; and that the minister, as upon other occasions, so at this time, if he be present, may put them in remembrance of their duty.'

The custom accordingly took hold in Lewis, in the conservative denominations and after the coffin has been lowered into the grave, that the minister give a very brief Gospel exhortation – a few remarks calling on all present to consider their latter end – and this, weather permitting, can be a powerful moment. This address is almost invariably in English, now, though at the funeral of Duncan John MacLeod from Carloway in November 2007 his minister gave a very warm little talk in Gaelic at the last act in Dalmore cemetery. The Church of Scotland generally have prayer at the grave, as – reflecting their United Free background – do the Free Church congregation on Scalpay.

But some districts resisted even this: Iain D. Campbell, inducted in 1995, is the first minister at Back to go to the cemetery at all. And with church attendance declining remorselessly in recent decades, ministers have felt naturally disposed increasingly to take advantage of funerals – the one occasion when the church may be full – with exhortation even in the building itself. The practice of the present minister in Shawbost, for instance, is to intersperse reading of chosen Bible portions – he usually reads out several – with appropriate remarks. The Free Presbyterian Synod moved firmly to suppress such developments in the 1990s.

There are other aspects of Lewis funerals that often startle the stranger: women very seldom go to the graveside (and, if so, only the closest relatives); there are often no flowers; and the atmosphere after the address usually and markedly lightens, at least if no women are present. In all the cemeteries of rural Lewis the men present help fill in the grave, bantering quietly, as others drift away one by one, or in pairs, for a smoke, or to look at the stones of relatives. These reflect the quiet realism of the culture, and the cruder aspects of burial long ago.

Dr Parman is fascinated by conversion, but presents it throughout in human terms: and, indeed largely interpreted by external ones, as a change in lifestyle and attitude visible to others and which redefines conduct, relationships, the intimate social circle and your place in the village scheme of things.[11] The colloquial Gaelic idiom for conversion, on both Lewis and Harris – and a long-mocked one at that – is *Tha an curam air* (literally, 'The concern is on him'), but with the same force and indeed flippancy of the English phrase, 'He's got religion.' The Gaelic has just the same grammatical construction an islander would use for diagnosing illness – *Tha an cnatan ort*, 'You have a cold' – and reinforces popular and fatalistic notions of the 'new birth' as something both random, pathological and even infectious. Ministers and most professing Christians favour a more reverent construction, *Tha e fo churam* – 'He's under concern,' under anxiety or unease about his immortal soul.

To Dr Parman, conversion is but one possible resolution to personal, existential crisis, in a northern, rural community of demanding weather, long hard winters and limited amenity, where nothing one says or does can pass without notice and comment – conversion only an alternative to, say, a drinking binge, a mental breakdown or deliberate exile to the mainland.

> A converted person 'has the curam' (has been saved, or is in a condition of conversion) or is *curamach* (converted). The word 'curam' means care, anxiety, responsibility; it means to be 'under concern' for one's state of mind and spiritual condition. The word 'curamach' means to be careful, solicitous, anxious, and attentive. In ordinary conversation the word may be used to mean being careful with your clothes; but in a religious context it means being careful and circumspect in your behaviour, evincing by your behaviour that you are living the 'good life'; your circumspect behaviour is a sign that you are among those chosen to be saved.
>
> Some non-curamach villagers refer jokingly to 'the big K' (from the brand name, Kellogg's, which appears in television and radio advertisements). A definitive sign of 'the big K' is when girls wear their hair in a bun and men stop drinking; and when they begin going twice a day to church and to Wednesday-night prayer meetings. The ultimate statement of conversion is to become a communicant . . . by taking Communion. Not all those who are curamach wish to take the highly visible step of becoming a communicant; but all who do so must be curamach. . . .
>
> Usually women move quietly and predictably into conversion, whereas men, who are expected to 'mix well' with other men in drinking groups, and who are expected to be less able to control themselves, often provide examples of dramatic conversion.

Dramatic conversions usually occur among the young, who convert in groups, and at middle age. 'She got it suddenly. She left halfway through a dance.' 'He converted suddenly, in the middle of a drink in the *bothan*.' Of the examples of dramatic conversion among females, most are associated with women who have lived away from the island and have returned to nurse an aging parent or to retire. 'I was working in the hotels. Then my mother got sick and I came back to nurse her; and when she died I couldn't leave my father there alone. Within a year I was converted.' Another woman lived for many years on the mainland, where she never attended church; when her husband died, she returned to the island and converted shortly afterwards.

There are external signs for a community to note – the newly *curamach* will start to attend the midweek prayer meeting; shun dances and the public house; and women – especially – may change their appearance, though the custom of growing one's hair long, abandoning a worldly 'bob', is now confined to the Free Presbyterians and enforced by their terms of Communion. Women are still expected to obey Pauline injunction and wear a 'head-covering' in public worship – indeed, until very recently, island women invariably wore some sort of head-covering in any public activity, such as the traditional scarf or *beannag*.[12]

One should dryly observe, though, that a head-covering is not head-decoration; and in any event the Scriptural custom is increasingly flouted in the larger island churches. But such markers of defined Christian conduct are essentially cultural; many Evangelical believers elsewhere would be aghast at Long Island toleration (in moderate use) of tobacco and alcohol, and there is a diverting story of some good Christian ladies flying from America for fellowship with others in Brazil. ('When the Brazilian women saw how much make-up the American believers were wearing, they were so shocked the cigars fell out of their mouths!')

One expects the ethnographer to record such communal criteria of holiness. But Dr Parman does include some striking conversion narratives, such as this account of a husband's great change by a Shawbost woman:

He was gone for his usual visit to the hotel, and on his way back he went in to speak to a friend who was in at a prayer meeting up the road. He saw them there sitting praying, all the young men, and he started crying. They looked so clean; he felt so dirty. I was at the window with his mother looking out for him. We saw him coming in the road staggering and I thought well he's drunk again, and when he comes in I'll make sure he doesn't go out again, I'll lock all the doors. But then I saw he was

crying. My heart went out to him; it was filled with tenderness. I said,
'What's wrong?' but he just cried and went into the bedroom and lay
down. He lay in bed for several days, very depressed, the handkerchief
over his eyes. Then I knew what it was – it was conviction of sin. His
mother was annoyed. All her life she had been a Christian [presumably
in a formal sense, one who went to church regularly but had no
experience of the 'new birth' and had never professed faith] and he
was the one who converted. You have to be plucked. Plucked like a
brand from the fire.

And this more immediate and autobiographical account:

Around the time of the [local] Communions, I was lying in bed around
midnight, not thinking about anything in particular. Then all of a
sudden I felt God talking to me. It's the strangest feeling to describe. All
of a sudden I didn't feel safe. I felt I was going to die; that with each tick
of the clock, time was running out, the universe was rushing towards its
end. For four days I was in a dazed, uncertain state, a state of not feeling
safe. I was talking to God but I didn't know what to do. I was in the mill
working but I didn't know what I was doing most of the time. Then all
of a sudden I had a vision of Christ on the cross who died for us. I had
been praying to God and here was my answer, trust in the Lord Jesus
Christ. God does everything for you. He makes you breathe, lifts your
lungs in and out, makes your blood flow. After I realised that, I could
take the days as they came, from one day to the next. God can do
anything. I saw the blackness of the life I was leading. I used to drink a
lot, but I didn't lie or steal. I used to rub shoulders with everyone, but
that life was leading me nowhere. I was black as that coal in the
fireplace, then lifted to light.

And, more dramatically still,

He was a hard worker but everything went to booze in the *bothan*. He slept
in the same room as his father, and his father used to lecture him, but he
closed his ears. Then his father died. One day a letter came for him. A
relative who had never sent him any money before sent him £10. He had
been trying to buy a suit on installment, but always spent the money on
drink. He went into town, got the suit, and wore it to church the next
Sunday. They saved his glass in the *bothan*, but he never went back.

Susan Parman's accounts of conversion are particularly valuable because, vouchsafed to a friendly stranger, they are entirely fresh, free of the

cant phrases and sentimentality of the sort of thing retailed in 'testimonies', detailed and sometimes flippant accounts of personal conversion,
which, largely as a consequence of the Faith Mission antics after the
Second World War, have become a vexing feature of island religion.
'Testimony' tends invariably to be marked by more talk of self than
Christ, to dwell rather more lusciously on the sinful past than on the
gracious present, and to be grossly atypical of Christian experience, not
least because those with the most dramatic stories are most often invited
to tell them. Yet even schoolchildren are now put under pressure to 'give
their testimony' in Christian gatherings or, still more imprudently, to
relate their conversion as part of, say, an evangelistic rally.

Conversion is one thing; to seek Communion is quite another. The very
language used in Highland Evangelicalism – 'to go forward', 'to do your
duty', 'to make public profession of faith' – is that of drama; of declaration; of setting oneself apart; almost an act of self-canonisation. And from
a very early point in the nineteenth century, at least, the sacrament of the
Lord's Supper became vested with extraordinary baggage.

In Lochs, for instance, at the height of the awakening under Robert
Finlayson, it is noted almost with pride that it had become practically 'a
mark of piety not to receive the sacrament.' When Roderick MacLeod
saw revival at Bracadale, at its height – out of a congregation of some
1,800 people – only eight actually partook of the Lord's Supper. Commenting of his native Skye late in the Evangelical period, Norman
MacLean – a Church of Scotland minister in early twentieth-century
Edinburgh – remarked unfairly that the 'success of a preacher of the
Gospel was judged not by the number he brought to the Holy Table, but
by the number whose consciences were so touched that they had not the
heart to come forward.'[13]

While something of this mentality was imported to Lewis by Alexander MacLeod, things never quite reached the extremes recorded elsewhere, especially in the Separatist culture of Sutherland and the east
Highland mainland, where John Grant himself declared that he would
allow no one past his own Session to the Table unless he himself,
personally and mystically, 'had them of the Lord' – much the same
grandiloquent mentality as, today, emboldens the occasional elder to
oppose a call to a given minister, even if the overwhelming majority of
communicants support it.

Attitudes certainly vary between denominations today, with the Free
Presbyterians taking generally a tougher attitude to membership than the
Free Church, and the Church of Scotland a more liberal one. But the real
constraint was not spiritual, but social; how would the community react if

you professed faith? If anything, in all denominations, things have eased as churchgoing has remorselessly dropped and, even on the Long Island, Christianity has grown increasingly marginal.

The paucity of communicants can be exaggerated. Though thought the strictest church in town, the Free Presbyterian congregation in Stornoway has still, in 2008, over sixty members on its roll. When Duncan MacGregor received his call to Stornoway Free Church in 1849, 685 male members had signed it, with another 851 female communicants 'concurring'. There are in fact, nowadays, very few believers in Lewis and Harris of any denomination who do not sit at the Lord's Table; and there is no imbalance in favour of the elderly – in the Free Church, there is probably more anxiety today that many recent new members are too young.

Yet there is one extraordinary Lewis twist. The definitive declaration that you believe yourself converted is not, in fact, seeking Communion but attending the midweek prayer meeting for the first time. This is rather less marked in Harris than in Lewis, and is deplored by the Free Presbyterians, who encourage as many people as possible to attend church midweek. But the lather of anxiety endured by someone thinking of 'coming out' – a phrase that is actually used – has become distinctly silly.

The step is not merely seen as definitive, but irrevocable. A woman in one Lewis congregation told me in 2005 that, when her 14-year-old son expressed eagerness to go to the meeting, 'I kept him in for three weeks, until I was sure it was serious.' 'To attend the prayer meeting was a huge step, for you were telling the community that you were concerned about your soul. It was almost a burning of the bridges behind you,' note Colin and Mary Peckham. 'Unbelievers, even though they may attend the church regularly, knew that they were not converted and did not frequent the prayer meetings. This resulted in people fearing to go to the prayer meeting, for if they went there, they would immediately be seen to be identifying with the people of God, and would be regarded as Christians, or as those who were earnestly seeking God. If they, at any time in the future, did not attend the prayer meeting, they would be regarded as having backslidden.' When Roderick MacKay of Tolsta Chaolais, *Ruaraidh a' Mhodel*, still only eighteen and increasingly 'under concern', made known his thoughts of going to the meeting in 1936, his mother's reaction was typical. 'Her discouraging warning struck me deeply, my faint heart failed me, and I did not attend, for she said, "If you go, you will have to keep going."'

Nevertheless, the lad did, weeks later, make his move. 'On my way to the prayer meeting, the Devil tried to turn me back, telling me what a fool I was. Why, the Free Church elders at the door would ask me why I had come. What on earth would I say to them? But when I got to the door I was welcomed with open arms. The relief and joy was wonderful . . .' But, 'When I reached home I was met with a barrage of criticism from my brothers. I had gone to the prayer meeting because I had heard that others were being converted and I was a sham!'[14] Yet *Ruaraidh a' Mhodel* was kept in the way; he died in Inverness early in 2007.

An enormous fuss is often made of such new arrivals, with Christians flocking about to hug the new converts or shake their hand, or descending afterwards on their home. This can be disconcerting. 'One woman who began attending Wednesday meetings was puzzled when people came up to congratulate her,' records Parman. ' "It's nothing you've done yourself; supposedly you're chosen." She was inundated with calls and visits, but she felt bothered by the difference between social pressure and what she expected conversion to be like.'[15] She had nevertheless 'started'; she had 'come out'; she had 'begun following', and in most respects this is really the moment of truth in Lewis, rather than admission to Communion.

But becoming a member remains difficult. For one, while Presbyterial order can in fact admit any individual at any time to the membership of a congregation, in Lewis and Harris it is popularly and culturally confined to the Communion season – a weekend of special services, unusual crowds, and heightened atmosphere. There is still another pressure on men: a male communicant is expected to be able to engage in public prayer, in the very formal structure of the midweek meeting, when the minister can 'put up' any individual he pleases. The quiet terror of this prospect, for many, is a real barrier to public profession. (There are unwritten rules: no man will be put up for the first time until after the Communion season following the one at which he professed; and – though elders frequently conduct the meeting in the minister's absence – the minister himself should put him up for the very first time.)

The local kirk session is constituted at the start of the weekend, and remains constituted until after the Monday thanksgiving service – its last act being to hear applications for baptism – and pulpit intimation is given, from the Friday evening onwards, that the session has been constituted and would be 'pleased to meet with anyone belonging to the congregation desiring to make public profession of faith for the first time'. Most seeking membership would request to meet the session after the Friday evening service – though opportunity is again given after the Saturday morning service, the Saturday evening prayer meeting and some have even been known, in the last gasp, to make their desire known before the start of the Communion service itself, on Sabbath morning. The boldest might simply remain in church after the benediction, and trot forward nervously to greet the elders; most go outside, pace about, and try and nip back in as discreetly as possible. To make matters worse, there are invariably inquisitive individuals who linger outside as long as possible, just to see what individuals might be going before the session (before, of course, dashing to a home or the nearest telephone to broadcast the news far and wide). And, though kirk session business is supposed to be strictly private, any elder can expect to be questioned wherever he goes through the Friday and Saturday whether anyone has gone forward, and whom.

There are other peculiarities of Highland Evangelicalism. For one, no one is admitted to the Lord's Table without giving a very clear 'conversion narrative'; he or she is expected to be able to relate what the Lord has done for their soul, and acceptably to answer questions on their experience. This was never historic practice in the Scottish Reformed order and in this respect the Highland church is actually much more akin to New England Puritanism, or even English congregationalism: again, it can probably be traced to Thomas Hog of Kiltearn, and his practice then honed still more rigorously by 'the Men' of the north; and, again, it seems to have been Alexander MacLeod who brought it to Lewis. The difficulty is that not everyone is able to say precisely when they were converted – especially those brought up in a Christian home and who have always, from childhood, lived an outwardly circumspect life – and the danger is that an elder or elders tend naturally to expect that the Christian experience of others should resemble their own.

The manual of *Practice and Procedure* finalised for the Free Church in 1886 by a committee led by a distinguished jurist, Sir Henry Moncrieff – still used by most island denominations today – is explicit. 'Without any inquisitorial minuteness, their outward conduct may be judged of, through the observation of the Minister, or one or more of the Ruling Elders. If there be nothing in what is thus seen decidedly inconsistent with their profession, and fitted to subject the parties to Church censure, and if no charge against them be brought before the Session, it is not competent for the Session to reject them merely on account of what the Minister or any Elder may conceive to be the state of their minds . . .'[16] But strong anecdotal evidence suggests this has not always been the case, to put it mildly. Ancient scandal may be disinterred. Parman records instances of men interrogated as to their alleged paternity, decades before, of a misbegotten infant. Candidates have been asked the most demanding questions on doctrine; during the Stornoway ministry of James Green- field, late in the nineteenth century, an eminent elder – Alexander Morrison – very properly erupted when a very young woman was asked such questions as, 'Did Christ suffer more in His soul than in His body?' There are still those who demand an applicant has a 'warrant' – a verse of Scripture laid on the mind as practically a command from Heaven that they profess. Such should be unhesitatingly slapped down by the presiding minister.

'Sadly, there is no doubt that in the Highlands, including Lewis, some ministers and elders applied the criterion too vigorously,' wrote my father in 1991, 'and went far beyond the powers conferred on them as *stewards* in the household of God. . . . but such excesses were rare and although instance could (and still can) be found of godly men and women never becoming communicants the fault usually lay not in harsh church discipline but with undue scrupulosity on the part of the individuals themselves. There are still those who regard the Lord's Supper as an ordeal rather than as a means of grace. But that problem is frankly far more prevalent on the mainland than it is in Lewis.'[17]

Inevitably, with so high a view of the Lord's Supper, a much laxer standard has been set for baptism. The infants of members in full communion are of course baptised in Highland Evangelicalism; but so are many – indeed, the great majority – of the infants of adherents, and there is no doubt at all – especially on Lewis and particularly in the mid twentieth century – that the dispensation of baptism became almost scandalous, with many parents seldom seen in church, or of empty heads and careless lives. (Driving home after a Stornoway kirk session that had granted baptism to a squad of rather casually connected men, Murdo MacRitchie saw one of them being thrown out of a pub.)

There are two aspects here that should be remembered. For one, contrary to widespread perception, a Presbyterian minister has very little actual power; admission to ordinances is a matter for the whole kirk session, and in many dubious cases it is fair to assume the minister was out-argued and out-voted by his elders. For another, church discipline in regard to baptism was fashioned in – and has been inherited from – the days of one, solid, Established Church, with very real civil power in a parish as well as spiritual authority. In the new century, with rampant denominationalism, parents were quite capable of leaving – and often did leave – the Free Presbyterians for the Free Church, or the Free Church for the United Free – to win there the sacrament withheld from them in their own church.

Explicit efforts have been made to justify a lower standard of qualification for baptism than Communion, most notably – and as long ago as 1869 – by Dr John Kennedy of Dingwall, in what is still the most revealing and, indeed, disconcertingly elegiac and defensive description of Highland religion ever written, *The Days of the Fathers in Ross-shire*. Before launching into a detailed and at times arcane discussion of the theological issues involved, he relates the practice with which he was familiar and which he himself fervently upheld.

The Ross-shire Fathers held that though in general the two sacraments were equally seals of the covenant of grace, they do in some respects differ even as sealing ordinances; that baptism being the door of admission into the visible Church, a larger exercise of charity is required in dealing with applicants for that sacrament than is called for in administering the other, which implies a confirmation of those who were members before; that the lessons of baptism are more elementary than those of the sacrament of the Supper; that the connection of the child and of both the parents, with an ordinary case of infant baptism, calls for peculiar tenderness on the part of Church rulers, and that the rule of Scripture requires baptism to be given on an *uncontradicted* profession of faith, while an *accredited* profession is required to justify the Church in granting admission to the table of the Lord. The result of carrying these views into practice is well known; the number of members in full communion is comparatively small, and parents who have never communicated receive baptism for their children.[18]

Kennedy's views should be set in context. For one, he describes an order which was long established and which he openly venerated. (A third of the book consists of an account of his own father, preacher at Assynt and minister of Killearnan.) Kennedy was writing, too, both when Highland Evangelic-alism was increasingly mocked by a wider Scotland; and he knew, besides, it was now largely marginalised in the Free Church. The position he outlines is remarkable. A man going to the Lord's Table must give an accredited profession of faith (with a conversion narrative that is clear, sincere, and which will stand up to questioning) but one seeking baptism merely an uncontradicted one (that is, a profession of faith founded on obvious knowledge of true religion, regular church attendance and a lifestyle that is not openly sinful.) It is worth stressing that he would be genuinely appalled at the carelessness in which baptism has too often since been granted, in Lewis and elsewhere. His views have besides been explicitly (if never formally, by resolution of Synod) incorporated in the Free Presbyterian Church, with Rev. William MacLean asserting them robustly in 1976:

We as a Church act on the principle which at one time was almost universal among the churches of the Reformation, the Church of Scot-land, the Presbyterian churches on the continent of Europe and most Protestant churches as the Church of England and the Congregationalist churches, that every baptised person not ex-communicated being a member of the visible church has a right to have his child baptised. 'Infants of such as are members of the visible church are to be baptised.' (Shorter Catechism, q.95)

We accordingly hold that the two sacraments are in general seals of
the covenant of grace, and that as such they are equally valid, but that
they do not *seal* the same measure of privilege, that the qualifications
therefore for baptism and for full communion are not identical, that
many may properly be admitted to the former who are not prepared for
the latter . . .[19]

Some early Reformed writings support this position – it seems to have
been the thinking of Samuel Rutherford,[20] and the 'Half-Way Covenant'
of New England Puritanism also articulates it.[21] But it is not Confes-
sional. The Westminster Standards grant baptism only to the infants
of 'members of the visible church' – and the plain meaning of that is
communicants. However, Highland churches have to contend with a
strong cultural reluctance to seek church membership and this long
established asymmetry between the two sacraments. The Free Presbyterian position is at least carefully thought through. For one, they uphold a
distinction even when dispensing adult baptism. Commenting on a recent
instance in one city congregation, the minister involved observed in my
hearing that 'he was examined as to his knowledge by the kirk session, but
he was *not* examined as to his experience.' For another, they insist on
regular church attendance. Despite MacLean's language, there is in fact
no absolute right to infant baptism if one is not a member in full
Communion. It is entirely at the discretion of the kirk session, who will
weigh every case before them on its merits and, by prudence and sheer
hunch, the individual seeking it.

The Presbyterian tradition has long and explicitly condemned superstitious notions of baptism. One gone-away-and-done-well Shawbost
native, Calum Smith, had been so dangerously ill after birth his parents
had won emergency baptism from the minister. 'The harsh brand of
Presbyterianism holding sway at the time saw nothing incongruous in the
belief that a fatherly and loving God should condemn a newly born child
to everlasting hellfire because he had not been subjected to the ritual of
baptism,'[22] Smith sneered in 2001. This is completely unjust and false;
the Free Church teaches no such thing and it is expressly repudiated in
the Confession of Faith, as is any suggestion of 'baptismal regeneration' –
that a baptised infant will by virtue of the sacrament be saved. The
children of believers do not become 'covenant children' when they are
baptised; they are baptised because they are already covenant children.

But there is no doubt that the distinctive practice of the Highlands is
an enormous pressure on ministers and that many island parents have won
baptism who had no credible entitlement to it. 'Spiritual mediocrity is one
thing,' wrote a Lewis-born theologian in 1998. 'Covenant repudiation

was quite another.'[23] Kenneth MacRae was aghast at the disorder he found on Lewis in 1931 – the most irregular parents expecting (and getting) the ordinance; a widespread insistence on baptism being administered in the home. It should never, any more than the Lord's Supper, be divorced from the preaching of the Word and, even if delicate circumstances call for a home service, it should be a public service and publicly intimated as such.

'Baptism is almost as much abused in the Free Church as the other sacrament is in the large Church,' sighed MacRae. 'It is astonishing how ignorant they are in Lewis as to the meaning of baptism.'[24] The most sensible practice, in the Highland context and in congregations – now mostly on Lewis and Harris – where there is still a considerable base of adherents, is that baptism only be granted to those who attend church regularly and whose lives are not marked by open misconduct of the sort that would invite comment and derision in the community; but even this calls for wisdom, sensitivity and sober judgement.

There is very little formal, judicial church discipline in the islands. True scandal is extremely rare and when official action does have to be taken, the cause will probably be lost and the member in question usually alienated. Most trouble is averted by a quiet, one-on-one word in the ear, and formal discipline is usually only invoked by criminal charges or the very rare event of sexual scandal.[25] It is important to remember that church discipline is meant expressly to induce repentance and that, if shame, confession and repentance are already manifest, there is no merit in further sanction.

Misconduct in a member is one thing, though; misconduct in an office-bearer quite another. A communicant is often allowed to remain in communion after admonition; an elder or deacon is invariably suspended from office and, if the offence is appalling, may be permanently deposed. To be 'suspended', or the Lesser Excommunication, is to be removed from the functions of office and from the right to 'sealing ordinances' (baptism and the Lord's Supper); while Presbyterial order does have the supreme sanction of the 'Greater Excommunication', it is unheard of in the Western Isles, can only be pronounced by the assent of Presbytery and is for offenders who are 'utterly recalcitrant and defiant'.

Pre-marital pregnancy – the sin is rather horribly termed 'antenuptial fornication' in Moncrieff's *Practice and Procedure* – has occasioned most formal discipline in the island church; a baby is, after all, definitive proof, and his baptism necessarily involved the kirk session, at least when baptism was still socially obligatory. But the deplorable custom of the couple being made to stand for public rebuke, before the congregation, before the sacrament could be granted – once universal in the old Kirk – survived on Lewis and Harris until very recent years. Many women, noted Parman in 1990, 'leave the island rather than submit to this public shaming,' and certainly – as a social spectacle – drew out the worst in human nature, the church being invariably packed for the *seasamh*, or 'standing', as the minister gave the hapless pair – usually very young – their character. Parman noted the remarks of one minister on such an occasion in 1971. 'You have brought shame upon yourselves, shame upon your children, and shame upon your parents. I cannot erase your shame. I can only hope that you ask Christ to forgive you, and that from now on you follow closely in the ways of the church.'

Shawbost, though, was unusual. John Morrison, minister of Cross Free Church from 1936 to 1966, flatly refused to hold the *seasamh*, maintaining that rebuke before the kirk session, in private, was quite sufficient. Kenneth MacRae, his Stornoway colleague, agreed – though held all such baptisms in the home. From the mid 1960s a forceful group of island ministers – Murdo MacAulay, Murdo MacRitchie and John MacSween – fought to eliminate the custom; social change and the very real fear that terrified young women might resort to abortion as preferable to such humiliation finally, mercifully saw its demise in all denominations by 1990. But it was, really, less a yielding to a new humanity than the tacit acknowledgement the Church had no longer general, definitive power in island communities.

One colourful minister at Back, Roderick MacKenzie, is still remembered for a *seasamh* some seventy years ago. The hapless wife was a big, strapping, formidable woman. She stood helplessly before him as he knocked ten bells out of her in scorn, invective and denunciation. The husband was a sad, wispy little bauchle of a fellow. MacKenzie had only one sentence for him, in conclusion. 'And as for *you*,' he said, with one withering glance, 'who would have thought you had it in you?'[26]

15

The Bebo Generation

Reverse and Renewal in the Twenty-first Century

The last years of the twentieth century were not easy for Christianity on the Long Island. The Free Church – to all intents and purposes the established parish church commanding most adherence – endured its own part in wider trouble. Bad headlines do not advance the Gospel. On the other hand, the ordeal largely dissolved a mounting, unattractive complacency.

The Presbytery had got into the bad habit – since the days of Kenneth MacRae and his latter search for 'Arminians' under the bed[1] – of throwing its weight around the wider Free Church, issuing dire reports, submitting rather menacing overtures to the General Assembly – such as a 1987 demand for renewed commitment to 'purity of worship', occasioned by an apocalyptic report in the *Free Presbyterian Magazine*[2] of averred remarks by Free Church ministers at a 'London Presbyterian Conference' – and apparently convinced, with ample congregations and contributing prodigiously to Free Church funds, it could now conduct itself as the policeman of the denomination.

We have seen how Christianity first reached the Hebrides and how – from 1820 – it exploded in Evangelicalism, renewed by repeated seasons of revival and transcending even the very difficult divisions of 1893 and 1900. We have seen, besides, the debt owed by the islands to a wider Church. The Gospel itself came from Ireland. While more might well have been done for the Highlands after the Reformation, there were real endeavours from Edinburgh (to say nothing of the fortuitous banishment of Robert Bruce). There were certainly mixed motives in the determined efforts to advance literacy and Presbyterianism after 1689 – not least to neutralise the Jacobite threat – but out of it came abiding good.

It is worth remembering besides how sacrificially people persevered in the face of opposition. Aeneas Sage of Lochcarron, the first Evangelical minister in the West Highlands, survived several attempts on his life.[3] Kenneth Morrison of Stornoway was almost borne off by thugs. SSPCK teachers battered on in very difficult situations, especially in the Great

Glen. Donald Morrison of Stornoway and Alexander MacLeod of Uig were only two of the many useful, conscientious ministers hounded by their own colleagues. Finlay Munro was repeatedly slandered. The persecutions of 1843, 1893 and 1900 are amply documented. Hebridean ministers in the 1980s were in no position to attack believers on the mainland as if they, themselves, were a self-generated branch of the True Faith with entire monopoly on spiritual discernment, and at times these attacks were personalised and vulgar. James Morrison of North Uist may genuinely have thought his Bishopbriggs colleague a 'caveman' – Alex MacDonald wore a beard, and hair rather longer than Morrison approved – but he had should not have got away with saying so on the floor of the 1980 General Assembly. MacDonald bore the smear with silent, Christ-like dignity. The Moderator did nothing.[4]

We have noted how times of spiritual refreshing continued and how the earliest Christian tradition still echoes – a tendency to venerate the past and the dead; a belief in prophetic gifts in alliance with faith; a superstitious view of the Lord's Supper and a real reluctance to partake – as frustrating for twentieth-century ministers as it was, 900 years earlier, for Queen Margaret. The civil powers enjoyed by Kirk ministers always irritated some Scots. In the Highlands, especially after the rise of Evangelicalism, the unpopular, often useless Moderates and their dependence on landlordism fostered still stronger feeling.

But sustained anticlericalism – a distrust of ministers as a species – is a marked Lewis phenomenon, certainly much more evident than it is on Harris. Its roots are obvious. Some ministers – even eminences like Alexander MacLeod – had been openly exploitative. Much more decisive was the Disruption. The people of Lewis had 'come out' almost to a man in 1843, following their four Evangelical ministers. Within eighteen months, three of those men had deserted their charges and the island, as had one of the abiding 'Auld Kirk' ministers; in the same year, 1844, the family who had owned and controlled the island since the days of James VI had sold out to a new and wholly unknown landlord, Sir James Matheson, who at that time – like landlords anywhere in the Highlands – could exercise near-untrammelled power over his tenants.[5] And Lewis had just been abandoned by its most respected natural leaders.

The scars of that go deep. It was only reinforced by the antics of Free Church ministers over the Declaratory Act – and spectacularly confirmed in 1900, when eleven of the twelve Free Church ministers on Lewis confidently strode into the United Free Church, followed by only a fragment of their people. For the most part, though, the quiet, unstated tension between laity and ministry has caused very little trouble. Some have wondered why the Charismatic movement – the widespread

Evangelical drift in Britain, from the 1970s, into exuberant and chaotic worship, strong lay leadership, and the ostentatious exercise of supposed spiritual gifts like 'speaking in tongues' – has never hit the Long Island or, indeed, the Free Church. While it has been imported by a few incomers, and may have the sympathy of one or two Church of Scotland ministers, it has otherwise got nowhere in Lewis or Harris. Why?

For one, anticlericalism had no real oppression to overthrow. A Presbyterian minister enjoys very little meaningful power. He has entire authority over his pulpit duties – and is accountable for them only to his Presbytery – and can assign the church building, on his own authority, for any act of public worship, and deny it to others. In everything else, save his civil function of marriage, he must act within the authority of the kirk session, which he only chairs and will, rarely, have the power of a casting vote. The session, not the minister, admits to baptism and the Lord's Supper, and examines candidates. For another, Highland Presbyterianism grants much scope to ordinary members. They can be elected as office-bearers. They usually lead the praise. They are involved in most ongoing congregational work. The fellowship meeting explicitly grants – in certain, at times uneasy constraints – a place for men who are not ministers to opine within even the Communion order. There, is besides, a great deal of built-in informality. The merry fellowships in houses, with men and women on equal terms, are as established a part of a Communion weekend as the services. There is even a very strong tradition, on Lewis, of writing and singing Gaelic hymns – it may well still be the strongest indigenous art-form on Lewis and Harris – and even MacRae, entirely thirled to exclusive psalmody, took pleasure visiting a home to sing such compositions. 'At night had supper in Domhnall Mhata's. Enjoyed the Gaelic hymns which were sung there. It is long since I have been out anywhere on New Year's Day. At the outset of my ministry it used to be a very dreary day for me,'[6] he noted on 1 January 1932. Free Presbyterians, too, take private comfort in 'uninspired hymns', one venerable minister once telling me how his own father, himself a minister of the Church, had sung English hymns of an evening by the fire.[7] The Charismatic movement gains traction best under a rigid liturgy in a sacerdotal order – such as the Church of England; in Lewis and Harris, it can have little opening.

One other reality contained anticlericalism in Lewis – and, when that reality changed, it became a more open and evident problem. Until after the First World War, surprisingly few Lewis or Harris men actually occupied Lewis and Harris pulpits. The island exported ministers; it did not hire them. None of the Evangelical ministers who featured in the 1820s' awakening – Alexander MacLeod, Finlay Cook and so on – were Long Island men. It was 1845 before a local son – Donald Murray, from

Melbost – was settled in an island charge, Knock Free Church.[8] It would be over forty years before another, Neil MacLean Morrison, from Leurbost, was settled as the first Free Church minister of Park. Lewis and Harris pulpits were filled with Lochaber men, Skye men, Wester Ross men, Sutherland men, Argyll men, even the odd Gaelic-speaking Canadian. They could draw on the resources of a great Gaelic-speaking realm. And when that realm contracted – as it began rapidly to do from the First World War, and catastrophically so after the Second – Lewis was thrown more and more on itself to fill its pulpits. Even had Free Church congregations wanted non-island men the acute shortage of Gaelic ministers amidst the new denominational competition of the twentieth century greatly limited their options. Several, indeed – Malcolm Gillies, James Tallach and Kenneth MacRae among them – had painfully learned the language.

There had also been another striking turnaround. From the 1820s to the Second World War, the island had been practically a desperate subsistence economy, enduring hardship more often than not, whose ministry and ordinances were of necessity supported by the wider Church. After the Second World War – the period from about 1947 to the mid 1970s is genuinely remembered as almost a 'golden age', when a welfare state, high employment and modern comforts were allied briefly to close-knit society and a vibrant Gaelic culture[9] – the position was very quickly reversed. By the 1960s, Lewis believers were bankrolling the Free Church. They would scarcely have been human had this not gone a little to their heads.

But new prosperity had consequences. The social gulf that had hitherto prevailed between ministers and people rapidly vanished. An island minister in the 1930s was usually the best housed, best schooled and almost the best paid man in the district, on a pedestal with the doctor and the schoolmaster. An unfortunate hangover of this is the continued tradition, in some charges, that the minister serve also as session clerk; an understandable provision when he was often the only man who could read English, but a very bad one today. By the 1980s, he might have the academic edge on many, but his other advantages had gone, and authority now hinged on the man rather than his office.

There were other curious changes. Congregations in or near Stornoway became distinctly suburban, with a high proportion of educated middle-class people. By the new century, the island church generally had a distinctly white-collar character, and the old democracy of Evangelicalism – weavers, fishermen, roadmen and so on, on equal terms in Presbytery and the kirk session – seemed to be fading. An underclass was emerging, especially in Stornoway (which had expanded massively in the 1970s, with acres of new public housing) with no meaningful church connection whatever. Car ownership, too, had effects. It reduced fellowship; people no longer walked to church in crowds and in knots, or piled onto the same bus. Islanders stopped going to Communions and staying for the whole weekend (though that culture has survived to some extent in the Free Presbyterians). It greatly increased the workload on ministers – they could now be, and often were, expected to preach on the same day in localities many miles apart, or take responsibility as interim-moderator for charges on the other side of the Clisham.

They had also the additional worry of a new language problem. The general demise of the Gaelic Shorter Catechism – and of family worship, conducted in Gaelic, in the home, from the 1970s – torpedoed the ability even of fluent speakers to follow a Gaelic sermon in its specialised religious vocabulary. An anglicised school-culture – and the advent of television in the 1970s, with profound impact on Hebridean culture – all but demolished it. By 1980, very few Lewis teenagers could have enjoyed (or substantially understood) a Gaelic service. By 1990, the matter was critical. The Church of Scotland has long been short of Gaelic ministers, though demand has slumped since 1970 as Gaelic largely collapsed on the mainland and Inner Hebrides. The Free Presbyterians have only ordained two since 1975 have only ordained two anywhere since 1975: Rev. Roderick MacLeod, to Tarbert, in December 1994 – now minister of St Jude's, Glasgow – and Rev. Allan MacColl, to Ness, in November 2008.[10] For over four years preceding Mr MacColl's settlement, not a single settled Free Presbyterian minister in the Western Isles could preach in the Gaelic language.

In contrast, the Free Church had the manpower and an abiding demand for Gaelic services in Lewis, but dragged its feet in making realistic, additional English provision and, considering the urgency of the Gospel, the failure was culpable. When John Morrison was inducted to Shawbost as recently as 1992 as Callum Matheson's successor, Shawbost had one English Sabbath service, one evening, a month. 'I'll have to consider the politics of this,' he joked to me in August 1992; but better arrangements were shortly made by his decisive leadership. As recently as 1996, the session on Scalpay made a serious bid to restrict English preaching to just one monthly service. A deacon, Roderick MacKenzie – brought up on the mainland and who could not have bought a packet of crisps in Gaelic – quickly organised a petition and carried the day against them.[11]

There was no easy solution. For most over the age of forty in the 1980s, Gaelic was the language of their hearts. Most born before the First World War had genuine difficulty in following an English service and Gaelic monoglots could be found in number even in the 1960s, one ancient lady expiring on Scalpay as late as 1991.[12] The island is still in language transition and the Free Church is still struggling conscientiously to handle it. No one can rejoice in the death-throes of a culture, and all efforts to succour Gaelic should be encouraged; but it is not the responsibility of Christians to save a minority tongue, but to proclaim Christ. That said, the pendulum had by 2008 swung rather too far the other way: a morning Gaelic service should not be punctuated with English summary, and in rural Lewis, with two annual Communion seasons in a district, could one not be conducted entirely in Gaelic, and vice versa?

There is an inevitable tendency to glamorise the past and to exaggerate church adherence in former days, as too many blithely (and absurdly) speak of universal church attendance in Victorian Scotland. My father's sober assessment of Shawbost, for instance, in the 1970s – when the Free Church was exceptionally strong and there were no incomers to speak of – suggests that around 50 per cent of adults in the village were in church at least once a month, probably as high a figure as it ever was.[13] Almost all children went to the Sabbath School, but – below secondary age, as a rule – only those of communicants were usually taken regularly to church; being shoved out the door to Sabbath School, of a Sunday afternoon, sufficing for most. In the late 1990s, a Lewis community survey suggested around a third of Barvas people went to church every week and perhaps 40 per cent once a month; in Point, a quarter went weekly, and a third monthly.

In a revealing note, one historian of the Free Church in Ness records that 'in 1912 complaints came to the Deacons' Court of children doing damage on the Sabbath while their parents were in church. A man was to be set aside in every township as a constable on the Sabbath.' Lewis had never boasted universal church attendance. But it has certainly fallen substantially since the 1970s and much of the blame for that – on top of television, social change, immigration and the spirit of the age – must rest on the failure, in time, to introduce adequate English preaching. Once the habit of churchgoing is lost, it is rarely recovered.

The sustained crisis in the Free Church in the late 1990s masked, though, some real local renewal. For one, the Free Church nationally had tightened up the educational standards required to enter her ministry, abandoning lenient 'Modified Course' arrangements tolerated, of necessity, after 1900. Only in the most exceptional cases – if a man was over forty, and had outstanding and proven gifts – was now allowed to enter the College without a university degree. From the early 1990s the ministers settled on the Long Island were well trained and in, several instances, of signal ability. The Church had also firmly addressed the language difficulty. By 1994 every congregation had a weekly, English evening service and those near Stornoway – such as Back and Crossbost – had begun a parallel English morning service in the hall. It was belated, but essential.

It is too easy to focus on these strains in the last fifteen years of the twentieth century. Though marked seasons of 'revival' had paused, the church continued to see, here and there, in ones and twos and threes, hearts touched, lives changed, and names added to her Communion roll. Sermons were preached, God's praise sung, and even in the most difficult circumstances of the 1990s Christian life went on and the line was generally held.

Since things settled, from January 2000 – there was some restructuring, most notably the merging of the Uist congregations with those of the Long Island in one Free Church Presbytery of the Western Isles – there has been sustained, sober and intelligent Free Church leadership, marked by an entire lack of self-righteous stridency and a new willingness to reach out and to adapt. If there were one bitter regret, it was the collapse of the last Free Church presence in Uig.[14] The 2002 General Assembly refused to continue special financial terms for Bernera – in another demonstration of anti-Lewis sentiment – and its young minister is now the Church of Scotland pastor of Lochmaddy. The Bernera congregation, or what was left of it, has been formally wound up. Contrary to the hopeful predictions of its enemies, the Free Church has had no difficulty replenishing Long Island pulpits with Gaelic preachers and the present generation of ministers is outstanding.

Murdo MacAulay died quietly, in Stornoway, in November 2001, in his ninety-fifth year. A few months before his death, he summoned my father to see him, and they spent a little time together that summer, supporting old age from either end – the old man lying on top of his bed in layers of clothing, the grand voice now a whisper, but his mind yet sharp and his dignity immaculate. Thus the torch was passed.

Recent schism had actually done very little damage to established denominational strength on Lewis. It is extremely doubtful if, between the two new denominations, a thousand people worship publicly at APC and FCC services on the Long Island. But, in the new climate of aggressive secularism – especially since the change of government in 1997 – the myth quickly took hold that the island church was riven in Calvinist splinters. MacAulay was barely buried before open assault was launched, in this new confidence, on the perceived privileges of island Christendom.

In the autumn of 2002, despite protests, scheduled Sunday flights began from Stornoway Airport. By the end of 2004, Western Isles Health

Board overturned long-standing chaplaincy arrangements at the Stornoway hospital. New, stringent requirements for disabled access were forced
on churches in the Western Isles as everywhere else, requiring expensive
works and forcing the closure of many district buildings – legislation
especially resented as many notable public buildings were exempt. Following certain atrocities, strict new laws were also imposed regarding the
appointment of anyone working with children or 'vulnerable adults' – all
students, ministers, office-bearers and any sort of youth worker had now
to complete elaborate 'disclosure' papers.

This often involved fatuous bureaucracy. One island communicant, in
2005, had to have six different sets of disclosure-papers because he was
involved in six different activities with children – a Sabbath School, a local
youth fellowship; a Stornoway youth fellowship; an autumn trip to the
mainland; a youth committee; and voluntary transport duties of a Sabbath
evening. Disclosure has since been much simplified; still, as a matter of
fixed principle, collecting youngsters for an activity, this jolly young man
would not travel alone with one child in his car – there had to be at least
two and, preferably, another adult. And the State, besides, steadily
amassed a database of individuals actively involved in Christian work.
If Scotland were again to see a totalitarian and persecuting order, the
implications were serious.

All this not only deterred volunteers, but raised real Disruption
principles. Ought the authority of the 'civil magistrate', with potential
power of veto over the appointment of ministers and office-bearers in the
church, to have been so lightly conceded? But there was little protest.
Churchmen were almost as risk-averse as their society. Though several
ministers are privately uneasy about disclosure legislation, a consequence
of such highly publicised outrages as the Dunblane massacre in 1996, they
were under enormous pressure from, for instance, insurance considerations to comply. So emotive are child protection issues in the new century,
anyway, it would be a brave man who publicly questioned them.

In April 2006 – it was the Sabbath morning of the Free Presbyterian
Communion season in South Harris – a Sunday car ferry service began
from North Uist to Leverburgh. By the end of 2007 there was a strident
clamour for Sabbath sailing between Stornoway and Ullapool. It was
notable, however, that the proposed service was adamantly opposed by
a majority of local councillors; that CalMac had broken past, repeated
assurances that they would only introduce Sunday services when invited
to do so by Comhairle nan Eilean Siar; that those locally leading the
campaign for them were at pains until late in 2008 to keep their identity
quiet; and that more people – 3,760 – had signed a petition against them,
completed by 27 November 2007 and confined exclusively to Long Island

residents, than had by 5 May 2008 signed a rolling Internet e-petition in demand for them – 1,505, including many people who did not live in the Western Isles, some who did not even live in the country, a heap of anonymous signatures (oxymoronic as that sounds) and dozens who had signed twice, thrice, and in one spectacular instance even four times.

In twenty years there had been evident change. For one, Presbyterial protest was remarkably muted. As of May 2008, only six island ministers had publicly protested against a Stornoway Sunday ferry service and not a single Free Church minister sat on the committee of the local branch of the Lord's Day Observance Society. The Free Church Continuing minister of Stornoway, David Murray, did lead a peaceful 2002 demonstration at Stornoway Airport, as the first Sabbath plane landed to the cheers of a crowing crowd. Few joined them. A few days later, the editor of a Sunday newspaper was tickled when a prominent island minister rang him 'to congratulate us for such balanced coverage.'[15]

Years of awful Free Church publicity in the late 1990s had probably begotten something of a 'Wee Free cringe'. Ministers were no longer eager to engage in public controversy or be identified with stereotypical Free Church stances. Indeed, the present campaign against Stornoway sailings was led by a Church of Scotland minister, Andrew Coghill of Lochs. Free Church clergy were hard worked as it was and battered after a long spell of bitter, personalised strife. Such timidity now reflected the general attitude of their people. Very few laity put their heads over the parapet either. There were other complexities. A good many Free Church people, including several office-bearers, were employed by Caledonian MacBrayne, and Sunday working was routine. On the mainland, pulpit-supply to such Free Church congregations as Strontian and Dunoon took Sabbath ferries to reach them. It was not uncommon for Free Church communicants on the mainland to catch Sunday flights to holidays in the sun,[16] and there were even – unsubstantiated – claims that some on the Long Island have used the ones from Stornoway. There was some anecdotal evidence of an 'alarming erosion of discipline, which (if it continues unchecked) will wreck absolute havoc in short order,' as one young office-bearer lamented by email in November 2007, but that was greatly complicated by the rights of appeal in a Presbyterial order and the return of overt, most subjective anti-Highland sentiments in the wider Free Church, with uncomfortable echoes of the Rainy era.

'Part of the trouble is that because the Free Church was dominated by the Western Isles in the 20th century, we ended up with the ridiculous situation of English psalms being sung in a Gaelic style. It is difficult to think of a more depressing and unedifying noise,'[17] lamented a city minister in September 2007. A month later, reporting an induction in Dunfermline, a Fife colleague was still bolder. 'This leaves us with the question of whether the Free Church is *able* to bring the Gospel to 21st-century urban Scotland? After fourteen years of trying, I think we can, but it is a far more difficult task than we tend to think. Non-Christians think we are too strict: Christians think we are legalistic. Sometimes we are seen as an enclave for exiled Highlanders. If we are to make progress in winning people to Christ, then we have to shatter these misconceptions. People think we are weird not because of our Gospel message but because of the way we speak, sound, dress and act. Chris McCune and his wife Liz, MTW missionaries who worked with us for four years in Dunfermline, did a great job in setting the foundation for a Free Church congregation that will be Gospel-focussed, relevant and open.'[18]

In stark contrast, it could be readily inferred, to an enclave of exiled Highlanders.

In January 1991, all local denominations in Harris had staged a massive joint prayer meeting in Tarbert – in the teeth of an explicit threat by Caledonian MacBrayne, who had timetabled Sunday ferries for that summer. The local Free Church, Free Presbyterian and Church of Scotland ministers united on stage to lead the singing, and men from all denominations took part. With the additional, convincing declaration by Scalpay fishermen that they would not hesitate to blockade a Sunday ferry into port, CalMac plans were subsequently abandoned on the express orders of the Secretary of State for Scotland, Malcolm Rifkind. This was dramatic evidence of the power of Christian unity. By contrast, in 2008, no such meeting has been organised. There are new denominational tensions, admittedly; but the real problem is a general lack of appetite, with the real fear that attendance at such a rally might be derisory.

There was, besides, now vast reverse-migration. Since the 1970s, people had been settling in Lewis and Harris in some number from England and the Scottish Lowlands. From 2001 – amidst a national property boom – it became a flood, even as island-reared youngsters continued to move out in large numbers. A Stornoway solicitor, Ken MacDonald, told one reporter that, in twenty-three years in the business, he had never known anything like it; in the past two months, in midwinter too, he had cleared twenty-five homes, with four more under offer. 'We have had people from as far south as Cornwall. The buyers are mainly from cities wanting to get out,' said MacDonald. 'We have had a lot of English, but also a high percentage of Scots. Unless these people are working from home I don't know where they will be making a living here because in the past employment has been poor.'[19]

Dozens and dozens of southerners duly settled on Lewis and Harris in the twenty-first century, with dramatic impact on house prices and still more on quiet rural communities. One Harris cottage, bought in 1992 for £20,000, sold on in 1995 for £23,000, was sold yet again in 2003 for £79,000. In the spring of 2008, it would be valued in six figures. Some incomers brought young families, initiative and enterprise. Many were older people, consciously 'down-shifting', no longer economically active. Some simply seemed in search of a cheap house. Few attended church, or integrated in any meaningful sense into the local community, and an alarming number made no secret of their contempt for Highland religion and were quick to agitate in the local press for Sabbath amenities.

This was wretchedly demonstrated in the comments of some incomers in the 'e-petition' for Sunday ferries in April 2008. 'The islands need to move with the time. Tesco's must operate 7 days a week and calmac will have to provide a 7 day service to cater for them,' wailed P. Brown Smythe. 'For me sunday is a leisure day for a supermarket shop, bar meal, visit to a art gallery pure heaven and i want it soon. Im not havin a minority dictating what i can and cant do! I came here to enjoy life.'

'As soons as Tescos opens,' burbled 'Stevie n Kara', or perhaps only Stevie, 'im going to get the manager to open on a Sunday. Weve moved from England and couldnt believe theres no shops open. We work Mon-Fri and need the shops open at weekend its our human rights.' 'We want Sunday ferries,' thundered Mick, 'Sunday Golf, Sunday Shopping n Sunday Sport. This is the 21st Century. I moved up from Oxford and demand my civil liberties.' And 'Victor n Margaret' were on their own righteous warpath. 'We had a holiday n Barra and the wee frees came outo church n went to shop n pub after service whats the difference n Lewis n Harris.'[20] The unfathomable, colonial arrogance of such remarks attest to the same, blinkered Englishness that has reduced some of the loveliest Mediterranean resorts to the Costa del Chips, complete with Ye Olde Englishe Pubbe.

That Sunday ferries would change their rural idyll, change it most quickly and change it irrevocably seemed entirely lost on many. News, in April 2008, that Tesco were taking over a Stornoway superstore did not bode well either for the traditional Lewis Sabbath, the company – one of the most aggressive and powerful in Britain – not being noted for its community sensitivities.[21]

By frantic endeavour, and by some deft manoeuvre behind the scenes, officebearers of the local Lord's Day Observance Society and a friendly journalist or two managed to prevent the launch of Sunday sailings from Stornoway in 2008. In May 2009, however – improbably invoking recent equality legislation, and legal advice they flatly refused to make public –

Caledonian MacBrayne announced piously that a Sunday service was now unavoidable, lest they be found in breach of discrimination law. It soon became evident that their position was backed by Scottish Government ministers and neither the local MP or MSP was prepared to make a stand for one side or the other on the issue, a cowardice that disgusted many of their constituents. The local newspaper – which, though its managing director was a Free Church elder, ran a blatant anti-Christian agenda with evident impunity – ran consistently unfair reports, and besides refused to print many letters of protest from island believers (though it happily published even anonymous epistles attacking them.)

Senior LDOS officebearers had retired the previous autumn, and it became pathetically apparent their successors had no real stomach for a serious fight. There was, besides, some denominational mischief-making within its unwieldy structure: the main Committee, for instance, had thirty-two members. A robust media campaign by two volunteers was nevertheless reluctantly sanctioned; a senior Scots advocate also furnished a robust opinion, running rings around CalMac's unconvincing argument. By the European Parliament election early in June, as documents later obtained under Freedom of Information law attest, CalMac managers were in a tizzy and Scottish Government officials in visible panic: the *West Highland Free Press* – which openly supported Sunday ferries, but granted Christians very fair coverage, openly conceded CalMac and their allies had been all but beaten – 'Politically and intellectually, their opponents have run rings around them.' Then – inexplicably – the LDOS shut the campaign completely down.

One West Side minister – the on-duty spokesman of the week – now flatly refused to authorise a proposed press-release: 'I don't want to get into politics here.' The LDOS chose thereafter not to issue any state- ments at all. Though some officials urged others to brave vituperative opposition on, for instance, the letters pages of a local news-website, they conspicuously failed to do so themselves. The new Chairman spent most of those critical weeks off the island at a round of Reformed conferences. The LDOS refused even to contemplate a local referendum (which they might well have won; significantly, Sunday ferry campaigners quite opposed any sort of poll) or apply for 'declarator' at the Court of Session on CalMac's dubious argument in law – squandering, through weeks of sloth and timidity, priceless advantages in the new 2009 situation. It did not take long for the authorities to recover the initiative. On 13 July 2009 – at just five days' notice – Caledonian MacBrayne announced Sunday sailings for the looming weekend, coinciding with the end of the Hebridean Celtic Festival and the departure of hundreds of visitors. Practically every Free Church minister was inexplicably off the island; the dreadful chore of braving cameras and reporters and explaining things to distant London radio shows fell almost exclusively on sturdy Free Presbyterians. The scenes that Sabbath afternoon on Stornoway Pier were, by all accounts, a gruesome circus, with smug CalMac directors, a mighty media presence, and even a piper or two. Worshippers in town that morning had already braved TV cameras outside church. Amidst the general triumphalism, one grizzled incomer strutted about in a specially printed T-shirt – 'LDOS – Let's Drink On Sundays in Ullapool!!!' As she finally backed out from the pier, to great cheering, the *Isle of Lewis* joyously blasted her whistle, in final and gratuitous contempt for Christian sentiment. There was entire silence from the local LDOS Chairman, save – two days before the first Sunday sailing – to post details of his holiday reading on his blog. Four days afterwards, he added a photograph of himself in John Calvin's Swiss pulpit, posed fetchingly in a Geneva gown.

By the end of 2002 it became evident that some schoolchildren in the Free Church congregation of Leverburgh had been converted and were earnest, enthusiastic Christians. A similar development was evident in Shawbost, where a Scripture Union group was formed in the village school. By the summer of 2005 evidence of a widespread spiritual movement among island schoolchildren – or at least widespread religious interest and an eagerness to become church members – could no longer be ignored. One or two lads who had professed faith, some as young as fifteen, emerged as forceful precentors, and by the end of 2006 nearly a hundred pupils at the Nicolson Institute flocked to meetings of the Scripture Union – approaching a tenth of the entire school roll. At times the school authorities struggled to cope.

At an Easter 2006 assembly in the Nicolson Institute, led by two senior pupils who were both Free Church communicants, the Gospel message was sincerely outlined. The lads were then blind-sided by an unexpected question. Did those who refused to believe in Jesus go at last to Hell? Well, yes, they replied nervously – and were fast summoned to the Rector's office, at the behest of one or two agitated teachers. No action was taken as, after all, the boys had only answered a question and had at no point been told by anyone they could not speak of eternal punishment. A fair point could be made to them – attendance at school assembly was obligatory; attendance at Scripture Union was voluntary, and what is said must reflect that sensitively – but the incident greatly disturbed many adult believers who heard of it, and remembered better days in island schools, to say nothing of what is still notionally a Christian country with a national Church and a sworn, Protestant Queen.[22]

All over Lewis, children began to appear at the midweek prayer meeting, to forsake former ways, to appear before kirk sessions seeking church membership. Children as young as eleven or twelve were admitted. Crowds of them went round the island Communion circuit, most formally dressed, jostling and enthusiastic. They filled entire pews at the Communion Table itself, as grizzled old adherents looked on in bemusement. In assorted gatherings at houses, on such sacramental occasions, they hunkered on the floor, squashed into sofas, said very little and listened a great deal. A striking feature of the awakening was the very high proportion of boys. Around half the new Christians were male – a marked contrast to many previous movements (though not Carloway in the 1930s) and in some congregations, such as Cross, boys seemed to be in the majority.

There were undoubted lapses. Some followed this tide, and then turned back, including one or two who had been admitted to membership. A significant element who carried on seemed determined to push certain Christian boundaries, in their society and amusements. One or two could be abominably rude. Christian parents could privately attest that Christian teenagers are no less prone to mood swings, insubordination, grunts, sulks and door slamming. The grounds of conflict changed, though: demands to be allowed out to a dubious dance becoming, for instance, a demand to attend a Christian youth evening event in Stornoway, as opposed to mucking out the byre or catching up on Higher modern studies homework.

The pages of young professing Christians on such social networking websites as Bebo[23] – which quickly became a very popular facility for contact and mutual support – are occasionally marred by aggressive exchanges, suggestive banter and, at times, frankly appalling language. However, the format of such websites in themselves, with opportunity to store music tracks and video-clips, to say nothing of novelties still more incomprehensible to anyone old enough to remember even the Thatcher government – is Pro Evo a person, a pop-group or a pill? – will inevitably make members appear much more flippant and materialist than they actually are. Few adolescents have secure self-awareness or much integration between a 'cool' public persona and a private, serious, vulnerable one.

It is also vital to remember that the pressures on twenty-first-century teenagers – if very different – are no less crushing than those of, say, the 1980s. Educational pressure, for instance, has actually increased. Most important of all, a child has 'childish piety'; and a teenager will have teenage piety; it is absurd to expect a boy of sixteen to have the attitudes and habits of an experienced, middle-aged deacon. The most that might

be said of young island believers is that they seem very Americanised in
their interests and even in their religion, readily blending avowed spiritual
commitment with, for instance, a taste for popular music and participation in competitive sports. And most adults might tacitly admit to a
certain, real envy of the young, at the very gate of their careers, looks
unsullied, infinite possibilities before them, untrammelled by mistakes
and regret – a phenomenon psychologists call the 'omnipotentiality' of
youth, which the older tacitly resent.

There were disconcerting aspects of the religious movement among
Long Island teenagers, Bebo lapses apart; though the picture was
complicated by the real difficulty, in some Christian social situations,
of ascertaining which milling youngsters, high on home-baking and cans
of pop, were professing Christians and which were not. Some were
conspicuously respectful of, for instance, ministers and office-bearers; but
there is an important difference between deference and humility. Besides,
by quiet consensus through the island, it was very rare for a teenage male
member to be asked to pray in public or even in a home, making it hard
for many to take the measure of their faith and their experience.

For a time the boisterous horseplay of some young male communicants
in public – jostling on a manse sofa, shoving one another and pinching –
caused acrid comment. What most alarmed folk – especially those who
went to speak at youth fellowships and so on – was the ready use of
mobile phones, Sabbath or no Sabbath, whipped from pockets, perched
on thighs, beeping ominously at intervals. 'I found myself wondering
if they were texting each other about what I was saying,' worried one
elder in March 2008. There was also, perhaps inevitable among believers
so young, little grasp of theological decorum. It is by no means uncommon to find such an online profile declaring, 'I recently became
a Christian – best decision I ever made,' not quite in the full-orbed glory
of the decrees of Calvinism. Fatuous remarks were occasionally made
to those who had just become members – 'You went forward!!!!
CONGRATULATIONS!!!!! xxx . . .' adorned the odd Bebo page.

When one did get to know some, though, they emerged generally as
anxious, conscientious people, struggling to find their bearings, who had
not lightly come out on Christ's side. One lad, who duly 'went forward',
had first attended the prayer meeting only a few days before, though he
had been following on the Communion circuit for months. He had
agonised until getting the mind and the will to leave a local rock-group –
he was a talented guitarist – and would not make a public move until he
had done so, lest he give unconverted friends traction to mock his religion.
This sort of conscientiousness was typical. And they had quite different
taboos to a past generation. Some liked playing cards, but they detested

smoking and often opposed even temperate alcohol use. Their enthusiasm for competitive sports and listening to popular music would have won strong objection from office-bearers in the 1980s and been unthinkable, as pursuits for professing island Christians, in the 1960s. Attendance at an organised dance within the island culture, or at a commercial rock-concert anywhere, does raise legitimate questions even in 2008.

But Christian veterans took tenderly to many of the new arrivals. First, 'they have enormous affection for another,' said a Ballalan elder. 'I was seeing them at Back Communion the other weekend – so-and-so had just gone forward, and there was a tremendous, a very tactile bond between them all, a sense that they are looking out for one another.' Anecdotal evidence confirmed that, in their own way, the new believers ran quite a doughty system of church discipline, rebuking offenders, trying to encourage backsliders, appalled if someone fell into bad company or spectacular scandal. Second, they were determined evangelists, eager to present an honest but appealing impression of their faith to classmates, fellow-apprentices and so on. Many had to endure real harassment – a surprising number of the new converts did not come from Christian homes – and Christian boys, especially (who by definition do not go about 'wenching', to use the island expression) were often horribly taunted, flippant references to homosexuality being generally a Bebo obsession.

This teenage trend was not universal. There were few such conversions in North Harris or Scalpay, and some congregations were more affected than others. There was also a marked lack of hysteria. There were no *cliobadaich*; swayings, swoonings, melodrama; though the hysterical public prayer delivery of one habitué of the Long Island Communion circuit – a breathless, ranting stream-of-consciousness – was affected sometimes by one or two teenage lads. Though they favoured English services, the young converts loved Gaelic psalm-singing and protested at Shawbost, in September 2006, when a Communion Table service did not feature it. (The presiding minister could not read Gaelic psalms, nor announce them.) The movement was not associated, as far as can be judged, with particular places, particular preachers or particular events.

Not everyone approved. There was that real if muted fear that religion had simply become fashionable. It is also much easier than it was, even two decades ago, to 'go forward' in Lewis, with examination generally brief and benevolent, refusal almost unheard of and discipline provoked only by sexual misbehaviour or criminal conduct.[24] Every true revival sees some degree of false conversion – precisely because religion, in that locality, has become the trend of the hour – and it would certainly be wise to wait a few years and see how these young people stand, not least as students in the big city. Schoolchildren in a close rural community, still under parental supervision, are seldom free to indulge in certain public sins, and the tramlines of professing Christian conduct in the Hebrides are as much social as ecclesiastical, reinforced by the ungodly as well as elders.

There had besides been a significant flood of very young communicants in the early 1980s – part of a wider trend across the whole Free Church, closely linked at that time to its summer youth camp programme – and the later declension had been appalling, many communicants simply apostatising on the mainland, one or two even emerging in the media openly to traduce their own spiritual culture. One son of the manse anxiously wondered, by email in April 2008, 'Has the understanding of conversion itself changed in Lewis in recent decades? . . . The formula of praying to "ask Jesus into your life" has been standard practice in the Scripture Union and Christian Union and evangelical churches in general in the last thirty years. It may well have been an experience some had on the road to the Cross, but is praying it actually conversion? Was there a tendency to see a sincere rendition of that prayer as automatically making you saved? Taken on its own, it doesn't fit well with the doctrine of effectual calling or the sovereignty of God.' Such 'easy-believism' is dominant in America and Duncan Campbell left more than a trace of it behind.

There were also, now, besides, new elements in the island religious scene – some small Charismatic groups, and a freelance Stornoway youth fellowship or two, under no congregational oversight. And there was a new Stornoway group called Stand In The Gap,[25] which claimed only to want to encourage closer fellowship between young believers of all churches with such events as a regular 'Big Breakfast' and Christian rock-music gigs called 'Xtreme' – which, in Stand In The Gap website media, sound exactly like any live rock-music event, in all its matchless ignobility. Stand In The Gap does seem – from what one hears of its events or can make out from its website – to emphasise a distinctly dumbed-down religion focused on fellowship, 'testimony' and very so-phisticated modern Christian music with booming backings and exuber-ant physical response. Even a Free Church minister well disposed to it concedes the fellowship is 'mildly Charismatic'. It was legitimately feared by others.

In December 2006, a 'praise-night' held in a rural community centre was certainly unconventional. Though carols were clearly advertised on the posters adorning local shops, only two traditional Christmas hymns were actually sung. Young women presided, and led in prayer. A minister in jeans gave a short talk. An older lady, with evident unease, stood and gave her 'testimony'. Schoolboys, an elder and a young crofter precented some psalms. A Christian rock-group performed some noisy items after much time fumbling with speakers, cables and mikes. There were a great many most modern 'choruses', with a ferocious digital soundtrack and pounding beat, which few over twenty seemed to know. A few hands floated in the air like the fronds of a hungry sea anemone, and one young woman made extraordinary noises, which may, or may not have been, speaking in tongues. This remarkable spiritual *smorgasbord* – something for every conceivable Christian tradition on Lewis, save Exposition of the Blessed Sacrament – attended largely by young people, some curious seniors, some bored women, typified Stand In The Gap, all love and cuddles, until you criticised it.

A simple questionnaire was emailed about a large group of island ministers in March 2008.[26] They generally took a positive view of the Bebo generation. 'I cannot comment on children outwith our own group,' observed one, 'but I know that at our Communions the children have visited the elders' homes and have fellowshipped with older Christians. We are going through our fourth Christianity Explored course . . . and we have a good mixture of old and young in our group. The discipleship of our young folk is vital. It is not about bringing in numbers but building up those children who have been converted in the faith to prepare them for the future. There may be boundary issues, but how will they know if they are not taught? I can only speak for our children here, but I believe that they are pretty level-headed, if you know what I mean.' A colleague noted a tendency for young people not to mix with older believers, 'but I think this is simply symptomatic of the fact that our society, as well as the church at large, has been attempting over the last couple of decades to place the children in the nursery with nanny.' 'Our boys,' said an older minister proudly, 'are conservative in their outlook and dress and, as far as I can see, very appreciative of Biblical teaching.' As to sheep-stealing religious influences, 'our young people here are aware of these influences and want no part of them'.

One Lewis pastor mused,

> I think that these young people are keener to bring the Gospel to their unsaved neighbours, whether at school or in the communities, than the previous generations of young people have been, so it may be that their engagement with 'the world' is perceived as being beyond acceptable boundaries. It is also the case that perceptions have changed (rightly or wrongly) in regard to what one wears to church, the extent to which believers may participate in social activities like 'ceilidhs' etc., and this no doubt gives rise to the view that these young people are too 'worldly'. I am concerned that certain groups . . . seem to be minimising doctrinal distinctives for the sake of outward unity with other groups such as our

own young people. This is one reason why the Presbytery were keen to set
up the course of 'discipling' meetings which have been held throughout the
winter. However, I have been glad to learn of our own young people's
awareness of this and on occasion how they have seen fit to leave a meeting
where events took on an unacceptable turn . . . a meeting in Stornoway at
which certain Charismatic phenomena were being practised, causing a
number of Free Church young people who were in attendance to leave.

He insisted besides that he had repeatedly asked groups for their views on
present Lewis worship – no instruments; Psalms only – and on every
occasion there 'was an endorsement of our current practice in the Free
Church'.

One man thought 'there was definitely an openness to consider
subjective experiences, but as you know this has always been a feature
of Highland piety'. He felt there was a 'greater commitment nowadays on
the part of the church to young people's development whilst growing up'.
Certainly, in the 1980s, there was a serious want of such mentoring and in
the 1970s open hostility even to congregational youth fellowships – which
Kenneth MacRae himself had always deplored.

The worries of another island clergyman, though, were evident in 2008.
'There are those who appear quite content restricting fellowship to their
own peer-group, and this is quite disturbing. Engagement with the world
is certainly an area of concern! For some, lifestyle is largely no different to
the life of the ungodly and the faithless. "I could see no difference
between them" is a not uncommon reaction in certain social situations.
This is always a difficult area to deal with and that sometimes results in a
reluctance to address certain issues. Inconsistency of instruction on the
part of the church in this area often leads to confusion and the church
needs to guard itself against . . . "making gods of our young people."'
There were, he thought, 'predatory influences around. The whole Stand
In The Gap movement along with its Xtreme events poses a real threat to
the stability and development of the young people. In a music-driven
generation such events are a powerful attraction and young people (and
older people) can get sucked into a charismatic, Pentecostal environment
without realising it.'

A colleague agreed, besides, that 'para-church groups and movements
have always been difficult to domesticate within local congregational life. If
there is one thing that has frustrated me personally, it is that most of my
preaching at Communion seasons has been in Gaelic, but few of the young
people have frequented Gaelic services. No doubt they are the better for not
having heard me preach, but that is not my point; it seems that few of the
local ministers have been heard or appreciated by the new Communion-

going generation, only because most of the English preachers on such occasions are from the mainland.' He added that 'one or two have not gone on in the faith, and have either lapsed or were not genuinely converted at all . . . a feature of revivals in the past, however much it has gone unreported . . . the sudden growth in our young membership was entirely unexpected,' but resulted 'in a reviving of local churches; that is to say, it encouraged those who were already members, young or old.'

It was widely observed, too, that a high proportion of the new Christians were exceptionally gifted, resourceful young people of strong personality. Quite a few were intensely committed to Gaelic and to Gaelic skills. One 16-year-old boy, practically in the course of a weekend, read a great Victorian volume of Spurgeon on homiletics. They had brains. They had spirit. And – yes – they were different to us, these pink, be-suited Communion goers, with their MSN messaging and Bebo skins that said things like 'Carlsberg don't do miracles, but if they did Celtic still wouldn't win the League.' What might they live to see, these pensioners of the 2060s, in a Britain where hatred for Christianity is increasingly strident?

In March 2007, one of these young believers sent a Bebomail. 'I have been enabled to see much of the sin within my own heart and beyond, within my heart of hearts also. It feels as if God has lifted much of the veil towards the secrets of my own heart . . . I personally have had my foundations dug up, and I've gone through enough of a variety of experiences, which I can look deeply into at all times whether they be extreme situations or simple ones, that makes me joyful at the work the Lord has done in my own heart. I rub my toes in anticipation and delight when I think of what's to come in the future, and I hope to be led by God wherever He wants me to go . . .'

Around 1877, in a place called Lingwick in the Canadian province of Quebec, a frail old man, Malcolm MacLeod, struggled out to the Friday fellowship meeting of the Highland Communion season. MacLeod, *Calum 'ic Thormoid* of Gress in Lewis, had in about 1820 gone out with his brother to hear Finlay Munro preach. They were both converted and they both, in these strained and difficult island decades, had emigrated to Canada. Though failing and forgetful, a half-century on, Malcolm MacLeod had a precious opportunity to hear again Daniel Gordon – the previous minister of Lingwick and to whom he was much attached – at this Communion, and insisted on coming out on this occasion, escorted by his wife and by Angus Morrison of Dell, who would voyage home to his native island the following year.

Gordon recognised the venerable old Christian and called on him to 'speak to the question'. Mrs MacLeod, frightened what her husband's wandering wits might come out with, tried firmly to hold him down even as Angus Morrison tried to help him up, and had to be sharply rebuked by the minister.

So *Calum 'ic Thormoid* with difficulty rose, and haltingly spoke.

'When I was young in Lewis, word came to the village one day that a service was to be held by a lad who was going about with a Bible. As the others were going to the service I followed them, and sat on the outer circle of the congregation. As the boy began to preach I became so enthralled by his teaching that I could not hold back my tears. As he went on I edged nearer and nearer to him, until at last – *shil mi uisge mo chinn, agus an ni a thòisich annam-sa an latha ud ann an Grias cha do dh'fhàg e riamh mi, agus chan fhàg ann an tìm na anns an t-sìorruidheachd* – I had shed a bowl-full of tears and found myself at his feet, and the work that began in my heart that day in Gress has not yet stopped, nor will it stop in time or in eternity.'[27]

Appendix 1

An Early, Important Article on Gaelic Psalmody

Rev. Donald Beaton (1939)

The psalmody of the Scottish Gael presents two distinctive features:
1. The ancient custom of 'reading the line' is still retained in such, and at
once arrests the attention of a stranger; 2. The tunes also, especially the
long ones, though known as Dundee, Elgin, French, London, Martyrs and
Stilt, are quite distinctive. The custom of 'reading the line', though now
almost wholly confined to the Highlands, had its origin elsewhere, and has
a history of its own. To hear the 'reading of the line' to full advantage, one
has to be present in a Highland congregation on the hillside during the
services of a Communion season. It is then, if a master of music is reading
the praise, and the people solemnised under the preaching of the Word, one
hears the 'reading of the line' to the best advantage. The plaintive musical
intonation of each line, before it is sung, has an impressive effect.

For the sake of those who have never heard that there was even such a
custom, a word or two of explanation may be given. According to the
present practice, after reading a few verses of a Psalm, the preacher
announces the number of verses to be sung, then reads the first line or
two. The precentor then rises, raises the tune, and the whole congregation
follow him until he comes to the end of the first or second line, as the case
may be. Then the congregation cease singing, while he chants with
musical intonation the words of the next line; the congregation again join
in with him and sing the line, and so on to the end of the verses given out
by the minister. In some places in the Highlands, the precentor reads two
lines at a time, but the ordinary practice was to read only one. So linked is
this custom with Gaelic psalm-singing that a Highlander can scarcely
conceive of Gaelic psalmody without it. It is a custom to which Highlanders cling tenaciously, though, strange to say, it came to Scotland from
England, and when introduced into Scotland it was only under certain
provisional conditions. The earliest reference to 'reading the line' is to be

found in Quick's 'Synodicon', where mention is made of a decree of the
French Synod of Figeac (1579), forbidding the churches which 'in singing
Psalms do first cause each verse to be read,' to continue 'that childish
custom' – the Huguenots reading each verse instead of each line. In the
Westminster Assembly the matter came under discussion during the
preparation of the 'Directory for Public Worship,' and from Lightfoot's
testimony it is evident, the Scottish Commissioners, at least Mr Henderson, disliked the clause giving permission to read the Psalm, line by line.
The matter was then referred to the Scottish Commissioners, and it is
probably owing to their influence that the Westminster *Directory of Public
Worship* reference is guardedly provisional.

'But for the present,' are its terms, 'where many in the congregation
cannot read, it is convenient that the minister, or some other fit person
appointed by him and the other ruling officers, do read the Psalm, line by
line, before the singing thereof.' The English Parliament sanctioned the
custom. In 1746, the General Assembly of the Church of Scotland took the
matter in hand and recommended that in private worship, families in
'singing the praises of God, go on without the intermission of reading the
line.' But it was in the Secession Churches that the real 'battle of the line'
was fought out. In the Army also the practice was honoured, in the
Highland regiments at any rate. It is related in the *Scots Brigade in Holland*,
that one of the chaplains in carrying out the instructions of the General
Assembly had discontinued the practice. The colonel at once gave orders
that the custom should be continued. The chaplain sent a respectful note, in
which he reminds the colonel in as gentle a way as he could, that he was
going out of his sphere. 'It will give us pleasure,' says the chaplain, 'to be
informed that you are satisfied with our conduct, though as a session, we
conceived that we were only accountable to a superior Court.'

The custom thus introduced through the Westminster *Directory* was
finally adopted in the Highlands, when the Gaels accepted Presbyterianism. In Gaelic psalmody, the custom was almost a necessity, owing to the
fact that the people could not read at the time. Even in the English services
in the northern counties, 'the reading of the line' continued until recent
times, and may be heard in some congregations in Caithness and Sutherland to this day, especially in those connected with the Free Presbyterian
Church. In the Gaelic services the 'line' is always read, and any attempt to do
away with the custom would probably cause trouble.

The other distinctive feature of Gaelic Psalmody mentioned was the
'long tunes'. These are rarely, if ever, heard now. Many attempts have
been made to explain the origin of these tunes, but none of the
explanations are altogether satisfactory. It has been said, that they are
relics of the Columban Church services; another theory is, that they were

brought to Scotland by Highland soldiers who served under Gustavus Adolphus. Probably the best explanation is that given by Mr MacBean, in his 'Highland Psalm Tunes'. 'Perhaps,' he says, 'the truth is, that these sacred strains are based on the common Psalm Tunes whose names they bear, and whose principal notes they generally retain; though, in accordance with the sombre and meditative mood of the Gael, the music has been lengthened out and elaborated, until its whole spirit and character is changed, and we have in effect new tunes.'

These tunes have different versions – Inverness-shire, Ross, Caithness and Sutherland having versions of their own. The different versions have from time to time been published; Mr MacBean – already referred to – has printed these old tunes in his 'Highland Psalm Tunes' with the other psalm-tunes sung by the Gael; these were reprinted in his 'Songs and Hymns of the Gael' (Eneas Mackay, Stirling, 1900.) Mainzer also deals with them in his 'Gaelic Psalmody of Ross-shire and Neighbouring Counties'. In 1856 William James Pasley Kidd issued his *Chorister's Text-Book containing Selections from the Psalmody of the Lowlands and Highlands and Islands of Scotland.* The work was dedicated to the Duke of Sutherland. Sutherland and Caithness and Inverness-shire and Ross-shire versions are given of Old French, Old Stilt, Old London, Old Elgin, Old Dundee, and Old Martyrs. Prof Kidd says of these Long Tunes: 'When the scale on which they are constructed is properly understood, and when heard in their beauty and simplicity, devoutly performed at a sacramental occasion by thousands of worshippers assembled in the open air, those competent to appreciate them will admit that they stand unrivalled. And lovers of sacred melody will concur with me in thinking that these relics of the ancient church of our forefathers, now rendered palpable by art, cannot be revered enough.' In 1910 the Free Church issued an edition of the Scottish Psalmody to which is appended *Seann Fhuinn nan Salm mar tha iad air an Seinn anns a Gaidhealtachd mu Thuath* [Old Psalm Tunes Sung in the North Highlands] taken down by T.L. Hately, precentor of the General Assembly of the Free Church of Scotland. These contain the versions of some of the tunes as sung in Ross-shire, Inverness-shire and Sutherland. Appended to the *Seann Fhuin* is the Sutherland version of the Six Long Gaelic Psalm Tunes taken down in 1909 from the singing of the Rev. Donald Munro, Ferintosh, by Mr W.F. Whitehead, ARCO, ARCM.

Free Presbyterian Magazine Vol. XLIV (May 1939), pp. 14–18.

Rev. Donald Beaton (1872–1953), born in Kilsyth, Stirlingshire, was one of the '1892 Students' who abandoned New College after the Free Church General Assembly passed the Declaratory Act, and subsequently adhered to the Free Presbyterian Church of Scotland at its formation in 1893. Unlike most who signed that bond – Alexander Stewart; John MacLeod; George MacKay; Alexander MacRae; John R. MacKay among them – he did not return to the Free Church after the Declaratory Act was repealed, and spent his entire career in Free Presbyterian service, being their theological tutor for a remarkable fifty-four years, editing the *Free Presbyterian Magazine* for quarter of a century, toiling as Clerk of Synod, making a heroic effort to learn Gaelic, and during the Second World War twice braving the U-boats to preach in Canada; all this on top of pastorates in Wick and Oban.

A noted scholar, his important works include a definitive paper on the 1720s' 'Marrow Controversy' – a theological row in the Kirk which gave birth to the Secession Church; a rare, much sought *Ecclesiastical History of Caithness* and a scrupulous series of biographical essays later published as *Noted Ministers of the Northern Highlands*. Mr Beaton – like MacLeod, Stewart and MacKay – should have died as a Doctor of Divinity.

Appendix 2

The Origin and Etiquette of Fellowship Meetings

Dr Donald Munro (c.1930)

Though I cannot lay hands on your letter, I can recall two queries it contained.

The first was with regard to the origin of the Fellowship Meetings in the Highlands. Many think they began during the ministry of Mr Hog in Kiltearn, and I am inclined to believe that such a commonly accepted opinion has a good basis of truth. In the life of Hog by the Free Church Publications Committee, shortly after the Disruption, it is stated that during his student days in Aberdeen Hog and some pious students had private meetings for prayer and conference and found them profitable. And is it not conceivable that on his settlement in Kiltearn, after souls were brought under the power of the truth, he should set up such meetings for the comfort and instruction of exercised people?

In Caithness, Sutherland and Easter Ross, and in the eastern glens of Inverness-shire and Nairnshire, there were private Saturday meetings at 12 noon. They were of a semi-private nature, for they were not open to all. Communicants could attend, but others were not admitted unless recommended by some of the leading 'Men' in the district. In some parishes there were two or three or more of such meetings, where they that led in prayer were specially seeking a blessing on the services of the Sabbath.

As to your second query, whether it was customary for the men to read the words of the Question before beginning to speak, I can give you a very definite answer. In the Gaelic-speaking parishes of Caithness, in Suther-land and part, at least, of Easter Ross and, I believe, in some of the glens of Inverness-shire, such a thing was unknown till the FP movement of 1893, and the Union of 1900. I venture to say without fear of contra-diction that no Gaelic-speaking native of Caithness, and no native of

Sutherland, ever did such a thing as to read the words of the Question before speaking, till 1893 or 1900. The thing was absolutely unknown.

My own firm conviction is that *Maighstir Fein* [Mr Self] was at the bottom of it. In the old days many of the 'worthies' were illiterate, and, of course, could not read. Then 'Maighstir Fein' had an opportunity of making a display, and might suggest to some that could read – 'Why not let the congregation see that you can read, and so you can move on a higher plane than those illiterate men.' The innovation began. Then in process of time, one and one followed, till eventually it came to be believed that it was inseparably connected with the Fellowship Meeting, and that it was the proper thing to do, whereas it was an uncalled-for innovation, which some of the outstanding ministers of the past would not tolerate.

Dr Aird [Gustavus Aird, FCoS, Creich] and others of the worthies of a past generation used to relate how effectively the great Mr Forbes [William Forbes], Tarbat, dealt with a conceited man, who seemingly had been in the south for a short time and wished to make a show on the Friday at Tarbat Communion. The large congregation met in the open air. After a number had spoken this man was called. Instead of giving marks of a work of grace, as he was supposed to do, he imagined he could throw all the preceding speakers into the shade by showing his powers of sermonising, and so he began by saying, *'Anns a' cheud aite,'* ['In the first place,'] Mr Forbes, in the tent, gave unmistakable signs of being displeased. The speaker went on to expatiate on his first head and then he announced his second head – *'Anns an daradh aite,'* ['In the second place,'], whereupon Mr Forbes got up in the tent but restrained himself. After holding forth for some time, the speaker came to his third head, when he said, 'Anns an treas aite,' ['In the third place,']. That was too much for Mr Forbes who brought down his ponderous fist on the book-board of the tent as he turned to the speaker, and said in stentorian tones, *'Anns a cheud aite, anns an daraidh aite, anns an treas aite ni thusa suidh,'* ['In the first place, in the second place and in the third place you will sit down now.']

The old fathers of the North objected to this innovation because:

It unduly prolonged the service, and thus when very many speakers were present it prevented some very worthy men from being heard. I have been at Question Meetings in Ross-shire, and the unnecessary time that some spent after being called till they actually began to speak to the Question was such that some of the good men of the past could have spoken to the Question and sat down in the time they took to the introductory part. They would try their pockets for their spectacles, then there was the opening of their cases, adjusting their glasses, looking for the passage, turning over the leaves of the Bible and then reading.

There is a well-founded tradition of a Communion in Golspie on the east coast of Sutherlandshire when 31 men from the parish of Farr alone spoke to the Question, and from the many other parishes that were represented from the county, and from Caithness and Ross-shire, more than another 31 men could have been called. Of course, reading of the Question was then unknown, but if all the speakers had adopted the modern way, it would have given bare time to the first 31 men to speak, let alone the other 30 or 40 more that followed. I had this information in my student days from a fine woman whose pious mother was present, more than 120 years ago.

A second objection the fathers had to this innovation was that it was a transgression of the 'marching orders', if one should use that term. The presiding minister never says to the speaker, *'Eiribh agus leughaibh an earran,'* but *'Eiribh, agus labhraidh ris a' Cheist,'* [never 'Rise and read the portion,' but 'Rise, and speak to the Question.']

Then this innovation might be regarded as a kind of reflection on the minister that opened the Question, as if he had not properly read the words of the Question.

In Sutherland, if a third minister spoke in the middle of the service, besides the minister that opened and the minister that concluded, he did not read the passage, nor sermonise. I remember a Communion in Rogart when many men and four ministers at least, besides the minister of the congregation, were present. Rev. Dugald Matheson, a Skye man, then in Kiltearn, was asked to speak in the middle and he neither read, nor made an attempt to give a lecture or sermon but gave briefly marks of them that were new creatures.

I am sorry to say that on the east coast of Sutherland, the innovation has been introduced since 1893 to some extent, I believe, among the younger Free Presbyterians, for a number of strangers at that time came from parts of the west coast of Ross-shire and they had the preliminary reading. Of course the good old men of Sutherland, who joined the FP Church, never would think of reading, but after they were called away, the younger FP speakers were so accustomed to see the men from Ross-shire read that some of them that were very young in the FP movement came to imagine that it was the proper thing for them to read.

The same thing has happened in the Free Church since 1900, and for the same reason. Men from Ross-shire began to attend Free Church Communions and they read. By and by the young Sutherland men, after the removal of the old local worthies, who, of course, did not read, were so accustomed to the innovation that they came to think that it was the proper thing to read.

Then also, for a number of years, nearly all the Free Church ministers in the east coast of Sutherland have been comparatively young men, belonging to districts where this innovation has prevailed, and so they naturally do not discourage it. The old way prevailed in the parish of Farr, for no strangers from Ross-shire attended the Communion there to introduce the innovation and as the minister, Mr Angus MacKay, once in Snizort, is a native of Farr, he would not encourage this new fashion.

The new style is now almost the order of the day in Lewis though I remember some of the good old men in Lewis of a past generation who had the North Country way, that is, they never read.

It was a pleasing surprise to me to see a few years ago a nice old man from Lewis, who stayed with his family for two or three years in Dingwall, follow the old way in the Burn of Ferintosh. And it was not because he could not read, for he was a missionary in Tarbert, Harris.

The same was true of some of the old men of Skye. Walter MacKay, of course, was a native of Sutherland, but Donald MacKendrie, a native of Strath and long a colporteur [a travelling agent distributing Christian literature] in Farr. I often heard him on a Friday and, I remember, he never read.

There was another habit that was once common in some of the large gatherings in Sutherland, Easter Ross and parts of Inverness-shire, and that was to have two Questions on the Friday at the same meeting. That gave variety to the speaking and then it had another advantage. If one of the outstanding speakers such as Sandy Gair, etc. were to 'give out' the first Question, he was not supposed to speak on that Question but he was free to do so at the second. There was a break in the middle of the service and the man that 'gave out' the first Question was called to pray. After singing, another Question was called for and opened and the same minister, as a rule, was asked to close the two Questions. That continued to my boyhood.

Now if I have been slow in answering your questions I have tried to make amends by the length of this letter.

This letter, probably written in the early 1930s, is addressed to Alexander MacAskill (1873–1965), an eminent elder and resident lay-agent of the Free Church of Scotland, born in Glen Brittle, Skye, and who spent most of his long life at Drynoch on that island, by Rev. Donald Munro DD (1860–1937). I have extracted it from a rare pamphlet, Kenneth J. MacLeay, *Alexander MacAskill*, Beauly, 1968.

Notes

1 Last Stronghold – Religion, Landscape and Pre-History

1. *Aspects of the Religious History of Lewis Up To the Disruption of 1843*, Rev. Murdo MacAulay, Stornoway, 1985. *An Eaglais Shaor Ann An Leodhas 1843–1900*, An t-Urr. Domhnall MacGilliosa, Knox Press, Edinburgh, 1979.
2. Obituary of Finlay Thomson from the *Free Presbyterian Magazine*, Vol. 112, May 2007, p. 149.
3. *Togail Tir: Marking Time – The Map of the Western Isles*, ed. Finlay MacLeod, Acair Ltd and An Lanntair Gallery, Stornoway, 1989; 'Early 19th Century Estate Plans', James B. Caird, pp. 49–77, for details of Harris boundary dispute.
4. *The Islands of Western Scotland – The Inner and Outer Hebrides*, W.H. Murray, Eyre Methuen, London, 1973.
5. *The Outer Hebrides – The Shaping of the Islands*, Stewart Angus, The White Horse Press, Cambridge, 1997.
6. *The Outer Hebrides – Moor and Machair*, Stewart Angus, The White Horse Press, Cambridge, 2001.
7. Obituary of Oighrig MacLean, *Free Presbyterian Magazine*, April 1932, Vol. 36, p. 492.
8. *Nis Aosmhor – The Photographs of Dan Morrison*, Acair Ltd, Stornoway, 1997. Seonaid or Jessie Gunn of Knockaird died in February 1961 in her hundredth year. Her son, Donald, *Am Patch*, dying late in 1990, outlived all but two other *Iolaire* survivors.
9. *The Teampall at Northton and the Church at Scarista*, Bill Lawson, Bill Lawson Publications, Northton, Isle of Harris, 1993.
10. *The County of Inverness – The Third Statistical Account of Scotland, Vol. XVI*, ed. Hugh Barron, Scottish Academic Press, Edinburgh, 1985. 'The Parish of Harris', pp. 562–589, Revs. Norman MacDonald and Murdo MacLeod, etc., updated by Rev. D.A. MacRae.
11. I have stuck to W.H. Murray's dating, placing Mesolithic activity no earlier than 3000 BC and Callanish not much earlier than 1800 BC. But see *The Archaeology of Skye and the Western Isles*, Ian Armit, Edinburgh University Press, Edinburgh, 1996.
12. *New Light on the Standing Stones of Callanish*, Gerald and Margaret Ponting, Callanish, 1984. Mrs Ponting is now married to Ron Curtis. *The Ancient Monuments of the Western Isles – A Visitor's Guide to the Principle Historic Sites and Monuments*, Noel Fojut, Denys Pringle and Bruce Walker, Historic Scotland, 2003.
13. *The Outer Hebrides and Their Legends*, Otta Swire, London, 1966.
14. *Calanais – The Standing Stones*, Patrick Ashmore, Urras nan Tursachan Ltd, Stornoway, 1995.

15. *Calanais*, ed. Ken Kennedy and Roddy Murray, An Lanntair, Stornoway, 1995. Especially the essays by Kenneth White, Iain Crichton Smith, Duncan MacMillan and Ron and Margaret Curtis.
16. *Callanish and Other Megalithic Sites of the Outer Hebrides*, Gerald Ponting, Wooden Books, 2002 (2nd edn 2007), Glastonbury.
17. See important entry, 'Paganism, survivals of' by Anne Ross in *The Companion to Gaelic Scotland*, ed. Derick S. Thomson, Gairm Publications, Glasgow, 2nd edition 1994.
18. Shawbost anecdotes from Angus J. Mitchell, *Aonghas Seorais*, b.1920; Jean MacIver, *Sine* Badhach, b.1912.
19. For Old New Year details, see *Pilgrim Souls*, Mary and Hector MacIver, Aberdeen University Press, Aberdeen, 1990, pp. 71–73; *Children of the Black House*, Calum Ferguson, Birlinn Ltd, Edinburgh, 2003, pp. 30–31.
20. *The Healing Wells of the Western Isles*, Finlay MacLeod, Acair Ltd, Stornoway, 2000. A Gaelic edition is also published.
21. *Healing Threads – Traditional Medicines of the Highlands and Islands*, Mary Beith, Birlinn Ltd, Edinburgh, 1995, 2004. Merits of *lus nan laogh* – Mrs Mary Etta MacDonald and Miss Donalda MacLeod, Carloway, conversation with the author, March 2007.
22. My late great-grandfather, Angus Thomson, *Aonghas Aonghais Alasdair* (1880–1971) of 3 Habost, Ness, and my great-aunt Mrs Marion MacLeod, *banntrach Choinnich Charlabhaigh* (1907–1991) of Melbost Borve – both seventh infants in their families and often besought for scrofula treatment.
23. Marion MacLeod (b.1915, Earshader) served as District Nurse of Brue and Barvas through the Second World War, and is among the last alive whose father died on the *Iolaire*.
24. *Scottish Highlanders – A People And Their Place*, James Hunter, Mainstream Publishing, Edinburgh, 1992, pp. 34–36, 61–63.

2 Pro Christo Peregrinari Volens – Myths and Reality of the Celtic Church, the First Millennium

1. *An Seann Cladh*, Comann Eachdraidh Nis, Habost, Isle of Lewis, 2004, Norman Smith, Anne MacSween et al. for details of Swainbost cemetery.
2. *A Desert Place In The Sea – The Early Churches of Northern Lewis*, Michael Robson, Comann Eachdraidh Nis, Habost Ness 1997.
3. *The Chapels in the Western Isles*, Finlay MacLeod, Acair Ltd, Stornoway, 1997.
4. *The Life of the Celtic Church*, James Bulloch, The Saint Andrew Press, Edinburgh, 1963. I have drawn very heavily on this lucid, engaging book for the general narrative here.
5. *The Quest for Celtic Christianity*, Donald E. Meek, The Handsel Press Ltd, Edinburgh, 2000. A splendid, deftly argued polemic against fashionable modern twaddle.
6. *Bede's Ecclesiastical History of the English People*, trans. Bertram Colgrave and R.A.B. Mynors, Clarendon Press, Oxford, 1969.
7. *Iona: Images and Reflections*, Neil Paynter and David Coleman, Wild Goose Publications, The Iona Community, 2007, for insight into modern 'Iona Community'. *George MacLeod – Founder of the Iona Community*, Ron Ferguson, Mainstream Publishing Ltd, Edinburgh, 1990, for its inter-war conception. *Praying With Highland Christians*, G.R.D. MacLean, with Foreword by Sally Magnusson, Triangle/

SPCK, London, 1999, typical of contemporary 'Celtic Christianity'. *Carmina Gadelica – Hymns and Incantations Collected in the Highlands and Islands of Scotland*, Alexander Carmichael, single-volume English-only edition, Floris Books, Edinburgh, 1992. Carmichael's methodology and integrity have been openly questioned – see sober Preface by John MacInnes, pp. 7–18; for recent assessment, *The Life and Legacy of Alexander Carmichael*, ed. Dohmnall Uilleam Stiubhart, The Islands Book Trust, Kershader, Isle of Lewis, 2006.

8. Again, *Archaeology of Skye and the Western Isles*, Ian Armit; *The Islands of Western Scotland*, W.H. Murray; *Scottish Highlanders – A People And Their Place*, James Hunter; *Aspects of the Religious History of Lewis*, Rev. Murdo MacAulay, especially for earliest Christian traditions and for optimistic claims for proto-Presbyterianism in the Columban order.

9. *The Companion Guide to Gaelic Scotland*, ed. Derick S. Thomson, especially entries on 'Celtic Church, The' by John W.M. Bannerman and G.W.S. Barrow; 'Celi De' and 'Dalriada', by Bannerman; 'Picts, pre-Union contact with the Scots' by Isabel Henderson; 'Maol Rubha', by Kenneth D. MacDonald.

10. *Adomnan of Iona – Life of St Columba*, trans. by Richard Sharpe, Penguin Books, London, 1995, especially introduction and notes.

11. *The Church In The Highlands*, John MacKay, Hodder and Stoughton, London, 1914, 'The Columban-Celtic Church, 563–1068.'

12. *The Burning Bush In Carloway – Its History and Revivals*, Murdo MacAulay, Carloway Free Church Deacon's Court, 1984.

13. For a fine little account of the most important Pabbay, in the Sound of Harris, see *The Teampall on the Isle of Pabbay – A Harris Church In Its Historical Setting*, Bill Lawson, Bill Lawson Publications, Northton, Isle of Harris, 1999.

14. *The Isle of Taransay*, Bill Lawson, Bill Lawson Publications, Northton, Isle of Harris, 1997.

15. *Harris In History and Legend*, Bill Lawson, John Donald Publishers (Birlinn Ltd), Edinburgh, 2002.

16. *Rona: The Distant Island*, Michael Robson, Acair Ltd, Stornoway, 1992, includes detailed discussion of the island's chapels; *The Ancient Monuments of the Western Isles*, Historic Scotland, 2003, for more information and illustration.

17. *The Literature of the Highlands*, Nigel MacNeill, first pub. 1892; Aeneas MacKay, Stirling, 1929; *Gleanings of Highland Harvest*, Murdo Campbell, Christian Focus Publications, Fearn, 1989 – esp. introduction by MacMillan, both quoted by Meek.

3 'Bitter is the Wind Tonight' – Norsemen, Rome and the Medieval Church, 795–1560

1. Murray and Armit have excellent, detailed study of the Norse occupation; Hunter has fine quotation from assorted Norse literature; Finlay MacLeod has detail of surviving Norse chapel ruins; Donald Meek records interesting material on Norse ecclesiology in Scotland; MacAulay has more early lore in *Aspects* and *Burning Bush*. I make extensive general use of all in this chapter. I am indebted to Bill Lawson's Taransay volume for the Irish couplet on Norse menace, and his 1992 Harris guide for demolition of the Armada myth.

2. *Lewis – A History of the Island*, Donald MacDonald, Gordon Wright Publishing, Edinburgh, 1978.

3. *An Eaglais Mhor (The Large Church)*, Angus Smith, Cross Free Church, 1992.

4. Articles in *The Companion Guide to Gaelic Scotland*, especially 'Gaelic, Norse influence' and 'Place-names, Norse' by Magne Oftedal; 'Scandinavia, contact with' by G.W.S. Barrow; 'Kenneth mac Alpan' by John W.M. Bannerman; 'Monastic orders, spread of' by G.W.S. Barrow.

5. *St Columba's Church at Aignish – (The Church of the Ui)*, Bill Lawson, Bill Lawson Publications, Northton, Isle of Harris, 1991, especially for concise account of the MacLeods.

6. Marsaili Mackinnon and family, Scadabay, Isle of Harris, 1998, for local Norse place-name traditions.

7. *A Short History of Scotland*, R.L. MacKie, 1962 edition (revised by Gordon Donaldson), Oliver and Boyd Ltd, Edinburgh.

8. *A History of the Scottish People 1560–1830*, T.C. Smout, Collins, London, 1969.

9. *The Lewis Chessmen*, James Robinson, The British Museum Press, London, 2004.

10. *Tales and Traditions of the Lews*, Dr Donald MacDonald, 1967; reprinted Birlinn Ltd, Edinburgh, 2004, pp. 41–44 on the Morrisons and the Brieves.

11. Smith, *An Eaglais Mhor*, for these Ness superstitions.

12. Series of articles, 'Notes On The Religion of Lewis', Rev. Malcolm MacPhail, Free Church (later United Free) minister of Kilmartin, Argyll; *The Oban Times*, Saturday July 16 1898 *et seq.* to August 1899. MacPhail had taught in Ness as a divinity student and is an invaluable source.

13. *St Clement's Church at Rodel*, Bill Lawson, Bill Lawson Publications, Northton, Isle of Harris, 1991; *The Ancient Monuments of the Western Isles*, Historic Scotland, 2003, for additional material.

4 'No Religion for a Gentleman' – Reformation and Presbyterianism, 1560–1742

1. I am indebted to Smout for robust, non-partisan analysis of the Reformation; to W.H. Murray for some detail of Dean Monro; to Lawson's Aignish booklet for detail of the fall of the MacLeods of Lewis; to Hunter (*Scottish Highlanders: A People and their Place*, Mainstream Publishing Ltd, Edinburgh, 1991) for detail on the anti-Highland hatefulness of James VI and the bloody enterprise envisaged for the Fife Adventurers; and, of course, to Murdo MacAulay.

2. *The Claim of Scotland*, H.J. Paton, George Allen and Unwin Ltd, London, 1968. 'The Legend of Scottish Intolerance', pp. 38–40.

3. *The Scottish Church 1689–1843*, Andrew L. Drummond and James Bulloch, The Saint Andrew Press, Edinburgh, 1973. The first glorious volume of an outstanding trilogy; followed by *The Church in Victorian Scotland 1843–1874*, Andrew L. Drummond and James Bulloch, The Saint Andrew Press, Edinburgh, 1975; and *The Church in Late Victorian Scotland 1874–1900*, Andrew L. Drummond and James Bulloch, The Saint Andrew Press, Edinburgh, 1978.

4. *The Jacobite Risings in Scotland 1689–1746*, Bruce Lenman, Eyre Methuen, London, 1980, pp. 228–230; *The Jacobite Clans of the Great Glen 1650–1784*, Bruce Lenman, Eyre Methuen, London, 1984, pp. 17–21, 75, for contemporary Highland religious realities.

5. See articles 'Gaelic speaking in Scotland, demographic history' by Charles W.J. Withers and Kenneth MacKinnon in *The Companion Guide to Gaelic Scotland*, above; also 'Carswell, John' by Derick S. Thomson; 'Monroe, Archdeacon Donald' by Ian Grimble; 'Bible, Gaelic translations of' by Donald E Meek; 'psalm tunes, Gaelic' by

Cedric Thorpe Davie; 'psalms, metrical' by R.L. Thomson. MacAulay (*Aspects*) also records in detail Synod of Argyll endeavours in Gaelic translation.

6. Drummond and Bulloch, Vol. 3, pp. 82–84, on Highland isolation and its consequences.

7. *The Diary of Kenneth A. MacRae – A Record of Fifty Years in the Christian Ministry*, ed. Iain H. Murray, The Banner of Truth Trust, Edinburgh, 1980 – hazards of Highland travel for a pastor, pp. 213–217, 248, 271–272.

8. A Bill Lawson anecdote, in a September 1993 'Feis na Hearadh' lecture at the Harris Hotel.

9. *Scottish Islands*, Ian Grimble, BBC, London, 1985, pp. 50–69 on bloody MacLeod intrigue and the Fife Adventurers.

10. Rev. Peter MacDonald, minister of Stornoway Free English from 1895, gave a series of lectures on 'The Religious History of Lewis' which were carried in *The Highland News* from 7 March 1896 to April 1896, devoted largely but not exclusively to the Evangelical era. Early Presbyterian ministry on Lewis and Harris is detailed by Rev. Malcolm MacPhail in a series of articles in *The Oban Times*, from 16 July 1898 to August 1899 – practically the ur-text of Lewis Evangelical history and all subsequent writers have borrowed from it, wittingly or otherwise; important material on the early Reformed ministers. Rev. Norman C. MacFarlane (Ness-born minister of Juniper Green, Edinburgh) wrote articles on Long Island ministers to the *Stornoway Gazette*, which ran from Friday 26 September 1930 to Friday 15 May 1931. All three men – as well as Rev. Alexander MacRae of Tong, Sutherland, as productive but less careful – entered the Union of 1900.

11. Charles I's comment on Presbyterianism – *History Of His Own Time*, London, 1818 edition, Gilbert Burnet, Vol. 1, p. 116.

12. MacPhail makes the point with evident relish, and gives excellent potted histories of all Lewis ministers from the Reformation to the Disruption.

13. *Rona: The Distant Island*, Michael Robson, Acair Ltd, Stornoway, 1991, pp. 8–9, 25–28 for account of visit by Rev. Donald Morrison to Rona; pp. 9–13 for the ordeal of Fr Cornelius Con.

14. Drummond and Bulloch (Vol. 10) cannot be bettered for an account of eighteenth-century Scottish religion and the complexities of patronage. For a wry, entertaining satire, see John Galt's 1821 novel, *Annals of the Parish*. Rather less neglected in a day desperate to mock Scottish religion is James Hogg's 1825 chiller *Private Memoirs and Confessions of a Justified Sinner*. Though popularly thought an exposé of Calvinism, it is really a psychological study of evil in a social context that happened to be Scottish and Presbyterian – 'an essay in morbid psychology' (Drummond and Bulloch, Vol. 1, p. 217) in the context of Scots Calvinism.

5 'Moderation is What Religion Enjoins' – Ministers and Moderates, 1742–1820

1. Surviving SSPCK material, including record of this Swainbost school, may be viewed at the Scottish Records Office, Edinburgh. I am indebted generally in this chapter to Malcolm MacPhail (1898–99 *Oban Times* series), Murdo MacAulay (*Aspects*), Angus Smith (*An Eaglais Mhor*), Finlay MacLeod (*The Healing Wells of the Western Isles*) for the Galson skull story William Matheson related to Anne Ross.

2. See article, 'schools, SSPCK' by John A. Smith in *The Companion to Gaelic Scotland*, above; and important entry on 'Roman Catholic Church' by Roderick MacDonald, relating exclusively to post-Reformation struggles and survival.

3. *A Desert Place in The Sea*, Michael Robson, pp. 18–19, 57–60, for the tedious Captain Dymes; pp. 50–67 generally for Teampall Mholuaidh traditions; Smith, pp. 3–6 on Teampall Mholuaidh and enduring paganism; Finlay MacLeod, *The Healing Wells of the Western Isles*, for the grisly Galson skull.

4. *When Piping Was Strong – Tradition, Change, and the Bagpipe in South Uist*, Joshua Dickson, John Donald (Birlinn Ltd), Edinburgh, 2006, ' "A Multitude of Papists" – Catholicism and the Preservation of Tradition in South Uist,' pp. 38–56. See besides the rather more partisan *Some Priests of Moidart*, Fr Jerome Ireland (ed. John Dye), Blackfriars Publications, Chapel-en-le-Frith, Derbyshire, 2000; and important entry on 'Roman Catholic Church' by Roderick MacDonald, *Companion to Gaelic Scotland*, ed. Derick S. Thomson, 2nd ed. 1994, relating exclusively to post-Reformation struggles and survival.

5. *Eigg – The Story of an Island*, Camille Dressler, Polygon, Edinburgh, 1998.

6. 'Pipe Major Donald MacLean of Lewis, 1908–1964 (Seaforth Highlanders)' article by Norman MacRitchie in *Fios a' Bhaile*, Comann Eachdraidh Bharabhais agus Bhru (Barvas and Brue Historical Society), December 2005.

7. 'Lochaber and its Evangelical Traditions', John MacLeod, *Northern Chronicle*, Inverness, 1920; reprinted in *Bypaths of Highland Church History*, ed. G.N.M. Collins, Knox Press, 1965 – unfortunately with the removal of all Gaelic text and some general editing; pp. 20–21; *Hector Cameron of Lochs and Back*, Murdo MacAulay, Knox Press, Edinburgh, 1982, pp. 1–3 for Lochaber and Cameron stories.

8. *The '45 – Bonnie Prince Charlie and the Untold Story of the Jacobite Rising*. Christopher Duffy, Cassell, London, 2003, for Rising; *Culloden*, John Prebble, Martin Secker and Warburg Ltd, 1961, later Penguin editions, for its aftermath; Bruce Lenman's studies (see notes to Chapter Four) for some social comment.

9. Drummond and Bulloch, Vol. 1 1688–1843 (above) remains the definitive study of patronage in the eighteenth-century Scottish Kirk and the 'Reign of the Moderates'.

10. Lectures by my father in Stornoway in 1991, on Lewis church history; Knockbain, 2003, on Highland church history. But see besides 'Moderator's Address,' Gustavus Aird, Free Church General Assembly, Thursday 24 May 1888, outlining earliest Highland Evangelicalism – PGAFCoS, 1888, pp. 3–12; and the rather neglected *The Evangelical Movement in the Highlands of Scotland – 1688 to 1800*, John MacInnes, The University Press, Aberdeen, 1951. MacInnes was minister of the Church of Scotland in Halkirk, Caithness, and the book is in the best tradition of parish-manse scholarship.

11. MacPhail details these later Morrison ministers. Lord Teignmouth's report of an Aignish funeral appears in MacAulay, *Aspects*, 1986, pp. 59–60.

12. MacAulay's posthumous instructions from *Harris in History and Legend*, Bill Lawson, John Donald Ltd (Birlinn), Edinburgh, 2002.

6 'The Boy with the Bible' – Finlay Munro and the Rise of Evangelicalism, 1820–1824

1. MacAulay (*Aspects*) and MacPhail ('Notes on Religion in Lewis', *The Oban Times*, July 1898–August 1899) remain principal sources for the early Evangelical era on the Long Island, both giving material on Finlay Munro and early converts. MacAulay (*Aspects*) has warm and detailed material on the Gaelic Schools.

2. Alexander MacRae, *Revivals in the Highlands and Islands*, date unknown, but early twentieth century, reprinted by Tentmaker Publications, Stoke on Trent, 1998.

Though not always reliable, these are colourful details of the pre-Evangelical Hebrides and of Roderick MacLeod's awkward night of hospitality.

3. *The Men of The Lews*, Norman C. MacFarlane, *Stornoway Gazette*, 1924, gives this unsettling tale in a characteristically earthy pen-portrait of Murdo MacDonald. But MacDonald's line sounds more like Lewis humour than prophetic imprecation.

4. *The People of the Great Faith – The Highland Church 1690–1900*, Douglas Ansdell, Acair Ltd, Stornoway, 1998; excellent material on SSPCK, Edinburgh Gaelic Schools Society, etc., pp. 90–108.

5. 'A Highland Evangelist – Finlay Munro', Principal John MacLeod, date unknown, probably 1920s, reprinted as appendix to *John MacLeod DD*, G.N.M. Collins, The Publications Committee of the Free Church of Scotland, Edinburgh, 1951, pp. 202–230. This is the best life of Munro we have much of the detail from Angus Morrison of Dell, whom the young MacLeod knew. MacAulay (*Aspects*, pp. 130–141) borrows very heavily from this account, though does have some original material. The early, pamphlet edition of this work included Gaelic and perhaps additional material. Letters of Munro, quoted by MacLeod, ended up in G.N.M. Collins' possession and have disappeared, probably destroyed during his notorious stewardship of the Free Church College library in the 1970s.

6. James Finlayson died on 3 November 1902, at the age of eighty. *Free Presbyterian Magazine*, December 1902, Vol. 7, p. 320.

7. This boy, Angus MacLean, *Aonghas Mhurchaidh Iain Og 'ic Iain Dubh* (1806–1874) was my great-great-grandfather. MacAulay records the anecdote in *Aspects* (1985) p. 137.

8. *Pronnagan mu Bharabhas*, John MacLeod, 4th edition, undated. A loose, anecdotal but engaging ramble of Gospel 'notes' in the Barvas district. I am indebted to my father for an English translation. This Rev. John MacLeod (1886–1963), a Free Church minister of Barvas, should not be confused with Rev. Principal John MacLeod (1872–1948).

9. *St Clement's Church at Rodel*, Bill Lawson, Bill Lawson Publications, Northton, Isle of Harris, 1991; *Harris Families and How To Trace Them*, Bill Lawson Publications, Northton, Isle of Harris, 1990, pp. 5–8; *The Teampull on the Isle of Pabbay*, Bill Lawson, Bill Lawson Publications, Northton, Isle of Harris, 1994; *Harris In History and Legend*, Bill Lawson, John Donald Ltd (Birlinn), Edinburgh, 2002, for details of nineteenth-century Harris misery.

10. *Skye: The Island*, James Hunter, Mainstream Publishing Ltd, Edinburgh, 1986, pp. 60–66, for vivid account of the kelp boom – and bust – on one Scottish island.

11. Bill Lawson quotes Carmichael on this Seilebost desecration: *Harris In History and Legend*, 2002.

12. *The Clearances In Lewis – Truth Or Myth?*, Bill Lawson, The Islands Book Trust/ Comann Eachdraidh na Pairc, 2006.

13. Murdo MacAulay (*Aspects*, pp. 113–115, 164–168) draws heavily in his account of John Morrison from biographical material appended to a post-war, Free Church edition of his Gaelic verse (including the silly line that Harris 'is the southern and most mountainous part of the Island of Lewis'). Though contemporary records (and his gravestone at Rodel) spell the Blacksmith's surname as 'Morison', I have deliberately used the standard spelling here, as his Harris relations do today.

14. MacAulay does not specify his source, but it was evidently an article in *The Scottish Christian Herald* by Alexander MacLeod, some years before the Disruption. A copy has eluded me.

15. Malcolm MacPhail outlines the excesses of this period in great detail, and is MacAulay's prime source. There is inextricable confusion as to when revival came to Barvas proper, but it certainly pre-dated any Evangelical awakening in Uig; if not the first fruits of Munro's work on the Broad Bay coast and John MacLeod's endeavours at Galson.

16. Murdo MacAulay, describing this last Munro sermon on Lewis, records (*Aspects*, pp. 139–140) that in 1947 the Free Church minister of Back and two companions, Murdo Graham and Alexander Neil Kennedy, 'visited this knoll . . . and sang some verses of a psalm.'

17. Short of deliberate, daily 'maintenance' – improbable over 180 years in a spot miles from any village – one explanation is 'visitor pressure', folk deliberately standing in the footprints and compressing the soil. But 'Finlay Munro's Footprints' are not well known and are not signposted; and there must be many days – even, occasionally, weeks – when no one sees them. In any event, natural or human cause would not vitiate Munro's prediction. They lie off the A887 highway from Inverness to Kyle of Lochalsh, via the village of Invermoriston – about two miles before the junction with the A87 from Invergarry and a mile after a local cafe and the former Free Church manse, now a guest-house; look for a tall wicket or 'kissing-gate' on the right-hand side, signposted for a local walk and a few yards from a convenient lay-by to leave your car. Proceed a few yards through the trees to the large low cairn that becomes visible; the footprints are right behind it; and there, indeed, nothing grows save a little occasional moss. Accounts vary as to the relatively recent vandalism, but it was not appreciated in the district. Some modern descriptions can readily be found on the Internet. Duncan MacLean (b.1982) is a grandson of the eponymous Free Presbyterian minister.

7 'No Finer Moral Spectacle' – Alexander MacLeod and Evangelical Ministry, 1824–1843

1. I again acknowledge anecdotes from Murdo MacAulay (*Aspects*) and Malcolm MacPhail, in his 1898–1899 *Oban Times* series. *Apostles of the North*, Norman C. MacFarlane, undated, *c*.1930, reprinted 1989 by Stornoway Religious Bookshop, pp. 31–40. This biographical essay on MacLeod includes much colour of Assynt background and the sensational elopement. MacFarlane had also heard MacLeod preach.

2. *Some Noted Ministers of the Northern Highlands*, Donald Beaton, Northern Chronicle, Inverness, 1929, pp. 200–211, for a more scholarly, sober account. A modern paperback reprint is available from Free Presbyterian Publications, Glasgow.

3. *Disruption Worthies of the Highlands – A Memorial of 1843*, ed. John Greig, pub. John Grant, Edinburgh, 1877, pp. 221–232 – this profile by George L. Campbell, FCoS minister of Lochs.

4. *Diary and Sermons of the Reverend Alexander MacLeod, Rogart (Formerly of Uig, Lewis) with Brief Memoir*, Donald Beaton, Inverness, 1925, especially the Diary, pp. 13–22 – such as was suffered to survive by MacLeod's heirs.

5. *A Brief Record of The Church In Uig (Lewis) Up to the Union of 1929*, John MacLeod, Carishader, Isle of Lewis, 2001, pp. 6–17. An important work of private scholarship, which was, alas, published posthumously.

6. *Aspects etc.*, Murdo MacAulay, Stornoway, 1986, for MacRitchie account, pp. 170–171.

7. *Aspects*, pp. 137–138, for MacLeod's encounter with Finlay. MacAulay credits this

story to Murdo MacLean, *Murchadh Chaluim Mor* (1891–1974), 4 New Shawbost, my late grandfather, and whose grandfather Angus had precented at Dalbeag for Finlay Munro.

8. *Bypaths of Highland Church History*, Principal John MacLeod, ed. Collins, Knox Press, Edinburgh, 1965, pp. 22–40, for account of Francis MacBean, originally published as a MacLeod pamphlet, *Lochaber and its Evangelical Traditions*, Northern Chronicle, Inverness, 1920.

9. *Aonghas nam Beann* was widely written up from the last years of the century. Several versions of the 'I lost the bit of lead' story: earliest in 'Angus of the Hills', John MacLeod, *Free Presbyterian Magazine* Vol. 2, p. 349, January 1898, pre-dating by some months Malcolm MacPhail's references in the *Oban Times*. Most versions of the story have MacLeod on his hands and knees searching in the heather for the missing 'bit of lead'. But see 'A Few Notes on Angus of the Hills', *Memoir, Biographical Sketches, Letters, Lectures and Sermons (English and Gaelic) of the Reverend Neil Cameron, Glasgow*, ed. Donald Beaton, Inverness, 1932, pp. 109–112; MacFarlane, *The Men of the Lews*, pp. 19–26. MacAulay draws heavily on MacPhail, for the most part, but has some original notes of his own, and not only precisely identified Angus MacLeod but located a photograph.

10. *Gleanings In The North*, David Stephen, Haddington, 1891, pp. 52–57, a generally unknown account of Finlay Cook in a rare Caithness memoir. Most material on the Cook brothers focuses on their mainland service: an edition of *Letters of Finlay and Archibald Cook* appeared in the 1890s and *Sidelights on Two Notable Ministries*, Free Presbyterian Publications, Glasgow, *c.*1973, is still readily available.

11. Beaton (pp. 212–223), MacFarlane, *Apostles*, pp. 20–30, and *Disruption Worthies*, pp. 145–152 (profile by Colin Sinclair, FCoS minister of Invergordon) all here augment MacAulay's account of Robert Finlayson, *Aspects*, pp. 84–85; 92–101. Though MacFarlane can be flippant, he gives more quotation of Finlayson than anyone.

12. *Disruption Worthies*, pp. 69–78, profile of Duncan Matheson by Kenneth Mac-Donald, FCoS minister of Applecross; *Apostles*, MacFarlane, pp. 41–49 on Matheson; MacAulay, *Aspects*, pp. 86–87.

13. See MacAulay on Morrison (*Aspects*) and MacLeod on MacBean (*Lochaber and its Evangelical Traditions*) on this unedifying row.

14. Premillennarian views are now generally deplored in Highland Evangelicalism, though hugely popular elsewhere and especially in America (Premillennial Dispensationalism). In early nineteenth-century Scotland, though, some eminent ministers were premillenarian, notably two reverend brothers, Horatius and Andrew Bonar, and – if less explicitly – Robert Murray McCheyne. The doctrine is not expressly repudiated in the Westminster Confession of Faith. Most Highland ministers of the period, though, were postmillennial, still the near-universal position in the Free Presbyterian Church, expecting Christ to return after a 'millennium' of vast spiritual revival and, especially, the conversion of the Jews. Most modern Free Church ministers are amillennial, doubting a 'millennium' at all.

15. *Lewis – A History of the Island*, Donald MacDonald, Gordon Wright Publishing, Edinburgh, 1978, p. 136, for some detail of the most elusive *Mac an t-Sronaich*. MacFarlane, *Apostles*, p. 23, for details of Mrs Finlayson's succour. She was a 'Miss MacAulay from Uig'. It is much more likely she made such provision for some less murderous fugitive who was a near-relation, than for a serial killer from across the Minch, and that the story has been 'improved' in the telling.

16. *Lewis In History and Legend*, Bill Lawson, Birlinn Ltd, Edinburgh, 2008, pp. 216–217.
17. 'A Revival of Religion in the Isle of Lewis,' unsigned, *The Scottish Christian Herald; Conducted Under The Superintendence of Ministers and Members of the Established Church*, Vol. 1, March 5–December 31 1836. Almost certainly the first reference in print to Lewis Evangelicalism. The usage 'Established Church' was then general, and I use it (or, on occasion, the 'Auld Kirk') in preference to 'Church of Scotland', which is substantially a post-1929 usage.
18. MacRae's verdict in MacAulay, *Aspects*, p. 179.

8 'The Church of Scotland, Free' – Big MacRae and the Disruption, 1843–1876

1. Beaton (*Noted Ministers of the Northern Highlands*, Inverness, 1929, pp. 265–270), MacFarlane (*Apostles of the North*, 1989 edition, pp. 7–15) and *Disruption Worthies of the Highlands*, ed. Greig, Edinburgh, 1877, pp. 115–126 – the profile is by his son-in-law, Donald MacMaster, FCoS, Back – all give studies of John MacRae. *Big MacRae*, G.N.M. Collins, Knox Press, Edinburgh, 1976 (new edition, 1977) is heavily indebted to *An t-Urramach Iain MacRath*, Nicol Nicolson, undated, late nineteenth century.
2. Beaton (*Noted Ministers*) gives excellent accounts of Aeneas Sage, pp. 65–75; Lachlan MacKenzie, pp. 76–86; and John MacDonald, pp. 157–170. MacFarlane *(Apostles)* profiles MacKenzie, pp. 95–99, and MacDonald, pp. 1–6.
3. Letter published in *Inverness Courier* on 15 December 1865, from Dr John Mac-Donald's son, D.G.F. MacDonald.
4. From *Piping Traditions of the North of Scotland*, (pp. 61–62). This may be an article, not a book. Unfortunately I have only the photocopy of two pages: possibly, *Transactions of the Gaelic Society of Inverness*, one reference suggesting it is post-1966.
5. Mrs MacDonald's funeral refreshment – *The Church in Victorian Scotland 1843–1874*, Andrew L. Drummond and James Bulloch, The Saint Andrew Press, Edinburgh, 1975, p. 25.
6. Beaton, 1929, p. 167 for MacDonald routine.
7. *The Apostle of the North*, John Kennedy DD, 1866; Free Presbyterian Publications, Glasgow, 1978, pp. 66–80 for St Kilda visit.
8. *St Kilda and its Church – A Hebridean Church in its Historical Setting*, Bill Lawson, Bill Lawson Publications, Northton, Isle of Harris, 1993; *The Life and Death of St Kilda*, Tom Steele, Fontana Books, London, 1975; for a new perspective, *An Isle Called Hirte*, Mary Harman, The Islands Book Trust, Kershader, Isle of Lewis, 1998; *St Kilda – Church, Visitors and 'Natives'*, Michael Robson, The Islands Book Trust, 2003; *The Decline and Fall of St Kilda*, The Islands Book Trust, 2005; *St Kilda – Myth and Reality*, John Randall, Bill Lawson, John Love, Michael Robson, The Islands Book Trust, 2006.
9. I am indebted to Norman Campbell, BBC Radio Radio nan Gaidheal, for supplying this stanza of MacDonald verse. It was quoted by Rev. Lachlan MacLeod, Free Presbyterian minister of Uig from 1953 to 1965, in his farewell service there.
10. *Annals of the Disruption*, Thomas Brown, Edinburgh, 1893, still the standard if appallingly partisan account of the event; *The Heritage of Our Fathers – the Free Church of Scotland: Her Origin and Testimony*, G.N.M. Collins, Knox Press, Edinburgh, 1974. For recent, more objective analysis, see *Scotland In The Age of the Disruption*, ed.

Stewart J. Brown and Michael Fry, Edinburgh University Press, Edinburgh, 1993, especially essay by Stewart J. Brown, 'The Ten Years' Conflict and the Disruption', pp. 1–27; and essay by P.L.M. Hillis, 'The Sociology of the Disruption', pp. 44–62.

11. Drummond and Bulloch give cool assessment of the 'Ten Years' Conflict' and the Disruption in Vol. 1, *The Scottish Church 1688–1843*, pp. 220–265; for thought on the emerging life and character of the Free Church of Scotland, see Vol. 2, *The Church in Victorian Scotland*, especially pp. 1–57, for Presbyterian landscape after 1843.

12. Drummond and Bulloch, *The Church in Victorian Scotland 1843–1874*, pp. 4–5, as to this planned Evangelical strategy. But – as Stuart J. Brown points out – even a General Assembly majority would not have sufficed for action so draconian; it would have had to go through the mechanism of the Barrier Act and be approved by a simple majority of Presbyteries, which the Evangelical Party never had.

13. *Memoir of Thomas Guthrie*, D.K. Guthrie and C.J. Guthrie, London, 1877, pp. 394–395. Guthrie (1803–1873) was not only the gifted minister of Free St John's, Edinburgh (now St Columba's Free Church of Scotland) – many thought only Chalmers eclipsed him as a preacher – but an important social reformer: a temperance campaigner and, most notably, founder of the 'Ragged Schools'. His statue stands on Princes Street, Edinburgh.

14. *Journal*, Lord Cockburn (2 vols), Edinburgh, 1874 – Vol. 2 p. 33.

15. *People of the Great Faith – The Highland Church 1688–1900*, Acair Ltd, Stornoway, 1997, excellent study of early Free Church and site-refusal and oppression, though rightly observes it was 'a minority of congregations that suffered,' pp. 56–89, with much detail of Lewis.

16. *A Brief Record Of The Church In Uig (Lewis) Up To The Union Of 1929*, John MacLeod, Carishader, 2001, pp. 13–21 for the 'Ten Years' Conflict', the Disruption, and the period from 1843 to 1875.

17. MacRae's graveyard diatribe recorded by John MacLeod, *Lochaber and its Evangelical Traditions*, Northern Chronicle, Inverness, 1920.

18. Ansdell gives much detail of the *Breadalbane*, pp. 74–75.

19. *Free Church Ministers in Lewis (Presbytery) 1843–1993*, Murdo MacAulay, Stornoway, 1993. MacAulay made use of *Annals of the Free Church of Scotland*, William Ewing DD, T. & T. Clark, Edinburgh, 1914, 2 vols, for pre-1900 information. *Annals of the Free Church of Scotland 1900–1986*, G.N.M. Collins, Knox Press, Edinburgh, is more heroic than reliable.

20. Mrs Marion MacLeod, Brue, b.1914, Earshader, told me this Uig tradition of how *Aonghas nam Beann* chose the Free Church site at Ceann Langabhat, in conversation in January 2008.

21. *The Burning Bush In Carloway – Its History and Revivals*, Murdo MacAulay, Carloway Free Church Deacons Court, 1984, pp. 14–21 for Disruption, Kenneth Ross and John MacLean; *The Men of the Lews*, MacFarlane, Stornoway, 1929, pp. 1–4 on Kenneth Ross.

22. Free Church middle-class censoriousness – Drummond and Bulloch, Vol. 2, p. 29.

23. Ansdell (p. 165) on Established Church recovery by the 1890s. John MacLeod's *Brief Record* is the definitive, detailed account of the 1875 division in Uig, pp. 26–30.

24. John MacPhail, though genial and pious, was a tight-wad. My late grandfather, Donald MacLeod, 'Foot' (1910–1986) of 28 Cross, spent a day working on the Established glebe in the early 1920s for an agreed hourly pittance. By sundown he had earned all of 10½d. MacPhail all but tore the manse apart, searching for small change, rather than give my grandfather a shilling. I am indebted to my father for this

anecdote, and besides for details of Bosville's sermon, which was probably a flippant performance for the children.

25. Peggy Gillies, *Peigi Iain Bho* (1914–2006) told me of an open-air Established Communion at Cross – the congregation overwhelmingly of Uig visitors – to which she and her brothers snuck down, still vividly remembered in conversation in June 2002 – with the most beautiful Gaelic singing she had ever heard. At a Free Presbyterian Communion on Raasay, in July 1992, Rev. Donald MacLean (b.1915), ordained to Portree in 1948, and from 1960 to 2000 minister of St Jude's, Glasgow, told me that Free Presbyterians in Uig, ex-Balnacille Parish Church, had still sung Gaelic psalms in four-part harmony on his Communion visits during his early ministry.

26. Drummond and Bulloch are acidulous on the United Presbyterian Church of Scotland (Vol. 2, pp. 44–52). Madeleine Smith (1835–1920) was acquitted of the murder of her lover, Pierre Emile l'Angelier, by Not Proven verdict in the summer of 1857; see *Square Mile of Murder*, Jack House, W. & R. Chambers, Edinburgh and London, 1961; Richard Drew Publishing, Glasgow, 1984, pp. 11–83.

27. *Donald John Martin*, Norman C. MacFarlane, Edinburgh, 1914. A warm but naturally uncritical assessment of a controversial Lewis minister of the 'Advanced Party'.

28. The history of the Scottish Episcopal Church in Stornoway was outlined by Dr Donald MacDonald in a genial speech later included in his book (*Tales and Traditions of the Lews*, Birlinn edition, 2004, pp. 249–251). See besides a recent and most interesting article, 'St Peter's Church, Stornoway', by Robin Mackenzie, *Back In The Day*, Stornoway Gazette Publications, May 2008, pp. 16–17.

29. Beaton, p. 269 (1929 edition) deplores John MacRae's early enthusiasm for union with the United Presbyterians. Collins (*Big MacRae*, pp. 83–88) has an involved but interesting account of MacRae's thinking and manoeuvres in this period.

30. MacAulay (*Burning Bush*) has warm notes on MacRae's Carloway ministry, pp. 21–22. G.N.M. Collins told me, with relish, of MacRae's pulpit habits over coffee in Edinburgh in August 1986.

9 'The Devil's Kitchen' – The Crisis of 1893

1. Gavin Crawford's unpleasant letter from *Sop as gach Seid*, Comann Eachdraidh Charlabhaigh, Carloway Historical Society – no. 33, August 2007, p. 33.

2. 'Opening of New Free Churches in Lewis by Principal Rainy', in *The Highland News*, Monday 20 October 1884. Though unsigned, 'our correspondent' was probably Alexander Lee, Free Church minister at Nairn and Rainy's chief Highland propagandist. See Wikipedia on 'Ronald Munro-Ferguson, 1st Viscount Novar'.

3. *The Free Church of Scotland 1843–1910*, Alexander Stewart and J. Kennedy Cameron, William Hodge and Company, Edinburgh and Glasgow, 1910. Cameron wrote chapters 14 and 15; Stewart everything else.

4. Theology: Calvinism is best understood as a Christian belief-system holding to the absolute sovereignty of God in all things, including salvation and the 'decrees' or doctrines of grace: the total depravity of man (unable to desire or obey God); unconditional election (those saved are preordained for salvation, from no merit of their own); limited atonement (Christ died only for a particular people, the 'elect'); irresistible grace (the elect are 'effectually called' to salvation, and cannot resist it) and perseverance of the saints (once saved, always saved). Yet the Gospel is to be freely

preached to everyone (the 'free offer of the Gospel'). Hyper-Calvinism denies the free offer of the Gospel and deplores indiscriminate evangelism. Arminianism – the dominant theology in global Evangelicalism – denies the 'decrees'; election is conditional on faith in Jesus and continued salvation is dependent on continued faith. Amyraldianism is 4-point Calvinism, denying a limited atonement – an incoherent attempt to reconcile election with the free offer of the Gospel. See *A Faith To Live By*, Donald Macleod, Christian Focus Publications, Fearn, 1998, esp. pp. 39–51; 129–148. For genesis of United Presbyterian Amyraldianism, see *Scottish Theology*, John MacLeod DD, 1943, 1946, reprinted Knox Press, Edinburgh, 1974, pp. 173–177. These views first articulated by a Highland Covenanting minister, James Fraser of Brea (1639–1698), but quickly suppressed. See Beaton, *Noted Ministers of the Northern Highlands*, 1929, on Fraser, pp. 31–37.

5. Drummond and Bulloch, Vol. 3, *The Church in Late Victorian Scotland 1874–1900*, on Moody campaign etc., pp. 9–18.

6. *The Diary of Kenneth A. MacRae*, ed. Iain H. Murray, chapter 2, 'Joining the Remnant', pp. 15–34, on Free Church declensions.

7. *The People of the Great Faith*, Douglas Ansdell, Acair Ltd, Stornoway – especially chapter 10, 'Secession', pp. 159–182. The word 'secession', though, is very loaded. For still more Lewis detail, see his excellent paper, 'The Disruptive Union, 1890–1900 in a Hebridean Presbytery', *Records of the Scottish Church History Society*, Vol. 26, 1996, pp. 55–103. Its only weakness is his extensive citation of readers' correspondence in the Highland press – frequently anonymous, often vituperative and not reliable.

8. *Noted Ministers*, Beaton, 1929, pp. 271–279 on Dr Kennedy; assessment from broader theological tradition in *Defending and Declaring The Faith: Some Scottish Examples, 1860–1920*, Alan P.F. Sell and James B. Torrance, Paternoster Press, Edinburgh, 1987. Kennedy conversation with Mrs C.R. Auld is quoted by Beaton in *Memoir and Remains of the Rev. Donald MacFarlane, Dingwall*, The Northern Counties Newspaper and Printing and Publishing Co. Ltd, Inverness, 1929, pp. 34–36 – citing a letter she submitted to the *Northern Chronicle*, written on 10 November 1894; but see items from Kennedy pamphlet, 'Unionism and the Union', *Heritage of Our Fathers*, G.N.M. Collins, Knox Press, Edinburgh, 1974, p. 95. For a little-known but striking biographical essay, see 'Dr Kennedy, of Dingwall', in *A Highland Editor – Selected Writings of James Barron*, Vol. 1, Robert Carruthers & Sons, Inverness, 1927, pp. 93–112 – originally published as an *Inverness Courier* article in 1893. Barron details an occasion when Dr Kennedy 'gave out' a paraphrase to be sung (in Dingwall, at C.H. Spurgeon's request); Kennedy's American jaunt in 1873 – when he was greatly taken with the prayers of the Dean of Canterbury – and other details of his breadth of mind that modern acolytes would rather suppress. Most famously, Dr Kennedy once heard a Requiem Mass in Rome for the late Pope Pius IX. Over a century later, at a Free Presbyterian Synod in 1989, this was raised in defence of Lord Mackay of Clashfern, an Edinburgh elder facing church discipline for attending one himself. 'Dr Kennedy was on holiday,' said an opponent dismissively. The Lord Chancellor was duly suspended from office and sealing ordinances, by six votes. Mackay has never formally joined another church.

9. *Disruptive Union*, Ansdell, p. 97 for Rainy's assessment of FCoS 1874 strength on Lewis.

10. Helen Macleod did not escape either. Many years later, the late Peggy Gillies told me, her house burned down and she lost all save the night-gown in which she fled the blaze. See my article on Duncan MacBeath, *The Herald* (Saturday magazine), 13 July 2002;

heavily edited version, 'The MacBeath Controversy', John MacLeod, *Criomagan*, Comann Eachdraidh Nis, Vol. 8, no. 30, May 2003, p. 4. Details of the Rona tragedy, *Rona – The Distant Island*, Michael Robson, Acair Ltd, Stornoway, 1991 (pp. 105–120); a whole book, *A Sad Tale Of The Sea – The Story of Malcolm MacDonald and Murdo MacKay on the Island of Rona*, Michael Robson, Port of Ness, 2006.

11. *The Second Disruption – The Free Church in Victorian Scotland and the Origins of the Free Presbyterian Church* (Scottish Historical Review Monograph No. 8), James Lachlan MacLeod, Tuckwell Press, East Linton, 2000. Unlikely to be bettered, this study of anti-Highland bigotry as a factor in the ecclesiastical politics of the day is particularly important.

12. *Social and Religious Life in the Highlands*, Kenneth MacDonald, R.W. Hunter, Edinburgh, 1902, pp. 247–248 for contemptuous Highland comment.

13. *The Life of Principal Rainy*, P. Carnegie Simpson, London, two volumes, 1909, Vol. 2, pp. 448–449 for more. One of the worst biographies of a Scottish churchman ever written – uncritical, bigoted and partisan, it entombed its subject.

14. *Proceedings of the General Assembly of the Free Church of Scotland*, 1891, Report XXIX, for text of the Declaratory Act.

15. *History of the Free Presbyterian Church of Scotland 1893–1970*, ed. Alexander McPherson, Free Presbyterian Church of Scotland, Glasgow, 1975, especially pp. 6–87. A turgid committee-job, very reliable if inevitably partisan, especially account of critical Free Church General Assemblies; also includes lectures on Declaratory Act by James S. Sinclair, which occasionally tend to the absurd; more Assembly detail, Drummond and Bulloch, Vol. 3, *The Church in Late Victorian Scotland*, pp. 267–273.

16. We have noted Beaton's 1929 *Memoir* of Donald MacFarlane. See too *Memoir and Remains of the Reverend Donald MacDonald, Shieldaig, Ross-shire*, Donald MacFarlane, John McNeilage, Glasgow, 1903; recent editions. See *John MacLeod DD*, G.N.M. Collins, Knox Press, Edinburgh, 1951, for a cautious account of MacLeod's activity in this period, pp. 32–49, and facsimile of Bond signed by 1892 students.

17. *Hector Cameron of Lochs and Back*, Murdo MacAulay, Knox Press, Edinburgh, 1982. Norman MacFarlane writes of Hector Cameron in the *Stornoway Gazette* (23 January, 15 May 1931, '50 to 70 Years Ago – Rural Ministers of the Old Free'.) Douglas Ansdell details Cameron's writhings in *Disruptive Union*, 1996.

18. *Popular History of the Origins of the Free Presbyterian Church of Scotland*, Donald M. Boyd, Inverness, 1988; some original detail on 1893.

19. Drummond and Bullough, Vol. 3, *The Church in Late Victorian Scotland 1974–1900*, p. 273.

10 'Israel and Judah' – The Crisis of 1900

1. *The Church In Late Victorian Scotland 1874–1900*, Andrew L. Drummond and James Bulloch, The Saint Andrew Press, Edinburgh, 1978, pp. 272–273, 313–315, for a surprisingly sympathetic take on the Free Presbyterians. This may, of course, reflect the loathing of many modern Church of Scotland ministers for the post-1900 Free Church.

2. *The Second Disruption: The Free Church in Victorian Scotland and the Origins of the Free Presbyterian Church* (Scottish Historical Review Monograph No. 8), James Lachlan MacLeod, Tuckwell Press, East Linton, 2000; *The Disruptive Union – 1890–1900 in a Hebridean Presbytery*, Douglas Ansdell, Records of the Scottish Church History Society, Vol. 26, 1996, pp. 55–103; *The Free Church of Scotland 1843–1910*, Alexander

Stewart and J. Kennedy Cameron, William Hodge & Co., Edinburgh, 1910; *The Heritage of Our Fathers*, G.N.M. Collins, Knox Press, Edinburgh, 1974; *Church and Creed in Scotland – The Free Church Case 1900–1904 And Its Origins*, Kenneth Ross, Rutherford House, Edinburgh, 1988. Website of the Free Church of Scotland – www.freechurch.org

3. The *Free Presbyterian Magazine and Monthly Record*, published monthly since April 1896, is an invaluable resource for students of her life and character. The name was shortened in 1970. See *History of the Free Presbyterian Church of Scotland 1893–1970*, ed. Alexander McPherson, Inverness, 1975; *One Hundred Years of Witness*, ed. Duncan R. MacSween, Free Presbyterian Publications, Glasgow, 1993; *Ministers and Men of the Free Presbyterian Church*, Neil Cameron, ed. Roy Middleton, Settle Graphics, Yorkshire, 1993, especially outstanding biographical essay, pp. ix–xl. Website of the Free Presbyterian Church of Scotland – www.fpchurch.org.uk

4. *The North Country Separatists*, John MacLeod DD, Inverness, 1930; reprinted in *John MacLeod DD*, G.N.M. Collins, 1951, pp. 78–162, but edited. In many respects the Free Presbyterian Church of Scotland is the ecclesiastical incarnation of the movement.

5. Early development of the Free Presbyterian movement on the Long Island from Ansdell, pp. 71–79.

6. *The Tolsta Townships*, Donald MacDonald, Comann Eachdraidh Tholastaidh, Stornoway, 1984.

7. *The Burning Bush In Carloway*, Murdo MacAulay, Carloway Free Church Deacons' Court, 1984, pp. 27–28 on Carloway Union tensions; *An Eaglais Mhor (The Big Church)*, Angus Smith, Cross, 1992, on those in Ness. Collins (*Heritage*, pp. 110–111) gives a more robust, if less neutral, account of the tussle over Cross Free Church than Ansdell (pp. 95–97); see also Stewart and Cameron, pp. 147–150. Though James Shaw Grant's long-running *Stornoway Gazette* column must always be treated with caution on religious matters, he gives a jolly account of the Ness building dispute, 'Why the "Polis" Went To Church' – see anthology, *Stornoway and the Lews*, James Thin Ltd, Edinburgh, 1985, pp. 103–104.

8. Mrs Margaret MacDonald, née Campbell, widow of Rev. Donald MacDonald of Greyfriars Free Church in Inverness, told me in 1989 how she routinely fled from *An Domhnallach* as a little girl.

9. I am indebted to Rev. James MacIver, MA Dip Th., Knock Free Church, for this material on the Union dispute in Knock. Ansdell's version is attributed to a *Stornoway Gazette* column by James Shaw Grant, 'In Search of Lewis', 10 June 1989.

10. Iain Murray quotes this strong letter from Archibald MacNeilage (*Diary of Kenneth A. MacRae*, p. 20). Stewart and Cameron give huge detail of case, pp. 151–240; on UF outcry, pp. 241–275; on property settlement, p. 276 *et seq.*

11. *Diary of Kenneth A. MacRae*, p. 22.

12. See assertive article, 'Our Edinburgh Congregation', by Rev. Alexander MacKay, October 1921, *Free Presbyterian Magazine*, Vol. 26, pp. 185–186, commenting of Alexander Stewart that the 'Free Presbyterian Church building, which he took over to the Free Church, and for which not a penny of all that was contributed by Free Presbyterians was refunded, was sold to be used as a motor garage, without even being offered, at any price, to the Free Presbyterians.'

13. *Memoir etc. of Rev Neil Cameron, Glasgow*, ed. Donald Beaton, Inverness, 1932, pp. 55–64.

14. Murdo MacRae's endeavours for Harris Tweed were documented by James Shaw Grant in another *Stornoway Gazette* column – see 'At the Sign of the Bull's Head', in

his second anthology, *Surprise Island*, James Shaw Grant, James Thin Ltd, Edinburgh, 1983, pp. 113–116.

15. MacAulay (*Burning Bush*) includes this engaging narrative of local revival and MacKay
    wedding romp, pp. 28–29. A distinguished grandson of Iain Amhlaidh, the Gaelic
    broadcaster Peter MacAulay, relates a slightly different 'version I heard from my uncle
    Finlay many years ago – these things happen in oral tradition. "*Le m'fhuil a fhuair mi iad,
    agus le m'fhuil a chailleas mi iad,*" was what I'd heard. "*Le m'fhuil*" means "with my blood"
    as opposed to simply "with blood". He was presented with the pipes after being
    wounded in battle in Crete as a young man in the early 20th century.'

16. *My Uncle George – The Respectful Recollections of a Backslider in a Highland Manse*,
    Alastair Phillips, George Outram Ltd, Glasgow, 1955. A new and very attractive
    edition from Richard Drew Publishing, Glasgow, 1984; Macmillan paperback,
    1986.

17. *Diary of Kenneth A. MacRae*, p. 173, recording this fellowship at Kyle of Lochalsh.

11 'That's What I Thought Too, When I Heard the Bell', 1914–1934

1. See an interesting interview with Donald MacCormick, *West Highland Free Press*,
   Friday 22 February 2008, emphasising the catastrophic consequences of the Great
   War on the Gaelic heartland.

2. *Sea Sorrow – The Story of the Iolaire Disaster*, Stornoway Gazette Ltd, 1972; *Call na
   h-Iolaire*, Tormod Domhnallach, Acair Ltd, Stornoway, 1978, with a fine English
   synopsis.

3. Peggy Gillies and I had several conversations about the *Iolaire* between May 2002 and
   April 2005. In May 2006 I interviewed Mòr MacLeod of Brue, whose father also died
   in the tragedy, for a feature in the *Scottish Daily Mail*.

4. Website of the Church of Scotland – www.churchofscotland.org.uk

5. Collins (*Heritage*) details these negotiations over the 1929 Union, pp. 146–156.

6. Website of the United Free Church of Scotland – www.ufcos.org.uk

7. See *Lord of the Isles*, Nigel Nicolson, Weidenfeld and Nicolson, London, 1960; reprinted
   Acair Ltd, Stornoway, 200; and *The Soap Man*, Roger Hutchinson, Birlinn Ltd,
   Edinburgh, 2003, for study of Lord Leverhulme's adventures on Lewis and Harris.

8. 'The Strond people were at fault there,' a senior minister remarked to me in 2002.
   Synod confirmed the division of Harris into two congregations in 1930 (*Free
   Presbyterian Magazine*, July 1930, Vol. 35, p. 90).

9. An unstable genius, by the end of Chisholm's life in 1957 his mind had entirely given
   way. His publications include the splendidly titled *A Defence of Reformation Principles
   In The Free Presbyterian Church Student Case*, the apocalyptic *Is There Not A Cause?*
   and the frankly bonkers *Wandering In Fields Of Dreams*.

10. My grandfather was very fond of the Chisholmites, who bequeathed a strongly
    separatist, hyper-Calvinist element to Lewis religion that still had power to rattle the
    Free Church in the 1990s.

11. Roderick MacInnes and Uig congregation detailed in official Free Presbyterian
    History, p. 164. See also *Free Presbyterian Magazine*, February 1931, Vol. 35,
    pp. 397–398. I am indebted to Rev. William MacLeod (Glasgow), Rev. David
    Campbell (Tolsta) and Mr Donald A. MacKay (Valtos) for repudiating the *fama* of
    alcoholism.

12. *The Diary of James Morrison*, ed. G.N.M. Collins, Knox Press, Edinburgh, 1984, for
    benevolent Scalpay detail.

13. D.J. MacAskill was loved in Harris and many anecdotes are locally retailed.

14. *Sorley MacLean – Critical Essays*, ed. Raymond J. Ross and Joy Hendry, Scottish Academic Press, Edinburgh, 1986, p. 218 in an important interview with Donald Archie MacDonald, 'Some Aspects of Family and Local Background.'

15. See *History of the Free Presbyterian Church of Scotland 1893–1970*, ed. Alexander McPherson, Inverness, 1975, p. 281, for tribute to Rev. James MacLeod. Anecdotes here from Kenneth MacSween, *Coinneach Shrannda*, Strond, and Kenneth Morrison, *Coinneach a' Phadaidh*, Seilebost, Isle of Harris.

16. *Fragments and Sermons of the late Rev. Malcolm Gillies, Stornoway*, ed. Dr Neil R. Gillies MB ChB., Stornoway, 1987, pp. 5–12.

17. Obituary of Dr Peter A. MacLeod, by Dr Hugh Gillies, in *Free Presbyterian Magazine*, February 1973, Vol. 78, pp. 45–47. William H.M. MacKenzie, Inverness, for the hospital anecdote, in 1988 conversation.

18. Miss Anna MacAulay, Leurbost, for anecdotes of Dr Hugh Gillies, related in North Uist in February 2004, transcribed and checked by her.

19. Additional James MacLeod anecdotes from Rev. Dr James R. Tallach, Raasay; Rev. Donald A.K. MacDonald, North Uist, in conversation with the author, 1998, 2004. Space does not unfortunately permit much account of Mr Tallach (1896–1960). See *Sermons and Meditations of the late Rev. James A. Tallach*, ed. E.D. Tallach, Dingwall, 1962, 2nd edition 1978; *Fraser: Not A Private Matter – A Human Story of Grace and Suffering*, Fraser Tallach with John and David Tallach, The Banner of Truth Trust, Edinburgh, 2003.

20. I am indebted to Rev. John MacLeod, Free Presbyterian minister of Stornoway from 1969 till translation to London in 2004 (b.1930) and Rev. Donald MacLean, lately Free Presbyterian minister of Glasgow (b.1915) for taking time on 20 June 2008 to share anecdotes of Pink and, in Mr MacLean's case, direct and rueful recollection. For a more worshipful view, see *The Life of Arthur W. Pink*, Iain H. Murray, The Banner of Truth Trust, Edinburgh, 2004 (revised and enlarged edition of his 1981 biography). The online catalogue description is revealing. 'Pink's biography, first written by Iain Murray in 1981, is here revised and enlarged with the benefit of new material, including some of Pink's own re-discovered manuscripts. It is the heart-stirring and compelling story of a strong, complex character – a "Mr Valiant-for-truth" who was also a humble Christian. In 1922 a small magazine – Studies in the Scriptures – began to circulate among Christians in the English-speaking world. It pointed its readership back to an understanding of the gospel that had rarely been heard since the days of C.H. Spurgeon. At the time it seemed as inconsequential as its author, but subsequently Arthur Pink's writings became a major element in the recovery of expository preaching and biblical living. Born in England in 1886, A.W. Pink was the little-known pastor of churches in the United States and Australia before he finally returned to his homeland in 1934. There he died almost unnoticed in 1952. By that date, however, his magazine was feeding several of the men who were leading a return to doctrinal Christianity, including Martyn Lloyd-Jones and Douglas Johnson (founder of Inter-Varsity) and, in book form after his death, his writing became very widely read across the world.'

21. On the Free Presbyterian Protest controversy (does a signed, dated Protest against a decision of the Supreme Court of a Presbyterian Church invariably and of necessity separate you from that Church?), see official *History*, ed. McPherson, 1975, pp. 175–177, 181–182, 185–186; pamphlets, *A Review of Events in the Free Presbyterian Church of Scotland 1925–1945*, A Committee of the Free Presbyterian Congregation,

17 Blythswood Street, Glasgow, May 1948; *The Right of Protest Against Decisions of Church Supreme Courts in Presbyterian Churches in Scotland – 1975*, Published by Authority of the Free Presbyterian Relief Congregation, 202 Renfrew Street, Glasgow, 1975; *The Ides of May*, S. Fraser Tallach, Kinlochbervie, 1981; *The Open Door*, S. Fraser Tallach, Weydale Publishing, Thurso, 1996.

22. *The Diary of Kenneth A MacRae – A Record of Fifty Years in the Christian Ministry*, ed. Iain H. Murray, The Banner of Truth Trust, Edinburgh, 1980.
23. Mr MacRae's grandson, Rev. Kenneth I. MacLeod (b.1952) has twice regretted in my hearing the impression of his grandfather conveyed in published *Diary*, recalling a playful, kindly and merry patriarch.
24. My grandmother, Alice MacLeod, née Thomson, *Alis Sheumais* (1912–1997), born at Habost in Ness, with whom I had many worthwhile conservations on the island Evangelical past.
25. My uncle Murdo Iain MacLeod, *Murdo Hydro*, b.1955.
26. See lyrics of two songs in *Flower Of The West – The Runrig Songbook – Words and Music for 1125 Songs*, Calum and Rory MacDonald, Ridge Books/Chrysalis Music Ltd/Storr Music, Aberdeen, 1st ed. 2000, pp. 46–47, 'An t-Iasgair', 'The Root From Off The Corn'.
27. My late grandmother, Alice MacLeod, detail of *dusgadh Roddy John*, the 1920s' spiritual movement in Ness, in conversation, 1989.
28. Donald MacDonald's travail at Cross kirk session is well known. Rev. Murdo Alex MacLeod writes of these trials, pp. vii–viii in biographical introduction to a posthumous volume of sermons, *Christian Experience*, Donald MacDonald, The Banner Of Truth Trust, Edinburgh, 1988. Mr MacDonald's widow, Margaret (who told me the 'football' story) discussed them with me on several occasions between 1989 and 1991.
29. Duncan John MacLeod (1915–2007) told me this story on several occasions, most recently in June 2007.

12 'Give the Swooners No Latitude' – Revival and Change, 1934–1999

1. Murdo MacAulay, *The Burning Bush in Carloway*, Carloway Free Church Deacon's Court, 1984, esp. pp. 30–53. Most of this material online – http://www.backfree-church.co.uk/history/macaulay.jsp
2. See Kenneth A. MacRae, *Diary*, esp. pp. 363–370, for this material.
3. I am indebted to Norman Campbell (and his aunt, Mrs Anne Ross, Laide) for the word *cliobadaich* and its meaning – email to the author, April 2008.
4. See Chapter 14, 'The Household of Faith', for a discussion of *curam*; a colloquialism for conversion or 'being under concern of soul'.
5. MacAulay, *Aspects*, p. 152, for reference to John MacIver's serenity in these circumstances.
6. These websites might be called Legion, for they are many. See, for instance, A Young Pastor's Perspective: Hebrides Revival – http://jonearls.blogspot.com/2007/02/hebrides-revival.html; The Hebrides Revival of 1949 – http://www.holytrinitynewrochelle.org/yourti19195.html; 1949 Revival in the Hebrides Islands, Scotland – http://www.firesofrevival.com/trevival/dcrevival.htm
7. *Excellence In Leadership – The Pattern of Nehemiah*, John White, Inter-Varsity Press, Leicester, 1986, p. 101. This howler aside, it is an excellent little book.
8. *Sounds From Heaven – The Revival On The Isle of Lewis 1949–1952*, Colin and Mary

Peckham, Christian Focus Publications, Fearn, 2004; Campbell biography pp. 37–46; his 'revival reports', pp. 47–73.

9. 'Vaguely evangelical' is fair comment on the Faith Mission, which has no clear doctrinal position; works largely through mainstream, theologically liberal churches; deploys women preachers; concentrates its endeavours largely in areas such as the Western Isles and Northern Ireland already replete in Evangelical ministry and ripe for proselytising; and has for so long been less than candid about events on Lewis in this period.

10. *The Lewis Awakening*, Duncan Campbell, The Faith Mission, 1954 and *Duncan Campbell – A Biography*, Andrew Woolsey, 1973, are both quoted to deadly effect by Iain H. Murray in *Diary*, MacRae; see pp. 444–449 for that detail and Kenneth MacRae's concerns on the movement. See, too, *God's Answer – Revival Sermons*, Duncan Campbell, The Faith Mission, Edinburgh, 1960, which also includes 'The Story of the Lewis Awakening'.

11. *The Diary of Kenneth A. MacRae*, p. 444.

12. 'Steadfastness In Conviction,' Duncan Campbell, http://articles.christiansunite.com/article10390.shtml

13. In this address, 'The Revival on the Hebrides Islands', Duncan Campbell does belatedly concede 'revival' had come to Barvas before his arrival; but his teaching on 'Spirit Baptism' is explicit, and his contempt for Free Church unease with it evident. http://www.etpv.org/1998/hebrides.html

14. *Duncan Campbell – A Biography*, Andrew. A Woolsey, Hodder and Stoughton Ltd, 1974; new edition, *Channel of Revival*, The Faith Mission, 1982.

15. The last operating Lewis bothan, at Habost in Ness, seems to have shut up shop in 2006. Though, despite a celebrated trial, they were never found illegal (no money changed hands), they should not be glamorised.

16. Mrs Margaret Anne MacLean, *banntrach Poco*, New Shawbost, b.1932, Arnol, recalling Campbell movement in April 2008.

17. See profile of this respected Lewisman, 'Murray, John (*Iain Moireach* (b.1938),' *Companion to Gaelic Scotland*, ed. Derick S. Thomson, 2nd edition, Gairm Publications, Glasgow, 1994.

18. *The Resurgence of Arminianism*, Rev. Kenneth A. MacRae MA, Stornoway, June 1954. MacRae could fairly observe that many Free Church people heard little intelligent teaching on 'Free Church principles', and raised the entirely legitimate question as to how men who had signed the Free Church Questions and Formula – avowing its form of worship – could then participate in and even lead services of hymn-singing and instruments in other denominations, a matter presently tormenting the Free Church in 2008. But none of this amounts to a 'resurgence of Arminianism' and the book badly damaged his own Free Church party in the General Assembly, delighting only the Free Presbyterians.

19. See interview with John Morrison, *Seonaidh a' Mhuilleir*, in *Lewis In The Passing*, Calum Ferguson, Birlinn Ltd, Edinburgh, 2007, pp. 39–61, for more detail of Brethren in Lewis.

20. *Our Holy Redeemer – Ar Fear-Saoraidh Naomh – Stornoway*, by Francis Thompson, Stornoway, 2007. A compact little history of the modern Roman Catholic congregation in the town, beautifully produced and illustrated.

21. See interview with Andrew Cabrelli, *Lewis In The Passing*, Calum Ferguson, pp. 62–69, for insight into this little Italian community on Lewis.

22. See *No Great Mischief If You Fall*, John MacLeod, Mainstream Publishing Ltd,

Edinburgh, 1993, for full if occasionally immature account of Lord Mackay affair and the formation of the APC. APC website – www.apchurches.org

23. For a wry, academic take on the birth of the 'Free Church Continuing', see 'Scenes of Ecclesiastical Theatre in the Free Church of Scotland 1981–2000', Fraser MacDonald, *Northern Scotland*, Vol. 20, 2000, pp. 125–148. FCC website – www.freechurchcontinuing.org

24. Agreement was wrought between Breasclete and Achmore in the early 1950s to combine under a joint Free Presbyterian ministry. Then someone asked where the manse would be built. The tenuous deal collapsed. Free Presbyterian elder, conversation with the author, April 1998. Services at Breasclete ceased after the fire in January 2010.

25. Kenneth MacRae's funeral was reported – with a striking photograph – in the *Scottish Daily Express*, 5 May 1964.

26. See obituary of Rev. Murdo MacRitchie by Rev. John N. MacLeod, *Monthly Record of the Free Church of Scotland*, July/August 1983, pp. 177–178.

27. Born at Lochcarron in 1907, William MacLean died in Stornoway in June 1985. Obituary by Rev. Donald MacLean, *Free Presbyterian Magazine*, December 1985, Vol. 90, pp. 378–385. I am indebted to William Fraser, Inverness; Mr Donald MacKenzie, Leverburgh; and the late Peggy Gillies for some other detail. Obituary of Edward Arthur Christensen (by Rev. J.A.T. van Dorp), *Free Presbyterian Magazine*, January 2003. In classic Free Presbyterian guardedness (being 'guarded' is highly esteemed), the beer is referred to coyly as 'refreshment'.

28. Mr Adam J. Johnson, conversation with the author, December 2000. Warm obituaries of 'Murdo Alick' appeared in several national newspapers.

29. There was a significant spiritual movement in Shawbost under Mr Matheson's preaching. In 1991 this genial, big-hearted figure accepted a call to Inverness, where his ministry was tragically brief – he died suddenly in June 1992, only forty-three years old.

30. Obituary of Donald A. MacRae by John MacLeod, *The Herald*, Monday 25 July 2005.

31. Obituaries of Murdo MacAulay – *Monthly Record of the Free Church of Scotland*, April 2002, pp. 12–13, Rev. Donald MacDonald (Carloway); and another by Mr Neil Murray, Back, in the *Ceann Loch a Tuath News*, a community newsletter, January 2002, p. 6. I also extract again from *The Burning Bush In Carloway*, pp. 36–37.

32. *The Burning Bush In Carloway*, Murdo MacAulay, Carloway Free Church Deacons' Court, 1984.

33. Rev. Donald MacDonald (Carloway, retired) told me this story – how the very old MacAulay mortified the young office-bearer – in April 2008.

34. Donald MacLeod, *Domhnall Chiulich*, Free Church elder at Shawbost, told me this prediction of Murdo MacAulay in May 2004.

13 The Table of the Lord – Aspects of Evangelical Worship

1. Chris Lawson of the '*Co Leis Thu?*' family-history centre at Northton, Harris, kindly identified Mrs MacAulay from the Uig civil registrar. This obituary, by Rev. Neil MacIntyre, from *Free Presbyterian Magazine*, October 1913, Vol. 18, pp. 215–217.

2. 'Towards a Spatial Theory of Worship: Some Observations from Presbyterian Scotland', Fraser MacDonald, *Social and Cultural Geography*, Vol. 3, No. 1, 2002.

3. My great-grandfather, Murdo MacLeod, *Murchadh Dhomhnall A' Phiobair*, 28 Cross

(1871–1953). For an interesting discussion of 'Sweets In Church', see *Re-Imagining Culture – Histories, Identities and the Gaelic Renaissance*, Sharon Macdonald, Berg (Ethnicity and Identity Series), Oxford, 1997, pp. 170–172.

4. Fraser MacDonald, pp. 75–76.

5. *Fragments and Sermons of the Reverend Malcolm Gillies*, ed. Dr Neil Gillies, Stornoway, 1987.

6. For discussion of the *seis*, see *Memories of a Wayfaring Man*, Murdoch Campbell, Highland Printers Ltd, 1974, pp. 30–31.

7. *No More Sea – Sermons and Addresses of the Rev. Angus Finlayson, North Tolsta, Isle of Lewis*, ed. Mrs I. Finlayson, Stornoway, 1975. See 'Biographical Introduction' by Donald MacLeod, pp. 7–10.

8. *The Diary of Kenneth A. MacRae*, ed. Iain H. Murray, The Banner of Truth Trust, Edinburgh, 1980, p. 271.

9. Angus M. Cattanach (b.1925, Edinburgh), ordained to mission in Southern Rhodesia, 1951; later FP minister of South Harris (Finsbay) from 1956 to 1979, of Staffin from 1988 to 1993. Since 1993 he has been minister of the consolidated Skye congregation of the APC. Duncan MacLean (1935–2006), a native of Lochcarron with strong family links to Skye, FP minister of Tolsta, 1972–1979, Finsbay (South Harris) 1979–1985. Men of real gifts and undoubted sorrows.

10. See *My Uncle George*, Alastair Phillips, 1984 edition, pp. 40–42. for jolly discussion of clerical collars.

11. *Free Presbyterian Church of Scotland – Proceedings of Synod*, May 1976, pp. 40–72, for an astonishing discussion of distinctive ministerial dress. This, perhaps significantly, was the last meeting of Synod reported verbatim for public consumption.

12. 'Psalm Tunes, Gaelic' by Cedric Thorpe Davie, *The Companion to Gaelic Scotland*, ed. Derick S. Thomson, Basil Blackwell Reference Ltd, Oxford, 1983 (first edition).

13. *Reading The Line: An English-language Lined-out Psalmody Tradition in Presbyterian Scotland*, Norman Campbell, Stornoway, 2005. See Drummond and Bulloch, Vol. 3, *The Church in Late Victorian Scotland*, for background to this South Clerk Street congregation, p. 146.

14. Marion MacLeod, Brue (b.1914, Earshader) remembers this psalmody class at Bernera.

15. In September 2006, Carloway Free Church dispensed with Communion tokens. *Aonghas nam Beann* was cited to this end from the pulpit.

16. *Bypaths of Highland Church History*, John MacLeod DD, ed. Collins, 1965, pp. 34–35, for details of literal fasting.

17. This Fellowship Meeting is first recorded by Malcolm MacPhail, and in more detail by John MacLeod DD, ed. Collins, 1965, pp. 23, 24.

18. My father's 1991 lecture, drawing on Gustavus Aird's Moderatorial address, outlines the origins of the Fellowship Meeting. See besides Beaton (1929) on Thomas Hog; Murdo MacAulay has interesting material in *Aspects of the Religious History of Lewis*, 1985, pp. 218–219.

19. Rev. Donald MacDonald cheerfully recalled this experience in conversation, in April 2008. It would be impolitic to name the congregation, the elder or the other minister.

20. Donald Morrison incidents related by MacAulay (*Aspects*), pp. 161–163. John MacRae's outmanoeuvring of Donald Duff from *Gleanings Of Highland Harvest*, Murdoch Campbell, 3rd edition, Ross-shire Printing and Publishing Co. Ltd, 1967, pp. 102–103.

14 The Household of Faith – Aspects of Evangelical Community

1. *Scottish Crofters: A Historical Ethnography of a Celtic Village*, Susan Parman; Thomson Wadsworth (Case Studies in Cultural Anthropology), 2nd edition, Belmont, California, USA, 2003. *The Living Past*, Donald Macleod, Acair Ltd, Stornoway, 2006, is a splendid portrayal of post-war Evangelicalism on Lewis.

2. *The Six Hills of Home*, Donald MacDonald (*Domhnall Dhonnachaidh*), 1998 (revised 2000, 2001), pp. 2–24 for valuable detail of Established Church and Church of Scotland in Shawbost.

3. MacAulay, *The Burning Bush In Carloway*, p. 23, for these details of Shawbost.

4. My aunt, Mrs Christina Montgomery, *Ciorstiona Mhurchaidh Chaluim Mhoir*, b.1926, has this account of a meeting on the beach. Parman records a version of the oatmeal incident in Carloway, pp. 139–140.

5. Report of the first Shawbost Communion from *The Highland News*, 11 November 1893; *Fuaran*, Comann Eachdraidh An Taobh Siar, autumn 2003, no. 5, p. 25.

6. George L. Campbell's induction date from MacAulay, *Burning Bush*, p. 23. Comment on Campbell's preaching from *Glimpses of Portrona*, Rev. R.M. Stephen MA, ed. Rev. R. Morrison Lit. A., *Stornoway Gazette*, undated, c.1920, p. 220.

7. MacFarlane's comment on Campbell from 'Rural Ministers (Old Free)', *Stornoway Gazette*, Friday 23 January 1931.

8. My aunt, Mrs Montgomery, for this folk-memory of Campbell in UF retirement. Shawbost Free Church ministers as follows – George L. Campbell (1895–1900), Nicol Nicolson (1902–1911), Murdo MacIver (1919–1950), John MacLeod (1951–1969), Alexander MacFarlane (1970–1979), Callum Matheson (1980–1991), John Morrison (1992–1999), Malcolm MacLeod (inducted 2000).

9. See Calum Ferguson, *Children of the Black House*, 2003; *Lewis In The Passing* (2007); Birlinn Ltd, Edinburgh, for detail of traditional island weddings. See Parman on 'Kinship, Courtship and Marriage', pp. 117–134; on death and funerals, pp. 148–152.

10. See *Priorities For The Church – Preaching and Unity*, Donald Macleod, Christian Focus Publications, Fearn, 2003, for these practical observations on ministerial participation in 'wakes'. The book is an edited collection of editorials from the *Monthly Record of the Free Church of Scotland*.

11. Parman on the Free Church, pp. 138–148; on conversion, pp. 162–170.

12. The greatly altered role of women, and new expectations, is an increasing factor in church life in the Highlands, from tension over the 'head covering' to the mobility and housing arrangements of ministers. Some now agitate openly for new arrangements and an enhanced stipend to allow (mortgaged) home ownership. See *The Monthly Record of the Free Church of Scotland*, 'What Would Chalmers do? – The Free Church in the 21st Century', James Eglinton, May 2008, pp. 14–15.

13. Quoted in *The Man in the Manse*, Ronald S. Blakey, Edinburgh, 1978. Blakey's evident contempt for Highland religion is not matched by his documentation; a succession of jibes and anecdotes billowing forth without citation. But see an engaging if equally anti-Calvinist memoir of childhood, *The Former Days*, Norman MacLean, Hodder and Stoughton, London, 1945. One wonders if MacLean's retreat from the 'old paths' was a reaction to paternal brutality; by his own account he was regularly thrashed by his father, an Established Church missionary, and the determinedly light tone of his autobiography must mark very dark feelings.

14. *Sounds From Heaven – The Revival On The Isle of Lewis 1949–1952*, Colin and Mary Peckham, Christian Focus Publications, Fearn, 2004, for these comments and Roderick MacKay's experience.

15. Parman's disconcerted new convert, p. 164. See, too, her important paper, 'Orduighean: A Dominant Symbol in the Free Church of the Scottish Highlands', Susan Parman, 1990, *American Anthropologist* 92(2), June 1990, pp. 295–305.

16. Current editions of Moncrieff include *The Practice and Procedure of the Free Church of Scotland In Her Several Courts*, Knox Press, Edinburgh, 1995; *A Manual of the Practice of the Free Presbyterian Church of Scotland*, Glasgow, 1999. The Church of Scotland manual, 'Cox's', is very similar.

17. My father's 1991 lecture on Stornoway religion includes the Alexander Morrison anecdote and these reflections on Lewis practice relating to membership.

18. *The Days of the Fathers in Ross-shire*, John Kennedy DD, 1861, new edition 1979, with biographical introduction by Neil M. Ross, Christian Focus Publications, Fearn; on baptism, see pp. 110–125, but Kennedy's efforts to reconcile Ross-shire practice with Scripture is more convenient than convincing.

19. These observations by William MacLean, *Free Presbyterian Church of Scotland – Proceedings of Synod 1976*, Glasgow, 1976, pp. 143–144, are the nearest the Free Presbyterian Church has ever come to granting Dr Kennedy's views on baptism canon-law status.

20. Samuel Rutherford (*c.*1600–1661), Scottish Presbyterian theologian and political philosopher: his *Lex Rex* ('The Law is King') is the earliest argument for limited government and written constitutionalism.

21. Jonathan Edwards (1703–1758) is one of America's most important philosophers. The 'Halfway Covenant', adopted by Synods of his church in 1657 and 1662, 'made baptism alone the condition to civil privileges in church membership, but not of participation in the sacrament of the Lord's Supper,' and from 1748 was at the root of tensions that finally destroyed Edwards' ministry in Northampton, Connecticut, only a few years after the 'Great Awakening' of 1739–1741.

22. *Around the Peat-Fire*, Calum Smith, Birlinn Ltd, Edinburgh, 2001, p. 3. Norman MacLean has a similar anecdote from Skye (*The Former Days*, p. 40) of a man whose family had assured him 'that all those who died unbaptised go to hell and that they are there roasted to all eternity'; but this must be treated with real suspicion – to this day, conservative Presbyterianism on Skye is noted for a marked, undue *reluctance* to apply for infant baptism (a legacy of Rev. Roderick MacLeod's extreme views), not a superstitious, intemperate demand for it.

23. See *A Faith To Live By – Christian Teaching That Makes A Difference*, Donald Macleod, Christian Focus Publications, Fearn, 1999, pp. 210–221, for theology of infant baptism.

24. *The Diary of Kenneth A MacRae*, ed. Iain H. Murray, The Banner of Truth Trust, Edinburgh, 1980, pp. 243, 246, 250, 257–258, 271–272 for MacRae's reflections on Lewis baptism.

25. While recent – or even historic – examples of church discipline on Lewis and Harris could readily be cited, it would be neither kind nor necessary.

26. Another diverting anecdote from my father's vast repository. MacKenzie is not remembered with respect on Lewis.

15 The Bebo Generation – Reverse and Renewal in the Twenty-first Century

1. *The Diary of Kenneth A. MacRae – A Record of Fifty Years In The Christian Ministry*, ed. Iain H. Murray, Banner of Truth Trust, Edinburgh, 1980 – Chapter 18, 'Leadership in the Policies of the Free Church', pp. 437–459.

2. *Free Presbyterian Magazine*, March 1987, Vol. 92 pp. 82–90, 'The London Presbyterian Conference – 1986', Roy Middleton.

3. *Noted Ministers of the Northern Highlands*, Donald Beaton, Inverness, 1929 – essay on Aeneas Sage, pp. 65–75.

4. *The Monthly Record of the Free Church of Scotland*, July/August 1980, p. 151.

5. *Highlanders – A History of the Gaels*, John MacLeod, Hodder & Stoughton, London, 1996, pp. 250–253, 258, for details of Sir James Matheson's most notorious factors, Donald Munro.

6. I am indebted to my father's 1991 lecture on Stornoway religion for most of these insights as to why the Charismatic movement never took hold in Lewis. *Diary*, MacRae, p. 244, for his 1932 New Year.

7. Rev. James S. Sinclair, one of the 1892 students and first editor of the *Free Presbyterian Magazine*, from 1896 to his sudden death in 1921. He was particularly fond of William Cowper's hymn, 'There Is A Fountain Filled With Blood.' Rev. Robert R. Sinclair (1898–1997), in conversation with the author, Wick, March 1989.

8. *Free Church Ministers In Lewis (Presbytery) – 1843–1993*, Murdo MacAulay, Stornoway, 1993 for details of Free Church ministers.

9. James Shaw Grant made this point emphatically – *Discovering Lewis and Harris*, James Shaw Grant, John Donald Ltd, Edinburgh, 1987, pp. 80–81. For a sadly neglected novel set in rural Lewis at this period, see the outstanding *Devil In The Wind*, Charles MacLeod, Gordon Wright Publishing, Edinburgh, 1978.

10. Allan MacColl, a native of Acharacle and of Free Church background, who had learned Gaelic to a high standard, was 'licensed to preach the Gospel' by the Southern Presbytery of the Free Presbyterian Church of Scotland on 11 June 2008. His settlement in the Ness congregation was expected in the autumn of 2008. MacColl is the author of an important and most readable book, *Land, Faith and the Crofting Community: Christianity and Social Criticism in the Highlands of Scotland 1843–1893*, Allan W. MacColl, Edinburgh University Press, Edinburgh, 2006.

11. Roderick MacKenzie's sister, Margaret Morrison, described this unrest to me in January 1996.

12. There has been no decennial Census question to identify Gaelic-only speakers in Scotland since 1971. That year, 477 were recorded, of whom a majority were probably pre-school children. There were 28,106 in 1901, out of an entire Gaelic-speaking population of 202,700. See 'Gaelic speaking in Scotland, demographic history,' by Charles W.J. Withers and Kenneth M. MacKinnon, *The Companion to Gaelic Scotland*, ed. Derick S. Thomson, 2nd edition Gairm Publications, Glasgow, 1994. My late great-grandmother in Cross, Mary MacLeod (nee MacDonald), 1876–1960, spoke nothing but Gaelic.

13. These are my father's calculations for church attendance in Shawbost around thirty-five years ago. For comprehensive demolition of supposedly universal churchgoing in the nineteenth century, see Drummond and Bulloch, Vol. 2, *The Church in Victorian Scotland 1843–1874*, pp. 110–114; Vol. 3, *The Church in Late Victorian Scotland 1874–1900*, pp. 139–149. Details of destructive children in *An Eaglais Mhor (The Big Church)*, Angus Smith, Cross, 1992.

14. Callanish Free Church is, in strict geography, in the post-1722 bounds of the parish of Uig. A new Free Presbyterian ministry in Uig is possible, but unlikely. On 27 June 2008, Rev. Hugh Maurice Stewart was ordained and inducted to the newly linked Church of Scotland charge, Uig with Lochs-in-Bernera. In April 2010 there were no Kirk vacancies on the Long Island.

15. The editor was Andrew Jaspan of the *Sunday Herald*, in conversation with the author, October 2002. It would be imprudent to name the minister.

16. The refusal of his Free Church session in Ullapool to support him in church discipline of individuals who had booked and taken Sunday flights for a package holiday was, according to Rev. Wilfred Weale, the main reason why he quietly demitted his charge in 2001 for the Free Presbyterians. He was inducted to their Staffin congregation later that year. Conversation with the author, February 2003.

17. *The Monthly Record of the Free Church of Scotland*, September 2007, p. 5.

18. *Monthly Record*, October 2007, p. 6. The increasing tendency to use induction reports as a platform for controversial, sometimes offensive editorialising is to be deplored.

19. 'Lewis lures urban castaways with two-for one home offer,' *Scotland On Sunday*, 9 February 2002.

20. This extraordinary petition – http://www.ipetitions.com/petition/Ferry7days/signatures.html

21. *Tescopoly: How One Shop Came Out On Top And Why It Matters*, Andrew Simms, Constable and Robinson Ltd, London, 2007.

22. The clever, cynical village schoolmaster – funny, active in left-wing politics, agnostic if not openly atheistic, often an enthusiast for Gaelic culture – has been a feature of island life since the First World War. Charles MacLeod of Shawbost (1921–1983), author of *Devil In The Wind*, is an affectionately remembered example, an outstanding headmaster in Shawbost and whose contribution to public life was considerable, sitting on – for instance – the Highlands and Islands Advisory Panel and the Broadcasting Council for Scotland, as well re-energising the Crofters Union to such effect it stymied an Act of Parliament. MacLeod, though, would have drawn the line at frightening teenage Christians.

23. There are several such social-networking websites, like MySpace and Facebook, but Bebo, founded in 2005 by Michael and Xochi Birch – it is a 'backronym' for 'blog early, blog often' – is by far the most popular with teenagers, being deftly designed and extremely easy both to use and to surf. 'Pro Evo' is a 'virtual football' computer game. By the end of 2007 most Long Island adolescents and most younger adherents of the Free Presbyterian Church (though their pages are much more strait-laced) had personal Bebo pages. I do not choose to document certain instances of bad language between young island communicants, but those sites should be more closely supervised by parents, and there is very little evidence they are. In April 2007, it was assessed that 85 per cent of Bebo users are under twenty-five. On 13 March 2008, Bebo was acquired by AOL for $850 million (£417 million.) As the Bebo fad waned steadily in favour of Facebook, by April 2010 AOL openly regretted the purchase, and the site's closure seemed increasingly probable.

24. There has been only one post-2000 instance, as far as can be ascertained, of an individual being refused membership in her local Free Church. She was accepted shortly afterwards as a member in the adjacent congregation.

25. The local Stand In The Gap website – http://sitg.t83.net/

26. I contacted most local Free Church ministers with the assurance of strict anonymity. I am grateful to those who replied courteously and with such helpful, interesting comments. It would be unkind to name those who replied rudely.

27. *Aspects of the Religious History of Lewis Up to the Disruption of 1843*, Murdo MacAulay, Stornoway, 1986, p 133. He has lifted the account from Principal MacLeod's little essay on Finlay Munro, *A Highland Evangelist*. I have slightly adapted their translation.

Index